Acing the New SAT

Breakthrough Strategies
for the Highest Scores

Marcia Lawrence

with Charles Piemonte

A PLUME BOOK

PLUME
Published by the Penguin Group
Penguin Books USA Inc., 375 Hudson Street,
New York, New York, 10014, U.S.A.
Penguin Books Ltd, 27 Wrights Lane,
London W8 5TZ, England
Penguin Books Australia Ltd, Ringwood,
Victoria, Australia
Penguin Books Canada Ltd, 10 Alcorn Avenue,
Toronto, Ontario, Canada M4V 3B2
Penguin Books (N.Z.) Ltd, 182–190 Wairau Road,
Auckland 10, New Zealand

Penguin Books Ltd, Registered Offices:
Harmondsworth, Middlesex, England

First published by Plume,
an imprint of Dutton Signet,
a division of Penguin Books USA Inc.
Earlier editions of this work published under the title *How to Take the SAT*.

First Printing, December, 1994
10 9 8 7 6 5 4 3 2 1

 REGISTERED TRADEMARK—MARCA REGISTRADA

LIBRARY OF CONGRESS CATALOGING-IN-PUBLICATION DATA
Lawrence, Marcia.
Acing the new SAT : breakthrough strategies for the highest scores /
Marcia Lawrence with Charles Piemonte.
p.   cm.
ISBN 0-452-27233-5
1. Scholastic aptitude test—Study guides. I. Piemonte, Charles. II. Title.
LB2353.57.L375   1994
378.1'662—dc20   94-14769
CIP

Printed in the United States of America
Set in Times Roman

Acing the New SAT

Breakthrough Strategies
for the Highest Scores

Leading authority Marcia Lawrence uses her expertise in this new home-study workbook to help students unveil the clues found in the actual test questions—thereby leading them to the answers hidden in the text. This follow-up guide to Lawrence's bestselling *How to Take the SAT* is designed to:

- Significantly increase your knowledge of the skills being tested

- Demonstrate concrete techniques for analyzing the question
  and narrowing down the answer choices

- Equip you with the skills you need to approach the SAT
  (and any other examination) with confidence

Unlike other SAT workbooks, *Acing the New SAT* offers more than just sample tests. It provides a complete course of home study for verbal and math tests, but more important, it enables students to understand the composition of the question. By the time you are finished reading this workbook, you will have learned how to zero in on the correct answers, how to check your answers out, and how to master an SAT test.

MARCIA LAWRENCE (M.A., Columbia) has worked in the field of education since 1962. She is the director of Lawrence Techniques of Test Taking, Inc., and is widely in demand for lectures and courses on this subject. She teaches English on the staff of John L. Miller Senior High School, Great Neck, New York.

CHARLES PIEMONTE (Ph.D., New York University), who assisted Marcia Lawrence on the math section, has published numerous articles on mathematics, computer science, and computer education. He taught high school mathematics for fifteen years and is presently the Director of the Village School, an experimental high school in Great Neck, New York.

To the Student

Several years ago, in a hit movie titled *Risky Business,* the hero, a high school student played by Tom Cruise, has a recurring nightmare. In it, our hero arrives late for his SAT and has only two minutes to complete the three-hour exam; his dream of going to Princeton is now impossible. Says the hero, "My life is ruined." This is a theme that is familiar to many juniors who are convinced that the SAT is their ticket to the future. They believe that whether they will or won't get into the college of their choice is going to be determined by what they get on this examination.

To complicate matters, there is so much concern over the new SAT that it has only added to student anxiety. But there is little reason for concern. Not only is the majority of the test exactly the same as it always has been, the changes are to your advantage. In fact, the test is even easier to prepare for.

Even if you have never taken an SAT, this book is the *only* resource you will need. It is designed to take you step-by-step through the SAT and show you how the test-makers construct each of the questions. *Taking a College Board Examination is a skill that can be learned,* but only if you master the test-taking techniques that you need in order to answer the questions. Without these skills you are forced, under the pressure of normal test-taking anxiety and tension, to make guesses on material that is not as simple as it appears.

As a result, many students do not do justice to their actual abilities on this crucial examination, whose score will determine to which colleges they can reasonably apply. Repeating the test several times or studying questions from prior examinations will not, by itself, improve your basic test-taking skills.

This book offers the test taker systematic methods for approaching each section of the Scholastic Assessment Test. It provides you with concrete techniques for analyzing each question, eliminating distractions and concentrating on those alternatives that offer the best possible answer. Armed with these skills, you can approach the examination with confidence, knowing that you can give it your best.

The Lawrence Techniques of Test Taking have been thoroughly tested in courses offered by the author and her associates since 1974 to thousands of college-bound students. They have discovered that this system has helped them take other examinations more successfully by teaching them to approach test questions with an *organized strategy.*

Acknowledgments

This book was made possible by the inspiration and assistance of many friends, colleagues, and students.

It is dedicated to Dr. Hans K. Maeder, faithful and encouraging teacher and friend to a generation of college-bound young people.

To my editor, Matthew Carnicelli, for his meticulous supervision of this book and many valuable suggestions.

To my agent and mentor, Charles Lieber, whose wit and wisdom has sustained and nurtured my efforts throughout these many years.

To Diana Freed, Lauren Golden, and Catherine Hong for their painstaking work on the manuscript.

To my children, Douglas and Suzanne, who motivated this creation.

—And especially, to Avraham.

Contents

Introduction to the New SAT

The Scholastic Assessment Test, formerly the Scholastic Aptitude Test, is one of the major criteria in the admissions process conducted by the college of your choice. The purpose of the test is to rate your ability to do college work in comparison with one million other high school students who will be taking these examinations at the same time you are.

However, there is little in the traditional high school curriculum that will prepare you for the SAT. It was not designed to test achievement, but how good a test taker you are, and how well you understand the examination questions and the intentions of the people who constructed this particular test.

Whereas for millions of students college acceptances often hang in the balance on the Scholastic Aptitude Test, educators continue to perpetuate the myth that the test cannot be studied for. But quite to the contrary, test-taking techniques are ACQUIRED SKILLS and scores can be significantly altered by learning the specialized skills that are needed on this examination.

The Scholastic Assessment Test, like any complex problem, must be approached with an organized strategy. It is important for you to know that each question type not only has a built-in clue that leads to the answer but requires a specific strategy for analyzing the question and narrowing down the answer choices. Consequently, any successful program must teach students how to master the strategies necessary to identify the correct answer.

The purpose of this book is to make maximum use of your potential by making you *test wise*. You might read extensively and have an excellent vocabulary. In that case, you might need only to master the techniques of test taking in order to use your present knowledge to its fullest. On the other hand, you might be a reader with a limited vocabulary, which puts you at a disadvantage even though you might have a natural talent for doing your best on tests. Finally, you might lack both verbal skills and test-taking skills.

We have taken all of these possibilities into account in creating this sequential learning program based on years of experience in SAT workshops helping students to improve their scores. Our course will offer you effective, personalized instruction. By the time you have finished this program, you will have learned how to tackle an SAT test, how to check out your answers, and how to zero in on the correct answer.

Once you begin this program, however, you have assumed a shared responsibility. There is no substitute for a good vocabulary, but by following the suggestions in this program regularly and using all of the material we have provided, you can substantially increase your chances of coming up with the right answers. It would be a good idea if you kept pencil and paper ready at all times. You should be constantly writing down clues and information, even when you are not specifically asked to do so.

There are a number of aspects of the SAT you should be particularly aware of.

1. ETS, the Educational Testing Service, which has produced the SAT exam, experiments with each test question for several years before allowing it to appear as a scoring question on a particular test. The purpose of these experiments is to reduce the margin for error in the selection of the right answer. In other words, there must be *clues* that are obvious enough to allow the majority of students taking the test to select the correct answer. It's your job to locate those clues, using the test-taking techniques this book will teach you.

2. What you may not realize, along with 90 percent of the students taking the Scholastic Assessment Test, is that you not only *can* but *must* write on your exam paper. You should cross out, underline, circle, and do whatever else you feel you need to

do right on your exam, in pencil. Remember, during the SAT itself you will be allowed no scratch paper.

3. All of the correct answers on the SAT should be arrived at by a *process of elimination*. Never think you've spotted the right answer immediately; there are subtle differences among the answers that need close analysis. If you think an answer is obvious, that might be just the reason the Educational Testing Service chose to include it. So *"back into" your answer* by first crossing out, with a pencil, all of the obviously incorrect answers.

4. If you narrow your answer down to two possibilities, guessing is usually to your advantage. However, if the entire question leaves you hopelessly baffled, even after you have applied all of the appropriate techniques, *do not guess*. You receive one point for each correct answer and no points for questions omitted. For questions with five answer choices, one-fourth point is subtracted for each incorrect answer. (One-third point is subtracted for questions with four answer choices, which sometimes appear in the mathematical part of the SAT. You receive both a verbal score and a mathematical score.)

5. It is important to learn to pace yourself through the examination. Questions range from easy to difficult and are often grouped so that the relatively easy ones come first. This is because the SAT is designed to cover a wide range of abilities. Make a notation next to any questions you have real difficulty answering, skip them, and go back to them after you have answered the others.

6. There are several versions of the SAT examination distributed at the same time, but your scores should not be affected by differences in these tests. Statistical measurements in scoring SAT examinations will adjust any differences among the various tests to ensure that your score is not affected.

7. Students who feel that their test scores are not indicative of their ability should plan to take the SAT examination again in November of their senior year. There can be a tremendous maturation over the summer. In addition, the student can use the time to study and internalize these SAT techniques and work on prefixes, suffixes, roots, and vocabulary.

8. One important item to note is that each test booklet contains one experimental section. Depending on which test you happen to receive, it could be in the verbal section or in the mathematical section. You will have no way of ascertaining which of your test sections is the experimental one, but *it does not count* toward your scores. This test is used to develop future SAT questions and maintain quality control.

9. One further point you might keep in mind is that there is no fixed rule about the order of the various sections within the verbal section or the order in which you must do them. The reading passages might or might not be the first set of questions on the test. Even when they are the first set of questions, many students who have not learned the reading comprehension technique offered in this handbook often leave them until last, and then, because these passages are tedious and complex, either guess at the answers or omit them altogether. But this is the section of the test that depends least on vocabulary, so it is to your advantage to learn the technique until you are proficient. Developing competence in this area will give you greater control over the material in the test and will allow you to move with confidence from one section to another. The remaining questions will include word relationships and sentence completions. You might consider alternating between these various groups of test questions, always keeping in mind that you must move at the fastest pace you can.

Particularly if you do skip from section to section and skip more difficult questions with the intention of coming back later, you must be very careful not to get confused on your answer sheet. Each time you answer a question, make sure the number on the question and the number on the answer sheet correspond. When you skip a question, it is surprisingly easy to forget to skip the corresponding answer space—and, of course, that could mean at best that you waste time correcting your error and at worst that you are scored wrong for all of the rest of the questions in the section.

10. Here is how to score the test. Each correct answer on an SAT verbal test receives one point. One-fourth point is subtracted for each incorrect answer.
To score the verbal test, use the following formula:

$$\text{raw score} = \text{correct answers} - \tfrac{1}{4} \text{ of incorrect answers}$$

To score the quantitative-comparison questions in the math section, use the following formula:

$$\text{raw score} = \text{correct answers} - \tfrac{1}{3} \text{ of incorrect answers}$$

Do not count any problems you skipped.

Typical Timetable for the SAT I

Total Time: 2 Hours, 30 Minutes

8:00 to **8:30**	Section 1	**Verbal Assessment Test**	9 Sentence Completion Questions 6 Word Relationship Questions 15 Reading Comprehension Questions
8:30 to **9:00**	Section 2	**Mathematics Assessment Test**	25 Questions
9:00 to **9:30**	Section 3	**Verbal Assessment Test**	10 Sentence Completion Questions 13 Word Relationship Questions 12 Reading Comprehension Questions
9:30 to **10:00**	Section 4	**Mathematics Assessment Test**	25 Questions
10:00 to **10:15**	Section 5	**Verbal Assessment Test**	13 Reading Comprehension Questions
10:15 to **10:30**	Section 6	**Mathematics Assessment Test**	10 Questions

Budgeting Your Time for the SAT

The SAT used to be a three-hour, six-section test. Now the SAT-I is a three-hour, seven-section test. The thirty minutes that used to be devoted to the Test of Standard Written English is now a fifteen-minute math section and a fifteen-minute verbal section. The other five remaining sections last thirty minutes each. But the important thing to know is that while the changes in timing will not affect you, budgeting your time is a crucial element in your SAT strategy for success. Planning a time budget in advance will relieve a great deal of test-day stress. Be sure to bring your own watch or stopwatch to the test. (Watches that beep are not allowed, though!)

VERBAL SECTIONS

Analogies and sentence completion questions can generally be answered in less than a minute (short questions). Each reading passage question usually averages more than a minute to answer (long questions).

Consider an 18/12-minute breakdown for each 30-minute verbal section, based on the short and long groupings. One verbal section has more reading passage (long) questions than the other, so there are two verbal time plans.

Verbal Section 1
(30 questions)
 6 Analogies
 9 Sentence Completions } 18 min
 15 Reading Passage Questions - 12 min.

Verbal Section 2
 (35 questions)
 13 Analogies
 10 Sentence Completions } 12 min.
 12 Reading Passage Questions - 18 min.

Verbal Section 3
(13 questions) - 15 min.

Reading passage questions will thus consume about half your total time on the verbal SAT. These questions are only worth about one-third of the points, though. Generally it is better to tackle the short questions first and save the reading questions until last.

MATH SECTIONS

You will have approximately one minute to answer each math question. If you think a question will take much longer than a minute to solve, or you don't know how to do it, put a check mark by it (in the test booklet, not on your answer sheet) and return to it later if you have time. Realize that in your area of strength (algebra, geometry, or arithmetic), even so-called "harder" questions at the end of the section might *not* be hard for you. Make sure you don't leave any "easy" approachable questions unanswered because you ran out of time. Leave the more difficult questions for last.

Do

- prepare for the SAT by sharpening reading and math skills.
- approach the test well rested and relaxed.
- eat breakfast the day of the test.
- bring your identification and your test ticket to the SAT.
- bring two sharpened #2 pencils to the test.
- familiarize yourself ahead of time with the directions to each type of question.
- wear light, comfortable clothing, and bring a sweater or jacket.
- arrive early to the test center so that you can choose a seat in a good location.
- save the most difficult questions until last.
- draw a diagram if it will help you answer a math question.
- bring a watch so that you can follow your time plan for the exam.
- answer easy questions first; they count just as much as hard ones.
- use a process of elimination to choose the best answer.
- use your pencil in the exam booklet; underline clue words, strike out incorrect choices, and circle the answer you select.

Don't

- try to cram for the test; the SAT measures aptitude, so cramming the night before the test won't help.
- make stray marks on your answer sheet; mark each answer in the correct spot on the answer sheet.
- get panicky if you miss a few questions; most students answer only about half the questions correctly.
- let your attention wander; it's important to stay focused.
- spend too much time on any one question; allow time to consider each one of the questions on the test.
- be afraid to guess if you can eliminate one or two answers.
- forget to consider all the possible answers; even if C is good, E might be better!
- rely on luck to raise your score; you must work to prepare yourself better if you hope to improve your score. (All of the scores are reported, not just the best ones.)
- bring a watch with a beeper.
- waste any extra time you might have at the end of a section; use the time to recheck your answers.

PART ONE

The Verbal
Assessment Test

Introduction to the New Verbal Assessment Test

If there was ever a good time to be taking the SAT since it was first mandated as a college entrance requirement, the time is now. For while the changes on the verbal section of the revised SAT are actually quite minimal, the new test is even easier to prepare for.

One of the most exciting changes in the new test is that the Antonym questions have been eliminated. Those were the questions on the old test in which you were given one word and asked to pick out its opposite from among five choices. Either you knew the word or you didn't. This is not the case with the new SAT. The vocabulary is now tested in the context of the reading comprehension passages where you are asked to find the dictionary definition of the word or its synonym, not its opposite.

The testing of vocabulary on the new SAT not only makes it easier to figure out the meaning of a word, the techniques used to determine its meaning are exactly the same as the techniques you will learn for the sentence completion questions—where the word is omitted and you have to decide what word, from among the five choices, fits the meaning of the sentence. Vocabulary tested in the reading comprehension is just like the sentence completion, only easier; you have already been given the word.

Furthermore, except for the number of questions, the sentence completion, as well as the word relationship sections on the new SAT are exactly the same as on the old test. Even if you are unfamiliar with these types of questions, in this book we will show you fail-safe methods and step-by-step techniques that will enable you to zero in on the correct answers.

One of the interesting changes in the new SAT is in the reading comprehension section, which the Educational Testing Service now refers to as Critical Reading. But the change in name is little more than window dressing. For while the passages are longer and followed by more questions, the fact remains that all reading is essentially the same and the new passages test the exact same skills as the old test. Even the amount of time you are given to read each passage and answer the questions has been adjusted to the length of the passage. So once you learn the techniques of how to handle this section of the test, you will have more than enough time to read the passages and find all the answers.

The most misunderstood part of the new SAT, the section that is replacing the Test of Standard Written English, is the fifteen-minute section dealing with the double reading comprehension passages, where in each pair of passages, the second passage will either support or contradict the opinions expressed in the first. This section can really be looked at as an extension of the reading comprehension section and can be handled in exactly the same way. You simply treat the double passages as if they were two separate passages. Since the questions are based on either one passage or the other, all that is necessary is to separate the questions as they apply to either passage.

Your score on the verbal section of the SAT reflects one measure of your ability to reason, to manipulate concepts, and to understand and articulate complex ideas. The techniques you are about to learn will help you excel in these areas. Nothing is left to chance. You are going to learn how to "dig out" the correct answers by working backwards from clues found in the questions to the answers hidden in the text. Furthermore, the verbal section of this book will give you all the information you will ever need to achieve your best scores. But keep in mind that the SAT is like any athletic event. No one with any desire to excel in any activity would enter the main event without grueling workouts and intense preparation. Any skill requires a concentrated effort. One thing is certain, however: the results are usually worth it.

ANALOGIES

The type of question treated in this section requires you to analyze word relationships and to recognize *analogies;* that is, things that are parallel in some way. The student is given two words that have a specific relationship, followed by five pairs of words, one pair of which clearly imitates the relationship between the first two.

To be able to choose the best parallel relationship from among the answers, the student must establish the relationship not only between the first two words but between the words in the answer choices. This part of the test calls on your knowledge of vocabulary, but there are also important ways of approaching words you don't know at all or perhaps know only vaguely. First we will explain the basic techniques to use when you *do* know the words, and then techniques you can resort to when you *don't* know the words.

If You Know Both Words

Step 1

Examine the following analogy question, paying particular attention to the relationship between the first two words.

> FEATHER:BIRD: : (A) fur:beaver (B) zebra:stripes (C) sky:cloud
> (D) goose:down (E) skin:man

Let's assume you know the meaning of the first two words, *feather* and *bird*. This, then, is what you are to do. On a separate sheet of paper, *make a sentence,* using the words *feather* and *bird.* Make your sentence as *simple* as possible and as *specific* as possible. Make certain it expresses the relationship between the first two words. Think about it for a minute. What does a bird have to do with feathers? Write your sentence in the space below, *before* reading further.

Chances are that you came up with either one of two sentences: *A bird has feathers* or *Feathers cover a bird.* (Of course, variations of either sentence are perfectly acceptable.)

Step 2

Now take your sentence and read it exactly as you have written it, only instead of the words *bird* and *feather,* substitute the choices given in A through E.

But this is important: The words must be in the same order. For example, if you had used the sentence *A bird has feathers,* you would have to say: (A) *A beaver has fur,* (B) *A stripes has zebra,* (C) *A cloud has sky,* (D) *A down has goose,* and (E) *A man has skin.*

As you read through your choices for the first time, take your pencil and *draw a line* through all choices that do not seem to make any sense or are impossible. *Go back* to the analogy and try it now. Do your crossing out right on this sheet.

Your analogy should look like this:

> FEATHERS:BIRD: : (A) fur:beaver (B) ~~zebra:stripes~~ (C) ~~sky:cloud~~
> (D) ~~goose:down~~ (E) skin:man

You probably eliminated (B), (C), and (D) because stripes do not have zebra, cloud does not have sky, and down does not have goose.

Step 3

Look at your remaining choices, (A) and (E). Now that you have narrowed your choices down to two, it is a good idea to work with one side of the analogy at a time.

Suppose you look at the left side first. *Fur,* choice (A), is more analogous to *feathers* than choice (E), *skin,* is—after all, birds, beavers, and men all have skin. So *skin* is probably too broad a word to express the analogy. But a *beaver* has *fur* in exactly the same way a *bird* has *feathers*. So (A) is the right choice.

Suppose you look at the right side first. *Beaver,* choice (A), seems to relate pretty well to *bird*—better than choice (E), *man,* in that beavers and birds are both animals, and men are usually not thought of as animals. This gives you the right answer too. But be careful in such situations! The distinction between man and animal, human and nonhuman, *might* be important in some analogies, but it is by no means always the determining distinction. Suppose the answer choices had been (A) *tail:beaver* and (E) *hair:man*. In this case, (E) would be correct.

Thus, by making a sentence that expresses the relationship between the first two words, it is usually possible to eliminate several of the analogy choices immediately without having to examine each one studiously; they will simply sound ridiculous in your sentence. If you have narrowed your answers down to two, both of which sound possible in your sentence, examine each part of the analogy individually. In some cases it might also help a lot to revise your original sentence to make it more specific. In the example above, revising your sentence to *Feathers grow from the skin of a bird* would quickly lead you to the right answer choice.

The following word-relationship questions represent the various types of analogies you are likely to have on the test. Handle them exactly the way you did the word relationship we just completed.

Time and Measurement

1. QUART:PINT: : (A) pound:ton (B) gallon:barrel
   (C) yard:inch (D) second:minute (E) yard:foot

If You Cannot Make a Sentence

2. SIAMESE:MOUSE: : (A) cat:goldfish
   (B) hunter:rabbit (C) greyhound:cat (D) dog:turtle
   (E) cobra:python

Synonyms

3. INTEREST:ENTHUSIASM: : (A) vanquish:defeat
   (B) irritate:annoy (C) anger:belligerence
   (D) ruthlessness:meanness (E) barbarous:savage

Antonyms

4. DISCORDANT:HARMONIOUS: :
   (A) impede:delay (B) friendly:congenial
   (C) crush:sever (D) opposed:compatible
   (E) flatter:trick

Animate and Inanimate

5. HUNTER:SPEAR: : (A) debater:argument
   (B) scientist:microscope (C) drill:dentist
   (D) cook:food (E) mathematician:integer

Genus, Class, Species

6. SNAKE:REPTILE: : (A) ape:baboon
   (B) bird:aviary (C) dolphin:whale
   (D) creature:beast (E) hamster:rodent

When One Answer Is Too Broad

7. POISON:ILLNESS: : (A) school:graduation
   (B) experience:growth (C) exercise:muscles
   (D) knowledge:maturity (E) freedom:wisdom

If Your Sentence Fits Them All

8. RANGER:BINOCULARS: : (A) physician:
   stethoscope (B) tractor:farmer (C) referee:whistle
   (D) pattern:seamstress (E) tourist:map

Here are the answers. Each answer is discussed in the explanations that follow.

1. (E)	2. (C)	3. (C)	4. (D)
5. (B)	6. (E)	7. (C)	8. (E)

1. (E) The type of sentence construction that often fits the time and measurement question and will help you arrive at the word relationship quickly is as follows: _____ is the largest part of _____. Go back to your example and try this now, *before reading further.*

Your sentence probably was *A pint is the largest part of a quart.* (We are assuming, of course, that you know liquids are measured in ounces, pints, quarts, and gallons.) If you substituted choices (A) through (E) in your sentence, you were probably able to eliminate (A), (B), and (D). A *ton,* choice (A), is not the largest part of a *pound;* a *barrel,* choice (B), is not the largest part of a *gallon;* and a *minute,* choice (D), is not the largest part of a *second.* With your remaining choices (C) and (E), you probably realized that in choice (C) the largest part of a yard is a foot, not an inch; an inch is the largest part of a foot. So (E) is the best answer.

There is one other type of time and measurement question that is sometimes asked on the SAT. The word relationship might be DECADE:YEAR: : (A) dollar:dime. If that is the case, use the sentence *There are ten years in a decade, just as there are ten dimes in a dollar.*

2. (C) What should you do if you cannot make a sentence? Look at the next example. Students waste too much time thinking of sentences such as *A Siamese chases a mouse,* but such trials don't get them very far. The fact is, of course, that such statements are not always true. Thus, it is important that your sentence be as simple and as factual as possible. You probably know that a *Siamese* is a particular type of cat and that a *mouse* is a member of the rodent family. Here, the best way to avoid wasting time is to define each word separately. In this example, your definitions would be *A Siamese is a specific and a mouse is a general.* Now substitute choices (A) through (E) in your sentence. Notice that if the *first word is not a type,* you need not bother with the second word; simply draw a line through the entire answer. Try this now before reading further.

You were probably able to eliminate (A) and (D) immediately, because neither (A), a *cat,* nor (D), a *dog,* is a specific. Left with (B), (C), and (E), you probably eliminated (E) next, because a *cobra* and a *python* is each a type of snake. Having narrowed your choices down to (B) and (C), you should have no trouble eliminating (B). Even though *hunter* and *greyhound* are both specific, a hunter is a human being and a greyhound and Siamese are both animals. The best answer is (B), in that a greyhound and a Siamese are both animal types.

3. (C) This question would have been easy, in that most people know the meaning of these two words. But it is not enough to know the definitions; it is important to recognize in as short a time as possible what the relationship is. This type of question is one of the most frequently used on the SAT. The synonym question lets you know that both words are similar. The instant you recognize a synonym question, you should use one of the following sentences: (A) _____ is the same as _____ or (B) _____ is stronger than _____. Go back to the example and see which sentence type best fits your word relationship.

You probably used the sentence *Enthusiasm is stronger than interest.* Now substitute your choices and see if you arrive at the answer. (Be certain the words *are in the same order.*)

You were probably able to eliminate (D) and (E), in that *meanness,* choice (D), is not stronger than *ruthlessness,* and *savage,* choice (E), is not stronger than *barbarous;* the words are in the reverse order. On closer examination, you would have eliminated

(B), in that *irritate* and *annoy* are about the same; neither word is more intense than the other. Left with (A) and (C), you might have had some difficulty with the word *vanquish,* which means "to conquer," but the words are in the wrong order. Thus (C) is the correct choice; *belligerence* means "warlike," the perfect word to express an extreme form of *anger* or intense displeasure.

4. **(D)** You should have no difficulty arriving at your sentence for the antonym question. It is _____ is the opposite of _____. Using this sentence, go back to the questions and substitute the choices in your sentence, eliminating those that are not possible. Do this now, without looking ahead.

   Because your sentence was *Discordant is the opposite of harmonious,* you were probably able to eliminate every answer choice but (D). *Opposed* and *compatible* are opposites, just the relationship you are looking for.

5. **(B)** This question should have been easy, in that most people know that *a hunter uses a spear.* But narrowing down your answer choices might have presented you with some difficulty. You were probably able to eliminate (C), in that a *drill does not use a dentist;* it's the other way around. Choices (A), (B), (D), and (E) seem to fit the sentence fairly well, so you had better take another look at the relationship and try to make a more *specific* sentence. One likely possibility might be *A spear is a tool a hunter uses.* That would eliminate (D), in that food is not a tool. Although an *argument,* choice (A), and an integer, choice (B), are used by a debater and a mathematician, respectively, they are not instruments but inanimate or abstract concepts. The best answer, therefore, is (B); a *microscope* is a tool used by a scientist in his work.

6. **(E)** There should be little problem making a sentence, in that most students know that *a snake is a type of reptile.* Substitution should easily eliminate (A), (C), and (D). Choice (A) is wrong because an *ape* is not a type of *baboon;* they are both from the same class. Choice (C) is also wrong, in that a *dolphin* is not a type of *whale;* both are aquatic mammals. A *creature,* choice (D), is not a type of *beast;* if anything, they are in the reverse order. Besides, this analogy is not dealing with biological classification. You probably left (B) as a possibility, in that you might not have known that an *aviary* is where a bird is kept. Even so, you probably picked (E) as the best answer, because you know that a *hamster* is a type of rodent.

7. **(C)** *Poison causes illness* is probably the simplest way to deal with this relationship. It should be apparent that the second word is the result of the first. Using this sentence, go back to the question and see if you can find the answer. Do this now, before reading further.

   You probably eliminated (E) without any difficulty, in that there is no cause-and-effect relationship between *freedom* and *wisdom.* But the remaining choices might have presented you with a problem because each of the second words in the answer choices can be a consequence of the first word. To get around this dilemma, you might follow another line of reasoning. Revise your original sentence this way: *Poison almost always causes illness.* Now try to substitute the choices in this revised sentence, eliminating those that are not possible. The answer, of course, is (C): *Exercise almost always causes muscles.*

   The other choices are simply too broad. *School,* choice (A), does not almost always cause graduation. School is a place where instruction is given; it does not mean that one has to graduate. (For that matter, a school could refer to a large number of fish.) *Experience,* choice (B), does not almost always cause *growth.* What type of growth? Mental growth? Physical growth? This answer is too broad. *Knowledge,* choice (D), is a body of information acquired by someone, and *maturity* can be taken in one of two ways—either as a state of complete physical development or as a way of behaving, usually associated with reason and intelligence. Neither definition has anything to do with knowledge. (C) is the best answer because it is *specific*. Even minimal exercise will develop muscles.

8. (E)   You might have started with a quite simple sentence, such as *A ranger uses binoculars.* Using this sentence, you would have eliminated (B) and (D) immediately, in that a *tractor* does not use a *farmer* and a *pattern* does not use a *seamstress.* At this point, the remaining choices all seem possible, so it might help to revise your sentence. With a longer sentence, such as *A ranger uses binoculars to make something clearer,* you probably eliminated (C), in that a *referee* does not use a *whistle* to make something clearer. You would have had some difficulty deciding between (A) and (E) because a *physician* does use a stethoscope to make something clearer—the patient's heartbeat—and a *tourist* does use a map to make something clearer (how to find his way to a particular destination). By more closely examining the relationship between your remaining choices, however, you could have detected a subtle distinction between the two relationships: a *ranger* and a *tourist* both use their eyes in order to make the object clearer, and a *physician* with a stethoscope uses his ears. The correct answer choice is therefore (E).

PRACTICE EXERCISES

Here are some analogies for you to practice on. Each question that follows consists of a related pair of words or phrases, followed by five lettered pairs of words or phrases. Practice making specific sentences. Substitute the choices in (A) through (E), eliminating those that are *not possible.* Then select the lettered pair that *best* expresses a relationship similar to that expressed in the original pair.

1. CHAPTER:NOVEL: : (A) epilogue:play
(B) stanza:poem (C) epigram:proverb
(D) rhyme:meter (E) verse:drama

2. PLUMBER:WRENCH: : (A) doctor:microscope
(B) surgeon:scalpel (C) car:brake
(D) sleeper:nightmare
(E) alcoholic:whiskey

3. ANGULAR:ROUND: : (A) vertical:horizontal
(B) straight:oblique (C) bend:notch
(D) jagged:curved (E) latitude:longitude

4. ANGER:FURY: : (A) infatuation:affection
(B) love:adoration (C) sullen:pouting
(D) acrimony:bitterness
(E) resentment:scowl

5. TIME:ETERNITY: : (A) year:chronology
(B) space:cosmos (C) factor:vector
(D) second:century (E) date:infinity

6. LASSO:CALF: : (A) captive:outlaw
(B) cage:lion (C) animal:trap (D) rodeo:cowboy
(E) handcuffs:prisoner

7. THERMOMETER:TEMPERATURE: :
(A) draftsman:compass (B) radar:navigator
(C) scale:weight (D) filter:water
(E) hypodermic:insulin

8. IMPULSIVE:CAUTIOUS: : (A) cruel:pitiless
(B) crooked:patriotic
(C) compassionate:indifferent
(D) bigoted:intolerant (E) soothe:pacify

9. TEAM:COACH: : (A) organization:chairman
(B) army:general (C) judge:court
(D) club:president (E) club:adviser

10. SCALES:FISH: : (A) tile:pattern
(B) wings:insect (C) wings:bird
(D) mane:lion (E) epidermis:man

ANSWERS AND EXPLANATIONS

1. (B)   2. (B)   3. (D)   4. (B)   5. (B)
6. (B)   7. (C)   8. (C)   9. (E)   10. (E)

1. **(B)**   This one should not be difficult. A sentence that seems to express the relationship well is *A chapter is part of a novel.* Substituting the choices in this sentence, you should have been able to eliminate (D) and (E). A *rhyme,* choice (D), is not part of a *meter,* and a *verse,* choice (E), is not part of a *drama.* You probably left (A) and (C), in that you might not have known that an *epilogue,* choice (A), is a speech given by one of the actors after the conclusion of a play, as opposed to a *prologue,* which is given at the beginning. In any case, you might have left this as a reasonable possibility because an *epilogue* is part of a play. You might also have left (C) if you did not know that *epigram* means "a witty or pointed expression." If you had known that definition, of course, you would have eliminated this as a possible answer, in that *epigram* and *proverb* are practically synonyms. Left with these choices, though, it would seem to make the most sense to select (B) as your answer, in that you know that stanzas are main divisions of a poem, just as chapters are main divisions of a book.

When you construct a sentence that expresses the relationship between words, try to avoid using the phrase *a part of.* This idea can lead you into trouble because many of the choices will seem reasonable. In most relationships, something is always a part of something else. You will probably have to revise your original sentence to show a more specific relationship. The analogy you have just finished illustrates this idea perfectly. An *epilogue* is part of a *play,* just as a *stanza* is part of a *poem.* But a *chapter* is a major division; that is the distinction you were looking for.

2. **(B)**   This sentence should not be difficult. Your sentence probably was *A plumber uses a wrench.* Thus, you should have eliminated (C) and (D), in that a *car,* choice (C), does not use a *brake* and a *sleeper,* choice (D), does not use a *nightmare.* In order to narrow your choices even further, it would have helped to revise your original sentence to make it more specific, such as *A wrench is a tool a plumber uses in his work.* Substituting the remaining choices in your sentence, you probably would have no difficulty backing into the right answer, (B). A *scalpel* is a tool a surgeon uses in his work. *Whiskey,* choice (E), is not a tool an *alcoholic* uses in his work, and in (A) a *doctor* uses a *microscope* in his work infrequently; it is not one of his primary instruments. (B) is therefore the more specific answer.

3. **(D)**   It should be obvious that the words *angular* and *round* are opposites; therefore, you might have started with the sentence *Angular is the opposite of round.* But you probably realized that choices (A), (D), and (E) all seem to fit this sentence fairly well. The best way to handle this type of relationship is to examine one side at a time. In that the word *angular* means "having angles," you could have backed into the correct answer, (D); *jagged* relates to *angular* and *curved* relates to *round.*

4. **(B)**   You might have started with the simple sentence *Anger is the same as fury.* That would have eliminated (C) and (E) because *sullen,* choice (C), is not the same as *pouting,* and *resentment,* choice (E), is not the same as *scowl.* (*Sullen* describes how one looks when one pouts, and *resentment* describes how one looks when one scowls.) You probably left (A), (B), and (D), in that each of these analogies deals with words that are similar. Whenever you have synonyms, one of the things you should be looking for is the degree of intensity: one word is often more intense than the other. Your original sentence could thus have been *Fury is stronger than anger.* Substituting (A) in this sentence, many students might realize that *affection* is not stronger than *infatuation;* these words have different meanings, for *infatuation* involves unreasoning passion, whereas affection means having genuine love. With (B) and (D) remaining,

chances are that you selected (B) as your answer; *adoration* is stronger than *love,* and *acrimony,* choice (D), is stronger than *bitterness,* not the other way around.

5. (B)   Your sentence for this analogy was probably something like *Endless time is eternity.* That should have easily eliminated (A), (C), and (D). An endless *year,* choice (A), is not a *chronology;* an endless *factor,* choice (C), is not a *vector;* and an endless *second,* choice (D), is not a *century.* You might have left (E) because of the word *infinity,* but the sentence does not fit; an endless *date* is not *infinity.* So you would go with (B).

6. (B)   There should have been little problem making a sentence, in that most students know that *a lasso is used to restrain a calf.* Using this sentence, you would have had to eliminate (A), (C), and (D). A *captive,* choice (A), is not used to hold an *outlaw;* an *animal,* choice (C), is not used to hold a *trap;* and a *rodeo,* choice (D), is not used to hold a *cowboy.* Now that you have narrowed your choices down to two, (B) and (E), it is a good idea to work with one side of the analogy at a time. On the left side, *lasso, cage,* and *handcuffs* are all means to control something, so there seems to be no way to narrow your choices any further. On the right side, although *lion* and *calf* are both animals, *men* are not usually thought of as animals; therefore, (B) is your best answer.
   But be careful in such situations. The distinction between man and animal, between human and nonhuman, *might* be important in some analogies, but it is by no means always the determining distinction.

7. (C)   This question should not have been difficult. A likely sentence is *A thermometer measures temperature.* You should have eliminated (A), (B), and (D) rather quickly. A *draftsman,* choice (A), does not measure a *compass; radar,* choice (B), does not measure a *navigator;* and a *filter,* choice (D), does not measure *water.* Narrowing your choice even further, a *hypodermic* is a syringe used to *administer* insulin, but it is not a measuring instrument. (C) is the best answer because a *scale* measures weight.

8. (C)   A simple sentence for this analogy is *Impulsive is the opposite of cautious.* Substituting the choices in this sentence, you more than likely backed into the correct answer, (C), in that the others can all be eliminated. *Cruel,* choice (A), is not the opposite of *pitiless;* they mean nearly the same thing. *Crooked,* choice (B), is not the opposite of *patriotic;* they are totally unrelated. *Bigoted,* choice (D), and *intolerant* are synonyms, not antonyms. *Soothe,* choice (E), is not the opposite of *pacify;* both words mean "to calm."

9. (E)   You might have started with a quite simple sentence, such as *A coach is the head of a team.* But this question is a good example of how easy analogies can sometimes lead the incautious student into an unsuspected trap. Substituting each of the five pairs in this sentence, you probably eliminated (A), (C), and (E). A *chairman,* choice (A), is not really the head of an *organization,* although he might be the presiding officer of a committee or meeting. A *court,* choice (C), is not head of a *judge;* if anything, it is the other way around. An *adviser,* choice (E), is not the head of a *club.* Your remaining choices, (B) and (D), probably led to an impasse; there is no way to eliminate one answer over the other. You had to go back to your original analogy. If you think about it, a *coach* is technically not the head of a team, the *captain* is. Whenever possible, use the words in the original analogy to make your sentence. This way, you leave nothing to chance. In this question, your sentence might then be *A coach coaches a team.* Now substitute the choices in this sentence. A *chairman,* choice (A), does not coach an *organization;* a *general,* choice (B), does not coach an *army;* a *court,* choice (C), does not coach a *judge;* and a *president,* choice (D), does not coach

a *club.* But an *adviser,* choice (E), does coach a *club,* just as a coach advises a team. The correct answer is (E).

10. (E) *A fish has scales* is probably the sentence you came up with. That should have eliminated (A) and (B), in that a *pattern,* choice (A), doesn't have a *tile* (if anything, it is the other way around) and an *insect,* choice (B), doesn't necessarily have wings; many insects don't have any. Having thus narrowed your answer down to (C), (D), and (E), it would have helped to revise your original sentence to make it more specific. Thus *Scales cover the body of a fish* would quickly lead you to the right choice, (E); *epidermis* covers the body of a *man.*

But be careful. You might have thought the answer was (C), in that all fish and birds are animals, and all birds have wings, just as all fish have scales. But the distinction between man and animal would have been important only if choice (C) had been *feathers:bird*

If You Know Only One of the Words

Examine the following analogy question, again paying particular attention to the relationship between the first two words.

> BIRD:AVIARY: : (A) tomb:headstone (B) actuary:lion
> (C) bridge:gully (D) prisoner:cell (E) money:safe

If you know what the word *aviary* means, make a specific sentence using both *bird* and *aviary* in the space below, *before reading further.*

What if you do not know what an aviary is? One way to discover what relationship *aviary* might have to *bird* is to *look over the choice of answers.* What choices do you have in this question? Two relationships you certainly know: a *prisoner* is locked up in a *cell* and *money* is locked up in a *safe.* Trusting yourself on this limited information, *you have to take a chance.* You have to make up a sentence with *bird* and *aviary* using these clues. Please do it now, using the space provided. You probably arrived at the same sentence you would have if you had known what the word *aviary* meant: *An aviary is where a bird is kept.* Now go back to the question and substitute the choices in your sentence, eliminating those that are *not possible.* Again, remember, *the words must be in the same order as in your original sentence.* Work on your analogy now, without reading ahead. The question should now look like this:

> BIRD:AVIARY: : (A) ~~tomb:headstone~~ (B) ~~actuary:lion~~
> (C) ~~bridge:gully~~ (D) prisoner:cell (E) money:safe

You probably eliminated (A), (B), and (C). A *headstone,* choice (A), is not where a *tomb* is kept. A *lion,* choice (B), is not where an *actuary* is kept. Even if you did not know that an *actuary* is one who calculates insurance premiums, you would realize that a *lion* is not a place. A *gully,* choice (C), is not where a *bridge* is kept. Again, even if you were not aware that a *gully* is a large trench worn in the earth, you would recognize immediately that a *bridge* is not kept anywhere.

Your remaining choices being (D) and (E), you might be puzzled because they both seem like good analogies. This *does* happen on actual SAT questions; not just students but their teachers might disagree on a particularly subtle question. You have to look for further distinctions that will make one choice better. For example, it should be apparent that (D) has an edge because *prisoner* is animate and *money* is inanimate. And there is another important distinction to keep in mind between (D) and (E) aside from animate and inanimate. That consideration aside, there are many things that are put into a safe besides money—such as documents, jewels, and so on—but *only* a prisoner is kept in a cell. So (D) is the *more specific* answer.

So far, you should have noted several important test-taking devices to keep in mind.

1. Make a *specific* sentence.
2. When substituting choices in (A) through (E), make certain that words are in the correct order.
3. Check for human and nonhuman, animate and inanimate—but remember that these are not primary considerations, they just help tip the balance where you have two choices that both seem good.
4. When left with a choice of two possible answers, be sure you select the more specific answer.
5. Look over your choices for clues to the relationship of the analogy being tested.

Step 1:   A person, a thing, or an idea

Examine the following analogy question, paying particular attention to the relationship between the first two words.

> PUGILIST:GLOVES: : (A) priest:religion (B) explorer:island
> (C) writer:book (D) navigator:map (E) architect:building

If you know what the word *pugilist* means, in the space below, form a specific sentence using both *pugilist* and *gloves*. Do this now, *before reading further*.

What if you do not know the meaning of *pugilist*? One way to discover what relationship *pugilist* might have to *gloves* is to ask yourself the question, Is the word *pugilist* a person, a thing, or an idea? One way to arrive at your answer is to look at the suffix *-ist*. Think of any words you know that end in these letters. Chances are you realized that the suffix *-ist* usually designates a person who does something, such as a *pharmacist* or an *anarchist;* the suffix means "practicer" or "believer." Even if you do not know that a *pugilist* is "a person who fights," just by knowing that the word refers to a person, you should go ahead and create a sentence. Try the sentence *A pugilist uses gloves.* Substituting the choices in your sentence, go back and try to find the answer. Do this now, *before reading further*.

You should have been able to eliminate (A), (B), and (E). A *priest,* choice (A), does not use *religion;* he is a person whose office it is to perform religious rites. An *explorer,* choice (B), does not use an *island,* though he might try to discover one. An *architect,* choice (E), does not use a *building,* though he might design one. Left with choices (C) and (D), you probably did not hesitate to choose (D) as the right answer, in that a *writer,* choice (C), generally creates, not uses, a *book.* A *navigator,* choice (D), uses a *map* in his profession, just as a boxer uses gloves in his.

Step 2:   Circle the prefix

Examine the following analogy:

> CIRCUMVENT:LAW: : (A) hasten:decision (B) censor:speech
> (C) evade:responsibility (D) argue:opinion (E) curb:temper

If you know what the word *circumvent* means, in the space below, make a specific sentence using both *circumvent* and *law*. Do this now, *before reading further*.

If you do not know what the word *circumvent* means, another technique you can use to arrive at the meaning is to *circle the prefix*. The prefix of *circumvent* is *circum-*, which means "around." You should have been able to figure this out in two ways. You are probably familiar with the word *circumference*, which means "the outer boundary of a circular area"; in fact, if you look closely at the prefix, you can recognize the word *circle*. Trusting yourself on this information, using the space below, go back to the question and make up a sentence showing the relationship between *circumvent* and *law* and see if you can arrive at the correct answer. Do this now, *before reading further*.

In either case, you probably arrived at some variation of the sentence *To circumvent the law is to go around it*. Based on substitution, then, you probably backed into the correct answer, (C). To *hasten,* choice (A), a *decision* is not to go around it but to hurry it up. To *censor,* choice (B), a *speech* is not to go around it; the word *censor* means "to suppress." To *argue,* choice (D), an *opinion* is not to go around it; on the contrary, it means to confront it head on. To *curb,* choice (E), a *temper* does not mean to go around it; the word *curb* means "to restrain or control." (C), of course, is the best answer. To *evade* a *responsibility* is to go around it. The word *evade* means "to avoid."

Step 3:   Circle the root

Examine the following analogy:

> PRAISEWORTHY:CULPABLE: : (A) abomination:loathing
> (B) extravagant:devotion (C) verify:contradict (D) biased:prejudiced
> (E) distrust:skepticism

If you know what the word *culpable* means, in the space below, make a specific sentence using both *praiseworthy* and *culpable*. Do this now, *before reading further*.

If you do not know the meaning of the word *culpable,* one way to determine its meaning is to circle the root *culpa-*. What familiar word can you think of that starts with similar letters? Chances are you came up with the word *culprit,* which means "one who is guilty of an offense." The root *culpa-* means "deserving blame." Go back to the original sentence completion and determine what the relationship is between the words *praiseworthy* and *culpable*. Make a sentence now, *before reading further*.

You probably realized that this word relationship is based on antonyms, a type of analogy we discussed earlier. Your sentence probably was *Praiseworthy is the opposite of culpable*. Now go through the choices and see if you can arrive at the correct answer.

By a process of elimination, you easily backed into (C), the correct answer. *Verify* is the opposite of *contradict;* the other choices are all synonyms.

Step 4: Look over your choices for clues to the definition

Examine the following analogy:

> TIME:SCYTHE: : (A) liberty:sickle (B) justice:scales
> (C) ignorance:chains (D) honor:testimonial (E) peace:dove

Even if you know what the word *scythe* means, you might have difficulty determining the relationship between the two words. It would be a good idea to look over your answer choices to see if you can figure out what they have in common. One way to do this is to examine the words on one side at a time. Suppose you look at the left side first. In what way are these words related? You probably realized that all of the words are abstract ideas. If you examine the words on the right side, you will notice that most of the choices are concrete objects that appear to have some relationship with the words on the left side; in fact, they represent those words. A sentence you might use is *A scythe is a symbol of time.* Substitute your choices in this sentence before reading further and see if you can find the right answer. But remember to use the second word first. Go back to the question and do this now, *before looking ahead.*

You probably eliminated (A) and (C), in that a *sickle,* choice (A), is one of the symbols on the Russian flag, which many people associate with tyranny and repression—not with liberty—and *chains,* choice (C), are a symbol not of *ignorance* but of bondage. Left with choices (B), (D), and (E), you probably had some initial difficulty. But consider that a *testimonial* is not a *concrete* symbol, as *scythe* is; a *testimonial* is something spoken or written as an expression of admiration. With choices (B) and (E) remaining, you would have had no trouble narrowing down your answer if you knew that a *scythe* is an implement with a long, curving blade, and is often used to symbolize Father Time. A *dove,* choice (E), is a familiar symbol of *peace,* but a dove is a bird; it is a living creature. The best answer is (B), in that *scales* are considered the symbol of justice and are inanimate objects, as a *scythe* is inanimate.

PRACTICE EXERCISES

Here are some analogies for you to practice on. Each question below consists of a pair of related words or phrases. Practice making specific sentences. In many of the original analogies, you will not know one of the words, or the relationship between them will not be clear to you, so try to use one or more of the techniques we have just discussed as a way to determine what the relationship could be. Then substitute the choices in (A) through (E) in your sentence, eliminating those that are *not possible.* Select the lettered pair that *best* imitates the relationship of the original pair.

1. EXPURGATE:IDEA: : (A) condense:book
   (B) filter:liquid (C) destroy:manuscript
   (D) improvise:speech (E) cancel:appointment

2. VIRULENT:DISEASE: : (A) enthusiastic:audience
   (B) stampeding:herd (C) incurable:liar
   (D) conspiracy:silence (E) acrimonious:debate

3. ABHORRENCE:ABOMINATION: :
   (A) offensive:action (B) altercation:disagreement
   (C) meek:arrogant (D) vigorous:imaginative
   (E) obtuse:intelligent

4. NEBULOUS:DECISIVE: :
   (A) despondent:dejected (B) impede:retard
   (C) deception:subversion (D) refusal:allowance
   (E) manifest:obvious

5. COVEY:PARTRIDGES: : (A) bunch:trees
   (B) gathering:congregants (C) swarm:bees
   (D) group:persons (E) riot:colors

6. EXPATIATE:IDEA: : (A) abridge:dictionary
   (B) level:building (C) analyze:document
   (D) focus:image (E) amplify:sound

7. MELLIFLUOUS:SOUND: : (A) incisive:wit
   (B) defamed:reputation (C) insipid:taste
   (D) beclouded:sky (E) saccharine:personality

8. DISSIDENT:GOVERNMENT: :
   (A) conformist:rules (B) hermit:solitude
   (C) iconoclast:tradition (D) fanatic:cause
   (E) philanthropist:charity

9. ENMITY:HATE: : (A) wearisome:refreshing
   (B) honor:courage (C) commodious:inconvenient
   (D) ignorance:fear (E) comity:friendship

10. TIMOROUS:FEAR: : (A) tranquil:uneasy
    (B) condone:forgive (C) worry:harm
    (D) resigned:hopeful (E) criticize:condemn

ANSWERS AND EXPLANATIONS

1. (B)	2. (E)	3. (B)	4. (D)	5. (C)
6. (E)	7. (E)	8. (C)	9. (E)	10. (B)

1. (B)   This analogy should have given you little difficulty, in that you know that the prefix *ex-* means "out of." (You could have figured this out by thinking of words beginning with that prefix). Your sentence was probably some variation of *When you expurgate an idea, you take it out.* You should have quickly eliminated (A), (C), and (D) for the following reasons. When you *condense,* choice (A), a book, you do not take it out; you make it more compact. When you *destroy,* choice (C), a *manuscript,* you do not take it out; you ruin it. When you *improvise,* choice (D), a *speech,* you do not take it out; you recite it on the spur of the moment.

Even if you did not know that the word *expurgate* means "to purify or cleanse" (in this case, to remove an offensive passage from a book) you would still have been able to eliminate (E). *Cancel* means "to put an end to" or "to make something invalid." On the other hand, *filter* is a verb form of the noun describing a device through which liquid is passed to take out impurities. So when you *filter* something, as when you *expurgate,* you purify it.

2. (E)   It is fairly easy to deal with this analogy by breaking down the word *virulent* in terms of its relationship with *disease.* You should recognize the beginning of the word *virus,* which is a highly infective agent. Your sentence was probably some variation of *When a disease is virulent, it is highly infectious or deadly.* You should then have been able to eliminate (A), (C), and (D). When an *audience,* choice (A), is *enthusiastic,* it is not highly infectious or deadly. It might be true that enthusiasm is contagious, but it should be obvious here that you are looking for a word that has negative implications. (C) is completely irrelevant, in that a *liar* is a person and *incurable* simply means that he is unable to change or rid himself of the habit. (D) is easy to eliminate, in that a *conspiracy* is a plot and you are looking for a negative adjective for the first word. (B) and (E) present an interesting choice. The word *stampede* means "sudden flight or rush," and its relationship with *herd* conjures up visions of hordes of animals running rampant—a situation in which the potential for danger is certainly real. But even if you do not know that *acrimonious* means "bitter" or "virulent," (E) is still the better choice. Not only do the words *disease* and *debate* both have negative connotations, but if you look at *acrimonious,* you might recognize it as related to the word *acid,* which means "sharp, biting." (B) is not specific enough. What type of herd? Geese? Sheep? Chances are you settled on (E); even though *stampede* means "sudden flight or rush," it does not suggest the idea of wild contamination, as *virulent* does.

3. (B)   It is obvious, if only from the prefix, *abhorrence* and *abomination* are synonyms. Therefore, you probably eliminated (A), (C), and (D) without any difficulty. *Offensive,* choice (A), is not the same as *action. Offensive* is an adjective that means "highly annoying," and *action* as a noun is a particular act. *Meek,* choice (C), is not the same as *arrogant; meek* means "submissive" and *arrogant* means "insolently

proud." *Vigorous,* choice (D), and *imaginative* have nothing to do with each other. Thus, you were probably left with choices (B) and (E) if you did not know the meaning of the words *altercation* and *obtuse.* If you look at *altercation,* choice (B), you will recognize the word *alter,* which means "to make different" or "to change." It should be obvious that in this analogy you are dealing with synonyms, not antonyms; in fact, an *altercation* is "a dispute." You have backed into the correct answer, (B). Can you think of any words beginning with *ob-* that tell you whether you have a positive or negative prefix? What about the words *obstruct* and *obstacle?* The prefix *ob-* is generally considered a negative prefix and means "against." You might have arrived at the fact that this is the choice you are looking for; *obtuse* means "dull" or "witless" and is the perfect antonym for *intelligent.*

4. (D) It should be apparent to you that the word *decisive* means "final" or "conclusive." If *nebulous* presented you with a problem, take a closer look at the word. Even if you don't know that *nebulous* means "vague" or "indistinct," you are probably familiar with the word *nebula,* which means "galaxy" or any other vast body in space. So it is obvious that this analogy involves antonyms. This should have eliminated (A), (B), and (C). Regardless of any other consideration, the prefix *de-* in (A) suggests that the words are synonyms (*de-* means "away" or "down from"). In (B), most students know that *impede* is similar to *retard;* both mean to "hinder" or "obstruct." Although *deception,* choice (C), and *subversion* have different meanings, they are usually closely related. *Deception* is the act of misleading, usually by a false appearance or statement, and *subversion* is usually thought of as an underhanded action taken in order to ruin or destroy something. In any event, the prefixes alone should have told you that you were dealing with synonyms, not antonyms, in that both are negative. With choices (D) and (E) remaining, you no doubt realize that (D) is the correct answer because *refusal* means "declining to accept something" and *allowance* means "permitting someone to accept something." Thus, you could have made this correct choice even if you didn't know that in (E) the word *manifest* means the same as *obvious.*

5. (C) Even if you do not know the meaning of the word *covey,* "small flock" or "group," you should have had no trouble recognizing that you are dealing with relationships wherein the first word is always used when there is a crowd or company of the second word present. This analogy is a bit tricky, unless you look for fine distinctions. You probably eliminated (B) and (D), in that *gathering* and *group* are general in their description, and *covey* seems to bear a more specific relationship to *partridges.* With (A), (D), and (E) remaining, you probably eliminated (A), in that most people associate the word *bunch* with small groups of things, such as flowers or grapes, that can be held in one hand. That leaves (C) and (E). You were probably confused about the word *riot,* which in this analogy means "to grow wildly" or a "brilliant display." However, the likely answer is (C); the familiar word *swarm* specifically relates to a *body,* or collection, of *bees.*

6. (E) If you do not know what *expatiate* means, this question was difficult. Looking over your choices, the only clue is that each of the first words seems to have some effect on the second word. If *expatiate* presented you with a problem, take a closer look at the word. One of the techniques we discussed earlier was to see if you can recognize the beginnings of words that might bear some relationship to *idea.* You might have circled the prefix *ex-,* which you know means "out of." Your sentence would then have been some variation of *When you expatiate an idea, you take it out or get rid of it.* However, if you look over your answers, you will see that none of the choices fits; therefore, it is important to look at the word again.

One of the techniques in recognizing familiar words is to use as many of the letters as you can. Sometimes you can miss an important word if you limit your analysis to the prefix. Take a few letters at a time and try to add other letters that will make a word that seems to fit the relationship. Chances are you recognized the word *expand,* which means to "spread out" or "enlarge." You should have had no trouble eliminating (B) and (C), in that *design* and *analyze* are irrelevant; neither word means to expand. You might have left (A) if under the pressure of time you mistakenly thought the word *abridge* means "to enlarge" rather than "to condense." However, with (D) and (E) remaining, the best answer is obviously (E). If you *amplify sound,* you enlarge it, just as you do when you expatiate an idea. There might be some students who chose (D) because they thought that *focus* means "to sharpen an image" the way *amplify* means to "sharpen a sound" by enlarging it. The problem is that *focus* involves concentrating or converging on a particular area; the process is one of narrowing, not widening. The better answer is therefore (E).

7. (E)   It should have been apparent to you that the word *mellifluous,* which means "having a smooth, rich flow," is a positive word. It consists of two words you can easily recognize: *mellow,* which means "gentle" or "rich," and *fluid,* which means "flowing." Your sentence might have read: *A mellifluous sound is sweet.* Looking over your choices, you should have easily been able to eliminate (B), (C), and (D). *Defamed,* choice (B), means "disgraced." You probably recognized that the prefix *de-* means "away" or "down from"; a *defamed reputation* would hardly be considered sweet. *Insipid,* choice (C), not only sounds negative, but the prefix *in-* should tell you that this is a negative word; in fact, *insipid* means "tasteless." *Becloud,* choice (D), means "to darken or confuse"; the word *cloud* is easily recognizable, and you probably thought of several words that begin with the prefix *be-,* such as *besiege, belittle,* and *begrudge.* The prefix *be-* means "about" or "around" and is used in a negative sense.

You might have left (A) and (E) if you did not know the meaning of *incisive* or *saccharine.* However, you could have easily arrived at the definition of *incisive* if you examined the word closely. What word do you recognize? You probably know that incisors are cutting teeth. That is just what the word means, "sharp" or "biting," so it is the word you are looking for. You have backed into the correct answer, (E). If you thought that *saccharine* means "artificial" because it is used as a substitute for sugar, you were following a false lead. Saccharine is four hundred times sweeter than cane sugar and is your best choice. A *saccharine personality* is of a sugary sweetness.

8. (C)   The *dis-* prefix in the original analogy should have clued you to the fact that *dissident* is a negative word; *dis-* means "apart from." Even if you do not know that *dissident* means "one who disagrees," the prefix should have made it easy for you to make a sentence. Your sentence was probably some form of A *dissident is one who disagrees with the government.* That would have eliminated (A), (B), (D), and (E). A *conformist,* choice (A), does not disagree with *rules;* he follows them. A *hermit,* choice (B), does not disagree with *solitude;* he lives in seclusion. A *fanatic,* choice (D), does not disagree with a *cause;* he embraces causes with unreasoning enthusiasm. A *philanthropist,* choice (E), does not disagree with *charity;* he is known for giving to others. You were able to back into the correct answer, (C), even though you might not have known that an *iconoclast* is a person who attacks or disagrees with cherished beliefs and *traditions.*

9. (E)   If you do not know that the word *enmity* means "a feeling of hostility," an easy way to deal with this analogy would have been to analyze the word in terms of its relationship with *hatred.* You should have recognized the word *enemy,* so it is obvious you are dealing with synonyms. This should have enabled you to eliminate (A), (B), and (D). *Wearisome,* choice (A), is not the same as *refreshing. Honor,* choice (B), is not the same as *courage;* it is possible to have honor without being courageous. *Ignorance,* choice (D), is not the same as *fear;* you can be ignorant without being afraid. (C) and (E) might have posed some difficulty if you did not know the meaning of *commodious* and *comity.* One way of narrowing your choices would have been to

look at the prefixes. You should have known that both *co-* and *com-* mean "with" or "together," which would indicate that you are dealing with positive words. Using this technique, you would have narrowed your choice to (E), in that *friendship,* choice (C), is also a positive word and *inconvenient* is negative.

There is still another approach you can use to test your answer. What is the opposite of *inconvenient*? It should be obvious that you are looking for a word that means "convenient" or "suitable." Now look at the word *commodious.* If you eliminate the suffix *-ious,* you are left with *commod.* What letters can you add to the beginning and end of *commod* that will give you a word similar in meaning to "convenient" or "suitable." The word is ACcommodATE, which means to "provide with room" or "make suitable." *Commodious* means "spacious" or "roomy." Therefore, (E) is the correct answer, in that *comity* means "civility" or "courtesy" and is related to friendship in the same way *enmity* is related to *hostility;* they are both synonyms. At any rate, you could have backed into the right answer, in that *commodious,* choice (C), is not a synonym for *inconvenient.*

10. (B)   Again, it is easy to deal with this analogy by recognizing the word *timid* in *timorous.* So it is apparent you are dealing with synonyms. You should then have been able to eliminate (A), (C), and (D). *Tranquil,* choice (A), is not the same as *uneasy;* tranquil means "peaceful." *Worry,* choice (C), is not the same as *harm,* and *resigned,* choice (D), is not the same as *hopeful;* they are both irrelevant. Your remaining choices (B) and (E) might have posed some difficulty if you did not know that *condone* means "excuse" or "forgive." That being the case, you probably moved to (E) as the right answer because *criticize* and *condemn* are synonyms. But think about these words. *Criticize* means to "find fault with," and *condemn* means to "express strong disapproval of," almost to the point of judging someone guilty. There are many forms of criticism. Teachers criticize the work of their students; parents criticize the behavior of their children; citizens criticize the actions of their government. In these examples, criticism can often be considered *constructive* or helpful, rather than destructive. The better answer would be (B); *condone* is the same as *forgive.* In any case, whenever you narrow your choices down to two, you should make an educated guess.

The only way that (E) might have been considered the correct answer is if the original analogy had been something like TIMID:COWARDLY. Then you could have assumed that although you were dealing with synonyms, they were based on degree of intensity; in that case, you could have gone with (E). It is important to recognize these fine distinctions on the SAT and to discern the subtle shades of difference between one answer and another so that ultimately you will be able to move confidently and successfully to the correct answer.

If You Do Not Know Either of the Words

Examine the following analogy question, noting the relationship between the first two words.

> INTROVERT:EXTROVERT: : (A) withdrawn:outgoing
> (B) loquacious:talkative (C) injurious:jinxed
> (D) despondent:depressed (E) arrogant:bumptious

Make a specific sentence using both *introvert* and *extrovert* and write it in the space below, *before reading further.*

Are you having difficulty with the words? Is it because you don't know what they mean? Well, you don't have to. Here is a perfect example of determining whether the words are positive or negative simply by examining the prefixes.

Ex- means "out of" and *in-* means "into." You could have figured that out by thinking of words beginning with those prefixes and thinking about what they mean—words such as *introduce, invite,* and *intramural,* and *extravagant, expel,* and *extract.* What is the difference between the words beginning with the prefix *ex-* and those beginning with the prefix *in-*? Do they have positive (good) or negative (bad) associations? Now that you have thought about the nature of words beginning with *in-* and *ex-,* you are ready for your sentence. Try to make one, writing it in the space previously provided.

You probably arrived at the most natural way to deal with an analogy of this type: *If I am an extrovert, I am not an introvert,* or *An extrovert is the opposite of an introvert.* Now go back to the question and substitute the choices in your sentence, eliminating those that are clearly not possible. *Do it now, without looking ahead.* The question should now look like this:

> INTROVERT:EXTROVERT: : (A) withdrawn:outgoing
> (B) loquacious:talkative (C) ~~injurious:jinxed~~
> (D) ~~despondent:depressed~~ (E) arrogant:bumptious

You probably eliminated (C) and (D) immediately. You know that both words in (C) have negative connotations. In other words, *injurious,* which means "tending to inflict injury," is similar to *jinxed,* which means "tending to bring bad luck." They are certainly not opposites. You probably also recognized that the prefixes of the two words in (D) are similar; therefore, you are probably not dealing with opposites here either (though *de-* can be a positive prefix, as in *delightful*). In fact, *despondent* means "hopeless."

Choice (E) should not have presented a problem, in that the word *bump* in *bumptious* should give you an obvious clue that it is a word with negative associations and therefore it is unlikely that it is an opposite of the word *arrogant;* in fact, the words mean much the same thing. Left with choices (A) and (B) and not having many clues to go on as to the meaning of *loquacious,* you still might naturally select (A), in that it is an obvious contrast. However, it is possible to deal with *loquacious* in two ways. The first is if you know that the root *loq-* means "talk." If you are not familiar with that root, it is still possible to work with the suffix *-ous,* which means "full of." In that *talkative* means "full of talk," there is a strong indication that *loquacious* is a synonym, not an antonym.

This is a good time to expand on the concept of positive and negative words. Positive words generally have good connotations; negative words generally have bad connotations. You can usually determine which type you are dealing with by the prefixes, such as *retro-,* ("backward"); *dis-,* ("apart"); and *ex-,* ("out of"). These are essentially negative words, whereas *pro-,* ("forward"), *syn-* ("with"), and *ad-* ("forward") are essentially positive words (at least for our purposes, in that there will obviously be significant exceptions to the suggestions developed in this book to help you make "educated guesses" on the SAT).

You will also have to make intuitive decisions. Trust your instincts as to whether a word is positive or negative. A word such as *irascible,* for example—how does it sound to you? Good or bad? Positive or negative?

Words are built on foundations. It is not an accident that *disturb* and *dissatisfy* begin with the same prefix. So another important technique for you to use in trying to define a word is to see if you can think of words beginning with the first few letters. In the case of *irascible,* such words include *irritate* and *irate.* These are all negative words.

Another technique you might try is putting the word in some context in which you might have heard it before. Consider the word *quixotic.* There is an entire range of associations, which could lead you to the meaning of the word. Do you remember the character Don Quixote in the Broadway show *Man of La Mancha*? The hit song from that show was "The Impossible Dream" and the hero was dreamy, or more specifically, impractically idealistic. And that is just what *quixotic* means.

Needless to say, the more roots you know, the easier time you will have identifying words. For example, the root *-lev-* is the basis for a great many words that have the sense of "lighten," such as *levity, elevator,* and *levitation.* What is most important is to use all of the possible techniques available to help identify the correct answer.

PRACTICE EXERCISES

Here are some analogies for you to practice on. Each question below consists of a related pair of words or phrases. Practice making specific sentences. In many of the original analogies, you might not know the meanings of the words being tested, but you might find some clues as to how best to deal with the relationship by examining the prefixes of the words. The first few letters can also offer you information about its definition.

1. IMPERTURBABLE:DISTRAUGHT: :
   (A) palpable:perceptible
   (B) comprehensible:inconceivable
   (C) ambivalent:ambiguous
   (D) evanescent:ephemeral
   (E) fulgent:radiant

2. EXTERN:INTERN: : (A) hoyden:hussy
   (B) extirpation:implantation
   (C) stipend:scholarship
   (D) feculence:fetidness
   (E) impartiality:objectivity

3. DISCREET:INJUDICIOUS: :
   (A) perturbed:agitated
   (B) pertinacious:obstinate
   (C) polluted:corrupt
   (D) qualified:competent
   (E) inhibited:exhibitionist

4. VERACITY:IMPOSTURE: :
   (A) precision:inaccuracy
   (B) hill:mound
   (C) perjury:falsehood
   (D) childbirth:delivery
   (E) chief:leader

5. SUPERNUMERARY:INSUFFICIENT: :
   (A) bombastic:pompous
   (B) lachrymose:tearful
   (C) sophomoric:immature
   (D) superfluous:inadequate
   (E) valance:drapery

6. PERSEVERING:PERSISTENT: :
   (A) prodigal:squandering
   (B) inherent:acquired
   (C) mediocre:outstanding
   (D) popular:aristocratic
   (E) heavenly:infernal

7. VERACIOUS:VERIDICAL: :
   (A) languid:active
   (B) tortuous:cruel
   (C) transient:lasting
   (D) prolific:fecund
   (E) trite:original

8. PROXIMITY:PROPINQUITY: :
   (A) garb:attire
   (B) recession:promulgation
   (C) reticence:conviviality
   (D) rift:juncture
   (E) revelry:sobriety

9. CENSURE:ACCLAIM: :
   (A) slattern:slut
   (B) precedence:anteriority
   (C) precursor:herald
   (D) obduracy:concession
   (E) sequel:supplement

10. VARIEGATION:COLOR: :
    (A) surveillance:liberty
    (B) tirade:speech
    (C) medley:music
    (D) harangue:discourse
    (E) democracy:absolutism

ANSWERS AND EXPLANATIONS

1. (B)	2. (B)	3. (E)	4. (A)	5. (D)
6. (A)	7. (D)	8. (A)	9. (D)	10. (C)

1. (B) It should be apparent to you that the word *distraught,* which means "harassed," is a negative word. Not only does the prefix *dis-* mean "apart from," but the word sounds like the word *distressed,* which is still another meaning. With the word *imperturbable* you must tread cautiously. You should recognize the word *perturb,* which even sounds like the word *disturb,* which is its definition. The prefix *im-* means "not"; hence, the word means "not perturbable." Therefore, you are dealing with antonyms. Your sentence might read: *A person who is imperturbable is not distraught.* You should then have been able to eliminate (A), (C), and (E) without too much difficulty. *Palpable,* choice (A), which is related to the word *palpate,* means "tangible" or "able to be touched." (Notice the first three letters of the word *palm,* which happens to be the part of the hand that does the touching.) *Perceptible* means nearly the same thing, "able to be recognized or perceived." Therefore, something *palpable* is *perceptible.* They are obviously not the antonyms you are looking for. In (C), even if you did not know that *ambivalent* means "uncertain" or "confused" and that *ambiguous* means "uncertain" or "vague," the prefix *ambi-* should make it easy because you know you are probably not dealing with antonyms; *ambivalent* is not the opposite of *ambiguous. Radiant,* choice (E), should have presented no problem because you know that the word means "shining brightly." Chances are you did not know that the word *fulgent* also means "shining" or "bright," but certainly the letters *ful-* should have given you some indication that you were dealing with a positive word, and that *radiant* and *fulgent* are not antonyms. With choices (B) and (D) remaining, you no doubt realize that (B) is the correct answer, because *comprehensible* means "able to be understood" and *inconceivable* means "not able to be understood"; therefore, something that is *comprehensible* is not *inconceivable.* You could have made the correct choice even if you did not know that in (D) the words *ephemeral* and *evanescent* both mean "short-lived."

2. (B) This analogy should have presented you with little difficulty, in that you know that the prefix *ex-* and the prefix *in-* suggest that you are looking for antonyms. Your sentence was probably some variation of *Extern is the opposite of intern.* You probably eliminated (A), (C), and (E). In (A), you might have had a hunch that *hoyden* and *hussy* are synonyms, not antonyms; they not only look similar but both sound negative, even if you don't know that both mean "boisterous girl." In (C), most students know that a *stipend* is similar to a *scholarship;* both are sums of money paid regularly. (E) *Impartiality,* choice (E), and *objectivity* also mean the same thing. Left with (B) and (D), it would be surprising if you did not take (B), in that you are again dealing with contrasting prefixes, which suggest antonyms even if you don't know that *extirpation* means "rooting out" and *implantation* means "planting firmly"; *extirpation* is the opposite of *implantation.* You are right if you assume that *feculence* and *fetidness* suggest synonyms, simply from the similarity of the initial letters and the way the words sound (both mean "smelly" or "foul").

3. (E) You probably know the definition for *discreet,* which is "cautious" or "having good judgment" (as distinguished from *discrete,* which means "separate"). If *injudicious* presented you with a problem, take a closer look at the word. You should recognize the beginning of the words *judge, justice,* and *judicial,* all referring somehow to "judgment." The prefix *in-,* however, makes the word negative: "not having good judgment." So you are obviously dealing with antonyms. That should have eliminated (A), (C), and (D), because someone who is *agitated,* choice (A), is *perturbed;* something that is *polluted,* choice (C), is *corrupt;* and someone who is *quali-*

fied, choice (D), is *competent.* Left with choices (B) and (E), your natural selection was no doubt (E), in that regardless of any other consideration, the prefixes *in-* and *ex-* suggest that you are dealing with opposites. Perhaps you knew the meaning of *pertinacious,* which is quite close to *obstinate*—so this pair are not opposites. The best answer, then, is (E), in that someone who is *inhibited* is not an *exhibitionist.* Also, *discreet* and *inhibited* both suggest refraining from some action; *injudicious* and *exhibitionist* both suggest engaging in some probably foolish action.

4. (A) Most students are familiar with the words *imposture,* which means "fraud" or "deception," and *veracity,* which means "truthfulness." Your sentence was probably some variation of *Veracity is the opposite of imposture* or *Veracity means "truth" and imposture means "falsehood."* You should have quickly eliminated (B), (C), (D), and (E). A *hill,* choice (B), is not the opposite of a *mound;* a hill is a mound. *Perjury,* choice (C), is not the opposite of *falsehood; perjury* means "lying" and is therefore a synonym. A *childbirth* is a *delivery.* A *chief* is a *leader.* (A) is obviously the correct answer in that it is the only pair of antonyms; *precision* is the opposite of *inaccuracy.*

5. (D) It is fairly easy to deal with this analogy by breaking down the word *supernumerary* in terms of its relationship with *insufficient.* The prefix *super-* means "going beyond," and you should have had no trouble recognizing the word *number.* Thus the definition is simply "going beyond the number" or "more than enough," which contrasts with *insufficient,* which means "not enough." Again we are dealing with antonyms.

   Please make a note. It is a good idea to use your analogy with the *definitions of the words* in addition to a general sentence such as *Supernumerary is the opposite of insufficient.* Your sentence should read: *Supernumerary means more than enough and insufficient means not enough.* You can eliminate (A), (C), and (E) because *bombastic,* choice (A), and *pompous* are synonyms; *sophomoric,* choice (C), and *immature* are synonyms; and an analogy with *drapery,* choice (E), could hardly have anything to do with "more than enough" and "not enough." In addition, a *valance* is something that a *drapery* is hung behind, not an opposite. If you did not know that *lachrymose,* choice (B), and *tearful* are synonyms, you might have had a problem. But probably you eased yourself into the obvious answer, (D). It fits so nicely; *superfluous* means "going beyond the necessary" and *inadequate* means "less than necessary."

6. (A) It is obvious that *persevering* and *persistent* are synonyms if just from the prefix alone. Therefore, you probably eliminated (C), (D), and (E) without any difficulty. *Mediocre,* choice (C), is not the same as *outstanding; mediocre* means "ordinary" and is therefore the opposite. *Popular,* choice (D), is not the same as *aristocratic* because *popular* refers to the masses of people and *aristocratic* refers to the upper class. *Heavenly,* choice (E), is not the same as *infernal;* they are opposites. The remaining choices, (A) and (B), might present a problem, in that it is likely that you know the meaning of the word *squandering* ("wasteful" or "extravagant") and the word *acquired* ("obtained"), but you might not know the meaning of the other words. If you look at the word *inherent,* you will note the prefix *in-,* which means "into." You might also recognize it as related to the word *adhere,* which means "stick to" (like adhesive tape). Chances are you worked out the meaning of *inherent,* which is "existing in someone or something as a natural quality"; that is, not *acquired,* which suggests something added on. In that analogy (B) is based on antonyms, the right answer is, of course, (A); in fact, *prodigal* means "wasteful," which is the same as *squandering.*

7. (D) You might have nothing more to go on except the hunch that two words beginning with *ver-* are synonyms. Your sentence probably is *Veracious is the same as veridical.* You probably eliminated (A), (C), and (E) immediately because *languid,*

choice (A), means "sluggish" and *active* is just the opposite; *transient,* choice (C), means "temporary" and *lasting* is just the opposite; and *trite,* choice (E), means "commonplace" and *original* is just the opposite. Of your two remaining choices, (D) might have stumped you completely unless you knew that *fecund* means "productive" or "fertile." Then, without knowing that *prolific* means "fruitful" or "producing many of a kind," you might consider the prefix *pro-,* which means "forward," and take a chance on (D) as your answer, which would be right. If you did not know what *fecund* meant, you might have turned to (B) as your first consideration. Take a closer look at the first word. In all likelihood you read this word as a form of the word *torture,* which is a common mistake. Look again. The word is not *torturous,* which means "causing torture." You are dealing with a completely different word, *tortuous,* which means "winding" or "twisted." Therefore, what you have in analogy (B) are actually two totally unrelated words. You have therefore backed yourself into the right answer, (D).

8. (A)   Again, the *pro-* prefix in the original analogy should have clued you in to the fact that you are looking for synonyms. Both *proximity* and *propinquity* happen to mean "nearness." *Proximity is the same as propinquity.* You were probably able to eliminate (B) and (D) without much difficulty. In (B), without knowing that *recession* means "going backward" and that *promulgation* means "announcing" or "making known," you are aware of contrasting prefixes; thus, *recession* is not the same as *promulgation.* In (D), most students know that a *rift* means a "split." It is obvious that a *rift* is not a *juncture.* If you were not sure of the word *juncture,* notice how much it is like *junction,* which is what it means. Left with three choices, (A), (C), and (E), you might be one of those fortunate ones who know that the words *garb* and *attire* mean the same thing and are therefore the synonyms you are looking for. But what if you do not know those meanings? There are still one or two clues left to enable you to get closer to the answer. Take another look at choice (C). The prefix *re-,* which means "back" or "again," generally has negative connotations, and the prefix *con-,* which means "with," generally has positive connotations. That might suggest that you are dealing with antonyms. You might also notice that the familiar word *vivacious* seems to have quite a lot in common with the word *conviviality.* Most students know that *vivacious* means "lively"; others might recognize the root *-viv-,* which means "live." The word *conviviality* literally means "festivity." As for *reticence,* you might not only sense negative connotations because of the prefix, but the word itself suggests others, such as *retire,* which is certainly not an "up" word. (C) should therefore be eliminated, in that *reticence* is not the same as *conviviality.* The word *sobriety* in choice (E) should immediately suggest the word *sober,* and similarly, *revelry* should suggest *revel.* These words are clearly not the same. So you probably backed into the right answer, (A): *garb* is the same as *attire.*

9. (D)   This analogy should not have presented a problem. If the word *censure* is unfamiliar, it should at least have reminded you of the more common word *censor,* which is someone who removes or prohibits anything that is unsuitable. The negative connotations are easily apparent; the word *censure* means "condemnation." In *acclaim,* most students would recognize the word *claim* and the prefix *ac-,* which is a variation of *ad-* and has positive connotations. The word *acclaim* literally means "shouted approval." What you are dealing with, then, are antonyms. Your sentence is probably *Censure is not acclaim.* You probably eliminated (A), (B), and (E) immediately. A *slattern,* choice (A), is a *slut;* they both describe women who are careless and sloppy in appearance and character. At any rate, in sound and form the words are highly similar and you might have taken a chance and eliminated this choice. *Precedence,* choice (B), and *anteriority* are both words that deal with the state of being before in time or place; you would have known that from the prefixes *pre-* and *ante-,* which both mean "before." *Sequel,* choice (E), and *supplement* are both words that

deal with the aftermath or what follows. You are then left with choices (C) and (D), probably because you did not know the meaning of the words *herald,* choice (C), and *obduracy,* choice (D). You probably had little difficulty with the word *precursor* because of the prefix *pre-,* which again implies something that comes before. You are also probably familiar with the meaning of *concession,* which is a yielding or giving in. Can you think of any word beginning with *ob-* that means "not yielding" or "holding out"? What about the word *obstinacy*? The definition for *obstinacy* is "stubbornness," and that is just what *obduracy* means. The prefix *ob-* is generally a negative prefix and means "against." Think of other words that begin with *ob-,* such as *obstruct* and *obstacle.* You might have arrived at the fact that this is the choice you are looking for; *concession* is the opposite of *obduracy.* In (C), the word *herald,* someone who proclaims or foretells, is one of those words you just have to know. Therefore, what you have in (C) are synonyms, which can be eliminated.

10. (C)   This initial analogy should not have presented too much difficulty, although the choices might have been more difficult. The word *color* is simple, and the word *variegation* is just as simple if you study it for a moment. The word you should recognize in *variegation* is *variety;* in fact, *variegation* means a "variety in appearance." Your sentence is probably some form of the following: *Variegation means many colors.* That would eliminate (A), (B), (D), and (E). A *surveillance,* choice (A), is not many *liberties; surveillance* means "watch" or observation." A *tirade,* choice (B), is not many *speeches;* a *tirade* is a long speech. A *harangue,* choice (D), is not many *discourses;* a *harangue* is a windy speech. *Democracy,* choice (E), is not many *absolutisms;* they are opposed concepts. The correct answer is (C), in that a *medley* is many pieces of *music.* Think of the word *medley* for a moment. Certainly you recognize the word *meddle,* which means "to mix in," and that is exactly what we call a variety of different musical compositions thrown together—a mix.

SENTENCE COMPLETIONS

This type of question tests your ability to use vocabulary and to recognize logical consistency among the elements in a sentence. Merely knowing the definition of a word does not guarantee success. Sentence-completion questions deal with one phase of reading comprehension and test your ability to recognize the implications of a sentence as well as your ability to select the word or pair of words that best fits the meaning of the sentence as a whole.

Although there are a variety of basic types of sentence-completion questions, it is important for you to know that every question has a built-in clue that points to only *one* of the five choices as the most appropriate or *best* answer. You should *back into the right answer* by eliminating those answers that are *not possible*—thereby reducing the choices. Whatever word you decide on for your answer, you should be able to go back to the question and justify your reason for selecting it; that is, to *locate the clue*. The answers on the SAT are *not* left to chance. Both the right and the wrong answers are carefully designed. Therefore, if you are going to make haphazard guesses without carefully examining each answer, you are apt to select an answer that *seems* appropriate on cursory reading only to fall into a carefully laid trap. A closer examination will reveal a *specific clue* for which only one choice is correct. It is important to learn how to locate that clue.

One-Word Sentence Completions

Sentence-completion questions might have two blanks or only one. Although those with two blanks actually contain more clues than those with one, the one-blank questions are easier to understand at first, so we will begin with them.

Step 1

Examine the following sentence-completion question and underline those words you feel are *key words*. Underline words you feel provide you with information or clues that will point you in the direction of the right answer. This technique is similar to the one we will teach you to use for reading-comprehension questions, but with one important difference. In reading-comprehension sections of the SAT, which are explained later in this book, the first thing you are advised to do is to look over the questions at the end of the passage. But in the sentence-completion sections, you are advised to analyze the question *before* looking at the choice of answers. That is, you should have a fairly good idea of what you are looking for before you examine the available choices. That is why the answer choices are omitted on the questions below. Underline key words in the sentence now, *before reading ahead.*

Children in poverty-stricken areas have a tendency to be ___*emaciated*___.

Chances are you underlined the words *children, poverty-stricken areas,* and *tendency* because children are a special category of people with special needs. It is important to know that you are talking about a particular group of children; namely, those from poor areas. *Tendency* implies that the children are probably something-or-other, but might not be.

Step 2

Now look at the sentence again and try to single out any word (or words) *of the ones you have underlined* that you think is an especially important clue to the answer. When you have made your choice, circle that word (or words) in the sentence. Do it now, *before reading ahead.*

Chances are the word you selected is *poverty-stricken,* because if you are looking for an attribute that all of these children have in common, it is going to be their poverty.

Step 3

Reread the sentence and fill in the blank with a word of your own. If you cannot think of a particular word, ask yourself this question: Is the word I am looking for *positive* or *negative*? That is, does the word you want have good connotations or bad connotations? You will probably have little difficulty in deciding that the word you are looking for is a negative word, in that something associated with children growing up in an impoverished area is not likely to be good.

Step 4

Go through the choices one at a time, drawing a line through those answers that are *not possible.* This will include, of course, any words you recognize as obviously positive, in that you are looking for a negative word. Please do it now, *before reading further.* (You might often find your eyes wandering down the page in search of the answer to such exercises as this. But to get the most out of the exercises, you must control your eyes! If you can't do it any other way, put a file card or small envelope over the page, moving it down only after you've followed the instructions.)

Children in (poverty-stricken) areas have a tendency to be _____.
(A) overfed (B) opulent (C) ostentatious (D) emaciated (E) affectionate

You probably eliminated (A), (C), and (E) immediately because a child from an economically deprived area is not likely to be *overfed,* choice (A); *ostentatious,* choice (C), means "showy," and it is not likely that a deprived child would have anything to brag about; and *affectionate,* choice (E), is a positive word and does not relate to the one clue, which is *poverty-stricken.* You might have left (B) because you did not know that *opulent* means "wealthy." If you did know the meaning, you certainly eliminated it. But with (B) and (D) remaining, your best choice would have been (D), in that most children from poverty-stricken areas do have a tendency to be physically wasted, or *emaciated.*

Here is another sentence-completion question for you to practice on. In this exercise, the answers will follow the sentence, but *do not look at the answers* until you have followed the steps in analyzing the question and have an idea of the word you are looking for.

His clothes are torn, his hair unkempt, his body unwashed; what a _____ sort!
(A) sporadic (B) spatial (C) slovenly (D) skittish (E) praiseworthy

This sentence completion is an example of a *definition question.* You are looking for an answer that describes the words expressed in the sentence. *Step 1:* Chances are you underlined the words *clothes, torn, hair, unkempt, body,* and *unwashed* because each of the words either means a part associated with the body or describes a condition those parts can be in. *Step 2:* You probably circled *torn, unkempt,* and *unwashed* because these words leave a strong impression. *Step 3:* The word you probably thought of to fill in the blank no doubt had negative connotations, in that all of the words that describe the person are negative. *Step 4:* Therefore, you probably eliminated (E) immediately, in that *praiseworthy* is a positive word. Chances are you eliminated (A) and (B) next, because *sporadic,* choice (A), means "infrequent" and is not relevant to the person's description, and *spatial,* choice (B), relates to "space" and is also irrelevant. You might have left (D) if you did know that *skittish* means "lively." But the best choice is (C), in that *slovenly* means "untidy"; in fact, if you add the letter *b* to the first three letters, *slo,* you have the word *slob,* which is an apt word for the person being described.

In its final diagrammed state, your sentence completion should look like this:

His <u>clothes</u> are ⟨torn,⟩ his <u>hair</u> ⟨unkempt,⟩ his <u>body</u> ⟨unwashed;⟩ what a _____ sort!
(A) ~~sporadic~~ (B) ~~spatial~~ (C) slovenly (D) ~~skittish~~ (E) ~~praiseworthy~~

Step 5

There is one additional sentence-completion technique you should keep in mind. Although recognizing the implication of a sentence and being able to isolate the clues that lead to the correct answer are the important skills you need to develop, the subtleties of usage also play an important part. That is, if you are left with a choice between two words, both of which seem possible (such as introductory and incipient, which are similar) read the sentence completion "out loud" with both words in the blank and select the one that *sounds* best. Yes, you can speak the sentence to yourself in a whisper or just pronounce it under your breath so that your neighbor will not be disturbed.

Here is another sentence for you to practice on. Remember, *do not look at the answers* until you have followed the steps in analyzing the question and have an idea of the word you are looking for.

The young businessman was _____. He had spent far more than he earned.
(A) indigent (B) imprisoned (C) despondent (D) anxious (E) optimistic

This sentence completion is another example of a *definition question;* you are looking for an answer that describes the words expressed in the sentence. *Step 1:* Chances are you underlined the words *businessman, was, had spent, far, more, than,* and *earned* because these words describe the state or condition of the subject. *Step 2:* You probably circled the words *spent, more, than,* and *earned* because these words specifically characterize the nature of his state. *Step 3:* The word you probably thought of to fill in the blank no doubt has negative connotations, in that the idea of living beyond one's means has serious implications. *Step 4:* Therefore, you probably eliminated (E) immediately, in that *optimistic* is a positive word. Chances are you eliminated (B) next, because *imprisoned* is not relevant to the businessman's condition. Besides, there is no clue to justify your answer. You might have omitted (A) if you did not know the meaning of *indigent,* thus narrowing your choices to (C) and (D). *Despondent,* choice (C), means "depressed" or "downhearted," and *anxious,* choice (D), means "showing great concern or worry." Either choice would be apt to describe one's state of mind if one spent *far more than one earned.* However, this should have been a signal that you were overlooking something important. You have just fallen into a familiar trap that is common to this type of question. You are being asked to find a synonym or word that means the same as the definition *spent far more money than he earned;* you are *not* being asked to find an adjective that describes how one feels when one spends more than one earns. Besides, there are no clues to justify (C) or (D) as answers. By using the process of elimination and by knowing that you must specifically prove or verify your answer, you have narrowed your choices down to (A), *indigent,* which means, "poor." When one spends more than one earns, one is broke. That is the reason we asked you *to not eliminate words that are unfamiliar to you.* By narrowing down your choices, you are often able to back into the correct answer even though you might not know the precise meaning of all of the words.

PRACTICE EXERCISES

Here are some one-word sentence completions for practice. The sentence completion section of the SAT has both one-word and two-word omissions. We will get to the two-word omissions later. Beneath each sentence are five words or sets of words. Choose the word or set of words that *best* fits the meaning of the sentence as a whole. Be certain to follow the five steps in analyzing the question *before* you look at the answers. Cover them up with a card, envelope, or sheet of paper if you find it difficult to resist sneaking a glance.

1. Although the men appeared to be reserved and even ____C____, they fought like furies.

   (A) belligerent (B) flushed (C) austere
   (D) poignant (E) relaxed

2. The president's most obvious handicap, his ____A____, is also a strength.

   (A) naivete (B) derision (C) expressivity
   (D) maturity (E) proficiency

3. Because she was obsessed with neatness, even the least bit of disorder made her feel ____A____.

   (A) anxious (B) cynical (C) magnanimous
   (D) reluctant (E) impetuous

4. All across the nation, outbreaks of cancer have been reported in conjunction with evidence of environmental contamination; yet firm proof of cause and effect remains ____D____.

   (A) obscure (B) perceptible (C) unavoidable
   (D) elusive (E) palpable

5. Although the mathematical proof of his theory was shown to be false, he ____D____ in his belief in the hypothesis.

   (A) vacillated (B) calculated (C) reciprocated
   (D) persevered (E) gravitated

6. Although his speech was ____D____ and delivered on the spur of the moment, it was one of the most sincere and compassionate I have ever heard.

   (A) infallible (B) indigent (C) impaired
   (D) impromptu (E) impetuous

7. Psychic automation is a form of free association in which the pen or brush is allowed to wander ____C____ by the conscious mind.

   (A) motivated (B) formed (C) undirected
   (D) muted (E) repressed

8. The local population was highly ____C____ after the accidental discovery of the toxic landfill.

   (A) indulgent (B) scattered (C) indignant
   (D) uniform (E) erratic

9. Enforcing rules is difficult when these rules are too ____B____.

   (A) decrepit (B) stringent (C) varied
   (D) subservient (E) permissive.

10. The scoutmaster was so proper and ____C____ that the parents were shocked to discover that he had been abusing the boys in his troop.

    (A) concerned (B) stimulating (C) circumspect
    (D) irascible (E) inflexible

ANSWERS AND EXPLANATIONS

1. (C)	2. (A)	3. (A)	4. (D)	5. (D)
6. (D)	7. (C)	8. (C)	9. (B)	10. (C)

It is likely that your sentence completion looks likes this:

1. (C) Although the men appeared to be reserved and even _____, they fought like furies.

The clue to this sentence completion resides in the words *and even.* The word *and* implies that whatever is on one side of the word *and*—in this case, the word *reserved*—there should be a word of similar import on the other side. The word *even* implies that the second word is *more intense.* You were probably able to eliminate (A) and (B) as irrelevant. The next step is to examine *reserved.* What does this word mean? You probably arrived at the idea that it means "to keep back" or "save for future use." In the context of this sentence, the word *reserve* refers to the way the men appeared; therefore, to show reserve would be to show self-restraint or to "hold back" in speech or actions. You would probably have eliminated (E), *relaxed,* because the word means "to loosen" in severity or self-restraint, and you are looking for a word that shows greater, not lesser, intensity. (C) and (D) might have posed some difficulty. You might not know that the word *poignant* is from the Latin word *pungere,* which means "to pierce," or that *austere* means "restrained in a serious or severe way." Having narrowed down your choices, if you had read them both out loud in the blank spaces, chances are you might have picked (C); *austere* simply sounds best in the sentence.

2. (A) The president's most obvious handicap, his _____, is also a strength.

In this sentence completion, the adjective you are looking for is a word that can be used as both a positive and negative word. If you concentrate only on the word *handicap,* you are falling into a trap. The context here is important; the word *strength* is as important as the word *handicap* in locating the right answer. The word must have both positive and negative qualities. You probably had no trouble eliminating (C), (D), and (E), in that none of these words has negative connotations. If you did not know the meaning of *naivete,* which means "unaffected simplicity" or "openness," and if you did not realize that, as a word, it can be considered both good and bad, depending upon the circumstances, you might have eliminated (B) anyway. You probably understood that the prefix *de-* in the word *derision* is negative and means "down from"; that leaves only choice (A). Besides, if you read both words out loud in the blanks, *derision* does not seem to be positive.

3. (A) Because she was obsessed with neatness, even the least bit of disorder made her feel _____.

The clue to this sentence completion is in the words *because, obsessed, neatness, least,* and *disorder.* It is obvious from the word *because* that whatever is stated in the second part of the sentence completion is a result of the first part. It should also be clear that you are looking for a negative word; if she was obsessed with neatness, anything out of order would upset her. Thus, you probably eliminated (B), (C), and (D) immediately, in that none of these words has the meaning you are looking for. *Magnanimous* is a positive word meaning "generous", *cynical* means "distrusting the motives of others," and *reluctant* means "unwilling." You might have had trouble with (E) if you did not know that *impetuous* means "to act impulsively or rashly." But if you had read these words out loud in the sentence, you would have realized that *anxious* is the best answer; it means to be "greatly troubled."

4. (D)   All across the nation, outbreaks of cancer have been reported in conjunction with evidence of environmental contamination, yet firm proof of cause and effect remains _____.

Chances are that if you were substituting your own words in the blanks before consulting the available choices, you came up with some variation of the word *vague.* The important clues in this sentence are the words *evidence* and *yet,* with the latter indicating that whatever is stated in the first part of the sentence is going to be contradicted in the second part. In this case, you are looking for a word that indicates a lack of concrete data to support the idea that certain factors in the environment cause cancer. You were probably able to eliminate (B) and (C) as irrelevant, but the three remaining choices might have presented you with a difficult choice. You might not know that *palpable,* choice (E), means "obvious," "plainly seen," or "that which can be touched or felt." There might be some students who have heard the form of the word *palpate,* which is used in medicine to describe an examination by the sense of touch. Others might recognize the word *palm,* which is actually the inner surface of the hand that does the touching. If you were still at a loss as to the meaning of *palpable,* you should have moved on to examine (A) and (D). These two choices present a good example of the need to distinguish subtle differences between words. At first glance, both words might have seemed possible. But if you had considered the word *firm* in the sentence, it would have helped you decide which word to pick. The word indicates that there might be grounds for believing in a cause-and-effect relationship between the environment and the disease, but *firm* implies that there is no fixed and explicit basis for that belief. Thus, you would have eliminated *obscure,* choice (A), in that the word means "remote" or "not readily seen." Choice (D), *elusive,* means "difficult to define"; that is, there is enough evidence, but it is difficult to say just what that evidence is.

5. (D)   Although the mathematical proof of his theory was proven to be false, he _____ in his belief in the hypothesis.

One of the important clues in this sentence completion is the word *although,* because it indicates that whatever is stated in the first part of the sentence is going to be contradicted in the second part. Upon examination of the question, you probably came up with some variation of the idea that he persisted in his belief that his theory was valid, even though it was proven false. Therefore, you probably eliminated (A), (B), and (C) because none of these words has anything to do with continuing in a course of action. Left with (D) and (E), you might have realized that even though *gravitate* means a natural tendency toward some point or object of influence, it connotes drifting, almost without effort. *Persevered,* on the other hand, clearly implies a determined effort to move in a particular direction *in spite of* strong opposing forces.

6. Although his speech was _____ and delivered on the spur of the moment, it was one of the most sincere and compassionate I have ever heard.

One of the important clues in this sentence is the word *and,* which implies that whatever is on one side of the word—in this case, the words *on the spur of the moment*—there should be a word of similar import on the other side. That is what you will be looking for among your choices. You should have eliminated all of the choices except (D) and (E), in that *infallible,* choice (A), means "incapable of error"; *indigent,* choice (B), means "impoverished" or "needy"; and *impaired,* choice (C), means "to make or become worse" or "weaken." You might have been unsure of the choice between (D) and (E), because one often associates *impetuous* with the idea of doing something without thinking; hence something done on the spur of the moment. But on closer scrutiny it is apparent that (D) is the better choice because *impromptu* actually means "made or done on the spur of the moment" or "improvised," and *impetuous,* choice (E), means "forceful" or "impulsive." Some students will be bothered by the fact that *impromptu* and *on the spur of the moment* mean almost exactly the same thing, because they know that it is usually poor writing style to repeat ideas in a sentence. So they will be drawn toward *impetuous,* choice (E), because this word does produce a more interesting sentence. But one of the important test-taking skills is being able to sense what the test makers are trying to test. In this case it is the meaning of the words, not the literary quality of the sentence.

7. (C)   Psychic automation is a form of free association in which the pen or brush is allowed to wander _____ by the conscious mind.

In this sentence completion it is obvious that the word missing in the blank has something to do with the word *wander.* You were probably able to eliminate (A), (B), and (E), in that none of these words relates to this idea. You probably left choice (D) because you might not know that the word *muted* means silent. The best answer is (C), *undirected,* which means "not guided."

8. (C)   The local population was highly _____ after the accidental discovery of the toxic landfill.

The understanding of this sentence completion depends largely on your familiarity with the word *toxic,* which means "poisonous." If you do not know this word, chances are that the words *accidental discovery,* which relates to *landfill,* gave you the feeling that the word you were looking for is *negative.* Thus, you were probably able to eliminate (A), (B), and (D) with little difficulty, in that *scattered* and *uniform* are irrelevant, and the word *indulgent,* which means "yielding to one's desires," would not be an adequate adjective to describe the people's attitude toward discovering something amiss in a landfill. Choosing between (C) and (E) might have presented you with some difficulty if you did not know that *erratic* means "wandering off course" and *indignant* means "angry." If you look at the word *erratic,* you will see that it is related to the word *error,* which means "deviation from accuracy"—certainly not the word you are looking for. You could have then backed into the right answer, (C). *Indignant* means "angry," the perfect word to describe the people's reaction to the discovery of toxic waste.

9. (B)   Enforcing rules is difficult when these rules are too _____.

If you substitute your own word in the blank before consulting the available choices, it is likely you came up with some variation of the word *hard.* It is virtually impossible to make people obey anything that is too severe. Thus, you could have narrowed your answer down to (B) and (D), in that the other choices have nothing to do with this idea. Choices (B) and (D) might have given you some difficulty, in that you might not know that *stringent* means "strict" and *subservient* means "inferior." You might have narrowed your choice down to (B) by one of two ways. The prefix of *subservient* is *sub-,* which means "under," and you probably recognized a variation on the word *servant* in the word. It is highly unlikely that this word would apply to a rule that is difficult to enforce. Besides, not only does the word *stringent* sound like *strict,* which could fit the adjective you are looking for, but when you read the two choices out loud in the sentence, (B) sounds best.

10. (C)   The (scoutmaster) was so (proper and) _____ that the (parents) were (shocked) to (discover) that <u>he</u> had been (abusing) the (boys) in his <u>troop</u>.

The clues to this sentence completion are the words *proper and*. The word *and* implies that whatever is on one side of the word—in this case, the word *proper*—should have a synonym on the other side. Therefore, you were looking for a positive word. You probably eliminated (B) and (E) without difficulty, in that neither of the words relates to *proper*. Left with (A), (C), and (D), you probably had some difficulty, especially if you did not know the meanings of *circumspect* and *irascible*. If you did not know the meaning of *circumspect,* you probably decided that (A) is a good choice, in that *concerned* means "to be interested or involved." You might have thought that a man who conforms to established standards, which is what the word *proper* means, would naturally feel an interest in, or responsibility for, the boys in his troop. If that was your thinking, you were led into a carefully designed trap. If you had thought about the word *concerned,* you might have realized that it expresses a person's *attitude* toward something, but, unlike the word *proper,* does not describe a person's *behavior.* You can be concerned about someone and show it in either a positive or negative way. For example, you could withhold certain things from someone because you feel it is in his best interest. It seems logical to infer from this sentence completion that the scoutmaster's interest or concern for the boys was from *negative, not positive,* motives. Otherwise, the parents would not have been *shocked.* If you had examined the word *circumspect,* you might have realized that the prefix *circum-* means "around" and *spect* means "to see." Hence the word literally means "to look around," which suggests the idea of caution. Therefore, the only possible answer choice is (C), *circumspect,* which is just the word you are looking for.

Two-Word Sentence Completions

The technique for dealing with the two-word sentence completion is basically the same as that for dealing with the one-word completion, but there are some special variations.

Step 1

Examine the sentence-completion question and underline key words.

Step 2

Single out any word, or group of words, of the ones you have underlined that you think is more important in providing clues to help you locate the answer. When you have made your choice, circle the word or group of words.

Step 3

Reread the sentence and fill in the blank with words of your own *before looking at the answer choices.* Determine if the words you are looking for are positive or negative; that is, have good connotations or bad connotations.

Step 4

Back into the right answer by going through the choices one at a time, drawing a line through those answers that are *not possible.* Leave words you do not know. Use "word attack" skills such as focusing your attention on prefixes and familiar roots to narrow down your choices.

Step 5

When you have narrowed down your choices, read the sentence out loud, substituting the remaining answers, in the space provided, and select the answer that sounds best.

Examine the following sentence-completion question. Underline and circle the key words in the sentence. Do it now, *before reading ahead.* Try to think of your own words to put in the blanks and determine for yourself whether the words you are looking for are positive or negative.

The military tribunal _____ the otherwise illegal action because the bravery of the soldier and the emergency of the situation _____ his guilt.

(A) enforced . . heightened (B) approved . . condemned
(C) condoned . . extenuated (D) extended . . retracted
(E) extradited . . increased

Try eliminating choices, dealing with one side of the sentence completion at a time. In other words, work with just the first omission as if it were a single completion and see how many choices on the left side you can eliminate. It is important to decide what type of word you need in the first blank. It is obvious that the important word here is *otherwise,* indicating that the military tribunal is treating in a less serious way something that ordinarily carries severe penalties. You are therefore looking for just such a word. That would eliminate (A), (D), and (E) immediately, because *enforce,* choice (A), means "compel obedience"; *extend,* choice (D), means "advance"; and *extradite,* choice (E), means "surrender an alleged criminal to another authority for trial." None of these words refers to treating an offense in a less serious manner. You realize, of course, that by eliminating *only one side,* you have eliminated the entire choice. That should simplify things.

If you are left with (B) and (C) as possible answers, and do not know that *condoned* means "excused," it should still seem highly unlikely that a military tribunal would *approve* an illegal action under any circumstances, so you would have backed into the right answer, (C). But leaving those two for a moment, let us see if we can work with the right side of those two choices and eliminate one of the answers more reasonably. You probably realized that the word you need in the second blank has something to do with lessening the soldier's guilt because of his bravery and because of the emergency. That would eliminate (B) immediately, in that *condemned* is the exact opposite of what you are looking for. Therefore, even if you did not know that *extenuated* means "lessened," you would have backed into the right answer. If you now read the sentence completion with your answer choice in the blanks, it should sound as though they were made for each other.

Your final diagrammed sentence completion should look something like this:

The military tribunal _____ the otherwise illegal action because the bravery of the soldier and the emergency of the situation _____ his guilt.

(A) enforced . . heightened (B) approved . . condemned
(C) condoned . . extenuated (D) extended . . retracted
(E) extradited . . increased

What you have done is first use one set of clues (the left-hand word in each pair) and then use the second set of clues (the right-hand word in each pair). It is because two-word sentence completions offer two sets of clues that they are actually easier than one-word sentence completions, permitting you to eliminate all of the wrong answer choices even though you might not know what all of the words mean.

Here is another two-word completion for you to practice on. Try eliminating the choices *one side at a time*. When you have narrowed your choices down as far as you can, try reading the sentence *out loud* with the choices in the blanks and select the one that sounds best.

> How can two brothers of the same family be so different; the one kind and
> _____, the other _____ and bitter.
>
> (A) mild . . truculent (B) mercantile . . avaricious
> (C) paranoid . . deluded (D) lackadaisical . . languid
> (E) unhealthy . . jaundiced

Note the importance of the word *and* following each of the blanks, which indicates that whatever word you select for the blank space must be similar to the word preceding the word *and*. The first blank, therefore, is asking for a word that is similar to *kind;* it will be a positive word. Therefore, you can eliminate (C), (D), and (E) immediately because they all have negative connotations. (B) can be eliminated because *mercantile* means "commercial" and is totally irrelevant; you should be able to see the connection between this word and *merchant*. The answer, therefore, is (A), because *mild* means "calm" and *truculent* means "fierce" and "destructive," a negative word, which is what is needed for the second omission.

Your final diagrammed sentence completion should look like this:

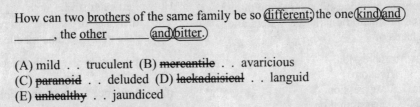

> How can two <u>brothers</u> of the same family be so (different;) the one (kind)(and)
> _____, the <u>other</u> _____ (and)(bitter.)
>
> (A) mild . . truculent (B) ~~mercantile~~ . . avaricious
> (C) ~~paranoid~~ . . deluded (D) ~~lackadaisical~~ . . languid
> (E) ~~unhealthy~~ . . jaundiced

Note that in this case, if you started trying to eliminate right-hand words in each answer choice, you doubtless had trouble, because all of the right-hand words are negative and make sense in the sentence. You should quickly have realized this and switched your attention to the left-hand words in each answer choice.

PRACTICE EXERCISES

Here are some sentence completions for you to practice on. Each sentence has two blanks, and beneath the sentence are five lettered sets of words. Choose the set of words that *best* fits the meaning of the sentence as a whole.

1. The systems of repression are identical—the arrests, the interrogations, the solitary confinements. One thing makes all dictatorships seem bizarre: Their _____ to allow the _____ to leave when he asks to go to another country.

    (A) refusal . . dissenter
    (B) desire . . hedonist
    (C) need . . criminal
    (D) resistance . . betrayer
    (E) unwillingness . . inquisitioner

2. The scientist who _____ at his task despite failure after failure, exemplifies _____ or strength of character.

    (A) persists . . determination
    (B) rejoices . . perseverance
    (C) balks . . humility
    (D) vacillates . . impatience
    (E) surrenders . . fortitude

3. Even if the solitary hero doesn't achieve anything immediate and practical, he stirs the waters and _____ the chains of _____.

    (A) weakens . . repression
    (B) fortifies . . freedom
    (C) intensifies . . aggression
    (D) alleviates . . determination
    (E) exemplifies . . democracy

4. In general, women in our society are taught to be submissive and dependent, yet their _____ of their situation is _____.

    (A) fear . . biased
    (B) portrayal . . comforting
    (C) consciousness . . changing
    (D) analysis . . passive
    (E) awareness . . abstract

5. By comparing the actual architectural _____ of the Greek temples with those given in ancient Greek texts, it is possible to _____ the overall descriptive accuracy of these texts.

    (A) dimensions . . falsify
    (B) devices . . revivify
    (C) designs . . ignore
    (D) blueprints . . initiate
    (E) details . . assess

6. Advertising is so _____ in our society that it is impossible not to be _____ by it.

    (A) impertinent . . solicited
    (B) persuasive . . accosted
    (C) ominous . . distracted
    (D) gratifying . . cajoled
    (E) pervasive . . manipulated

7. Whether we agree with the political position or not, the anticapitalist bias in John Dos Passos' *U.S.A.* makes the work _____ and _____ and helps to shape our feelings about the characters and the world they live in.

    (A) coherent . . accessible
    (B) plausible . . remote
    (C) amorphous . . harmonious
    (D) significant . . trivial
    (E) meaningful . . necessary

8. He waited each stroke with _____ and _____. The intervals of silence grew progressively longer; the delay became maddening.

    (A) intimidation . . belligerence
    (B) fortitude . . calm
    (C) impatience . . apprehension
    (D) anticipation . . indignation
    (E) apathy . . disinterest

9. The amount of radioactive material was very small, yet the _____ shield did not _____ the researcher.

    (A) powerful . . protect
    (B) thin . . envelop
    (C) broad . . detect
    (D) apparent . . safeguard
    (E) bare . . endanger

10. Political questions about literature can _____, even _____, the reader because the answers are so complex.

    (A) enrage . . anger
    (B) denigrate . . arouse
    (C) perplex . . disturb
    (D) confuse . . delight
    (E) soothe . . pacify

ANSWERS AND EXPLANATIONS

1. (A)	2. (A)	3. (A)	4. (C)	5. (E)
6. (E)	7. (A)	8. (C)	9. (A)	10. (C)

1. (A)   The systems of repression are identical—the arrests, the interrogations, the solitary confinements. One thing makes all dictatorships seem bizarre: Their _____ to allow the _____ to leave when he asks to go to another country.

The important clue in this sentence completion is the word *bizarre,* which means "odd" or "strange"; it indicates that you are looking for words that contradict the actions one would expect from a repressive regime. However, if you do not know the definition and tried substituting your own words in the blanks before consulting the available choices, it is more than likely you came up with some variation of the idea that the opponents of repressive governments are not permitted to emigrate, even though it might seem that they would pose less of a problem to the government if they did. Therefore, looking over your choices for the first omission, you probably eliminated (B) and (C), in that the words *need* and *desire* imply some action taken for the benefit of the individuals the government wishes to keep under control. This idea totally contradicts the actions of dictatorships, as described in this first sentence. In the second omission, you are looking for a word to describe the type of person a government would be likely to refuse permission to leave the country. This would eliminate (E), in that it is irrelevant. Choices (A) and (D) both seem likely possibilities. However, even if you were not certain of the word *dissenter,* which has come to suggest determined opposition to authority, (D) would not be possible. There is no clue to support (D) as an answer. The answer is (A).

2. (A)   The scientist who _____ at his task despite failure after failure, exemplifies _____ or strength of character.

It is important to decide what type of word you need in the first blank. It is obvious that the important word here is *despite,* which always emphasizes a contrasting idea. In this case, the author is indicating that even though the scientist has experienced repeated failure in his work, there is some positive aspect he wants you to recognize. The missing word should also have something to do with the idea of repetition. If you substituted your own words in the blank before consulting the available choices, it is likely you came up with some variation of the idea of one who stays or *keeps at his task despite failure after failure.* Therefore, looking over your choices for the first omission, you probably eliminated (B) and (E), in that neither of them is even a remote possibility. Of course, you might not know that *balk* means "to stop short and stubbornly refuse to go on" and *vacillate* means "to sway" or "to waver." *Perseverance* and *fortitude* are acceptable alternatives to *determination,* but the words they are paired with do not fit the context; therefore, you can immediately eliminate (B) and (E) from consideration.

The words you substituted in the second omission were probably some variation of the idea that the scientist was firm in his commitment to continue his work. So your choice would naturally be (A), for the word *determination* is the most suitable choice. Note the importance of the word *or* following the second blank, which indicates that whatever word you select for the blank space must be similar to the word preceding the word *or.* If you now read the sentence completion with your answer choice in the blanks, it should sound as though they were made for each other.

3. Even if the solitary hero doesn't achieve anything immediate and practical, he stirs the waters and _____ the chains of _____.

In this sentence completion, it is easier if you begin with the second omission. It is obvious that you need a negative word that has something to do with the symbolic meaning of *chains,* in that all of the words on this side are abstract concepts. Chances are you eliminated (B), (D), and (E), in that they are all positive words. Reading (A) and (C) in the sentence, you probably selected (A) as the correct answer. Your major clue in the first blank is *even if,* which indicates that the word in the first blank will contrast with the idea expressed in the first part of the sentence completion. Thus, even though the individual does not achieve tangible results for his effort, he does make some contribution in helping to remove the chains that are holding men in bondage. The word *intensifies* is exactly the opposite of the idea you want to express, for it suggests that not only is the hero unable to *achieve anything immediate and practical,* he even makes the problem worse. The only possible choice is (A).

4. (C)   In general, women in our society are taught to be submissive and dependent, yet their _____ of their situation is _____.

One of the important clues in this sentence completion is the word *yet;* it tell us immediately that the missing words are going to contrast with the ideas implicit in the first part of the sentence. The words you are looking for will challenge the fact that women have simply accepted what they have been *taught*—in this case, to play a *submissive* and *dependent* role. Looking over your choices, you probably had no difficulty in eliminating (A) and (B) for the first omission, in that neither word has anything to do with the idea of turning away from what one has learned. In the second omission, a word is needed that indicates some form of movement away from women's traditional roles. That would eliminate (D) and (E), in that neither of these words fits the description of what we are looking for. The answer, of course, is (C); *changing* does give the idea that women's awareness of their situation is making a difference in how they behave.

5. (E)   By comparing the actual architectural _____ of the Greek temples with those given in ancient Greek texts, it is possible to _____ the overall descriptive accuracy of these texts.

It should be clear from your diagramming of this sentence completion that the clues to the two omissions are well defined. In the first blank it is obvious that we are looking for a word that has to do with some architectural aspect of a particular structure. You probably eliminated (B), in that the word *devices* implies an invention or contrivance—not generally the basis for comparing an actual structure with its description in a book. Left with the remaining choices as distinct possibilities, you then moved to the second omission. The important clues for the second blank are the words *compare* and *possible to.* These clues indicate that you are looking for a word that will describe what one is able to do if one compares an actual Greek temple with its description in a text. The answer, of course, is (E), in that none of the other choices fits this result.

6. (E)   Advertising is so _____ in our society that it is impossible not to be _____ by it.

You know that the word you are looking for in the first blank has something to do with advertising in our society. If you were substituting your own word in the blank before consulting the available choices, you would have been likely to come up with some variation of the word *widespread.* Thus, you would probably have eliminated (A), (B), and (D), in that you know that none of these words means "widespread." Turning to the second omission, we see that the clue is tricky; it is a double negative, so that the words *it is impossible not to* mean "it is possible to." This would be a good time to read the sentence completion out loud to yourself with your choices (C) and (E) in the blank spaces, in that how well the words sound in the context of the reading will help you arrive at your answer. The answer, of course, is (E); the word *manipulated* is directly related to advertising.

7. (A)   Whether we agree with the political position or not, the anticapitalist bias in John Dos Passos' *U.S.A.* makes the work _____ and _____ and helps to shape our feelings about the characters and the world they live in.

The clue for both the first and second omission in this sentence completion is the word *shape*. The words you are looking for are not only both positive words but are close to being synonyms. Looking over your choices for the first omission, you probably found it difficult to eliminate any of them, unless you know that *amorphous* means "formless." Turning to the second omission, you were probably able to eliminate (B), (D), and (E). Something that is *remote,* or far removed, is not going to help us understand the characters or the world they live in. *Trivial* is irrelevant to the idea of shape or form, as is *necessary.* Left with (A) and (C), read the sentence out loud with the words for both choices in the blank spaces and select the one that *sounds better.* Even if you did not know what *amorphous* means, chances are you backed into (A), the correct answer. *Coherence* means "logical" or "consistent," and *accessible* means "capable of being reached."

8. (C)   He awaited each stroke with _____ and _____. The intervals of silence grew progressively longer; the delay became maddening.

The most important clues in this sentence completion are the words *intervals . . . grew* and *delay became maddening.* It should be apparent that you are looking for words that mean essentially the same thing; that is, words that have something to do with tension or anxiety. Looking over your choices for the second omission, you probably eliminated every one but (C) because *apprehension* is the only answer that indicates uneasiness about something that might happen.

9. (A)   The amount of radioactive material was very small, yet the _____ shield did not _____ the researcher.

One of the important clues in this sentence completion is the word *yet* because it indicates that whatever is stated in the first part of this sentence is going to be contradicted in the second part. This, then, is another common type of sentence completion; it is based on a contrast between the ideas expressed in the first part of the sentence and those expressed in the second part. Therefore, it is important that you circle all connecting words and phrases in every sentence completion. If you were substituting your own words in the blanks before consulting the available choices, it is likely you came up with some variation of the word *protect,* which happens to be the answer in (A) for the second omission. In this instance, you're correct; but don't be misled. One of the common traps testers have set for you is to include a word that seems correct. It is always a good idea to follow the process of narrowing down your answers, just to be sure.

10. (C)   Political questions about literature can _____ even _____ the reader because the answers are so complex.

From the clues you have isolated, it should be apparent that the words you are looking for in this sentence completion are not only both negative words but are close to being synonyms, differing only in intensity. We know they are negative because of the word *complex.* That would eliminate (E), in that *soothe* is a positive word. Turning to the second omission, you probably eliminated (D) and (B), in that *delight* is a positive word and *arouse* is irrelevant. Now you have narrowed your choices to (A) and (C). Because the word *even* means that the word in the second blank must be of greater intensity than the first word, you would have selected (C) as the correct answer. In choice (A), the first word, *enrage,* is more intense than *anger.*

READING COMPREHENSION

The most significant changes in the SAT are now in the Reading Comprehension section because that is the basic skill required for college work. The invention of the printed word is the key device by which our culture has most successfully transmitted its knowledge from generation to generation. There is no avenue of study or course of inquiry that does not depend on your ability to understand your reading.

For this reason, the largest portion of the Scholastic Aptitude Test is devoted to reading comprehension. The reading comprehension test *does not* evaluate the candidate's *knowledge* of subjects included in the secondary school curriculum. It seeks, rather, to *measure the skills* you will need in order to read with understanding at a college level. These include accurate and precise perception, and the ability to reason and draw inferences, to sense subtle nuances of thought, to weed out irrelevancies, and to make judgments, all within a reasonable framework and close to what might be required for college reading.

In the reading comprehension section of the SAT, students are asked to read highly complex passages that range from approximately four hundred to nine hundred words. They are also required to make critical judgments by comparing two contrasting passages on the same subject. Many students are turned off by the highly analytical nature of passages having to do with intricate subjects in science and technology. Furthermore, even students who find that articles of a complex nature are relatively easy might expect clarity and organization in reading matter, so the SAT, part I, will prove difficult for them, too.

Stylized Traps

SAT passages are riddled with repetitive ideas and irrelevant sentences. Material designed to distract a student from the main point of the discussion is inserted within what should be a logical sequence of ideas. In addition, students who carefully work at mastering the reading techniques that enable them to comprehend such passages might discover that they are being asked to find the answers to five questions of which most, if not all, have been carefully constructed to trick the test taker into a wrong answer.

No speed-reading course could ever prepare a student to deal with these products of a seemingly inhuman imagination. The reading-comprehension questions are stylized traps and have to be approached as if you were maneuvering through a minefield. But once you have the blueprint identifying the mine sites, you can negotiate the passage effortlessly.

Simplifying the Confusion

It is important that you master the technique of dealing with the reading-comprehension part of the test because it is the section of the test that depends least on your knowledge of vocabulary. What is even more in your favor is that *every answer you need will be built right into the passage.* You are given all the information you need. It is just a question of learning how to read each passage and of familiarizing yourself with the technique of digging out the answer.

Many workbooks spend time teaching various methods of how to read a passage. There is *only one way* to read an SAT passage. The writers of these pieces deliberately set out to do two things: confuse you with their rhetoric and bore you with the dry and tedious nature of the subject matter.

But you are going to learn how to simplify the confusion and overcome the difficulty that most students have; they remember little, if anything, they have read after only four or five lines into the passage. You are going to have the decided advantage of knowing that when you have finished the reading selection, you are not only going to understand what you have read, you will know where every answer can be found.

It is important for you to keep in mind that the techniques for the reading comprehension passages involve detailed notation. Unless you master these techniques *prior* to the Scholastic Aptitude Test, the process might exceed the time allotted for each passage. However, if you practice these techniques faithfully, you will find that when you take the actual SAT, you will automatically read with greater speed and understanding, while minimizing the need to outline your passage in such great detail.

Part I
Techniques of Reading Passages

Step 1

Following the sample passage below, there are three questions. Read the *questions* first, *not the answers,* and underline any words you think will enable you to recall the entire question by just looking at those words. Those words you underline are called "Key" words. Try it now.

The decade of the twenties, or more precisely the eight years between the postwar depression of 1920–21 and the stock-market crash in October of 1929, were prosperous ones in the United States. The total output of the economy increased by more than 50 percent. The preceding decades had brought the automobile; now came many more automobiles and also roads on which they could be driven with reasonable reliability and comfort. The downtown section of the mid-continent city—Des Moines, Omaha, Minneapolis—dates to those years. It was then, more likely than not, that what is still the leading hotel, the tallest office building, and the biggest department store went up.

These years were also remarkable in another respect. For as time passed, it became increasingly evident that the prosperity could not last. Contained within it were the seeds of its own destruction. Herein lies the peculiar fascination of the period for a study in the problem of leadership. For almost no steps were taken during these years to arrest tendencies which were obviously leading, and which did lead, to disaster.

1. The main idea of this passage is best expressed as

(A) the fabulous twenties
(B) prosperity and decay in the twenties

(C) the problem of leadership in the twenties
(D) the decade of the twenties as a picture of doomed prosperity
(E) prosperity as reflected in urban development

2. The word *remarkable* as it is used in the first line of the second paragraph most nearly means

(A) catastrophic
(B) ironic
(C) distinctive
(D) prosperous
(E) problematic

3. The author implies

(A) that unchecked prosperity is likely to lead to bad results
(B) that during this period of prosperity all portents of disaster were ignored
(C) that the germinating qualities that lead to success eliminate the fear of failure
(D) that the economy more than doubled during the period that preceded the decade of the twenties
(E) that the twenties ushered in the beginning of what is now familiarly known as urban renewal

Your questions probably look like this:

1. The <u>main idea</u> of this passage is best expressed as
2. The word *remarkable* as it is used in the first line of the second paragraph <u>most nearly means</u>
3. The <u>author implies</u>

In question 1, the important thing you want to remember is that you are being asked to find the *main idea* of the paragraph.

In question 2, you want to keep in mind, if you can, that you are going to be asked to define the word *remarkable* as it is used in the context of the sentence.

In question 3, you are asked to locate something the author suggests. This is a familiar type of question. Again, the answer will be *stated within the passage*.

Step 2

Go back to the paragraph and read the *first* sentence. Underline any key words. Use the same reasoning process for selecting the words to be underlined as you did with the questions at the end of the passage. Do it now, *before reading further*.

Your sentence should look something like this:

The <u>decade</u> of the <u>twenties</u>, or more precisely the eight years between the <u>postwar depression</u> of <u>1920–21</u> and the <u>stock-market crash</u> in <u>October 1929</u>, were prosperous ones in the <u>United States</u>.

You have no doubt singled out the above words to underline, in that they possess important information; that is, that the "decade" of the twenties, which the writer reduces to an eight-year period, was a prosperous time in the United States.

There is one thing you should keep in mind: there is no single correct way to underline, so do not be overly concerned about whether or not you are selecting the right words. You are doing something that is far more important. You are *thinking about what you are reading.* In addition, you are underlining words that will enable you to recall the meaning of a sentence even after a lapse of many weeks. This is a technique you will use to advantage in college, where you might often have to review hundreds of pages of reading for an exam. Thus you are participating in a threefold process. First, you are thinking about your choice; second, you are making it possible to remember huge chunks of material by a single glance at your underlined words; third, by actually doing the underlining, you are helping to reinforce, in your mind, the ideas you have just read.

There are many students who find themselves completely detached from what they are reading, and because the SAT passages are designed to permit such detachment, this is not surprising. Students complain that the passages are boring and that there is no way they can relate to them. These students have not learned to underline and do not become *active* and *involved* participants. As a result, they constantly report that they can read and reread the same passage without having the slightest idea of what it is about. But you must persist. It is a slow process in the beginning but, in time, you will find yourself in the enviable position of being able to zigzag through the paragraphs with the ease of a slalom racer.

Step 3

Go back to the *first* sentence and *circle* those underlined words you feel are *most important* in terms of what the sentence means. Do it now, *before reading further*.

Your sentence probably looks something like this:

The ⟨decade⟩ of the ⟨twenties⟩ or more precisely the <u>eight years between</u> the <u>postwar depression</u> of <u>1920–21</u> and the <u>stock-market crash in October 1929</u>, were ⟨prosperous⟩ ones in the ⟨United States.⟩

If you are like many other students, you will have a tendency to underline many words in a sentence when you read it for the first time, and that is as it should be. There are many key words in a sentence that carry important information. Yet, if we want to crystallize the ideas conveyed in those underlined words, it is often possible to find several that seem to summarize the entire point of the sentence. You probably realize that the main idea the author of this sentence is trying to convey is, simply, that the decade of the twenties was a prosperous period in the United States.

Before we go on to step 4, go back to the *second sentence* in the paragraph and follow steps 2 and 3. Underline the key words in the sentence and circle those underlined words you feel are more important in terms of what the sentence means. Do it now, *before reading further.*

Your second sentence probably looks like this:

The <u>total output</u> of the ⟨economy⟩ ⟨increased⟩ by <u>more than</u> ⟨50⟩ ⟨percent⟩

You might have circled and underlined slightly differently, but the important thing is that although your underlining and circling will not always be the same as our examples, you are following similar processes and for the same reason: to condense the important ideas of each sentence in consecutive stages.

Step 4

This is one of the most important steps in mastering the reading-comprehension technique. Although it is particularly applicable to the SAT passage, proficiency in this area will make you a more discerning reader.

Determine what the second sentence has to do with the first sentence. If it is a *new idea* or there is a *change in point of view,* put ‖ (double lines) wherever the change occurs. It might happen between sentences or between words in the sentence. Go back to the first and second sentences and decide what the relationship is between the two and whether or not you will use double lines. Do it now, *before reading further.*

You probably decided against using double lines, and for good reason. The second sentence is an elaboration of the first. It gives support to the original idea that the twenties was a prosperous decade by citing by what percentage the economy increased.

Step 5

Whenever you come across connecting words or phrases—such as *furthermore, on the other hand, in addition,* and *but*—be sure to circle them *immediately.* These words will indicate whether or not the author is moving on to a completely new idea, or whether he has switched his point of view.

Before we go on to step 6, go back to the passage and read the third sentence. Follow steps 2, 3, and 4. Do it now, *before reading further.*

This is the way your sentence probably looks:

‖ The ⟨preceding⟩ ⟨decades⟩ had brought the ⟨automobile;⟩ ‖ ⟨now⟩ came ⟨many⟩ more ⟨automobiles⟩ and ⟨also⟩ ⟨roads⟩ on which they could be <u>driven</u> with reasonable ⟨reliability⟩ and <u>comfort</u>.

The reason for the double lines before the sentence is that the author is moving to a new idea: he reaches back to the previous decades to discuss the introduction of the automobile. However, you could just as well have omitted the double lines, deciding that this sentence is another, more specific, elaboration of the one preceding it. The reason for the double lines between *automobile* and *now* is that the author is comparing the previous decades to the decade of the twenties. Whereas there were some automobiles before, the prosperous twenties saw a tremendous increase in their number.

Step 6

If the author lists examples in his paragraph, indicate each one in the following way: Ex. 1, Ex. 2, Ex. 3, and so on.

Go back to the paragraph and read the fourth and fifth sentences. Follow steps 2, 3, 4, 5, and 6 wherever possible. Do it now, *before reading further*.

This is probably the way your third, fourth, and fifth sentences look:

∥ The preceding decades had brought the automobile; ∥ now
                    EX. 1   EX. 2
came many more automobiles and also roads on which they could be driven with reasonable reliability and comfort. The downtown section of the mid-continent city—Des Moines, Omaha, Minneapolis—dates to these years. It was then, more likely than
                                                EX. 3   EX. 4
not, that what is still the leading hotel, the tallest office building, and
                        EX. 5
the biggest department store went up.

When you have finished reading an SAT passage, it is wonderfully reassuring to look back and see that a major part of the reading is simply a neat succession of examples. It makes it much easier to locate the answers to the questions, because you are secure in your knowledge about the information in at least one section of the passage. The six examples in this paragraph are illustrations to support the idea that the twenties were, indeed, a time of prosperity.

However, not every SAT passage will include statements you can call examples; some passages will simply read straight through, keeping very close to the subject or using generalities rather than specific examples. It is still worthwhile to try step 6, though, because when you discover that there *are* no examples, you will automatically have increased your comprehension of the passage and of the way the writer has organized his statements.

Now go back to the passage and read the first sentence of the second paragraph. Follow steps 2 through 6 wherever possible. Do it now, *before reading further*.

This is the way your sentence probably looks:

∥ These years were also remarkable in another respect, for as time passed, it became increasingly evident that the prosperity could not last.

Although it would appear that this sentence is a continuation of those that precede it, describing another aspect of prosperity, we soon realize that the word *another* takes on the meaning of "different" or "contrasting"; hence the double lines before *these*. The point of this sentence is that there was increasing evidence that the prosperity could not last.

Now go back to the passage and read the *second sentence* in the second paragraph. Follow steps 2 through 6 wherever possible. Do it now, *before reading further*.

Your sentence probably looks like this:

Contained within it were the seeds of its own destruction.

This sentence is, obviously, a continuation of the idea that just preceded it. This sentence gives the *reason* the prosperity could not last: it was somehow unsound and would destroy itself.

Now go back to the passage and read the *third sentence* in the second paragraph. Follow steps 2 through 6 wherever possible. Do it now, *before reading further*.

Your sentence probably looks like this:

Herein lies the peculiar fascination of the period for a study in the problem of leadership.

In this sentence the author shifts to a different aspect entirely; that is, the attraction this period has for someone studying the problem of leadership.

Now go back to the passage and read the *last sentence* in the second paragraph. Follow steps 2 through 6 wherever possible. Do it now, *before reading further*.

Your sentence probably looks like this:

For almost no steps were taken during these years to arrest tendencies which were obviously leading, and which did lead, to disaster.

It should be obvious to you that the concluding sentence is a continuation of the idea in the one that preceded it. This sentence indicates what the particular problem of leadership was—that there was none. No one assumed the responsibility of preventing disaster.

Now that you have concluded diagramming the passage, take a long, hard look at what you have outlined. You will not only have little difficulty reassembling the various parts of the passage into a cohesive whole, but you should have a full understanding of what the paragraph means.

Step 7

There is one final technique in reading comprehension. Look over the passage and place an asterisk (*) before the main idea. There is an easy way to determine what the main idea is: if by reading the sentence you have selected you have a fairly good idea of what the *entire* passage is about, that is probably your best choice.

Go back to the paragraph and place an asterisk before the sentence you think is the main idea. Do it now, *before reading further*.

You probably selected the first sentence for the reason you were asked to keep in mind: the first sentence tells you what the entire paragraph is about. Even the content of the second paragraph—about the collapse of prosperity—is foreshadowed by the mention of the stock-market crash at the end of the prosperous period. Let's put it another way: every sentence in the next two paragraphs relates in some way to the idea that the decade of the twenties was a prosperous period in the United States.

But do not be misled. *The main idea might occur anywhere in the paragraph.*

How to Answer "Main Idea" Questions

Now we are ready to discuss the SAT questions. Follow the directions carefully and soon you will feel confident of your ability to deal with this part of the test.

Most of the SAT paragraphs have, as one of their questions, a title question, which deals with the *main idea* of the paragraph. There are always five choices from which to select your answer, but *the title question has a specific variety of choices that none of the other questions has.* The choices for the title question generally fall into the following categories:

1. *One answer might be too broad.* That will be an answer that is very general, going much farther than the statements in the passage itself.
2. *One answer might be too narrow.* This answer is easy to eliminate because it is a statement that would hold true for only one or two sentences in the passage.
3. *One answer might be irrelevant.* It will have nothing whatever to do with the passage you have just read.
4. *One answer might be out of context.* Actual words are lifted from a sentence in the passage and used as an answer. That is presumably to throw the student off guard. He might remember having seen the statement somewhere in the passage and assume, too readily, that it is the right answer. That is exactly the trap the testers have in mind.
5. *One answer is the correct one.* This is not as obvious as you might think. It must fulfill two requirements. It must *deal with most of the sentences* in the passage and it must *be specifically related* to the subject being discussed. That means if five sentences deal with one idea and six sentences deal with another idea, you must choose that answer that deals with the largest number of sentences.

You might not have one answer of each type; you might have two choices that are too narrow or two choices that are out of context, or any combination. But whatever the combination is, these are the only types that will be used.

You are to work through the choices by drawing a line through them one at a time, eliminating those answers that are *not possible.* Look at the title question; then look over each choice and decide whether it is (1) too broad, (2) too narrow, (3) irrelevant, (4) out of context, or (5) possibly the right answer. *At any time, if you think the answer is possible or you are not sure, leave it. But draw a line through all of the other choices as you dismiss them.*

Now go back to the paragraph and read the first question. This is the title question. Follow the instructions on how to narrow down your choices. Until you have internalized your knowledge of the various types that might be included in the title question, refer back to your list. Do it now, *before reading ahead.*

Chances are your question looks like this:

1. The main idea of this passage is best expressed as

   (A) the fabulous twenties
   (B) ~~prosperity and decay in the twenties~~
   (C) ~~the problem of leadership in the twenties~~
   (D) the decade of the twenties as a picture of doomed prosperity
   (E) ~~prosperity as reflected in urban development~~

You probably eliminated (B), (C), and (E) without difficulty. (B) is *irrelevant* because there is no direct mention of decay in the passage. (C) is both *out of context* and *too narrow* because it is only mentioned in one sentence. It does seem possible that "leadership in the twenties" would *become* the main topic *if the passage continued,* because the writer has carefully led up to the statement about leadership. But you cannot make assumptions of this type; *all of the answers are somewhere in the passage.* (E) is too narrow because urban development is mentioned in only two sentences; it is used as an example of prosperity but is not the main point. You probably left (A) because as you went through your choices it seemed possible. If one considers the great prosperity of this decade as "fabulous," this would seem like a reasonable answer. You probably left (D) because the passage does describe the twenties as a decade of prosperity.

If you are left with a choice of two possibilities, chances are that one of these choices is *too broad.* You probably left that answer as a possibility not only because it seemed possible, but because you didn't yet know if any other answer would be more specific. Now go back to choices (A) and (D) and select the answer that more specifically relates to the paragraphs as a whole. Do it now, *before reading further.*

The answer, of course, is (D), in that it is the more *specific* answer of the two. The decade of the twenties might be considered fabulous not only because of its prosperity, but because it is the idea of prosperity alone that is discussed throughout this passage, even to accounting for its eventual demise.

How to Answer All Other Questions

For every question you have to answer, *other than the title question,* go back to the paragraph and find the answer. If you cannot verify the choice you have selected somewhere in the passage, it *cannot* be your answer.

Work through the choices on all questions by a process of elimination. *Do not use* the technique of determining whether some choices are too broad, too narrow, out of context, or irrelevant; this technique is only for the title question. In the other questions, you eliminate answer choices for one reason only: *they are not mentioned in the passage.*

Go back to question 2. Read the question and back into the correct answer by drawing a line through those choices that are *not possible.* Do it now, *before reading further.*

You are asked to define the word *remarkable* as it suits the context or spirit of the sentence. Rereading the first sentence of that paragraph, it is clear that the word *also* is a clue in defining this word. The first paragraph discusses the special quality of the twenties, namely its prosperity. The word *also* must imply that the author would like to describe *another* special or unique quality of this decade that makes it remarkable. You will be looking for a word synonymous with *special* or *unique. Catastrophic,* choice (A), means "disastrous"; it does not mean "special" or "unique." You should have drawn a line through that answer. *Ironic,* choice (B), describes some type of incongruity; as, for example, when the actual result of something is quite different from the expected result. It does not mean "special" or "unique." You should have drawn a line through that answer. *Distinguished,* choice (C), means "separate" or "different"; it is close in meaning to "special" or "unique," and you should have left it as a possibility. *Prosperous,* choice (D), would not fit after the word *also* because the passage goes on to mention a decline in prosperity, and you can't have a prosperous decline of prosperity. Besides, *prosperous* does not mean "special" or "unique." You should have drawn a line through that answer. You have backed into the only possible definition for *remarkable,* answer (C).

Now turn back to question 3. But remember that even though the question asks you to determine something the author *implies,* you must still be able to locate your answer choice within the confines of the passage. Go through the choices one at a time, eliminating those that are *not possible*. Do it now, *before reading further*.

You probably eliminated every choice except (B), because none of the other answer choices was mentioned in the passage. The answer to question 3 is found in the last line of the second paragraph. The exact words are "tendencies which were obviously leading to disaster." The word *obviously* means that there were signs people could see; and in the answer, the word *portents* means "things that foreshadow a coming event." In other words, there were signs that foreshadowed disaster.

PRACTICE EXERCISE 1

Now look at the passage below. Handle it exactly as you did the passage we have just completed. Read the passage, following steps 1 through 7. Step 1, remember, begins with underlining key words in the *questions* following the passage. Underline the passage just as you will underline the SAT passage on the official examination. (It is perfectly permissible to write on both the verbal and math sections of the SAT.) When you are finished marking your test, and before you answer the questions, compare your diagrammed passage with the one here. Read the following example now, beginning with the questions and following steps 1 through 7, *before reading further*.

1 The adult, even in his most personal and private
2 occupation, even when he is engaged on an inquiry
3 which is incomprehensible to his fellow-beings, has
4 continually in his mind's eye his collaborators or opponents,
5 members of his own profession to whom sooner or later
6 he will announce the result of his labors. This mental
7 picture pursues him throughout his task. The task itself
8 is henceforth socialized at almost every stage of its
9 development. Invention eludes this process, but the need
10 for checking and demonstrating calls into being an inner
11 speech addressed throughout to a hypothetical opponent,
12 whom the imagination often pictures as one of flesh and
13 blood.When, therefore, the adult is brought face to face
14 with his fellow-beings, what he announces to them is
15 something already socially elaborated and therefore roughly
16 adapted to his audience, i.e., it is comprehensible. Indeed,
17 the further a man has advanced in his own line of
18 thought the better able is he to see things from the point
19 of view of others and make himself understood by
20 them.

1. The author of this selection feels that men are essentially

   (A) isolated from one another
   (B) social animals
   (C) desirous of being alone
   (D) difficult to understand
   (E) unable to communicate ideas easily

2. According to the author, the inventive man has a continual dialogue in his mind with

   (A) a potential critic
   (B) himself
   (C) his audience
   (D) those who are going to fund him
   (E) nobody

3. The author believes that a person is able to communicate his creation to others easily because

   (A) he speaks to those in his own field
   (B) all men are in constant communication with one another
   (C) he has already communicated in his mind as his work progresses
   (D) even his opponents are willing to listen
   (E) men are primarily social beings

4. The writer considers that the more advanced a man is in his own field

   (A) the less he is able to make himself understood
   (B) the more he understands how others see things
   (C) the more he works with others
   (D) the more his opponents criticize him
   (E) the more he likes other human beings

5. This passage implies that an essential characteristic of man is

   (A) the need for isolation
   (B) a vivid imagination
   (C) the need to communicate to his fellow man
   (D) inventiveness
   (E) the need to oppose and criticize inventions

1* The adult, even in his most personal and private
2 occupation, even when he is engaged on an inquiry
3 which is incomprehensible to his fellow-beings, has
4 continually in his mind's eye his collaborators or opponents,
5 members of his own profession to whom sooner or later
6 he will announce the result of his labors. This mental
7 picture pursues him throughout his task. The task itself
8 is henceforth socialized at almost every stage of its
9 development. // Invention eludes this process, // but the need
10 for checking and demonstrating calls into being an inner
11 speech addressed throughout to a hypothetical opponent,
12 whom the imagination often pictures as one of flesh and
13 blood. // When, therefore, the adult is brought face to face
14 with his fellow-beings, what he announces to them is
15 something already socially elaborated and therefore roughly
16 adapted to his audience, i.e., it is comprehensible. Indeed,
17 the further a man has advanced in his own line of
18 thought, the better able is he to see things from the point
19 of view of others and make himself understood by
20 them.

1. The author of this selection feels that men are essentially

   (A) isolated from one another
   (B) social animals
   (C) desirous of being alone
   (D) difficult to understand
   (E) unable to communicate ideas easily

2. According to the author, the inventive man has a continual dialogue in his mind with

   (A) a potential critic
   (B) himself
   (C) his audience
   (D) those who are going to fund him
   (E) nobody

3. The author believes that a person is able to communicate his creation to others easily because

   (A) he speaks to those in his own field
   (B) all men are in constant communication with one another

   (C) he has already communicated in his mind as his work progressed
   (D) even his opponents are willing to listen
   (E) men are primarily social beings

4. The writer considers that the more advanced a man is in his own field

   (A) the less he is able to make himself understood
   (B) the more he understands how others see things
   (C) the more he works with others
   (D) the more his opponents criticize him
   (E) the more he likes other human beings

5. This passage implies that an essential characteristic of man is

   (A) the need for isolation
   (B) a vivid imagination
   (C) the need to communicate to his fellow man
   (D) inventiveness
   (E) the need to oppose and criticize inventions

You probably put an asterisk alongside the first sentence (lines 1–6), in that it neatly summarizes what the entire passage is about: man is a social being, and no matter what he does, he thinks about what the reaction of other people will be, particularly those in his own profession. The second sentence (lines 6–7) reiterates and elaborates on the same idea. You probably put double lines between the third and four sentences because the fourth sentence (lines 9–13) switches to a new idea: when an individual first conceives of something new as an "invention," he does *not think* in social terms. The word *eludes* means "escapes from." There are double lines, however, between *process* and *but* because the writer returns to the point that once the "invention" stage is passed, the social stage takes over. A person begins to think about the comments of other people like himself, those of *flesh and blood*.

There are double lines between the fourth and fifth sentences because the fifth sentence (lines 13–16) deals with the person in actual contact with his audience, rather than just thinking about them. Because he has been thinking about his audience through every stage in the development of his idea, he can now relate to them in a way that makes him thoroughly understood. The last sentence (lines 16–20) reiterates and elaborates on the sentence that precedes it.

Now you are ready to answer the questions. Review the technique and handle them exactly as you handled the questions in the previous passage. Do them now, and compare your answers with Answers and Explanations when you are finished.

ANSWERS AND EXPLANATIONS

1. (B)   2. (A)   3. (C)   4. (B)   5. (C)

1. (B)   You could have backed into the correct answer by a process of elimination. The only answer mentioned in the passage is (B). It is stated strongly in lines 7 through 9 with the words *the task itself is henceforth socialized at almost every stage of its development.*

2. (A)   You probably narrowed your answers down to (A) and (C), in that (B), (D), and (E) are never mentioned in the paragraph. But the answer is (A), in that the question asks with whom *the inventive man has a continual dialogue in his mind.* You must always go back to the statement where the question is being discussed and search out the answer. In this case the answer at first seems to be in lines 3 and 4. *Opponents* is just another way of saying *potential critics.* That's (A). But *collaborators* confuses the issue a bit. Perhaps *his audience,* choice (C), is the right answer after all, in that *audience* could include both opponents and collaborators. But read further, to lines 10 and 11: *an inner speech addressed throughout to a hypothetical opponent.* This is one of the major ways the tester can confuse the test taker; he gives clues that might make you choose the wrong answer if you aren't careful. It is your job to find the words in the passage that relate *more directly* to the question. Here it is lines 10 and 11, not lines 4 and 5. Answer (C) is not exactly wrong, in that critics are part of the audience, but it is nowhere near as precise as (A): *continued dialogue in his mind with a potential critic* is exactly the same thing as *inner speech addressed throughout to a hypothetical opponent.* So if you chose (C), you have a pretty good idea what the passage is saying—but you haven't been suspicious enough, and you'll be scored wrong.

3. (C)   Answer (C) can be found in lines 13 through 16. The key word is *therefore,* indicating that all of the inner communicating the person has done with his imaginary opponent throughout the development of his project makes what he has to say to his actual audience *comprehensible.*

4. (B)   The clue to this answer is in the question. You were told that one way to locate an answer is to go to the sentence where the question is discussed. That is obvi-

ously in the last sentence. You probably noted that answer (B) is simply another way of saying *the better able is he to see things from the point of view of others.* Also, none of the other answers can be found in the passage.

5. (C) Answer (C) is the only answer applicable to the passage. Lines 6 and 7 express it best: *this mental picture pursues him throughout his task.* The word *pursue* indicates a deep need that it is necessary to deal with at all times. Again, however, none of the other answers is remotely possible in answering the question: what *essential characteristic of man* is expressed throughout the passage? Remember, even though the question asks what the author *implies,* the *answer must be found within the passage.*

PRACTICE EXERCISE 2

Now look at the passage below. It is the type of reading passage you are going to have on the SAT in terms of length and the number of questions that follow. It is also comparable in the nature of the subject matter and its level of sophistication. Handle it exactly as you handled passages we have just completed.

Read the questions and the passage, following steps 1 through 7. Step 1, remember, begins with underlining key words in the questions following the passage. When you are finished and before you answer the questions, compare your diagrammed paragraph with the one here.

1   One of the values of a college experience can be the exposure it offers
2   to unfamiliar views and attitudes. Throughout elementary and
3   high school years, one meets and studies alongside students from
4   environments generally homogeneous with one's own. Going away to
5   college requires us to confront the fact that some of our most cherished
6   precepts are not shared by intelligent confreres whose background
7   diverges from our own.
8   We find ourselves in class after class, in a dormitory or social deliberation,
9   forced to question the accustomed axioms of our childhood. In
10   addition, we find that many respected instructors esteem the views of our
11   colleagues above our own, often subjecting us to public humiliation and
12   ridicule. Accustomed for years, in grade after grade, to the respect
13   accorded the oral and written expressions of a school's most eminent
14   students, we now find ourselves in competition with classmates more
15   adroit in their arguments than we, better read, more resourceful.
16   // Or we find ourselves forced to rub elbows with a classmate whose
17   racial or religious background is so dissimilar from our own that he
18   challenges our every premise, forcing our daily life into an almost nonstop
19   debate. We feel harassed and attacked; what began as a love of learning is
20   transformed into a deep hate of a fellow learner.
21   The simplest way to assuage our frustration is to indulge in the opiate
22   of prejudice to ease our own sense of inadequacy by attributing our
23   shortcomings to presumed characteristics inherent to the background of the
24   hated—his race is crafty, aggressive, arrogant, underhanded . . . And like
25   a snowball, our prejudice attracts the stray twigs and dead leaves of
26   additional justification: He is uncouth, malodorous, a radical, too loud, too
27   studious . . .
28   If such a transformation is possible in a liberal young person,
29   open to all experience and eager for it, what hope is there for the less
30   intelligent, more provincial citizenry, who never depart their natal
31   insularity?

1. The author believes that

   (A) our childhood experiences are unfortunate because they always cause us to become prejudiced when we go to college
   (B) we become prejudiced simply because we cannot tolerate differences
   (C) we begin to become prejudiced when we try to ease the pain of our own shortcomings by projecting our weaknesses onto others
   (D) prejudice causes immense frustration on a college campus
   (E) none of us is prejudiced when we are in high school

2. According to the author

   (A) a college experience is valuable because it exposes us to students brighter than ourselves
   (B) college causes us to feel harassed and consequently to hate learning
   (C) in college we are forced to become friendly with those of other races and religions
   (D) in college we improve by mingling with those more adroit in arguments than ourselves
   (E) our high school experiences do not prepare us to meet people of equal intelligence who have different backgrounds and values

3. The author is concerned that

   (A) we learn to cope with our frustrations in the easiest way possible.
   (B) if liberal college students can become prejudiced, what about the large number of people who never get beyond their own backyards?

(C) college instructors easily become prejudiced
(D) we become friendly with those of different religions and races while in college
(E) we feel inadequate because we are prejudiced against those of other races

4. Which of the following statements is best supported by the article?

   (A) Prejudice is caused by liberal students becoming too conservative when they arrive on campus.
   (B) Our feelings of inadequacy are caused by our high school teachers.
   (C) Those whose background is different from ours often challenge the basic precepts of our thinking.
   (D) College instructors often humiliate their colleagues.
   (E) Those who are different from us in background always disagree with us on intellectual matters.

5. Which of the following ideas are considered in this passage?

   I. the nature of prejudice on a college campus
   II. the inadequacy of our high school experience in preparing us to meet those of dissimilar backgrounds
   III. the reasons one must become friendly with those of dissimilar backgrounds
   IV. the causes of frustration on a college campus

   (A) I, II, IV (B) I, II (C) I, IV (D) IV
   (E) I, II, III

1   One of the values of a college experience can be the exposure it offers
2 to unfamiliar views and attitudes. // Throughout elementary and
3 high school years, one meets and studies alongside students from
4 environments generally homogeneous with one's own. // *Going away to
5 college requires us to confront the fact that some of our most cherished
6 precepts are not shared by intelligent confreres, whose background
7 diverges from our own.
8   We find ourselves in class after class, in a dormitory or social deliberation,
9 forced to question the accustomed axioms of our childhood. In
10 addition, we find that many respected instructors esteem the views of our
11 colleagues above our own, often subjecting us to public humiliation and
12 ridicule. // Accustomed for years, in grade after grade, to the respect
13 accorded the oral and written expressions of a school's most eminent
14 students, // we now find ourselves in competition with classmates more
                    EX. 1   EX. 2
15 adroit in their arguments than we, better read, more resourceful.
    EX. 3
16   // Or we find ourselves forced to rub elbows with a classmate whose

17 racial or religious background is so dissimilar from our own that he
18 challenges our every premise, forcing our daily life into an almost nonstop
19 debate. We feel harassed and attacked; what began as a love of learning is
20 transformed into deep hate of a fellow learner.
21 || The simplest way to assuage our frustration is to indulge in the opiate
22 of prejudice to ease our own sense of inadequacy by attributing our
23 shortcomings to presumed characteristics inherent in the background of the
             EX. 1   EX. 2   EX. 3   EX. 4
24 hated—his race is crafty, aggressive, arrogant, underhanded . . . And like
25 a snowball, our prejudice attracts the stray twigs and dead leaves of
                              EX. 5   EX. 6   EX. 7   EX. 8
26 additional justification; he is uncouth, malodorous, a radical, too loud, too
        EX. 9
27 studious . . .
28 || If such a transformation is possible in a liberal young person,
29 open to all experience and eager for it, what hope is there for the less
30 intelligent, more provincial citizenry, who never depart their natal
31 insularity?

1. The author believes that:

   (A) our childhood experiences are unfortunate
       because they always cause us to become
       prejudiced when we go to college
   (B) we become prejudiced simply because we
       cannot tolerate differences
   (C) we begin to become prejudiced when we try
       to ease the pain of our own shortcomings by
       projecting our weaknesses onto others
   (D) prejudice causes immense frustration on a
       college campus
   (E) none of us is prejudiced when we are in high
       school

2. According to the author

   (A) a college experience is valuable because it
       exposes us to students brighter than ourselves
   (B) college causes us to feel harassed and
       consequently to hate learning
   (C) in college we are forced to become friendly
       with those of other races and religions
   (D) in college we improve by mingling with those
       more adroit in arguments than ourselves
   (E) our high school experiences do not prepare
       us to meet people of equal intelligence who
       have different backgrounds and values

3. The author is concerned that

   (A) we learn to cope with our frustrations in the
       easiest way possible
   (B) if liberal college students can become preju-
       diced, what about the large number of people
       who never get beyond their own backyards?

   (C) college instructors easily become prejudiced
   (D) we become friendly with those of different
       religions and races while in college
   (E) we feel inadequate because we are prejudiced
       against those of other races

4. Which of the following statements is best supported
   by the article?

   (A) Prejudice is caused by liberal students be-
       coming too conservative when they arrive
       on campus.
   (B) Our feelings of inadequacy are caused by
       our high school teachers.
   (C) Those whose background is different from
       ours often challenge the basic precepts of
       our thinking.
   (D) College instructors often humiliate their
       colleagues.
   (E) Those who are different from us in
       background always disagree with us on
       intellectual matters.

5. Which of the following ideas are considered in
   this passage?

    I. the nature of prejudice on a college campus
   II. the inadequacy of our high school experience
       in preparing us to meet those of dissimilar
       backgrounds
   III. the reasons one must become friendly with
       those of dissimilar backgrounds
   IV. the causes of frustration on a college campus

   (A) I, II, IV (B) I, II (C) I, IV (D) IV
   (E) I, II, III

You probably put an asterisk alongside the third sentence (lines 4–7), in that it discusses an idea elaborated on, in one way or another, throughout the passage: that the elementary and high school years do not prepare us for one of the most valuable experiences of college, which is meeting people of equal intelligence who have different backgrounds and values. It is possible that you put an asterisk alongside the first sentence because it says the same thing in a more general way, but the better choice would be the third sentence. There are double lines between the first and second sentences because the writer contrasts college with the elementary and high school years. There are double lines between the second and third sentences because the author shifts back to college. Lines 8 through 12 reiterate and elaborate on the idea discussed in the topic sentence. There are double lines between the words *ridicule* and *accustomed* in line 12 because the author again shifts his subject from college to high school, and between the words *students* and *we* in line 14 because he shifts back again. The idea, however, is always the same: in elementary and high school one associates with students of the same background, and the student who excels is accorded the respect due him; however, at college, this same student is confronted with peers of similar intelligence who do not share his values and beliefs, and he is constantly challenged. There might be some disparity of opinion about putting double lines at the beginning of line 16. On the one hand, the writer continues his discussion of what the individual might face in his college experience, but differences in terms of not only values and beliefs but race and religion. On the other hand, one might consider the shift to color and religion sufficiently discussed or grand enough in its impact to deserve double lines, indicating a total shift, even though the writer is still talking about what a student is forced to confront on a college campus.

There are double lines between *learner* and *the* on line 21, in that the writer shifts his discussion to the way one can relieve or *assuage* his frustration—by prejudice. The key idea inherent in the remainder of this discussion is the fact that one of the characteristics of prejudice is attributing our own shortcomings to someone else; in this case, the person who is dissimilar to us. Finally, there are double lines between *studious* and *if* in line 28 because the author poses a question, the result of his discussion on prejudice: if a liberal young person who has a zest for learning can become a narrow-minded bigot, then what hope is there for those who have none of the positive qualities to begin with?

Now you are ready to answer the questions. Review the techniques and handle the questions exactly as you handled the questions in the previous passages. Do them now, and compare your answers with the ones here.

ANSWERS AND EXPLANATIONS

1. (C)   2. (E)   3 (B)   4. (C)   5. (A)

1. (C)   You probably eliminated (A) because it never states in the passage that our childhood experiences are *unfortunate,* and it never states in the passage that our childhood experiences are responsible for our prejudices when we go to college. Choice (B) is never mentioned in the passage. The answer (C) is stated in lines 21 through 24. Choice (D) is never stated in the passage. The passage does deal with prejudice and it does mention how one might *ease* his frustration, but it never makes the sweeping generalization that *prejudice causes immense frustration on a college campus.* If you think it does, there is always a simple way to test yourself: find it and read it out loud. If you cannot, it is not the answer. (E) is easily eliminated, in that it is never stated in the passage.

2. (E)   Choice (A) is easily eliminated, in that the passage never states that students are *brighter;* (B) can be eliminated in that the passage never says that *college* is what

makes students *harassed* (it is, rather, the contact with students of different races and religions); (C) can be eliminated because nowhere in the passage does it say that a student is *forced to become friendly;* and (D) can be eliminated because *improve* has nothing to do with the passage (only negative effects of the college experience are discussed). The answer is (E), in that it is clearly stated in the first paragraph.

3. (B)   Choice (A) can be eliminated, in that the author never expresses any such concern. (B) is a concern of the author's and is expressed in lines 28 through 31. Again the author changes words around. In that *natal* means "pertaining to birth" and *insularity* means "narrowness" or "the state of being an island," *people who never get beyond their own backyards* can be said to have a *natal insularity;* the forms of expression are quite different, but the meaning is the same. (C) is never mentioned in the passage. (D) is not mentioned either. (E) is tricky; the passage never says that we feel inadequate because we are prejudiced, but rather that we are prejudiced because we feel inadequate (lines 22–27).

4. (C)   You should have been able to back into the correct answer for this question, in that none of the choices except (C) was mentioned in the passage. (C) can be found in the first paragraph (lines 4–7).

5. (A)   The only answer choice not mentioned in the passage is (III); we are never given any such reasons or even told that being friendly with those of dissimilar backgrounds is desirable. The writer might well be able to give such reasons, but in the passage he did not.

Practice Reading-Comprehension Passages

Here are some reading-comprehension passages for you to practice on. Each passage is followed by questions based on its content. Follow the directions explained above for reading the questions and the passages. Answer all of the questions following a passage on the basis of what is stated or implied in the passage. Arrive at your answer by a process of elimination by drawing a line through all answers that are *not possible.* Remember that except for the title question you must be able to locate the answer within the passage.

PASSAGE 1

The *Divine Comedy* is an allegory. But it is fortunately that special type of allegory wherein every element must first correspond to a literal reality, every episode must exist coherently in itself. Allegoric interpretation does not detract from the story as told but is rather an added significance which one may take or leave. Many readers, indeed, have been thrilled by the *Inferno*'s power with hardly an awareness of further meanings. Dante represents mankind, he represents the "Noble Soul," but first and always he is Dante Alighieri, born in thirteenth-century Florence. The whole poem purports to be a vision of the three realms of the Catholic otherworld—Hell, Purgatory, and Paradise—and a description of "the state of the soul after death"; yet it is peopled with Dante's contemporaries and, particularly in the materialistic realism of the *Inferno,* it is torn by issues and feuds of the day—political, religious, and personal. It treats of the most universal values—good and evil, man's responsibility, free will and predestination—yet it is intensely personal and political, for it was written out of the anguish of a man who saw his life blighted by the injustice and corruption of his times.

The *Divine Comedy* is classically referred to as the

epitome, the supreme expression, of the Middle Ages. If by this is meant that many typically medieval attitudes are to be found in it, it is true; the reasoning is scholastic, the learning, the mysticism are those of the author's time. But if from such a statement one is to infer that the poem is a hymn to its times, a celebration and glorification of them, then nothing could be more misleading. The *Comedy* is a glorification of the ways of God, but it is also a sharp and great-minded protest at the ways in which men have thwarted the divine plan. This plan, as Dante conceived it, was very different from the typically medieval view, which saw the earthly life as "a vale of tears," a period of trial and suffering, an unpleasant but necessary preparation for the afterlife where alone man could expect to enjoy happiness. To Dante such an idea was totally repugnant. He gloried in his God-given talent, his well-disciplined faculties, and it seemed inconceivable to him that he and mankind in general should not have been intended to develop to the fullest their specifically human potential. The whole *Comedy* is pervaded by his conviction that man should seek earthly immortality by his worthy actions here, as well as prepare to merit the life everlasting.

1. The author of this passage suggests that the main theme of Dante's *Divine Comedy* is

    (A) to express the author's view of life and culture in the Middle Ages
    (B) to argue against the way in which humanity has thwarted God's plan for the world
    (C) a celebration and glorification of the religion of the Middle Ages
    (D) to depict life as a "vale of tears"
    (E) to give us a view of the three realms of the Catholic otherworld

2. According to the author of this passage, Dante's world view includes all but one of the following:

    (A) Life is a period of trial and suffering, necessary to prepare for the afterlife.
    (B) The world is one in which individuals can and should seek to develop their potential.
    (C) The world was created according to a divine plan.
    (D) Political and religious feuds influenced the cultural and economic climate.
    (E) Corruption and injustice caused pain and suffering.

3. According to the author of this passage, the *Divine Comedy* deals with all but one of the following:

    (A) good and evil
    (B) free will
    (C) pain and suffering
    (D) political corruption
    (E) the value of learning

4. The *Divine Comedy* is primarily meant to be read

    (A) as an allegory
    (B) as a comment on the political and religious corruption of its time
    (C) on many different levels
    (D) as a description of life in the otherworld
    (E) as a cultural and economic picture of the Middle Ages

5. According to this article, Dante believed that immortality is

    (A) earned in life on earth
    (B) predestined
    (C) impossible
    (D) dependent on one's involvement in political and religious issues of the day
    (E) intensely personal

PASSAGE 2

The hallmark of the New Deal was its experimental nature. Its planners and supporters were agreed on only one goal—ending the Depression. Beyond that, there was no agreement on what type of relationship ought to exist between big business and big government; or the desirability of a welfare state; or the extent of federal spending; or the role of big labor; or on whether an attempt should be made to encourage the redistribution of wealth. These vital issues were left to the workings of the politicians. Gradually a consensus emerged. Capitalism would indeed survive, though with increased regulation by the federal government

in cooperation with business; in many cases, however, the standards to be enforced were actually set by the industries to be regulated. The creation of Social Security symbolized the new role of government as the protector of the individual in good times and bad. The gradual acceptance of concepts like deficit spending—that is, spending more money, obtained by borrowing, than comes in from taxes—symbolized the same kind of federal role for the economy as a whole. In general, the ideas of the New Deal amounted to an extension of the old Progressive ideas.

In spite of the massive federal intervention in the

economy, the New Deal failed in its primary purpose of ending the Depression. Only the coming of World War II accomplished that feat. In the late 1930s, the deteriorating international situation turned the attention of the intellectuals decisively to Western Europe, where the democracies and their allies seemed to be in retreat from Hitler. Traditional isolationism coupled with memories of World War I competed with the view that democracy (and ultimately the United States) was in a fight for its life against the totalitarian regimes of Nazi Germany and Fascist Italy. This debate ended in the same way as the debate about how to get out of the Depression; both were suddenly made irrelevant by the Japanese attack on Pearl Harbor.

1. The primary purpose of the New Deal was

   (A) the enhancement of the relationship between big business and big government
   (B) the creation of a welfare state
   (C) combating isolationism
   (D) combating the Depression
   (E) preparing for World War II

2. Deficit spending was created to

   (A) manipulate the economy in order to protect the American people during bad times
   (B) socialize the economy

(C) protect the country for the duration of World War II
(D) prevent inflation
(E) rebuild the economy

3. The New Deal

   (A) accomplished its goal of ending a depressed economy
   (B) did not accomplish its goal
   (C) led directly to World War II
   (D) encouraged the redistribution of wealth
   (E) encouraged isolationism

4. The Depression was ended by

   (A) the end of isolationism
   (B) the advent of World War II
   (C) the creation of Social Security
   (D) the regulation of capitalism
   (E) the creation of deficit spending

5. According to this passage, the survival of capitalism depended on all but one of the following:

   (A) increased regulation by government
   (B) cooperation between government and big business
   (C) the creation of a Social Security system
   (D) increased taxation
   (E) concepts such as deficit spending

PASSAGE 3

In the second decade of the twentieth century, American poets were gathering in two centers, Chicago and London, and although there were many close ties between these two centers, it is possible to make meaningful distinctions between them. Of the two groups, the Chicago poets, as their location would suggest, were by far the more self-consciously American. They saw themselves, as the Beats would later see themselves, as heirs of the mystical nationalism of Walt Whitman, and much of their verse bears the mark of Whitman's influence. They wished to create a new culture for and of the American heartland.

Of the poets who gathered in London, many were associated with the Imagist movement, for a time under the leadership of Ezra Pound. Imagism was an attempt, inspired in part by study of modern French poetry and Japanese haiku, to codify the principles for writing a new kind of poetry. Having no understanding of the language, and little knowledge of the culture, Pound's understanding of haiku was confined to the imagistic technique, and to the condensation and suggestiveness which are so much a part of the method

of haiku. This resulted in Pound's super-pository technique which he defined as "the one image poem" where "one idea is set on top of another," a method which the haiku employs to overcome the limitations of its brevity.

F. S. Flint, a minor British poet who appeared with Pound in the original Imagist anthology (1913), listed three rules for Imagists: direct treatment of the "thing" whether subjective or objective; to use absolutely no word that does not contribute to the presentation; as regarding rhythm: to compose in the sequence of the musical phrase, not in the sequence of the metronome. Pound wrote: "An 'Image' is that which presents an intellectual and emotional complex in an instant of time . . . It is the presentation of such an image which gives the sense of sudden liberation; that sense of freedom from time and space limits; that sense of sudden growth, which we experience in the presence of the greatest works of art."

There were many debates over just what rules an Imagist should follow—especially over whether or not it was necessary to abandon regular meter and write in free verse. But behind these debates there was general agreement that the popular poetry of the time was vapid and sentimental, addicted to imprecise language and vague emotions. The Imagists proposed to describe concrete objects with precision and to evoke states of feeling only through carefully established scenes and objects.

1. The main theme of this passage is

(A) a description of twentieth-century American poetry
(B) a description of the poetry of Ezra Pound
(C) an analysis of the major objectives of the Imagist movement
(D) an explanation of why Chicago and London became the two centers of early twentieth-century American poetry
(E) the origins of twentieth-century American poetry

2. According to the writer, all but one of the following factors influenced the Imagist movement:

(A) modern French poetry
(B) a dislike for sentimental poetry
(C) mystical nationalism
(D) haiku
(E) the desire to write a new kind of poetry

3. According to the writer, the leader of the Chicago poets was

(A) Ezra Pound
(B) Walt Whitman
(C) F. S. Flint
(D) the Beats
(E) none of the above

4. According to the writer, Imagist poets argued over

(A) whether or not to write in free verse
(B) the mystic nationalism of Walt Whitman
(C) the difference between them and the Chicago poets
(D) whether or not to use imprecise language and vague emotions
(E) whether or not to describe concrete objects with precision

5. The writer implies that the Chicago poets attempted to

(A) define mystic nationalism
(B) argue with their counterparts in London
(C) create a new kind of American poetry
(D) discredit Ezra Pound
(E) codify the principles for writing a new kind of poetry

ANSWERS AND EXPLANATIONS, PASSAGES 1–3

Passage 1
1. (B)   2. (A)   3. (E)   4. (C)   5. (A)

Passage 2
1. (D)   2. (A)   3. (B)   4. (B)   5. (D)

Passage 3
1. (C)   2. (C)   3. (E)   4. (A)   5. (A)

Passage 1

1. (B) Choice (A) is incorrect; the author never says this. In the second paragraph, the author states that if one is to infer that the "*Comedy* is a supreme expression of the Middle Ages, then nothing could be more misleading." (B) can be found in the fourth sentence of the second paragraph. The author explicitly states that the *Comedy* is a "sharp and great-minded protest at the ways in which men have thwarted the divine plan. (C) is wrong; the passage totally contradicts this idea. Dante's poem was not a "glorification" of the religion of the Middle Ages but a protest against the medieval view that saw the earthly life as a "necessary preparation for the afterlife." (D) is incorrect for the same reason as (C); that is, the poem is a protest against "the typically medieval view (of religion), which saw the earthly life as a "vale of tears." (E) is totally irrelevant. The three realms of the Catholic otherworld are mentioned in the first paragraph as an example of what some readers of the *Comedy* erroneously perceive as the theme of the poem.

2. (A)   The question is telling you that four of the five answer choices can be found in the passage. The one that is not is the correct answer. You could have backed into choice (A), in that this answer is never stated in the passage. (B) is in the next-to-last sentence in the passage. (C) is stated in the middle of the second paragraph. (D) can be found in the next-to-last sentence in the first paragraph. (E) is in the last sentence of the first paragraph.

3. (E)   This question also states that four of the five answer choices are explicitly stated in the passage. Choice (E) is the only answer that is not mentioned by the author.

4. (C)   Although the author states in the second line of the passage that the *Divine Comedy* is an allegory, he contradicts choice (A) in the next sentence. The author clearly states that "allegoric interpretation does not detract from the story as told," a story that specifically "deals with issues and feuds of the day." (B) is given in the last line of the first paragraph as Dante's motivation for writing the *Comedy,* but the author never gives this as the primary reason for reading it. (C) is the correct answer. The author states that the *Divine Comedy* is not merely a personal statement, nor does it only treat the most universal values but is also a "glorification of the ways of God." (D) is incorrect. Although the poem presents *a vision of the three realms of the Catholic otherworld,* the author never gives this as the primary reason why one should read Dante's work. (E) is irrelevant. The passage never mentions the cultural and economic aspects of medieval life as themes in the poem.

5. (A)   Choice (A) is explicitly stated in the last sentence of the passage. According to the author, Dante believed *that man should seek earthly immortality by his worthy actions here.* None of the other answers is given in the passage.

Passage 2

1. (D)   If you put an asterisk alongside the first and second sentences, you would have selected the correct answer without any difficulty. The second sentence states that the one goal of the New Deal was to end the Depression.

2. (A)   You were told that one way to locate an answer is to find where in the passage the question is discussed. That is obviously in the last six sentences in the first paragraph. However, this could be misleading, in that answer (A) seems to apply to the idea of Social Security, not deficit spending. If you look closely, however, the sentence before that states that the creation of Social Security symbolized the role of government as protector of the *individual,* whereas in the next to the last sentence in this paragraph, the words *some kind of federal role* imply that both Social Security and deficit spending were created for the same reason: to protect the American people both on a personal as well as societal basis. This is one of the ways the test makers can confuse the test taker; they present their information in a way that requires you to look more closely. This is precisely why the most efficient way to arrive at your answer choice is by a process of elimination. You could have narrowed your answer to (A) because the other choices are never mentioned in the passage.

3. (B)   This is the only answer applicable to the passage. The first sentence of the second paragraph expresses it best: In spite of the massive federal intervention in the economy, the New Deal failed in its primary purpose of ending the Depression.

4. (B)   Answer (B) can be found in the second sentence of the second paragraph, which explicitly states that the coming of World War II accomplished what the New Deal could not—that is, end the Depression.

5. (D)   The clue to the answer is in the question. The words *all but one* mean that you should be able to locate four of the five answer choices in the passage; therefore, the one that is not mentioned is the correct answer. You probably narrowed your answer down to (D), in that (A) is in the third sentence of the passage, (B) is in the second half of the same sentence, (C) is in the fourth sentence, and (E) is in the fifth sentence in the paragraph.

Passage 3

1. (C)   Choice (A) is incorrect because the answer is too narrow; *American poetry* is only mentioned in the first paragraph. (B) is also too narrow because the only discussion of the poetry of *Ezra Pound* is presented in the second paragraph. (C) is correct because the analysis of the *objectives* of the Imagist movement begins in the second paragraph and continues to the end of the passage. (D) is irrelevant; the author never explains *why* Chicago and London became the two centers of early twentieth-century American poetry. (E) is also irrelevant; there is no mention of the *origins* of twentieth-century American poetry.

2. (C)   This question is telling you that four of the five choices are true; they are stated in the passage. Only *one* answer is *not* true. You could have backed into choice (C) by a process of elimination. (A), (D), and (E) are all found in the second sentence of the second paragraph. The author states that *Imagism was an attempt, inspired in part by study of modern French poetry and Japanese haiku, to codify the principles for writing a new kind of poetry.* (B) is in the next to the last sentence in the passage. The author clearly states that the one thing over which there was "general agreement," not "debate," was *that the popular poetry of the time was vapid and sentimental.* Choice (C) is correct because although the passage does mention "mystical nationalism" in the first paragraph, its influence was on the *Chicago* poets, not the *Imagists* who gathered in London.

3. (E)   The author never tells us who the leader of the *Chicago* poets was, so (A), (B), (C), and (D) are obviously wrong.

4. (A)   The answer to this question is in the last paragraph. It is the only part of the passage where the author mentions that the Imagists debated. The answer is stated almost word for word in the first sentence. *There were many debates over just what rules an Imagist should follow—especially over whether or not it was necessary to abandon regular meter and write in free verse.* Choices (B) and (C) are irrelevant; the Imagists never argued over "mystic nationalism" or "the difference" between them and the Chicago poets. While choices (D) and (E) are both mentioned in the last paragraph, the Imagists never debated over questions of "imprecise language" or "whether or not to describe concrete objects with precision." The answer is clearly stated in the last sentence of the passage, where the author states *The imagists proposed to describe concrete objects with precision and to evoke states of feeling only through carefully established objects.*

5. (A)   Remember that even though the question asks what the author implies, you must still be able to locate the answer in the passage. You could have backed into choice (A) by a process of elimination. However, the answer is found in the first paragraph, in which the author points out that the Chicago poets set forth the nature and meaning of mystic nationalism in their poetry. (B) is incorrect; it never says that the Chicago poets *argued* with their counterparts in London. (C) looks good at first, but note that in the last sentence of the first paragraph the words are "create a new *culture*" not "a new kind of American *poetry*." (D) is simply wrong; the passage never states that the *Chicago* poets attempted to "codify the principles for writing a new kind of poetry"; on the contrary, it was the *Imagists*. The answer is explicitly stated in the second sentence of the second paragraph.

Part II
Vocabulary in Context

In an effort to make the vocabulary section of the SAT I more accessible for students, the designers of the test have decided to test student vocabulary proficiency in a more natural or realistic way. Instead of presenting students with questions that are completely dependent on vocabulary—where you are simply given a word and asked to find its opposite, or antonym, among the five words that follow—the vocabulary has been integrated into the reading-comprehension questions.

> The author uses the word *accessible* in the first sentence to mean:
> (A) challenging (B) conclusive (C) manageable (D) superfluous
> (E) precise

This vocabulary question is a typical example of the form used on the SAT I. What you might not have realized is that tested in this way, the vocabulary becomes an extension of the techniques for *backing into the right answer* for the *sentence-completion question*. But in this case, you've already been given the "missing" word. It is no longer necessary to depend solely on having to know the exact meaning of the word. Now there are built-in textual clues that will enable you to deduce the meaning. So if you skipped over the sentence-completion section in this book (or, for that matter, the reading-comprehension section), we suggest you turn back to it now before you begin this section.

One of the advantages of handling the vocabulary in this way is that you have already underlined the key words in the passage as you read it through for the first time. This should make it easier for you to identify the clues for the vocabulary question that will lead you to the right answer.

Techniques for Answering Vocabulary Questions

Step 1: Identifying Key Words

If you have not already done so, go back to the opening paragraph of this section and underline and circle the key words in exactly the same way as if you were reading the passage for the first time. (These are also the first steps in diagramming the sentence-completion question).

In its final diagrammed state, your paragraph should look like this:

In an effort to make the vocabulary section of the SAT I more accessible for students, the designers of the test have decided to test student vocabulary proficiency in a more natural or realistic way. // Instead of presenting students with questions that are completely dependent on vocabulary—where you are simply given a word and asked to find its opposite, or antonym, among the five words that follow—// the vocabulary has been integrated into the reading-comprehension questions.

You probably realized that one of the important clues in this paragraph are the words *Instead of,* which imply that whatever is stated in the first sentence is going to be contradicted in the next sentence; therefore, you should have set off the words *In-*

stead of with double lines. Furthermore, in that the words *Instead of* begin an entirely new sentence, you know that the second part of the sentence is going to explain specifically the exact nature of that contrast. It should be obvious that the information set off by the double lines explains the way antonyms were tested on previous SATs compared with the format on the newly redesigned test.

Step 2:   Determining the Connotation

Reread the first paragraph and ask yourself the question: Is the word *accessible* a positive or a negative word? What type of word could I substitute in its place? You will probably have little difficulty in deciding that the word you are looking for is positive, in that the key words used to describe the new format are *more natural* and *realistic.*

Step 3:   Narrowing Your Choices

Go through the choices one at a time, drawing a line through those answers that are *not possible*; that will, of course, include any words you recognize as obviously negative, in that you are looking for a positive word. (Try to use as many of the techniques you have learned from the earlier sections of this book as you can to narrow down your choices.)

Please go back to the question. Back into the right answer by eliminating all of those words that are *not possible.* Follow the procedure just outlined for you. Do it now, *before reading further.* Your question probably looked like this:

> The author uses the word *accessible* in the first sentence to mean:
> (A) ~~challenging~~ (B) ~~conclusive~~ (C) manageable (D) ~~superfluous~~ (E) precise

You probably eliminated (A) immediately, in that the words *more natural* suggest the idea of questions that are "tester friendly"; in other words, they are easier to figure out in some way, rather than more difficult or challenging. Besides, *challenging* is a negative word. You were probably able to eliminate (B) and (D) because you realized that the word *conclusive* is irrelevant. Even if you did not know that *superfluous* means "being over and above what is sufficient or required"—in other words, "unnecessary"—you probably recognized the prefix *super,* either as a slang word meaning "fine" or "extremely great" or as a prefix meaning "of superiority." In either case, the word does not seem to fit the definition we are looking for. Left with choices (C) and (E), you might have realized that the word *precise* means "definite" or "exact," which suggests that students are being asked for a fixed definition. But that is the exact opposite of what the new format for the vocabulary question is designed to test. Instead, students are being asked to determine the way the word is used in the context of the paragraph. (C) is the perfect choice.

Here is another vocabulary question. Try it now, *before reading further.*

> He <u>drove</u> in <u>silence,</u> the reins loosely held in his left hand, his brown, seamed profile, under the helmet-like peak of the cap, relieved against the banks of the snow like the bronze image of a hero.
> The author uses the word *relieved* to mean: ~~(A) enclosed~~ (B) unburdened ~~(C) compressed~~ (D) outlined ~~(E) solidified~~

In its final diagrammed state, your sentence should look something like this:

> He <u>drove</u> in <u>silence,</u> the <u>reins loosely held</u> in his left hand, (his) brown, seamed (profile,) (under) the <u>helmet-like peak of</u> the (cap,) (relieved) (against) the (banks) (of) the (snow) (like) the (bronze) (image) of a <u>hero.</u>

To the unsuspecting student, the question might seem to pose little difficulty, in that most students know that the word *relieved* is a form of the word *relief,* which means "to ease" or "to free from pain or fear." So *unburdened,* choice (B), would seem to be the obvious choice. But even if you know the meaning of the vocabulary word, *do not attempt to answer the question without first going back to the passage.* Remember, you were asked to determine its definition by the way it was used in the sentence. Besides, a word might have a meaning with which you are unfamiliar. Rereading this sentence, you probably realized that you could eliminate *enclosed,* choice (A), as irrelevant because the word *against* suggests the idea of leaning into something rather than being contained or shut up in some way. Although the words *banks of snow* and *bronze image* seem to convey the idea of something solid or compact, neither *compressed,* choice (C), or *solidified,* choice (E), fits into the meaning of the sentence as a whole. It is clear from this sentence that the writer is attempting to describe the driver of a horse-drawn vehicle. But his only view of the man is his "profile" or "image," which is set off "against the banks of snow." If you substituted your own word in place of *relieved,* the best possible choice is (D), *outlined.* The word *relieved* as it is used in this sentence means "to bring into prominence"; in other words, "to stand out." It fits the context perfectly.

A WORD OF CAUTION. This method of testing vocabulary has its advantages and disadvantages. A student might select the wrong answer simply because he is familiar with the word and assumes that he understands its meaning; however, his interpretation might not be what the author intended.

Words often mean different things to different people. In this type of example, it is important to examine the context in which the words are used. *The context will determine their meaning.* Furthermore, the Educational Testing Service (ETS) has constructed the test choices so that several might vary by shades of difference. Answers are so often apparently similar that they might seem arguable. In order to ensure your best performance on these questions, approach each one systematically. Firmly eliminating choices will sharpen your perception in making fine, and final, decisions.

When You Do Not Know the Word

There are additional techniques you can use when even clues in the context of the passage are unable to help you arrive at an approximate definition of the word being tested. Look at the following example:

PITHY: (A) concise (B) verbose (C) irritable (D) spread out (E) callous

The first step in dealing with a word you do not know is to *circle the prefix, root, and suffix* if you can. (A later section in this book, Building Your Vocabulary, will be of great help in learning to do this.) If you cannot identify any parts of the word, circle either any word you recognize (which might be the root), or any group of letters that might suggest a word you know. Go back to the question and do it now.

Most students will be able to circle the word *pit,* and others will recognize the word *pith.* Both suggest the meaning of something being central or in the center. Please go back to the question. Back into the right answer by eliminating all words that are *not possible.* Do it now, *before reading further.* Your question probably looks like this:

PITHY: (A) concise (B) verbose (C) ~~irritable~~ (D) ~~spread out~~ (E) callous

You probably eliminated (C) and (D) immediately because (C) has nothing to do with a fixed or central point and (D) conveys just the opposite meaning. (B) and (E) should have been easy to eliminate. If you did not know the meaning of the word *verbose,* notice in it the word *verb,* which is a shortened version of the word *verbal. Verbose* means "wordy" or "talkative," which has just the opposite connotation of "fixed" or "central point." If you did not know the meaning of the word *callous,* think of any context in which you can place the word. How about the callus a person acquires on his hands and feet as a result of hard work? What is a callus? It is a layer of tough skin, and *callous* means "having calluses," or hardened or tough. So *callous* is not the word you are looking for. The answer is *concise,* choice (A). Actually, *pithy* means "concise" or "to the point," so the words are indeed synonyms. Look at the following example.

DISAFFECTED (A) ambivalent (B) amicable (C) estranged (D) irascible (E) devoted

Answer the question by following the procedure just outlined for you: (1) if you do not know the meaning of the word *disaffected,* circle the prefix, root, and suffix if you can; (2) if you cannot identify any parts of the word, circle any words you recognize or any group of letters that might suggest a word you know.

An additional technique: if you cannot arrive at an approximate definition of the word being tested, *determine whether or not the word is positive or negative* on the basis of either the prefix, root, or words suggested by the first few letters. If you are working with a negative word, you will eliminate all positive choices. If you are working with a positive word, you will eliminate all obviously negative choices. Go back to the question and back into the correct answer by eliminating all words that are *not possible.*

You probably recognized the prefix *dis-* and circled it, along with the root *-affect.* If you knew that the prefix *dis-* means "away," "off," "down," or "opposing," you realized you are dealing with a negative word. If you did not know what the prefix means, you might have thought of words beginning with those letters, such as *disassemble* and *disappoint.* You probably also recognized the root word *affect,* which means "acted upon" or "touched," so you would have realized that the word *disaffected* has something to do with breaking away from or opposing some influence. Because you know that you are looking for a negative word, the first step, then, is to go through the question, eliminating all positive choices. Your question probably looks like this:

DISAFFECTED: (A) ambivalent (B) ~~amicable~~ (C) estranged (D) irascible (E) ~~devoted~~

You probably eliminated (B) and (E) immediately because they are clearly positive words. The next step should have been to circle the prefix, root, and suffix of the remaining words. The words should have looked like this: (A) ambivalent (C) estranged (D) irascible.

Although many students do not know that the prefix *ambi-* means "both," most students are familiar with the word *ambidextrous,* which means "skillful with both hands," so the meaning of "both" might be arrived at in that way. The word *ambiguous* might also have come to mind, a word that suggests something that can be taken in two ways or is unclear. The word *ambivalent* will therefore pose a problem, in that *ambidextrous* suggests certain positive qualities and *ambiguous* certain negative ones. You probably left it and went on to the word *estranged.* You might have known that the prefix *e-* is a variation of *ex-,* meaning "out of" or "from," and that the word *strange* means "unsure" or "out of one's natural environment." You probably left it as a possible answer. The word *irascible* might have at first seemed a likely choice because the prefix *ir-* means "not," or "opposing." Furthermore, if you look closely at the first few letters of the word, you will notice the beginning of the word *rascal.* But these clues should only have reinforced your feeling that *irascible,* which means "irritable," is probably not the answer you are looking for. Left with (A) and (C), you probably decided on the correct answer, which is *estranged,* a word that means "to turn away in feeling or affections." This is the perfect synonym for the word *disaffected* and is closest to the idea conveyed in the prefix *dis-,* meaning "to be separated from" in some way, which is what the word *disaffected* means.

PRACTICE EXERCISES

Here are some vocabulary questions for you to practice. They are based on excerpts from various passages. Follow the steps outlined; the answers and explanations will follow. In that some of the questions require you to distinguish fine shades of meaning, consider all of the choices before deciding which is best. Remember, if this were the real test, once you have narrowed down your choices, *you must go back to the reading-comprehension passage. The answer you choose will depend on the way it is used in the context of the sentence.*

1. He seemed a part of the mute melancholy landscape, an incarnation of its frozen woe with all that was warm and sentient in him fast bound below the surface, but there was nothing unfriendly in his silence.

   Which of the following best captures the meaning of the word *sentient*? (A) unyielding (B) restrained (C) feeling (D) unconscious (E) deadened

2. He stamped and swore that he was going to have blood and breathed indictments, jail, publicity, and lawsuits. His fires, however, were pretty soon banked. Not that in the end it didn't cost him some change. But in the end, the whole transaction was conducted without noise.

   The author uses the word *banked* to mean: (A) impaired (B) protected (C) redirected (D) disposed of (E) satisfied

3. The author professed her desire to write books that were enormous naturalistic novels with unhappy endings, full of detailed descriptions and arresting imagery.

   In this context, the author uses the word *arresting* to mean: (A) delayed (B) unfocused (C) precise (D) striking (E) thoughtful

4. What gave his activities unity and power was his passionate sense of the tragedy of life, irony of history, and fallibility of humans—and his deep conviction of the duty, even in face of these realities, to be firm in the right as God gives us to see

the right. Humility, he believed, must temper, not sever, the nerve of action.

   The word *temper* most nearly means: (A) inflame (B) subdue (C) excite (D) restrict (E) inhibit

5. She walked quickly, straining her eyes to detect anyone who might be coming along the street, but before reaching the house in which direction she was headed, she crossed over the sidewalk to the edge of the curb in order to avoid the light of the window. Whenever she was unhappy, she felt herself at bay against a pitiless world, and a kind of animal secretiveness possessed her. But the street was empty.

   The phrase *at bay against* most nearly means: (A) indignant toward (B) pitted against (C) pursued by (D) confused by (E) frightened by

6. A novelist's chief concern is to be as unconscious as possible. He has to induce in himself a state of perpetual lethargy. He wants life to proceed with the utmost quiet and regularity.

   The word *lethargy* most nearly means: (A) invisibility (B) rashness (C) mediation (D) detachment (E) reflection

7. He seemed to behave in an irrational manner. It was most noticeable in the spare and almost unreasonable way he handled expenditures, even to the point where he refused to provide decent living conditions for himself.

   The word *spare* most nearly means: (A) cautious

(B) generous   (C) stinting   (D) considerate
(E) thoughtless

8. Immediately she saw that the pin she had chosen for herself was a mere trifle compared to the small round stone, blue as a mountain lake, with little sparks of light all around it. She blushed at her want of discrimination.

Which of the following best captures the meaning of the word *want:* (A) awareness (B) desire (C) resentment (D) lack (E) promise

9. The idea of a curriculum based on women's studies can mean that women are led to read mediocre or peripheral books by women rather than the great books of humanity in general. The danger is in separating women from the mainstream thinking of the human race.

The word *peripheral* most nearly means: (A) commonplace (B) significant (C) exaggerated (D) superficial (E) informative

10. When social animals are gathered together in groups, they become qualitatively different creatures from what they were when alone or in pairs. Single locusts are quiet, meditative, sessile things, but when locusts are added to other locusts, they become excited, change color and intensify their activity.

The word *sessile* most nearly means: (A) provocative (B) segregated (C) fixed (D) disconnected (E) inconstant

ANSWERS AND EXPLANATIONS

1. (C)   2. (D)   3. (D)   4. (B)   5. (B)
6. (D)   7. (C)   8. (D)   9. (D)   10. (C)

1. (C)   He seemed a part of the mute melancholy landscape, an incarnation of its frozen woe with all that was warm and sentient in him fast bound below the surface, //but there was nothing unfriendly in his silence.

One of the important clues in this sentence is the word *and,* which implies that whatever is on one side of the word—in this case, the word *warm*—there should be a word of similar import on the other side. That is what you will be looking for among your choices. Chances are you eliminated *deadened,* choice (E), in that you are looking for a word that has emotional connotations. If you examined the sentence further, you probably realized that it is based on a contrast between the ideas expressed in the first part of the sentence and those expressed in the second part. More specifically, the individual in the first part of the sentence is described as *part of the frozen landscape,* which indicates that you are looking for a word that contradicts the word *frozen.* Choices (A), *unyielding;* (B), *restrained;* and (D), *unconscious,* might at first seem likely possibilities. However, *unyielding* and *restrained* both convey the idea of holding back or keeping down in some way, and *unconscious,* choice (D), means not to know or be aware of something. All three choices convey the idea of a dormant or unemotional state, just the opposite meaning of the word you are looking for. The answer, of course, is (C).

2. (D)   He stamped and swore that he was going to have blood and breathed indictments, jail, publicity, and lawsuits. His fires, //however, were pretty soon banked, //Not that in the end it didn't cost him some change, //But in the end, the whole transaction was conducted without noise.

There are many vocabulary words that have more than one meaning. *Banked* is one of those words. You probably realized that the writer of this sentence is using the idea of banking in terms of emotional expenditure. But even if you did not, you probably noticed that one of the important clues in this passage is the word *however;* it indicates that whatever is stated in the first part—in this case, a description of inflammatory behavior—is going to be contradicted in the second part. In the final sentence, the writer specifically states that *the entire transaction was conducted without noise.* Therefore, we can assume that the word you are looking for is a word that suggests the idea of something being diminished or quieted down in some way. Looking over your choices, it would be possible to eliminate every answer but (D), in that (A), *impaired;* (B), *protected;* (C), *redirected;* and (E), *satisfied,* do not fit the description of the word we are looking for. *Disposed of,* choice (D), most nearly approximates the idea of covering up or putting away.

3. (D)   The author professed her desire to write books that were enormous naturalistic novels with unhappy endings, full of detailed descriptions and arresting imagery.

In this excerpt, you might have had some difficulty in recognizing the clues: *enormous* and *full of.* These words convey the idea of power and immensity. Recognizing the implications in this sentence is the important skill you need in order to arrive at the correct answer. You probably realized that the writer wants to create images that are as equally grand and forceful as her "endings" and "descriptions." So you know you are looking for a word that not only has positive connotations but exudes energy. Since you know you are looking for a positive word, you could have eliminated (A), *delayed,* and (B), *unfocused,* in that both words are obviously negative. Left with (C), (D), and (E), you probably eliminated (E), in that the word *thoughtful,* which means "considerate" or "reflective," seems to lack the dramatic intensity of the word you are looking for. Left with choices (C) and (D), at first glance, *precise,* choice (C), might seem like a good possibility because of its relationship to the word *detailed* in the sentence. But although *detailed* suggests descriptions that are fully and distinctly related, *precise* means "definite" or "exact"; the word has rigid or mechanical associations, just the opposite meaning of the word you are looking for. It should be obvious that the author wants to create compelling images—visual pictures that are exciting and will catch the reader's attention. The perfect choice is *striking,* choice (A), in that *arresting* means "any seizure by force" or "the act of stopping." It is clear that in this context the word *arresting* is used in a psychological sense; that is, the author wants to create figurative descriptions that will capture the reader's attention. The word *striking* means "impressive" or "attractive."

4. (B)   What gave his activities unity and power was his passionate sense of the tragedy of life, irony of history and fallibility of humans—and his deep conviction of the duty, even in the face of these realities, to be firm in the right as God gives us to see the right. Humility, he believed, must temper, // not sever, // the nerve of action.

In diagramming this excerpt, you probably isolated the word *not* in the final sentence as an important clue. It tells us immediately that we are looking for a word that in some way contrasts with the word *sever,* which means "to separate" or "to break apart"; a word such as *join* or *connect.* Yet if you look over your choices, there is no word that has this meaning. So it is important to go back to the passage and to reread the last sentence. One technique that might help you move closer to the right answer is to try reading this sentence by first omitting the words *not sever.* You will discover that the word *humility* turns out to be a very important clue. You probably know that humility means "modesty" or "humbleness" and is therefore a positive quality. So you also realized that the word *temper* has more than one meaning, and that in this context it is closely related to the idea of humility. Most students know that the word *temper,* as a noun, has to do with a state of mind usually associated with outbursts of anger. Less familiar is the verb form of *temper,* which means "to soften" or "tone down." If we mean by "nerve of action" having the courage or the strength to act, in this context the word *temper* is used to suggest a more moderate or less extreme form of action, as opposed to forcibly breaking off all action completely. So we are looking for a word that suggests moderation. You could have easily eliminated *inflamed,* choice (A), and *excite,* choice (C), in that both words mean to make more violent and are contrary to the idea of modesty or humility. *Restrict,* choice (D), and *inhibit,* choice (E), might seem like possible choices because they mean "to confine" or "to restrain," but those definitions are too similar to the idea of preventing or stopping action, rather than to simply tone it down. The best answer is *subdue,* choice (B), which means "to soften," a definition well suited to the spirit of the passage.

5. (B) She (walked)(quickly,)(straining) her (eyes) to (detect)(anyone) who might be coming along the street, // (but)(before)(reaching) the (house) in which direction she was headed, she (crossed) over the (sidewalk) to the edge of the curb in order to (avoid) the (light) of the window. // (Whenever) she was (unhappy,) she (felt) herself (at)(bay)(against) a (pitiless)(world,) and a kind of (animal)(secretiveness) possessed her. // (But) the (street) was (empty.)

This question should have presented few problems even if you did not know the meaning of the word *bay.* There are ample clues throughout the passage to help you arrive at the correct answer. Looking over your choices, you could have easily eliminated (A), (D), and (E). The word *indignant* means "to show displeasure at something one thinks is unworthy." It also suggests a certain degree of strength and feeling of superiority. You probably realize that it does not fit the description of what we are looking for. You could have also eliminated (D), in that the answer is simply irrelevant. There are no clues to support the idea of any confusion. At first glance, (E) might seem as if it were a likely possibility because someone who behaves in a secretive manner to avoid detection and makes every effort to keep from being seen can be considered *frightened,* but there is nothing to support the idea that fear is the motivating factor in her behavior. Choice (C) is very appealing because the passage seems to suggest that she is being hunted or tracked like an animal, but nowhere in the passage is this stated. On the contrary, the author clearly states that the street was empty. Choice (B) seems the likely way to go. The word *pitted* means "to set in opposition," as "one against another." *Pitted against* perfectly expresses the idea of someone "held in check" or "confronted" by a world that in this case has no compassion.

6. (D) A (novelist's) chief (concern) is to (be) as (unconscious) as possible. He has to (induce) in himself a (state) of (perpetual)(lethargy.) He (wants) life to proceed with the utmost (quiet) and (regularity.)

It should be clear from your diagramming that there are several important clues in this sentence, including the words *quiet* and *regularity,* but the most important clue is the word *unconscious,* which means "not to be aware of something" or "not known or perceived by." You could have easily eliminated (B) and (E). *Rashness* means "acting too hastily" or "impetuous," the exact opposite of the meaning you are looking for. The word *reflection* means "to consider carefully"; it is an active process and represents the exact opposite of the author's stated requirement, which is "to be as unconscious as possible." You might have left *mediation,* choice (C), if you confused it with the word *meditation,* which means "to engage in contemplation," often thought of as spiritual or prayerful. (This is one of the common traps the SAT testers have set for you. It is always a good idea to check the spelling just to be sure.) Because *mediation* is an "action to bring about an agreement" or a "peaceful settlement between parties," it is obvious that choice (C) is irrelevant. Left with (A) and (D), you might have realized that *invisibility,* which means "withdrawn from sight" or "unseen," just doesn't fit. The best answer is *detachment,* choice (D), which suggests "aloofness" or "lack of concern or interest"—a completely unemotional state of being very close to the meaning of *lethargy,* "a state of dullness" or "sluggish inactivity."

7. (C)   He seemed to behave in an irrational manner. It was most noticeable in the spare and almost unreasonable way he handled expenditures, even to the point where he refused to provide decent living conditions for himself.

This is the type of vocabulary question that is deceptive in its simplicity because the word *spare* has more than one meaning. If you thought that *spare* means either "to leave uninjured" or "to hold in reserve," you might have had a difficult time answering this question, wasting valuable time in a search for the answer. The way to approach this question is to look over the clues you isolated in your diagramming. Note the importance of the words *and almost* in the second sentence. They indicate that you are looking for a word that has to do with some form of extreme behavior that is close to being unreasonable. It should also be apparent that the word you are expected to find in some way reflects an inability or unwillingness to spend money. You could have easily eliminated (B), *generous,* and (D), *considerate,* in that the word we are looking for has negative, not positive, connotations. But you might have been somewhat unsure of the choice between (C), *thoughtful,* and (E), *cautious,* because both words are adequate explanations for an individual's unwillingness to spend money, although cautious would be the more reasonable choice. But (A), *stinting,* is the correct answer. It is the only choice that has to do with money, particularly the idea of "restricting oneself as to an amount," with "a particular emphasis on getting along on a scanty allowance."

8. (D)   Immediately she saw that the pin she had chosen for herself was a mere trifle compared to the small round stone, blue as a mountain lake, with little sparks of light all around it. She blushed at her want of discrimination.

One of the most important clues in this passage is the word *blushed* because it suggests that we are looking for a negative word, one that would have the effect of causing someone embarrassment. You probably also realized that the word *want,* which in its verb form means "to feel a need" or "desire for," must have more than one meaning. In this context it seems obvious that the word *want* implies "something lacking," which is what the noun form of the word *want* means. What is lacking is the ability to discriminate between things or to make fine distinctions or judgments. You could have eliminated every answer except (D) because none of the other words conveys the idea of a deficiency or absence of something.

9. (D)   The idea of a curriculum based upon women's studies can mean that women are led to read mediocre or peripheral books by women, // rather than the great books of humanity in general. The danger is in separating women from the mainstream thinking of the human race.

It should be clear from your diagramming of this passage that the clues to the words you are looking for are well defined. The phrase "rather than" is a very important clue. It indicates that whatever is stated in the first part of this sentence is going to contrast in some way with the idea presented in the second part. Therefore, it is important that you circle all connecting words and phrases in every sentence. Looking over the passage, you probably came up with some variation of the idea that a women's studies program would be likely to prevent women from reading great books of intellectual thought. The word *or* in the first sentence is another important clue; it suggests that you are looking for a word that is similar to the word *mediocre,* which means "ordinary." Many students know the meaning of the prefix *peri-* from the word *perimeter,* which means "the circumference" or "outer boundary." In fact, *peri-* means "around" or "apart," so you could have eliminated (B), (C), and (E). *Significant,* choice (B), and *exaggerated,* choice (C), are irrelevant, and *informative,* choice

(E), might be a valid description of a women's studies program, but it's beside the point; all books are informative. Left with (A) and (D), you might have picked (A) as your answer. Choice (A) seems perfect; the word *commonplace* certainly suggests "mediocrity." But if you look again at the clues you have diagrammed in the passage, you will see that what you want is a word that is related to "mediocre" but not a synonym. That is the danger in selecting an answer choice that is not based on its meaning in the passage. The last sentence clearly indicates that we need a word that means "separated" or "apart from the mainstream"; (D), *superficial,* is the perfect choice.

10. (C)   When social animals are gathered together in groups, they become qualitatively different creatures from what they were when alone or in pairs. || Single locusts are quiet, meditative, sessile things, || but when locusts are added to other locusts, they become excited, change color, and intensify their activity.

Even if you are totally unfamiliar with the word *sessile,* there are several important clues to help you narrow down your choices. The most important clue is *but,* which indicates that whatever word or group of words follows, the word you are looking for is going to contrast in meaning. Therefore, we are looking for a word that means the opposite of "excited" or to "intensify . . . activity." Furthermore, it is also a word that essentially means the same thing as "quiet" and "meditative." That would eliminate (A) and (E), in that both words mean just the opposite. *Provocative* means "to stir" or "arouse" and *inconstant* means "changeable" or "variable." You could also have eliminated (B) and (D) because *segregated* means "to separate" or "set apart" and *disconnected* means "severed" or "detached"; neither word comes close to the meaning of the word we are looking for. The best choice is (D) because the word *fixed* means "permanently placed" or "made fast or firm"; it fits perfectly.

Building Your Vocabulary

There is no substitute for having a substantial vocabulary. For that reason we have compiled several important lists for you to learn. The lists include words that are often mistaken for similar-looking words, and prefixes, roots, and suffixes that frequently appear in the English language. The longest list is composed of words that appear especially frequently in college entrance examinations.

If you really want to score well on the SAT, you can use the lists to make "flash cards." A good method is to cut up ordinary file cards; one 3 × 5 file card will make five 1 × 3 flash cards. On each flash card, write one root, prefix, suffix, or vocabulary word. Then write the definition on the reverse side. Making the flash cards might seem tedious, but it is not wasted time. On the contrary, writing each word or word element and its definition will go a long way toward fixing the information in your memory. Shuffle these cards so that they are in random order and put them together with a rubber band or paper clip. Set yourself a reasonable number of cards to learn each week. A reasonable number would be anywhere from 25 to 40. As you go through each stack, put the ones you get right aside, but put the ones you get wrong on the bottom of the stack. Eventually you will get them all right. Then go back through the entire stack again to make sure you really know them all. Remember, there might be many you already know. Carry these cards with you and use any spare moments you have to study them. You might want to keep the complete words in a separate stack and learn all of the prefixes, roots, and suffixes first because these will make it possible for you to figure out, for yourself, the definitions of many thousands of words.

If you do not want to make flash cards, you can merely study the lists in the book, covering the definitions with a file card or small envelope. Whichever method you use, keep it up until you can go through all of the words, prefixes, suffixes, and roots without error. This might take you only a few hours or several days—but however long it takes, you will be well rewarded not only by a much higher SAT score but by a greatly increased vocabulary that will benefit you throughout your life.

Words Commonly Confused with Each Other

Let's start with this short list of commonly confused words. Most of them are words you probably think you know, because when you see them in context you do not misunderstand them. However, when you see such words in word-relationship questions, they might fool you—just what the makers of the SAT are expecting them to do. Also, if you are nervous and hurrying, as most of us are to some degree in a test, you can misread a word you really do know very well.

ARBITER	a supposedly unprejudiced judge	ARBITRARY	prejudiced
ASCETIC	self-denying	AESTHETIC	pertaining to beauty
AVERSE	disinclined	ADVERSE	opposed
BAN	prohibition	BANE	woe
CENSURE	to find fault	CENSOR	to purge or remove offensive passages
COMPLACENT	self-satisfied; smug	COMPLAISANT	kindly; submissive
CONTEMPTIBLE	despicable	CONTEMPTUOUS	scornful

COSMOPOLITAN	sophisticated	METROPOLITAN	pertaining to the city
CREDIBLE	believable	CREDITABLE	worthy of praise
DEMURE	modest	DEMUR	to hesitate; raise objections
DEPRECATE	to disapprove regretfully	DEPRECIATE	to undervalue
DISCREET	judicious; prudent	DISCRETE	separate
DISINTERESTED	unprejudiced	UNINTERESTED	not interested
DIVERS	several	DIVERSE	varied
ELICIT	to extract	ILLICIT	unlawful
EMEND	to correct a text or a manuscript	AMEND	to improve by making slight changes
EXULT	to rejoice	EXALT	to raise; praise highly
GOURMET	lover of good food	GOURMAND	glutton
EQUABLE	even-tempered	EQUITABLE	just; fair
INDIGENT	poor	INDIGENOUS	native
INGENIOUS	clever	INGENUOUS	frank; naive
INTERNMENT	imprisonment	INTERMENT	burial
MAIZE	corn	MAZE	confusing network
MARTIAL	warlike	MARITAL	pertaining to marriage
MENDACIOUS	untruthful	MENDICANT	begging; beggar
PERSONAL	private	PERSONABLE	attractive
PERSPICACIOUS	shrewd	PERSPICUOUS	clear; lucid
PRODIGAL	wasteful	PRODIGIOUS	extraordinarily large
REGAL	royal	REGALE	to entertain lavishly
SANCTION	authorization; penalty	SANCTITY	holiness
SOCIAL	pertaining to human society	SOCIABLE	companionable
URBAN	pertaining to the city	URBANE	polished; suave
VENAL	corrupt; mercenary	VENIAL	pardonable

Prefixes

Prefixes would be very simple if each one always had only one meaning. Unfortunately, this is not the case. Some of the most common prefixes have several meanings—sometimes even opposite meanings. For example, the prefix *in-* sometimes means "not," as in *inactive,* but it can also mean "very"; that is, it can intensify rather than reverse the meaning of the word root it precedes, as in *insurgent.* It can also mean "in" or "on," as in *infer.* To complicate matters further, the prefix *in-* sometimes changes its form to *il-, im-,* or *ir-,* depending on the word root it is combined with. Thus *illegitimate, imply,* and *irradiate* all have the same prefix, *in-,* but it both takes a different form and has a different meaning in each word. Finally, English takes its prefixes from several older languages, and identical prefixes can vary depending on which language they came from. Thus the *a-* prefix in *averse* is from Latin and means "away" or "from"; the *a-* prefix in *amoral* is from Greek and means "without" or "not"; and the *a-* prefix in *aboard* is from Old English and means "on" or "in."

Does this make it impossible to determine the meaning of a prefix when you see it in a particular word? No. As your verbal skills increase, you will find that you almost always sense the *correct* meaning of a prefix if you know all of the things it *can* mean. For example, the word *irradiate,* which was mentioned above, might confuse you if you had only a partial understanding of the prefix *in-;* you might think the word meant "not radiate." Such a meaning would not make much sense in typical contexts. But if you know that *in-* can intensify as well as reverse the meaning of the root word, you would have very little difficulty understanding *irradiate* in context; you would sense that "radiate" rather than "not radiate" was the basic meaning, even if you had never seen the word *irradiate* before.

Consequently it is well worth your while to study the prefixes listed here. At first you might think that you are only confusing yourself. Actually you are increasing your awareness of words and their structure. The confusion will lessen if you persevere.

The list has been divided into prefixes of Old English, Latin, and Greek origin. Usually Latin prefixes go with Latin roots and Greek prefixes go with Greek roots, but there are many exceptions.

PREFIX (AND VARIANTS)	GENERAL MEANING	EXAMPLES OF USE
Prefixes of Old English origin		
a-	in, on, of, up, to	astride, afoot
be-	around, about, away, very	behead, beset, beloved
for-	away, off, from	forsake, forbid
fore-	before, previous	foreword, forethought
mis-	badly, not, poorly	misfit, misfire
over-	over, excessively	overthrow, overcast
un-	not, opposing	unfold, unknown
Prefixes of Latin origin		
ab-, a-, abs-	from, off, away	abdicate, averse, abstract, abstain
ad-, ac-, af-, ag-, al-, an-, ap-, ar-, as-, at-	to, toward, very	advocate, accede, affiliate, aggression, allude, annul, appear, arrogate, assent, attempt
ambi-	around, both	ambition, ambidextrous
ante-, anti-	before, previous	antecedent, anticipate
bi-	two, twice	bisect, bilateral
circum-	around	circumvent, circumspect
com-, co-, col-, con-, cor-	with, together, very	commotion, complicate, coexist, collate, congenital, corrupt
contra-	against, opposing	contradict, contravene
de-	away, from, off, down	demur, demolish,
demi-	half	demigod, demitasse
dis-, di-, dif-	away, off, down, opposing	dissent, digress, diffident, diffuse
ex-, e-, ef-	away, from, out	excise, expulsion, eradicate, efface
ex-	former	ex-husband, ex-convict
extra-, extro-	outside, beyond	extramural, extrovert
in-, il-, im-, ir-	in, into, within; not, opposing; very	induct, illumine, immigrate, irrigate; incapable, insoluble, inutile, illicit, implacable, irreverent; insurgent

PREFIX (AND VARIANTS)	GENERAL MEANING	EXAMPLES OF USE
inter-	among, between	intercede, intersperse, intermittent
intro-, intra-	inwardly, to the inside, within	introvert, introduce, intravenous
non-	not	nonessential, nonentity
ob-, oc-, of-, op-	over, against, toward, very	obtrude, obstruct, occlude, offend, opposite
per-	through, thoroughly	permeate, pernicious,
post-	after, following	postpone, postscript
pre-	before	prevent, preclude
pro-	forward, forth, favoring, in place of	protract, profuse, proslavery, pronoun
re-	back, backward, again	revoke, recede
retro-	back, backward	retroactive, retrospect
se-	away, aside	secede, seclude
semi-	half	semiannual, semiconscious
sub-, suc-, suf-, sug-, sum-, sup-, sus-	under, beneath	subsist, subjugate, suggestive, summon, sustain, succinct, suffuse
super-	over, above, extra	supervise, superscript
trans-	across, beyond	transfusion, transcend, transient
ultra-	beyond, excessive	ultramodern, ultraviolet

Prefixes of Greek origin

a-, an-	lacking, without, not	amorphous, anarchy
amphi-	around, both	amphibian, amphitheater
ana-	back, throughout, against	anagram, anachronism
anti-	against, opposing	antipathy, antithesis
apo-	from, away	apology, apostate
arch-, archi-	chief, first	architect, archbishop
cata-	down, away	catalyst, catastrophe
dia-	through, across, apart	diameter, diagnose
en-, em-	in, within, among	endemic, empirical
epi-	on, over, outside	epigram, epidermis
eu-	good, well	eulogy, euphemistic
hemi-	half	hemisphere, hemiphase
hyper-	excessive, over	hypercritical, hyperbole
hypo-	under, beneath	hypodermic, hypothesis
meta-	change of, over	metamorphosis, metaphor
para-	beside, beyond	parallel, paraphrase
peri-	around, near	periscope, perimeter
pro-	before	prognosis, program
syn-, sym-, syl-, sys-	together	synchronize, sympathy, syllogism, systematic

PREFIXES DENOTING NUMBER

A special class of prefixes are formed from the Latin and Greek words for numbers. Usually Latin prefixes are used with Latin roots and Greek prefixes with Greek roots. Latin prefixes also tend to be used with roots that are neither Greek nor Latin.

NUMBER DENOTED	LATIN PREFIX	EXAMPLE	GREEK PREFIX	EXAMPLE
half	semi-	semicircle	hemi-	hemisphere
one	uni-	uniform	mono-	monograph
two	bi-	bilateral	di-	dimeter
three	tri-	trireme	tri-	tricycle
four	quadr-	quadruped	tetra-	tetrahedron
five	quinque-, quint-	quintuple	penta-	pentagon
six	sex-	sextet	hexa-	hexameter
seven	sept-	September	hepta-	heptameter
eight	oct-	October	octa-, octo-	octopus
nine	nona-, novem-	November	ennea-	ennead
ten	dec-	decimate	deca-	decalogue
twelve	duodec-	duodecimo	dodeca-	Dodecanese
hundred	cent-	centennial	hecto-	hectograph
thousand	milli-	millennium		

Roots

In a loose sense, a root word is simply an ordinary word to which prefixes and suffixes can be added. For example, *antidisestablishmentarianism* is merely the word *establish* with an unusual number of prefixes and suffixes. But in a stricter sense, *establish* itself is constructed on the root *-stab-*. The more of these basic roots you know, the better able you will be to deal with unfamiliar words.

ROOT	MEANING	EXAMPLES
Greek roots		
-agog-	lead, leader	demagogue, synagogue
-anthrop-	man, mankind	anthropology, misanthrope
-arch-	ancient, chief	archaeology, monarch
-astr-, -aster-	star	astral, astrology, asterisk
-auto-	self	autonomy, autocratic
-bibli-	book	Bible, bibliography
-bio-	life	amphibious, biology
-chrom-	color	chromosome, chromatic
-chron-	time	synchronize, anachronistic
-cosm-	order, world	cosmic, microcosm

ROOT	MEANING	EXAMPLES
-crac-, -crat-	power, rule	democracy, aristocrat
-crypt-	secret, hidden	cryptic, cryptogram
-cycl-	wheel, circle	tricycle, cyclic
-dem-	people	democracy, demagogue
-derm-	skin	epidermis, dermatology
-dox-	belief, teaching	orthodox
-dyn-	force, power	dynamic, dynasty
-erg-	work, power	energy, energetic
-gam-	mate, marry	bigamy, monogamous
-gen-	kind, race	genealogy, eugenics
-geo-	earth	geometry, geology
-gon-	corner, angle	diagonal, trigonometry
-gram-	write, writing	telegram, epigram
-graph-	write, writing	graphite, geography
-heli-	sun	heliotropism, helium
-hem-	blood	hemorrhage, hemophilia
-hetero-	other, different	heterogeneous, heterodox
-homo-	same	homogeneous, homograph
-hydr-	water	dehydrate, hydrant
-iatr-	heal, cure	iatric, geriatrics
-iso-	same, equal	isotope, isosceles
-lith-	rock	monolithic, lithography
-log-	speech, word, study	theology, epilogue
-mega-	large, enlargement	megalomania
-metr-, -meter-	measure	diameter, trigonometry
-micr-	small	microbe, microscope
-mon-	one, single	monotonous, monologue
-morph-	form	metamorphosis, amorphous
-necr-	die, dead	necrology, necromancy
-neo-	new	neolithic, neophyte
-nom-	law, rule	autonomy, economy
-onym-	name	anonymous, pseudonym
-orth-	straight, correct	orthodontist, orthodox
-pan-	all, entire	panorama, panacea
-path-	feeling, suffering	apathy, sympathy
-ped-	child	orthopedic, pediatrician
-phil-	like, love	philanthropic, bibliophile
-phon-	sound	phonetics, phonglogy
-phor-	bear, bearing	euphoria, phosphorous
-phot-	light	photostat, photograph
-pod-	foot	tripod, podiatrist
-poly-	many	polygon, polytheistic
-proto-	first	protocol, prototype
-psych-	mind	psychology, psychosomatic
-pyr-	fire	pyromania, pyrotechnic
-scop-	seeing, watch	telescope, microscope
-soph-	wise, wisdom	sophomore, philosopher
-tax-, -tac-	arrange, arrangement	taxidermy, syntax
-techn-	art, skill	polytechnic, technology
-tele-	far, distant	telegraph, telepathy
-the-	god	theist, atheist, theology
-therm-	heat	thermal, thermometer

ROOT	MEANING	EXAMPLES
-tom-	cut	atom, epitome
-urg-	work, power	metallurgist
-zo-	animal	protozoa, zoology, zodiac

Latin roots

-ac-, -acr-	sharp	acute, acrid
-ag-, -act-	do, drive, impel	agent, active, transact
-agr-	field	agrarian, agriculture
-ali-	other	alien, alibi, alias
-alter-, -altr-	other, change	alternate, alter ego, altruism
-am-, -amic-	love, friend	amity, amicable
-anim-	mind, soul, spirit	animosity, animate
-annu-, -enni-	year	anniversary, perennial
-apt-, -ept-	adjust, fit	adapt, inept, aptitude
-aqu-	water	aquarium, aqueduct
-arm-	arm, weapon	army, disarmament
-art-	skill, craft, art	artisan, artificial
-aud-, -audit-	hear	auditory, audience
-aur-	gold	aureole, aureate
-bel-, -bell-	war	rebel, bellicose
-ben-, -bene-	well, good	benefit, benediction
-brev-	short, brief	brevity, abbreviate
-cand-	white, glowing	incandescent, candor
-cap-, -capt-, -cept-, -cip-	take, seize	capture, captivate, intercept
-capit-	head	per capita, decapitate
-carn-	flesh	incarnate, carnivorous
-ced-, -cede-, -cess-	go, yield	secede, intercede, precede
-cent-	hundred	century, centipede
-cern-, -cert-	perceive, decide, make certain	discern, certify
-cid-, -cis-	cut, kill	homicide, incision
-cit-	summon, impel	excite, citation, incite
-civ-	citizen	civilian, civilize
-clam- (-claim-)	shout, cry out	clamor, proclaim
-clar-	clear	clarify, clarity
-clin-	bend	decline, recline
-clud-, -clus-	close, shut	preclude, seclusion
-cogn-	know, be acquainted	recognize, cognizant
-corp-	body	corpuscle, corpulent
-cred-	belief, trust	credible, credulous
-cruc-	cross	cruciform, crucify
-culp-	fault, blame	culpable, culprit
-cur-	care, care for	accurate, curator
-cur-, -curr-, -curs-	run, course	concur, cursory, curriculum
-dec-	ten	decimal, decimate
-dent-	tooth	dentist, indent
-dic-, -dict-	say, speak, word	indicate, diction, predict
-dign-	worth, worthy	dignify, condign
-doc-, -doct-	teach, prove	doctrine, docile
-du-	two	duet, duplicate
-duc-, -duct-	lead	reduce, conduct, deduct
-dur-	hard, lasting	durable, obdurate

ROOT	MEANING	EXAMPLES
-ego-	I, self	egotist, egoist
-equ-	equal	equity, equilibrium
-err-	wander	erratic, aberration
-ev-	time, age	medieval, longevity
-fac-, -fact-, -fect-, -fic-	do, make	facile, facsimile
-fer-	bear, yield	fertile, transfer
-ferv-	boil, bubble	fervor, effervescent
-fid-	belief, faith	fidelity, infidel
-fin-	end, limit	final, infinite
-firm-	strong	confirm, affirm
-flect-, -flex-	bend, twist	reflection, flexible
-flor-	flower	floral, florid
-flu-, -fluct-	flow	fluent, fluctuate
-form-	form, shape	formative, transform
-fort-	strong	fortify, effort
-frag-, -fract-	break	fragile, fragment, refract
-fus-	pour	transfuse, effusive
-gen-	birth, origin, kind	generate, progeny
-grad-, -gress-	step, go	egress, gradual, digress
-grat-	please, favor	gratitude, gratify
-grav-	weight, heavy	grave, gravitation
-greg-	flock	congregate, aggregate
-her-, -hes-	cling, stick	adhere, coherence
-it-	go, travel	exit, transit, circuit
-jac-, -ject-	throw, hurl, cast	eject, projectile
-jud-	judge	judicious, prejudice
-junct-	join	juncture, adjunct
-jur-	swear	perjury, conjure
-labor-	work	laboratory, elaborate
-leg-	law	legislate, legitimate
-leg-, -lig-, -lect-	choose, read	legible, negligible, election
-lev-	light, rise	levitation, elevate
-liter-	letter	literal, illiterate
-loc-	place	locality, locus
-loqu-, -locut-	talk, speech	elocution, colloquial
-luc-	light	lucid, translucent
-magn-	large	magnitude, magnify
-mal-	bad	malady, malevolent
-man-, -manu-	hand	manual, manacle
-mar-	sea	marine, maritime
-mater-, -matr-	mother	maternity, matriarchy
-medi-	middle	mediocre, mediate
-merg-, -mers-	dip, plunge	submerge, immersion
-min-	less, little	minus, minimize
-mit-, -miss-	send	admittance, transmission
-mob-, -mot-	move	mobile, remote
-mon-, -monit-	warn	admonish, monitor
-mor-	custom	morality, mores
-mor-, -mort-	die, death	moribund, mortuary
-multi-	many	multiple, multifarious

ROOT	MEANING	EXAMPLES
-mut-	change	immutable, commute, transmute
-nav-	ship, sail	naval, navigate
-neg-	deny	negate, negative
-nomen-, -nomin-	name	nominate, nomenclature
-nov-	new	novelty, renovate
-ocul-	eye	oculist, binocular
-omni-	all	omnipotent, omnivorous
-ora-	speak, pray	orate, oracular
-orn-	decorate	ornate, ornament
-par-	equal	par, disparity, disparate
-pater-, -patr-	father	paternal, patriotic
-ped-	foot	pedal, quadruped
-pel-, -puls-	drive	repel, compulsion
-pend-, -pens-	hang, weigh	suspend, suspense, propensity
-pet-	seek	petition, competitor
-pon-, -pos-	place, put	postpone, interpose
-port-	carry	transport, importation
-pot-	power	impotent, omnipotent
-press-	press	compress, express
-prim-	first	primary, primeval, primitive
-quir-, -quis-	ask, seek	inquire, inquisition
-reg-, -rig-, -rect-	rule, straight, right	regent, directive, incorrigible
-rid-, -ris-	laugh	ridiculous, derision
-rog-	ask	abrogate, interrogative
-rupt-	break	rupture, abrupt, interrupt
-sanct-	holy	sanction, sanctuary
-scrib-, -script-	write	transcript, manuscript
-sed-, -sid-, -sess-	sit, seat	sedentary, residual, session
-seg-, -sect-	cut	segment, dissect
-sent-, -sens-	feel	sensory, sentient
-sequ-, -secut-	follow	sequel, subsequent, consecutive
-sol-	alone	solitude, solitaire
-solv-, -solu-, -solut-	loosen, free	solvent, solution, dissolute
-son-	sound	resonant, unison
-spec-, -spic-, -spect-	look, see	specimen, perspicacity
-spir-	breathe	expire, inspiration
-stab-	firm, standing	stable, establish
-string-, -strict-	bind tight	stringent, constrict
-struct-	build	structure, construct
-suad-, -suas-	advise	persuade, dissuade
-sum-, -sumpt-	take	resume, presumption
-tang-, -ting-, -tact-, -tig-	touch	tangible, contingent, tactile
-tempor-	time	contemporary, temporary
-ten-, -tin-, -tent-	hold, contain	tenure, detention, retentive
-tend-, -tens-, -tent-	stretch	distend, tendency, pretense
-tenu-	thin	tenuous, extenutate
-terr-, -ter-	land	terrestrial, subterranean
-test-	witness	testify, testimony
-tort-, -tors-	twist	distort, contortion
-tract-	draw, pull	extraction, distract

ROOT	MEANING	EXAMPLES
-trib-	assign	attribute, contribution
-trud-, -trus-	thrust	obtrude, abstruse
-turb-	agitate	turbid, turbulence, disturbance
-umbr-	shade	umbrella, adumbrate
-und-	wave	undulant, innundate
-uni-	one	unity, uniform, unison
-urb-	city	urban, suburban
-vac-	empty	vacant, evacuate
-vad-, -vas-	go	pervade, evasion
-ven-, -vent-	come	intervene, event
-ver-	true	veracity, verisimilitude
-verb-	word	verbose, verbal
-vert-, -vers-	turn	convert, aversion
-vest-	dress	vestment, divest
-vid-, -vis-	see	visualize, provident
-vinc-, -vict-	conquer	victor, convince
-vit-	life	vitality, vitamin
-viv-	life, lively	vivacious, survivor
-voc-, -vok-	call	vocal, provoke
-vol-	wish	volition, volunteer
-volv-, -volu-, -volut-	roll, turn	evolve, revolve
-vulg-	common	vulgar, divulge

Suffixes

Suffixes are somewhat simpler than prefixes because there are fewer of them and their forms do not change as much. Usually a suffix determines what part of speech a word is. For example, -*ment* added to the verb *establish* makes the noun *establishment*. Consequently, a suffix not only affects the meaning of a word but determines the role the word plays in the sentence of which it is a part. This makes suffixes particularly valuable as clues to meanings of sentences and entire passages.

ADJECTIVE AND NOUN SUFFIXES

SUFFIX	SPEECH PART	MEANING	EXAMPLES

Suffixes of Old English origin

SUFFIX	SPEECH PART	MEANING	EXAMPLES
-dom	n.	state, rank, condition	wisdom, serfdom
-en	adj.	made of, like	wooden, golden
-er	n.	doer, actor, maker	writer, swimmer
-ful	adj.	full of, marked by	grateful, careful
-hood	n.	state, condition	manhood, statehood

SUFFIX	SPEECH PART	MEANING	EXAMPLES
-ish	adj.	rather, suggesting, like	warmish, girlish
-less	adj.	without, lacking	hopeless, senseless
-ly	adj.; adv.	like, in the manner of	friendly, meanly
-ness	n.	quality, state	greatness, smallness
-ship	n.	condition, office	friendship, clerkship
-some	adj.	showing, tending to	lonesome, bothersome
-t	n.	act, state, quality	flight, weight
-th	n.	act, state, quality	breadth, growth
-ward(s)	adj.; adv.	in the direction of	forward, backward
-y	adj.	showing, suggesting	hilly, wavy

Suffixes of foreign origin

SUFFIX	SPEECH PART	MEANING	EXAMPLES
-able	adj.	able, fit, likely	capable, tolerable
-age	n.	state, place, process	passage, bondage
-al	n.; adj.	pertaining to doing; act	animal, capital
-an	adj.; n.	one belonging to	human, Asian
-ance, -ancy	n.	act, state, condition	acceptance, allowance
-ant	adj.; n.	doing, showing; agent	servant, pendant
-ar	adj.; n.	pertaining to; marked by	regular, capitular
-ard, -art	n.	one doing	wizard, braggart
-ary	adj.; n.	belonging to; showing	adversary, primary
-ate	n.	rank, office	delegate, sublimate
-ation	n.	action, state, result	occupation, manifestation
-cy	n.	state	accuracy, democracy
-ee	n.	one showing	employee, refugee
-eer	n.	worker at, maker, doer	engineer, auctioneer
-ence, -ency	n.	act, state, condition	emergency, evidence
-ent	adj.; n.	doing, showing, agent	confident, solvent
-er	n.	doer, for; action, result	buyer, fencer
-ery	n.	action, skill, state	robbery, surgery
-escent	adj.	beginning, becoming	obsolescent, quiescent
-ese	adj.; n.	of a place, style, language	Chinese, Japanese
-esque	adj.	in the style of, like	statuesque, grotesque
-ess	n.	feminine	governess, lioness
-et, -ette	n.	diminutive; feminine	midget, suffragette
-fic	adj.	making, causing	terrific, beatific
-ian	adj.; n.	pertaining to; marked by	Asian, reptilian
-ible	adj.	able, likely, fit	edible, incorrigible
-ic	adj.; n.	dealing with, like, caused by; person or thing showing	cosmetic, alcoholic
-ice	n.	act, state, quality	justice, service
-id	n.; adj.	marked by, showing	solid, rancid
-ile, -il	adj.; n.	marked by, showing	juvenile, fossil
-ine	adj.; n.	marked by, dealing with	canine, marine
-ion	n.	action, state, result	fusion, opinion
-ism	n.	act, manner, state, doctrine	barbarism, socialism
-ist	n.; adj.	practicer, believer, doer	anarchist, atheist
-ite	adj.; n.	formed, showing, marked by	favorite, composite
-ition	n.	action, state, result	malnutrition, expedition
-ity	n.	state, quality, condition	acidity, placidity
-ive	adj.; n.	belonging to, tending to	defective, detective

SUFFIX	SPEECH PART	MEANING	EXAMPLES
-ment	n.	result, means, action	refreshment, adornment
-mony	n.	resulting state, condition	matrimony, ceremony
-or	n.	doer, office, action, state	elevator, honor
-ory	adj.; n.	doing, pertaining to	accessory, olfactory
-ose	adj.	marked by, given to	bellicose, morose
-ous	adj.	marked by, given to, full of	religious, riotous
-ry	n.	condition, practice	dentistry, rivalry
-tion	n.	action, state, condition	relation, creation
-tude	n.	quality, state, result	fortitude, multitude
-ty	n.	quality, state	activity, enmity
-ure	n.	act, result, state, means	culture, signature
-y	n.	result, action, quality	jealousy, inquiry

VERB SUFFIXES

SUFFIX	MEANING	EXAMPLES
-ate	become, form, treat	separate, sublimate
-en	become, cause to be	deepen, darken
-esce	grow, continue, become	convalesce, acquiesce
-fy	make, cause, cause to have	glorify, fortify
-ish	do, make, perform	punish, embellish
-ize	make, cause to be, treat with	sterilize, cauterize

Word List

The words that follow are particularly apt to appear on the SAT. The definitions are necessarily brief; if you do not understand a definition, look the word up in a regular dictionary.

Abase	to humiliate	Abut	to touch, to border on
Abate	to lessen	Accolade	honor, award
Abdicate	to give up	Accrue	to accumulate
Abet	to aid	Acerbity	bitterness
Abeyance	inactivity	Acme	peak
Abhor	to hate	Acrimony	acerbity
Abominate	to abhor	Adamant	unyielding
Aborigine	original inhabitant	Adjudicate	to decide a case
Abort	to miscarry	Adjunct	assistant
Abrade	to scrape out	Admonish	to warn
Abrogate	to abolish	Adroit	skillful
Abscond	to run off	Adulation	praise
Absolve	to pardon	Advocate	to recommend
Abstract	summary	Aesthetic	pertaining to beauty
Abstruse	hard to understand	Affable	friendly; courteous

Affinity	attraction
Affluence	wealth
Affront	insult
Aggrandize	to enlarge
Agility	quickness, nimbleness
Agnostic	one who believes God is unknowable
Agrarian	pertaining to farming
Alacrity	liveliness
Alimentary	supplying food
Allay	to calm; to reduce intensity
Allegory	narrative using figurative language
Allocate	to set aside; to apportion
Allude	to refer to indirectly
Altercation	angry dispute
Altruism	unselfish devotion
Ameliorate	to improve
Amiable	pleasant; kind
Amnesty	pardon
Amulet	object worn to ward off evil
Anachronism	something out of its proper time
Anarchy	absence of government
Anathema	ban, curse
Animate	to move to action
Animosity	hatred; dislike
Annals	historical records
Anneal	to toughen
Anomaly	irregularity; exception from the norm
Anthology	collection of literary pieces
Antipathy	dislike
Antipodes	opposite side of the earth
Antithesis	direct opposite
Apathy	indifference; lack of interest
Aphorism	brief statement; proverb
Aplomb	self-confidence
Apoplexy	sudden loss of consciousness
Apostate	one who forsakes one's principles
Apothecary	druggist
Appall	to terrify; to shock
Apposite	appropriate
Arabesque	ornate design; ballet position
Arable	able to be plowed
Archaeology	study of remains of past cultures
Archaic	no longer in use
Archipelago	group of islands
Archives	place where records are kept
Arduous	difficult
Arrears	in debt
Articulate	to speak clearly; to write
Artifice	trickery
Ascendant	rising
Aspersion	slanderous remark
Assay	to test; to analyze
Assiduity	care; diligence
Assuage	to make less severe; to calm
Astral	pertaining to the stars
Astute	shrewd
Atheist	one who denies the existence of God
Athwart	across
Atoll	island that encloses a lagoon
Atrophy	to waste away
Attest	to confirm
Audacious	bold
Audible	able to be heard
Augment	to increase
Augur	to predict
August	majestic; imposing
Auspices	protection
Auspicious	favorable
Austerity	severity
Authoritative	commanding
Autocratic	arrogant
Autonomy	self-government
Auxiliary	giving aid
Avarice	greed
Avoirdupois	weight
Avow	to declare openly
Awry	off the right course
Badger	to harass; to nag
Balk	to hinder; to stop short
Balm	something that soothes
Banal	meaningless, commonplace
Bandy	to exchange (as words)
Bane	a curse; denunciation
Baneful	creating destruction; ruinous
Beatitude	state of bliss
Beguile	deceive
Bellicose	warlike
Benediction	blessing
Beneficence	kindness
Benign	harmless, kindly
Benignant	gentle; kindly
Benison	blessing
Beset	to attack
Bestial	savage
Bestow	to present (as a gift)
Bestride	to mount
Bewitch	to charm
Bicker	to quarrel
Biennial	occurring every two years
Bilk	to cheat
Bland	mild
Blasphemy	a profane remark about God
Blatant	objectionably loud
Blazon	to adorn; to proclaim
Blithe	gay

Bluster	to speak boastfully
Bondage	slavery
Boorish	rude
Botch	to ruin through clumsiness
Bounty	reward
Bourgeois	pertaining to the middle class
Bovine	pertaining to the ox, cow, etc.
Brandish	to wave menacingly
Breech	lower part of the body, buttocks
Brigand	robber
Broach	to introduce (a subject)
Browbeat	to intimidate
Bruit	to spread news
Brusque	abrupt in manner
Bucolic	pertaining to the country
Buffoon	clown
Bullion	gold or silver (as in bars)
Bumptious	arrogant
Bureaucracy	government through bureaus
Burlesque	to represent in a ridiculous way
Burnish	to polish
Butte	hill
Cacophony	harsh sound
Cajole	to coax
Caliber	degree of worth
Caliph	head of a Moslem state
Calumny	slander
Cant	tilt; whining speech
Canter	to trot
Canvass	to make a survey
Capitulate	to surrender
Caprice	an impulsive change of mind
Captious	finding fault
Captivate	to fascinate
Careen	to swerve
Caret	sign ∧ meaning "it is missing"
Carnage	slaughter
Carnivorous	flesh-eating
Carp	to complain constantly
Carrion	decaying flesh
Castigate	to punish
Cataclysm	a violent change
Cathartic	cleansing
Cavil	to quibble
Censure	to criticize sharply
Centrifugal	moving away from the center
Chaff	worthless matter
Chagrin	embarrassment
Chamberlain	chief steward
Charlatan	faker
Chaste	morally pure
Chauvinism	fanatical patriotism
Chattel	slave
Chicanery	deception
Chide	to scold

Chilblain	inflammation
Chimerical	imaginary
Chronicle	record of historical events
Circumspect	watchful
Citadel	fortress
Civility	politeness
Clandestine	secret
Claret	dark red
Clime	climate
Coerce	to force
Coffer	strongbox
Cogent	convincing
Cogitation	meditation
Cognate	related
Cognizant	aware
Collate	to put together in proper order
Collocation	arrangement
Colloquy	conversation
Collusion	secret agreement to defraud another
Commensurate	proportionate
Commissary	a store selling food and equipment
Commodious	spacious
Compassion	pity for distress of another
Complacent	contented
Compunction	uneasiness; remorse
Concatenation	act of linking together
Conclave	secret meeting
Concomitant	accompanying
Condolence	expression of sympathy
Configuration	shape; arrangement
Congeal	to freeze solid
Congenital	existing from birth
Congruent	agreeing
Coniferous	cone-bearing
Conjecture	to guess; to suppose
Connote	to suggest; to imply
Connubial	pertaining to marriage
Conscript	to force into service
Consort	husband or wife companion; to be in agreement
Constellation	group of stars
Consternation	sudden confusion; panic
Constrict	to shrink
Contemn	to despise
Contiguous	adjacent; touching
Contingent	possible
Contumely	rudeness
Conundrum	riddle
Convivial	sociable; jovial
Convoke	call together
Convolution	coiled state
Copious	abundant
Corollary	inference; result

Corona	crown; luminous circle	Digress	to stray away from the subject
Corporeal	pertaining to the body	Dilate	to make wider or larger
Corpulent	fat	Dilemma	difficult situation
Corroborate	to confirm	Diligent	industrious
Covenant	contract	Diocese	church district
Covert	concealed; secret	Disconcert	to disturb
Cower	to cringe in fear	Disconsolate	without hope
Cozen	to trick	Discountenance	to disapprove of; to dismay
Crabbed	ill-tempered	Discursive	rambling
Crag	steep, projecting rock	Disdain	to scorn
Credible	believable	Disparage	to belittle
Credulity	gullibility; readiness to believe	Disparity	difference
Crimp	to bend into shape	Disseminate	to spread widely
Crony	close friend	Dissident	disagreeing
Crux	vital point	Dissipate	to scatter wastefully
Cudgel	club	Dissonant	out of harmony
Culpable	deserving blame	Diurnal	daily
Cult	group sharing a common interest	Diverge	to branch off
Curry	to seek favor by flattery	Divers	several
Cursory	superficial	Divest	to deprive
Dank	chilly and wet	Docile	easy to handle
Daunt	to discourage	Doggerel	poorly written verse
Dearth	scarcity	Dogmatic	arrogant; unyielding
Debase	to lower in rank	Dolorous	mournful
Debauch	to corrupt	Dormant	asleep; inactive
Debility	weakness	Dour	gloomy
Decadence	decay	Dregs	leftovers
Decant	to pour	Dross	waste matter
Declivity	descending a slope	Ductile	easily molded
Decorous	proper	Dudgeon	sullen resentment or anger
Decrepit	weakened by age	Dulcet	pleasing to the ear
Defection	desertion	Duplicity	deception
Deference	respect	Duress	force; compulsion
Definitive	explicit; conclusive	Dynamic	energetic
Deleterious	harmful	Ebullition	bubbling over
Delineate	to describe	Eclat	brilliance
Delta	mouth of a river; Greek letter	Eclogue	poem about the country
Demeanor	behavior	Edify	to enlighten
Demure	shy	Effete	worn out
Deplore	to regret	Efficacious	potent to produce an effect
Deposition	removal (as from office)	Effigy	a dummy
Depraved	sinful	Effrontery	boldness
Deprecate	to disapprove	Egregious	outstanding
Depreciate	to lessen in value	Ejaculate	to exclaim
Derision	ridicule	Elicit	to draw forth
Descant	discussion; melody	Emaciated	haggard
Descry	to discover	Emanate	to issue forth
Desecrate	to profane	Embezzle	steal
Desiccate	to make dry	Emollient	softener
Desist	to stop doing something	Empirical	experimental
Desultory	disconnected; rambling	Emulate	to excel or imitate
Dichotomy	division into two parts	Encomium	praise
Dictum	a positive statement	Engender	to cause
Didactic	instructive	Enhance	to increase
Diffident	shy	Enigma	puzzle

Enjoin	to prohibit
Ephemeral	short-lived
Epicure	lover of good living
Epitaph	writing on a tombstone
Epitome	brief statement
Equable	calm; uniform
Equitable	just; fair
Equivocal	uncertain; obscure
Erotic	tending to arouse sexual love or desire
Erratic	wandering
Erudite	learned
Esoteric	relating to knowledge
Ethical	accepted standards of conduct
Ethnic	relating to races of people
Eulogy	high praise
Euphony	sweet sound
Exacerbate	to make more violent or bitter
Excise	to remove by cutting out
Exculpate	to clear from blame
Execration	to denounce; curse
Exigency	urgency
Exonerate	to clear from blame
Exotic	strikingly different
Expatiate	wander
Expectorate	to spit
Expedient	advisable under the circumstances
Expiate	to atone for
Expound	to state in detail
Expunge	to erase
Extant	in existence
Extol	to praise highly
Extradite	to surrender a prisoner to another authority
Extraneous	not belonging
Extricate	to free
Extrinsic	not an essential part
Fabricate	to construct; to devise a deception
Facade	front part of a building
Facetious	humorous
Facile	easy
Factitious	artificial
Fastidious	hard to please
Fatuous	foolish
Feasible	possible
Fecund	fertile
Felicity	great happiness
Ferret	to hunt out
Fervent	emotional; ardent
Fetid	stinking
Fetish	an object believed to have magical powers
Fettle	good condition

Fiasco	complete failure
Fief	estate held in feudal times
Fiord	long, narrow inlet from the sea
Flaccid	soft and flabby
Flagitious	vicious; wicked
Flagrant	shocking
Flail	to thrash
Flamboyant	showy
Flaunt	to show off
Fledge	to grow feathers
Florid	rosy-colored; excessively ornate
Foible	a minor weakness
Foment	whip up
Font	basin
Forensic	pertaining to debate
Formidable	huge; dreadful
Forte	strong point
Fortitude	courage
Fortnight	two weeks
Fortuitous	by chance
Fray	(v.) to unravel; (n.) noisy quarrel
Frizzle	to curl
Frugal	thrifty
Fulmination	violent explosion; severe censure
Fulsome	disgusting
Furtive	stealthy; foxy
Galaxy	large system of stars such as the Milky Way
Gambol	to romp; to frolic
Gamut	entire range
Garble	to distort
Garrulous	talkative
Gauntlet	medieval glove
Generic	pertaining to a class or group
Germane	related; fitting
Ghoul	demon; grave robber
Gibe	to scoff; to jeer
Gird	to encircle
Glib	fluent; smooth
Goad	to spur
Gradient	slope
Gratuitous	without charge; without justification
Gregarious	sociable
Grist	grain to be ground
Grueling	very tiring; severe
Guild	organization of persons with common interests
Halcyon	calm; peaceful
Hale	healthy
Hallow	to make holy
Hallucination	illusion
Hapless	unfortunate

Harangue	long speech
Harass	to annoy by repeated attacks
Harbinger	omen
Hearth	floor or a fireplace; home
Heinous	hateful; abominable
Herbivorous	feeding on plants
Heresy	antireligious opinion
Heretic	person who maintains opinions contrary to church doctrine
Heterogeneous	different in kind
Heyday	period of success
Hiatus	gap
Hibernal	wintry
Hirsute	hairy
Histrionic	theatrical
Hoax	joke
Holocaust	destruction by fire
Homily	sermon
Homogeneous	essentially the same
Horticulture	study of how to grow plants
Hurtle	to speed
Husbandry	study of raising crops and animals
Hybrid	mongrel; mixed breed
Hydrophobia	rabies; fear of water
Hyperbole	exaggeration
Hypochondriac	one who worries about his health
Iconoclast	destroyer of idols or images
Idyl	short poem describing simple living
Ignoble	dishonorable
Ignominious	shameful
Illicit	unlawful
Imbibe	to absorb
Imbroglio	confused state of affairs
Immutable	unchangeable
Impalpable	vague; not understandable
Impasse	dead end; difficult situation
Impeach	to accuse
Impecunious	poor; penniless
Impertinent	irrelevant; rude
Implicit	absolute; suggested
Importune	to trouble with requests
Impugn	to attack by words; to challenge as false
Impute	to attribute something bad to another
Incendiary	inflammatory
Inchoate	just begun; rudimentary
Incipient	just beginning to appear
Incongruous	not harmonious; inappropriate
Incredulous	skeptical
Increment	increase
Incubus	nightmare
Indigent	poor

Indolent	lazy
Indulgence	act of pampering
Ineffable	beyond words; unspeakable
Ineluctable	inevitable
Ineptitude	awkwardness
Inert	without power to move or react
Inexorable	unyielding
Infernal	hellish; outrageous
Infidel	unbeliever
Ingenuous	innocent
Inherent	inborn
Iniquitous	unjust
Injunction	judicial order
Innate	inherent
Innocuous	harmless
Insidious	treacherous
Insipid	dull
Insolvent	bankrupt
Insular	pertaining to an island
Intangible	not able to be touched; impalpable
Interdict	to prohibit
Interminable	endless
Interpolate	to insert something additional
Interregnum	interruption in continuity
Intransigent	refusing to compromise
Intrepid	fearless
Intrinsic	essential
Intuition	insight
Invective	denunciation
Inveigle	to entice
Investiture	act of bestowing rank or office
Inveterate	firmly established
Invidious	causing ill will; offensive
Irascible	easily angered
Ironic	contrary to what was expected
Isthmus	a narrow strip of land having water on either side
Iterate	to say or do something repeatedly
Itinerant	traveling from place to place
Jargon	meaningless talk; gibberish
Jaundice	yellowness of the skin
Jetty	wall built out into the water
Jocose	joking; humorous
Juxtapose	to place side by side
Kaleidoscopic	constantly changing as in form
Ken	range of vision or knowledge
Labyrinth	maze
Lachrymal	pertaining to tears
Laconic	using few words; concise
Laity	all the people as distinguished from the clergy
Lampoon	strong satire in written form
Languid	lacking in spirit or interest

Lascivious	full of lust; oversexed
Latent	hidden; dormant
Lethargic	sluggish
Levity	lack of seriousness
Levy	to impose a tax, fine, etc.
Lexicon	dictionary
Libretto	words of an opera
Licentious	lewd; immoral
Liege	feudal term for lord or subject
Limpid	clear, as air or water
Litany	prayer with responses
Lithe	bending easily; flexible
Litigation	lawsuit
Liturgy	form of public worship
Livid	discolored due to bruise; dull blue
Loquacious	talkative
Lucid	shining; easily understood
Lucre	money (in a bad sense)
Ludicrous	ridiculous
Lugubrious	mournful
Lymph	clear, yellowish fluid
Machiavellian	crafty; cunning
Machination	evil design
Magnanimous	generous; noble
Malevolent	wishing evil; malicious
Malign	to slander
Malinger	to pretend sickness
Martinet	very strict disciplinarian
Maudlin	tearfully sentimental
Maw	mouth
Maxim	short statement of a truth
Mellifluous	smoothly flowing
Mendacious	untruthful
Mendicant	begging; beggar
Menial	servile; low
Meretricious	showily attractive; tawdry
Mesa	flat-topped land with steep sides
Metamorphosis	change of form
Metaphysics	philosophy that is subtle and difficult to comprehend
Mete	to allot
Mettle	spirit; courage
Microcosm	world in miniature
Mien	manner; way of carrying oneself
Misanthrope	hater of mankind
Misgiving	doubt
Missal	book containing prayers
Mnemonic	assisting in the memory
Mollify	to appease
Monetary	pertaining to money
Moot	doubtful; debatable
Moribund	dying
Mosque	Mohammedan temple
Mulct	to punish by fine

Mundane	pertaining to the world; commonplace
Muting	to muffle the sound
Myriad	very great number
Nadir	lowest point
Narcissism	self-love
Nativity	birth
Nebulous	vague; indistinct
Nefarious	extremely wicked
Neophyte	beginner; convert
Niggardly	stingy
Nocturnal	pertaining to night
Noisome	offensive; harmful
Nuance	delicate variation in meaning, tone, shade
Nugatory	worthless
Nurture	to feed; to bring up
Obdurate	stubborn
Obeisance	show of respect
Oblation	offering of a sacrifice
Obscure	not clear
Obsequious	overly submissive
Obsolescence	passing out of use
Obstreperous	boisterous
Obtrude	to intrude
Obtuse	stupid
Obviate	to prevent
Odious	hateful; disgusting
Officious	meddlesome
Oligarchy	government by a few
Ominous	threatening
Omnivorous	eating all kinds of food
Onerous	burdensome
Opprobrious	shameful
Opulence	wealth
Oracular	predicting
Orbit	path
Organic	fundamental; essential
Orifice	opening; mouth
Ornate	overadorned; showy
Orthography	spelling
Ossify	to change into bone
Ostentatious	pretentious
Ostracize	to banish
Overt	not concealed
Palatable	tasty
Pall	to become wearisome
Palpable	obvious
Palsy	paralysis
Panacea	cure-all
Pander	to act as a go-between in intrigue
Parable	short story to convey a moral
Paradox	seemingly absurd statement that is nevertheless true
Parsimony	stinginess

Pastoral	pertaining to shepherds
Patent	evident
Pathos	quality of arousing pity
Patriarch	father-ruler of a family or tribe
Patrician	aristocratic
Patrimony	property inherited from one's father or ancestors
Paucity	scarcity
Pavilion	building used for exhibits
Peccadillo	minor sin; slight fault
Pectoral	pertaining to the chest
Pecuniary	pertaining to money
Pedant	one who possesses mere book learning; narrow-minded teacher
Perdition	hell
Peremptory	dictatorial; unconditional
Perennial	enduring; lasting all year or year after year
Perfidious	treacherous
Perforce	of necessity
Perfunctory	mechanical; indifferent
Periphery	outside boundary
Pernicious	destructive; fatal
Perpetuate	to cause to continue
Perquisite	something additional to regular pay
Perspicacious	having insight
Pert	forward; impertinent
Perturbation	agitation
Pervade	to spread throughout
Philanthropist	lover of mankind
Philistine	narrow-minded person
Phlegmatic	calm; not easily disturbed; dull
Pinnacle	peak
Piquant	pleasantly tasting; stimulating
Pithy	concise
Placate	to pacify; to conciliate
Placid	peaceful; calm
Platitude	trite remark
Plebian	common
Plethora	overabundance
Poignant	keen; moving
Portend	to foretell
Portentous	ominous; serious
Portly	stately; stout
Pragmatic	practical
Prate	to speak foolishly
Precarious	risky
Preclude	to shut out; to eliminate
Precursor	forerunner
Prevaricate	to lie
Probity	incorruptibility
Proclivity	inclination; natural tendency
Prodigal	wasteful
Prodigious	huge; enormous
Profligate	dissipated; wasteful
Prolific	abundantly fruitful
Prolix	verbose; drawn out
Propensity	natural inclination
Propitiate	appease
Prosaic	commonplace
Protract	prolong
Proximity	nearness
Prurient	lascivious in thought or desire
Pseudonym	pen name
Puerile	childish
Pugnacious	combative
Puissant	powerful
Pulchritude	beauty
Punctilious	laying stress on form; precise
Pungent	stinging; caustic
Punitive	punishing
Purge	to clean by removing impurities
Purport	intention; meaning
Pusillanimous	cowardly
Quaff	to drink with relish
Qualms	misgivings
Quay	dock; landing place
Quell	to put down; quiet
Querulous	whining
Quintessence	purest and highest state
Quixotic	idealistic
Quizzical	bantering
Rabid	like a fanatic; furious
Rampant	unrestrained
Rancid	offensive
Rancor	bitterness; hatred
Rant	to rave
Rapacious	excessively grasping
Raucous	harsh and shrill
Ravenous	extremely hungry
Raze	to destroy completely
Recalcitrant	stubborn
Recant	to repudiate
Reciprocal	mutual
Recluse	hermit
Recondite	abstruse
Recreant	coward
Rectitude	uprightness
Redolent	fragrant
Redress	remedy
Refractory	stubborn
Refulgent	radiant
Relegate	to banish; to consign to an inferior position
Relevance	pertinence
Relinquish	to abandon
Remonstrate	to protest; to admonish
Renegade	deserter

Replenish	to fill up again	Squalid	dirty; neglected
Reprehensible	deserving blame	Stentorian	extremely loud
Reprobation	severe disapproval	Stoic	person who is indifferent to feeling
Repugnance	loathing		
Requisite	necessary requirement	Stolid	dull; impassive
Rescind	to cancel	Strident	loud and harsh
Respite	delay in punishment	Stringent	binding; rigid
Reticence	reserve; unwillingness to speak	Stupor	state of apathy
Ribald	wanton; profane	Suavity	urbanity; polish
Rococo	ornate; highly decorative	Subservient	behaving like a slave; servile
Roseate	rosy; optimistic	Sublimate	to refine; to purify
Rote	repetition	Subsistence	existence; means of support
Rotundity	roundness	Subterfuge	pretense; evasion
Ruminate	to ponder	Succinct	brief; terse
Ruse	trick; stratagem	Succor	aid; assistance
Sacrilegious	profane; desecrating	Suffuse	to spread over
Sagacious	having insight; wise	Sully	to tarnish; to soil
Salubrious	healthful	Sultry	sweltering
Sanguinary	bloody	Supercilious	contemptuous; haughty
Sanguine	cheerful; optimistic	Supine	lying on back
Sardonic	disdainful	Supplicate	to entreat; to beseech
Sate	to satisfy to the full	Surfeit	to overfeed; to cloy
Saturnine	gloomy	Surly	rude
Schism	division	Surreptitious	secret
Scintillate	sparkle	Surveillance	watching; guarding
Scourge	whip; severe punishment	Sycophantic	servilely flattering
Scrupulous	conscientious; honest	Sylvan	rustic; pertaining to the woods
Scurrilous	obscene; indecent	Tacit	understood; not put into words
Secular	worldly; not pertaining to the church	Taciturn	silent
		Tactile	pertaining to the sense of touch
Sedate	composed; grave	Talisman	a charm
Sedentary	requiring sitting; inactive	Tantalize	to tease
Sedulous	diligent	Tautological	needlessly repetitive
Semblance	outward appearance	Temerity	boldness; rashness
Sententious	full of meaning; pompous	Tenacious	holding fast
Serrated	having a sawtoothed edge	Tenet	doctrine; dogma
Servile	slavish; cringing	Tentative	provisional; experimental
Severance	division	Tenuous	thin; rare; slim
Shibboleth	slogan	Tepid	lukewarm
Simile	comparison of one thing with another using "like" or "as"	Terse	concise; abrupt
		Testy	irritable
Simulate	feign; pretend	Thrall	slave; bondage
Sinecure	well-paid position with little responsibility	Thwart	to block; to oppose
		Timidity	lack of self-confidence
Sinuous	winding	Tirade	scolding; denunciation
Sloth	laziness	Toady	to flatter for favors
Slovenly	untidy	Torpid	dormant; dull; lethargic
Somnolent	almost asleep	Tortuous	winding; full of curves
Sonorous	resonant	Toxic	poisonous
Specious	seemingly reasonable but incorrect	Tractable	docile
		Transcend	to exceed; to surpass
Spectral	ghostly	Transcribe	to copy
Splenetic	spiteful, irritable	Transient	fleeting
Sporadic	occurring irregularly	Translucent	partly transparent
Spurious	false; counterfeit	Transmute	to change

Travail	painful labor
Tremulous	trembling; wavering
Trenchant	cutting; keen
Trepidation	fear
Trite	commonplace; hackneyed
Truculent	aggressive; savage
Tumid	swollen; pompous
Turbid	muddy; having the sediment disturbed
Turbulence	state of violent agitation
Turgid	swollen; distended
Tyro	beginner; novice
Ubiquitous	being everywhere; omnipresent
Umbrage	resentment; anger
Unbridled	violent
Uncouth	outlandish; clumsy
Unctuous	oil; bland
Undulate	to move with a wavelike motion
Unequivocal	plain; obvious
Unkempt	disheveled
Unmitigated	harsh; severe
Untenable	unsupportable
Upbraid	to scold; to reproach
Urbane	suave; refined
Usury	lending money at illegal rates of interest
Uxorious	excessively devoted to one's wife
Vacillation	fluctuation; wavering
Vacuous	empty; inane
Vagary	caprice; whim
Vainglorious	boastful
Validate	confirm; ratify
Vanguard	forerunners
Vantage	position given an advantage
Vapid	insipid; inane
Variegated	many-colored
Vaunted	boasted; bragged
Veer	to change direction
Vehement	impetuous
Venal	capable of being bribed
Veneer	thin layer; cover
Venerate	revere
Venial	forgivable; trivial
Veracious	truthful
Verbose	wordy
Verdant	green; fresh

Verity	truth; reality
Vernal	pertaining to the spring
Vertigo	dizziness
Vestige	trace
Vicarious	acting as a substitute
Vicissitude	change of fortune
Vie	to contend; to compete
Vigilance	watchfulness
Vilify	to slander
Vindicate	to clear of charges
Virago	shrew
Virile	manly
Virtuoso	highly skilled artist
Virulent	extremely poisonous
Visage	face; appearance
Viscous	sticky; gluey
Vitiate	to spoil the effect of
Vitriolic	corrosive; sarcastic
Vituperative	abusive; scolding
Vivacious	animated; gay
Vociferous	noisy; talkative
Volatile	explosive; changeable
Volition	act of making a conscious choice
Voluble	fluent; glib
Voluptuous	gratifying to the senses
Voracious	ravenous
Votary	follower of a cult
Vulnerable	susceptible to wounds
Waggish	mischievous
Wan	having a pale or sickly color
Wane	to grow gradually smaller
Wanton	unruly; excessive
Wary	very cautious
Whet	to sharpen; to stimulate
Wily	cunning; artful
Winsome	agreeable; gracious
Wizened	shriveled
Wont	custom; habitual procedure
Wraith	ghost; phantom of a living person
Wreak	inflict
Wrest	to pull away; to take by violence
Zealot	fanatic
Zenith	point directly overhead in sky; summit
Zephyr	soft gentle breeze; west wind

Part III
Reading Comprehension Techniques for Passages of Extended Length

For most students, it is not the reading of the passages on the SAT that presents the greatest problem, but understanding what they have read. This is particularly true for the passages of extended length. For some students, trying to follow and integrate the ideas in passages of 800 to 900 words might be an altogether difficult and frustrating experience. But there is no need to panic. In the first place, even though the passages are long, the time allotted for the reading comprehension has also been extended. Furthermore, you have already learned many of the techniques that will help you understand these longer passages. Generally speaking, all reading is the same. Although the length of the passages may vary, and although one passage might seem more difficult than another because of its subject matter or the way the ideas are presented, every reading-comprehension passage requires the same basic skills in order to process the information and answer the questions.

The Organizing Principle

A writer might find many different ways to organize his ideas, but it is your job to figure out what the writer is up to. Most students tend to look at the individual words, instead of the organizing principle that pulls all the words together. That is just what this section of the book is designed to do, to help students process the information.

Visualization

One way to do this is through visualization. Most students are visually oriented. Visualization is a process of creating pictures in your mind, similar to the way in which you view a film or TV program. In visualizing, you draw upon the intuitive, emotional part of yourself, tapping into your imaginative powers. This is an important dimension in reading the SAT passages: to project an image in your mind as you read, as if you were a director creating images on a screen. Visualization is a technique valuable for all of the reading passages on the SAT, even for the passages of related or opposing viewpoints. But whereas visualization is an important adjunct in helping students process information, its emphasis is on abilities directly opposite the verbal and analytic skills required for the reading-comprehension passages, which are intricate in design and complex in information.

Tracking the Relationship Between Paragraphs

In this section, we will concentrate on techniques that are most important; techniques that will enable you to develop your ability *to track the relationship between the ideas* the author develops throughout the passage, and *to perceive the underlying patterns or themes* that constitute the main idea of the passage as a whole. These are techniques that will help keep you focused, targeted, and involved. By concentrating on these techniques and by constant practice, you will discover that you are able to minimize the detailed diagramming of each passage and to process the information easily and with full comprehension. But remember, there is no substitute for practice. The more you practice, the faster you will progress.

Step 1: Summarizing the Main Idea in the Opening Paragraph

One of the most important parts of any passage is the opening paragraph. It is here the author establishes his tone, point of view, and main idea. It is important that you *carefully diagram this paragraph, using the techniques you have already learned.* You should also try to familiarize yourself with the many types of openings an author might begin with, such as a "direct quotation" or direct statement; he might also open his passage with a leading question or a challenge, even a conversation. When you have finished outlining the opening paragraph, try to *summarize the main idea* to see if you can recognize the author's attitude about the subject.

Step 2: Diagramming Transitions: Beginnings and Endings

Paragraphs are the building blocks the author uses in developing his main idea. Just as sentences tie together, so paragraphs must also be related in some way. The connecting device used to link paragraphs one to the other are called transitions, the purpose of which is to make logical connections between ideas. So one important way to diagram these longer passages, in addition to using any of the techniques you have already learned, is to *diagram the first and last sentence in each paragraph throughout the passage.*

Just as there are many types of opening paragraphs, an author might rely on several types of transitions in developing his subject. Transitions are sign posts an author uses to enable the reader to follow or track the development of the topic. He might, for example, develop his theme through a sequence of events or present an idea and prove it with examples. He might use the principle of cause and effect or build on a certain time sequence, such as first, second, third, and so on. He might use contrasts or comparisons to develop his main point. The question to ask yourself as you move from one paragraph to another is, "How are the paragraphs logically related?"

It is essential that you know how the paragraphs are linked one to another. Once you understand the organizing principle or pattern the author uses to develop his idea, you will be able to easily and fully comprehend the passage and access the information you will need in order to answer the questions.

Step 3: Summarizing the Main Idea in the Concluding Paragraph

The concluding paragraph functions somewhat like your opening paragraph. Both focus the topic for the reader and usually state it with some forcefulness. It is the conclusion that is uppermost in the reader's mind when he finishes the passage. A concluding paragraph is usually well focused, unified, and significant. This is the last opportunity the author has to persuade the reader on some point he has been trying to make throughout the passage. (It is rare, though not inconceivable, that the author would write a final paragraph that did not, in some way, summarize the main points in the passage.) Therefore, an important technique to use on the extended passages is to *diagram the concluding paragraph, using detailed notation, the same way you did for the opening paragraph.* When you are finished outlining the conclusion, try to summarize the main points.

PRACTICE EXERCISES

Now you are ready to handle the following practice passages. In addition to using any of the techniques you have previously learned, concentrate on the techniques just outlined: step 1, diagram the opening paragraph and summarize the main idea; step 2, diagram the transition sentences and underline and circle the first and last sentence in each paragraph; and step 3, diagram the concluding paragraph and summarize the main idea. Do the following exercises now, and when you are finished, compare your answers with our Answers and Explanations.

PASSAGE 1

The passage below is followed by questions based on its content. Answer the questions on the basis of what is *stated* or *implied* in the passage, and in any introductory material that might be provided.

The following passage is primarily concerned with the parts of the sea known as the continental shelves.

The first European ever to sail across the wide Pacific was curious about the hidden worlds beneath his ship. Between the two coral islands of St. Paul and Los Tiburones in the Tuamotu Archipelago, Magellan ordered his sounding line to be lowered. It was the conventional line used by explorers of the day, no more than 200 fathoms long. It did not touch bottom, and Magellan declared that he was over the deepest part of the ocean. Of course he was completely mistaken, but the occasion was nonetheless historic. It was the first time in the history of the world that a navigator had attempted to sound the depths of the open ocean.

Now hundreds of vessels are equipped with sonic sounding instruments that trace a continuous profile of the bottom beneath the moving ship. Soundings are accumulating much faster than they can be plotted on the charts. Little by little, like the details of a huge map being filled in by an artist, the hidden contours of the ocean are emerging. But, even with this recent progress, it will be years before an accurate and detailed relief map of the ocean basins can be constructed.

The general topography is, however, well established. Once we have passed the tide lines, the three great geographic provinces of ocean are the continental shelves, the continental slopes, and the floor of the deep sea. Each of these regions is as different from the others as an arctic tundra from a range of the Rocky Mountains.

The continental shelf is of the sea, yet of all the regions of the ocean it is most like the land. Sunlight penetrates to all but its deepest parts. Plants drift in the water above it; seaweeds cling to its rocks and sway to the passage of the waves. Familiar fishes—unlike the weird monsters of the abyss—move over its plains like herds of cattle. Much of its substance is derived from the land—the sand and the rock fragments and the rich topsoil carried by running water to the sea and gently deposited on the shelf. Its submerged valleys and hills, in appropriate parts of the world, have been carved by glaciers into a topography much like the northern landscapes we know, and the terrain is strewn with rocks and gravel deposited by the moving ice sheets. Indeed many parts (or perhaps all) of the shelf have been dry land in the geologic past, for a comparatively slight fall of sea level has

sufficed, time and again, to expose it to wind and sun and rain. The Grand Banks of Newfoundland rose above the ancient seas and were submerged again. The Dogger Bank of the North Sea shelf was once a forested land inhabited by prehistoric beasts; now its "forests" are seaweeds and its "beasts" are fishes.

Of all parts of the sea, the continental shelves are perhaps most directly important to man as a source of material things. The great fisheries of the world, with only a few exceptions, are confined to the relatively shallow waters over the continental shelves. Seaweeds are gathered from their submerged plains to make scores of substances used in foods, drugs, and articles of commerce. As the petroleum reserves left on continental areas by ancient seas became depleted, petroleum geologists look more and more to the oil that may lie, as yet unmapped and unexploited, under these bordering lands of the sea.

The shelves begin at the tide lines and extend seaward as gently sloping plains. The 100-fathom contour used to be taken as the boundary between the continental shelf and the slope; now it is customary to place the division wherever the gentle declivity of the shelf changes abruptly to a steeper descent toward abyssal depths. The world over, the average depth at which this change occurs is about 72 fathoms; the greatest depth of any shelf is probably 299 to 300 fathoms.

Nowhere off the Pacific coast of the United States is the continental shelf much more than 20 miles wide—a narrowness characteristic of coasts bordered by young mountains perhaps still in the process of formation. On the American east coast, however, north of Cape Hatteras the shelf is as much as 150 miles wide. But at Hatteras and off southern Florida it is merely the narrowest of thresholds to the sea. Here its scant development seems to be related to the press of that great and rapidly flowing river-in-the-sea, the Gulf Stream, which at these places swings close inshore.

The widest shelves in all the world are those bordering the Arctic. The Barents Sea shelf is 750 miles across. It is also relatively deep, lying for the most part 100 to 200 fathoms below the surface, as though its floor had sagged and been downwarped—further evidence of the work of the ice. The deepest shelves surround the Antarctic continent, where soundings in many areas show depths of several hundred fathoms near the coast and continuing out across the shelf.

Once beyond the edge of the shelf, as we visualize the steeper declivities of the continental slope, we begin to feel the mystery and the alien quality of the deep sea—the gathering darkness, the growing pressure, the starkness of a seascape in which all plant life has been left behind and there are only the unrelieved contours of rock and clay, of mud and sand.

1. According to the passage, the great fishing grounds of the world seas are

   (A) all confined to the continental shelves
   (B) found only where there is seaweed
   (C) the most important resource of the continental shelf
   (D) found mostly in the shallow waters of the continental shelves
   (E) becoming scarcer as we dig more and more for oil

2. According to the author, the dividing line between the continental shelf and the slope to the ocean is

   (A) the 100-fathom contour
   (B) twenty miles from the low-tide mark
   (C) where the shelf begins to descend abruptly
   (D) at about 150 miles out to sea on the east coast of the United States
   (E) at about 300 fathoms

3. The reason given for the narrowness of the continental shelf on the Pacific coast is that

   (A) the Gulf Stream comes close in shore there
   (B) the depth goes beyond 100 fathoms
   (C) the slope declines gradually rather than abruptly
   (D) this is common in areas where mountain ranges are probably still being formed
   (E) the shelf begins at the tide lines and extends seaward with a gentle slope

4. The article implies that the continental shelf on the east coast, north of Cape Hatteras, probably

   (A) is more valuable to man than the continental shelf south of Cape Hatteras
   (B) will not offer the possibility of much oil
   (C) is 300 fathoms deep
   (D) is influenced quite a bit by the nearness of the Gulf Stream
   (E) is caused by the continental formation of new mountains

5. According to the article, which of the following are true?

   I. The continental shelf of the United States is in some places as much as 150 miles wide.
   II. Geologists think the continental shelf might yield oil.
   III. The narrowest part of the continental shelf is along the Pacific Ocean.
   IV. Products made from seaweed are part of our economy.
   V. The Gulf Stream comes close inshore north of Cape Hatteras.

   (A) I, II, III (B) II, IV, V (C) I, II, IV
   (D) II, IV (E) I, IV

6. Which of the following is the most significant aspect of Magellan's voyage?

   (A) He used a sounding line more than 200 fathoms long.
   (B) He was the first European to sail to St. Paul.
   (C) He discovered the Tuamotu Archipelago.
   (D) He tried to sound the ocean depths.
   (E) He discovered the deepest part of the ocean.

7. The author's comparison of the fishes of the continental shelf to herds of cattle is a(n)

   (A) simile
   (B) exclamation
   (C) question
   (D) pronoun
   (E) allegory

8. According to the passage, the deepest continental shelves in the world

   (A) border the Arctic
   (B) line the Pacific coast
   (C) buffer the island of Los Tiburones
   (D) are located near Cape Hatteras
   (E) surround the continent of Antarctica

9. The author expects that the process of constructing an accurate map of the ocean basins will be

   (A) protracted
   (B) annoying
   (C) timely
   (D) discursive
   (E) immediate

10. The author suggests that the topographical features of the continental shelf might have been caused by

    (A) rock fragments
    (B) glacial activity
    (C) algae
    (D) prehistoric beasts
    (E) continental slope movement

11. To emphasize the "stark" nature of the sea, the author might also describe it as

(A) moderate
(B) harmonious
(C) severe
(D) derogatory
(E) temperate

12. The tone of the last paragraph suggests that the author is

(A) determined to explore continental slopes
(B) amused by the rock contours of the continental shelves
(C) afraid of the creatures that inhabit the continental shelves
(D) contemplating the wonders of the sea
(E) startled by the declivities of the continental slope

PASSAGE 2

The passage below is followed by questions based on its content. Answer the questions on the basis of what is *stated* or *implied* in the passage, and in any introductory material that might be provided.

The following passage focuses on the major contributions of Sigmund Freud in the field of psychoanalysis.

From our present vantage point it now appears that what Freud was trying to accomplish during the thirty years between 1890 and 1920, when the unconscious mind reigned as the sovereign concept in his psychological system, was to discover those determining forces in personality that are not directly known to the observer. Just as physics and chemistry make known that which is unknown about the nature of matter by means of experiment and demonstration, so the task of psychology for Freud was to seek out those factors in personality of which we are ignorant. This seems to be the meaning of Freud's statement that "our scientific work in psychology will consist in translating unconscious processes into conscious ones, and thus filling in the gaps in conscious perceptions." Freud is merely acknowledging the well-known fact that the goal of all the sciences is to substitute knowledge for ignorance. For example, man is not directly aware of the process of digestion. This knowledge does not enable him to perceive (be directly aware of) his own digestive processes as they are occurring; nevertheless, he knows (understands) what is taking place. In a similar manner, one is not aware of unconscious mental processes, but psychology can teach him about what is going on below the level of awareness.

For example, a person who has an accident is usually not aware that the accident may represent a desire to hurt himself. Yet this is precisely what a number of studies have shown. Or a person who has an abnormal craving for food or liquor is ordinarily not conscious of the fact that the craving may grow out of a frustrated desire for love. Yet this is often the case. Even when a person learns that there is a relationship between accident proneness and feelings of guilt or between alcoholism and frustrated love, he probably does not become directly conscious of this relationship as it exists in him.

The First World War opened the eyes of official medicine to the value of the psychoanalytic idea. While the medical profession still was careful to keep its distance, it came at last, through the observation of war neurosis, to a recognition of the significance of psychic factors in producing neurotic disturbances. Some of the psychoanalytic conceptions, such as "the advantage of being ill" and the "flight into illness" suddenly became popular. By the end of the war it was evident even to medical diehards that "shell-shock," so-called, was not necessarily caused by physical concussion, and that the many arms, legs, and trigger fingers were rooted not so much in the conscious desire to malinger as in the unconscious mechanisms which Freud first described. The last psychoanalytic congress, held at Budapest in 1918, before the German collapse, was attended by official representatives of the allied governments of the Central European powers, and they agreed to the establishment of psychoanalytic stations for the treatment of war neurosis. Although the war ended before this could be put into effect, a psychoanalytic institute and clinic for veterans was established in Berlin in 1920, and Ferenczi, during the Bolshevist rule in Hungary, conducted a successful course of psychoanalytic instruction at the University of Budapest.

By the early 1930s the psychoanalytic approach to human problems had tinctured the thinking of the world. Whether people completely understood what they were saying or not, Freudian terms such as *complex, libido, sublimation,* and *fixation* had crept into their everyday language. In the 1920s, awareness of Freud and his discoveries had been limited to the *avant-garde* and to the so-called intelligentsia. By the next decade the Freudian word had seeped down to pulp magazines, comic strips, musical comedies, and advertising copy. Learned journals and technical articles designed for scientists referred to his doctrines.

Whether or not people agreed with Freud's concept of the Oedipus complex, they were prone to trace their current difficulties back to their childhood situations. Whether they preferred the age of innocence to the era of infantile sexuality, Freud's doctrines had so far revolutionized the field of child psychology that they were beginning to rear their children in a spirit diametrically opposed to the rigid authority which characterized Freud's own childhood. Where their sex life had been a subject neither for conscious consideration nor discussion, where it had been blanketed under centuries of traditionally imposed reticence and guilt, people were emerging from an era of sexual licence (which had been their first understanding of what Freud was saying) into a more sane, more balanced recognition of their fundamental natures.

These attitudes and these points of view came to them not from a study of Freud's work but indirectly, through novels, plays, magazines, and newspapers. Revolutionary as Freud's concepts proved to be in the field of normal and abnormal psychology, his influence in the arts was greater. And of all artists the writer (because his preoccupation, like Freud's, is with men's motivation) was most influenced by Freudian concepts. Whether it be the novel or poetry, drama or biography, historical literature or surrealist outpourings, detective fiction or movie scripts which are examined, there is apparent not only in the content but increasingly in the form an overwhelming concern with those unconscious emotional forces in human behavior and society which Freud first charted for his era.

Art and literature, which had been primarily concerned with a depiction of the surface world of reality, began to penetrate below the surface in order to expose the hidden motives and drives which Freud had uncovered. The working of the unconscious mind began to take precedence, as a matter of concern to artists, over the description of the conscious mind.

Freud believed that if psychology were to justify itself as a science it would have to discover the unknown causes of behavior. That is why he made so much of unconscious causation or motivation in the early years of psychoanalysis. For Freud, what is unconscious is what is unknown.

1. The main theme of this passage is

    (A) the development of Freud's theories of psychoanalysis
    (B) Freud's preoccupation with the causes of neurotic behavior
    (C) Freud's attempt to make psychology a respectable science by translating unconscious processes into conscious ones

    (D) the reasons psychology remains an inexact science
    (E) Freud's methods of psychoanalysis

2. According to this writer, the goal of science is

    (A) the translation of unconscious processes into conscious ones
    (B) to replace ignorance with knowledge
    (C) to determine the unconscious causes of behavior
    (D) to create systematic bodies of knowledge
    (E) to make intellectual sense of unconscious emotions

3. According to this writer, the most important concept in Freud's theory was

    (A) conscious behavior
    (B) factors constituting personality
    (C) the unconscious
    (D) the validation of psychology as a science
    (E) finding a cure for neurosis

4. This writer implies that the primary goal of chemistry and physics is to

    (A) dispel ignorance
    (B) discover the nature of matter
    (C) make psychology a respectable science
    (D) study the physical processes in man, just as psychology studies the emotional processes
    (E) help individuals understand how their physiology works

5. According to the writer, all but one of the following words or phrases describe Freud's view of the unconscious

    (A) hidden from the conscious mind
    (B) influencing behavior
    (C) a physical process
    (D) a factor in personality
    (E) causing a gap in conscious perception

6. According to Freud's theory of the unconscious,

    I. an individual with feelings of guilt will often unconsciously subject himself to accidents.
    II. when an alcoholic realizes that his craving stems from a desire for love, the alcoholism will be cured.
    III. neurotic behavior is the inevitable result of traumatic war or traumatic childhood experiences.
    IV. the connection between behavior and unconscious desire is so strong that an

individual might not perceive it occurring in himself.

   (A) IV, I (B) III only (C) III, IV
   (D) I, II (E) I, II, III

7. The establishment of psychoanalytic stations by the allied governments for the treatment of war neurosis after World War I

   (A) allowed for the development of new psychotherapy for treatment of shell-shock, trigger finger, and other war neuroses
   (B) occurred before the German collapse
   (C) came about only after months of diplomatic negotiation between official representatives
   (D) allowed the treatment of shell-shocked soldiers from both World War I and World War II
   (E) signaled a new era of modern medicine, in which the medical profession began to acknowledge the value of psychoanalysis

8. According to the passage, what was the main difference between the Freudian legacy of the 1920s and the 1930s?

   (A) In the 1920s, psychiatrists were more interested in curing war neuroses, and in the 1930s, the Oedipus complex was the primary neurosis of the public.
   (B) Freud's theories had been known by relatively few in the 1920s; by the 1930s, awareness of his work had reached a wider population.
   (C) Large psychoanalytic stations, such as were established in the 1920s by governments for war veterans, gave way to smaller, private psychiatric offices in the 1930s.
   (D) The 1930s saw a sharp increase of various neuroses.
   (E) People became more sexually liberated in the 1930s after they learned Freud's theory of the unconscious.

9. *Avant-garde* and *intelligentsia* in paragraph 4 refer to

   (A) individuals who are trained psychologists
   (B) individuals who are well traveled and wealthy
   (C) individuals who are generally more intelligent than others
   (D) individuals who are on the cutting edge and intellectual
   (E) individuals who are involved in the state intelligence organization

10. According to the writer, Freud's theories had an especially great influence on arts and literature because

   (A) artists and writers were more likely to have heard of his theories
   (B) Freud's theories were increasingly gaining wider acceptance among the public
   (C) Freud believed the arts and the sciences had many similarities
   (D) art and literature are often concerned with issues of motivation
   (E) Freud's theory of the Oedipus complex lent itself easily to art and literature

11. According to the writer, which of the following were *not* influenced by Freud's theories?

   I. sexual attitudes
   II. childbearing
   III. popular culture
   IV. historical literature

      (A) I (B) II (C) none of the above
      (D) II, III (E) IV

12. The word *reticence* in paragraph 5 most nearly means

   (A) rules
   (B) suffering
   (C) celibacy
   (D) silence
   (E) fear

PASSAGE 3

The passage below is followed by questions based on its content. Answer the questions on the basis of what is *stated* or *implied* in the passage, and in any introductory material that might be provided.

The following passage analyzes the role of Negro folk music in the development of blues and jazz.

Legitimate Negro folk music lived through the various efforts to water it down and became one of the decisive elements in that most American of musical styles, jazz. Yet jazz itself is a hybrid form of musical expression; it has evolved through many stages, from a variety of traditions, both European and neo-African.

During the 1870s and 1880s, various elements of Negro folk music and pseudo-folk music came together in ragtime, the earliest ancestor of jazz that we know about. Ragtime, or rag, combined the cakewalk, march rhythms, and the idiom of the banjo. In its heyday (1895–1915), rag was written out in full rather than improvised and was published in great quantity for the piano. It became so respectable that it actually moved toward the outer fringes of classical music. Moreover, many of the early rags were recorded on player-piano rolls, so it is possible to hear exactly how someone like the black composer-pianist Scott Joplin (1868–1917), the "King of Ragtime," actually performed his music. Rag is the earliest American music of which this can be said.

What has been called "classic blues" was the result of more diverse sociological and musical influences than any other kind of American Negro music called the blues. Musically, classic blues showed the Negro singer's appropriation of a great many elements of popular American music, notably the music associated with popular theater or vaudeville. The instrumental music that accompanied classic blues also reflected this development, as it did the Negro musician's maturing awareness of more instrumental style, possibly as a foil to be used with his naturally vocal style. Classic blues appeared in America at about the same time as ragtime, the most instrumental or nonvocal music to issue from Negro inspiration. Ragtime is also a music that is closely associated with the popular theater of the late nineteenth and early twentieth centuries. Although ragtime must be considered as a separate kind of music, borrowing more European elements than any other music commonly associated with Negroes, it contributed greatly to the development of Negro music from an almost vocal tradition to one that could begin to include the melodic and harmonic complexities of instrumental music.

Socially, classic blues and the instrumental styles that went with it represented the Negro's entrance into the world of professional entertainment and the assumption of the psychological imperatives that must accompany such a phenomenon. Blues was a music that arose from the needs of a group, although it was assumed that each man had his *own* blues and that he would sing them. As such, the music was private and personal, although the wandering country blues singers of earlier times had from time to time casual audiences who would sometimes respond with gifts of food, clothes, or even money. But again it was assumed that anybody could sing the blues. If someone had lived in this world into manhood, it was taken for granted that he had been given the content of his verses.

Given the deeply personal quality of blues singing, there could be no particular method for learning blues. As a verse form it was the lyrics which were most important, and they issued from life. But classic blues took on a certain degree of professionalism. It was no longer strictly the group singing to ease their labors or the casual expression of personal deliberations on the world. It became a music that could be used to entertain others formally. The artisan, the professional blues singer, appeared; blues singing no longer had to be merely a passionately felt avocation, it could now become a way of making a living. An external and sophisticated idea of performance had come to the blues, moving it past the casualness of the "folk" to the conditioned emotional gesture of the "public."

The blues, a type and style of vocal music that grew out of the field hollers and work songs of the rural South, coexisted with and fertilized the early jazz style. The blues entered the consciousness of the general public only in the years immediately following World War I, through singers like Ma Rainey (1886–1939) and Bessie Smith (about 1900–1937). The early jazz musicians took over the blues form as well as the vocal style of blues singing, with its great flexibility of pitch, rhythm, and tone color.

The primitive blues was still very much a vocal music; the singers relied on the unpredictability and mobility of the human voice for their imaginative catalysts. But the growing use of European instruments such as brass and reeds almost precluded song, except as accompaniment or as an interlude. When Negroes began to master more and more "European" instruments and began to think musically in terms of their timbres, as opposed to, or in conjunction with, the voice, blues began to change, and the era of jazz was at hand.

"Jazz began in New Orleans and worked its way up the river to Chicago" is the announcement most investigators of mainstream popular culture are apt to make when dealing with the vague subject of jazz and its origins. And while that is certainly a rational explanation, charmingly simple, it is more than likely untrue. Jazz, or purely instrumental blues, could no more have begun in one area of the country than could blues. The mass migrations of Negroes throughout the South and the general liberating effect of the Emancipation make it extremely difficult to say just exactly where and when jazz, or purely instrumental blues (with European instruments), originated. It is easy to point out that jazz is a music that could not have existed without blues and its various antecedents. However, jazz should not be thought of as a successor to blues, but as a very original music that developed out of, and was concomitant with, blues and moved off into its own path of development. One interesting point is that although jazz developed out of a kind of blues, blues in its later popular connotation came to mean *a way of playing jazz,* and by the swing era the widespread popularity of the blues singer had already been replaced by the jazz player's. By then, blues was for a great many people no longer a separate music.

There was always a border beyond which the Negro could not go, whether musically or socially. There was always a possible limitation to any dilution or excession of cultural or spiritual references. The Negro could not ever become white and that was his strength; at some point, always, he could not participate in the dominant tenor of the white man's culture. It was at this juncture that he had to make use of other resources, whether African, subcultural, or hermetic. And it was this boundary, this no man's land, that provided the logic and beauty of his music.

1. The author describes ragtime as

    I. music that is primarily improvised
    II. an early, simply constructed ancestor of jazz
    III. an outgrowth of African folk songs
    IV. the first American music recorded on player-piano rolls
    V. a combination of several different musical elements

    (A) I, III, IV (B) I, II, III (C) I, III, IV, V
    (D) IV, V (E) III, IV, V

2. What does the word *appropriation* mean in paragraph 3?

    (A) use
    (B) appreciation
    (C) presentation
    (D) understanding
    (E) enjoyment

3. According to the passage, which of the following statements is true?

    (A) Jazz is a successor to blues.
    (B) Early jazz could also be termed "instrumental blues."
    (C) Ma Rainey and Bessie Smith were two early jazz singers.
    (D) The earliest jazz appeared in the 1870s and 1880s.
    (E) Jazz began in New Orleans and spread north.

4. What does the author mean when, in paragraph 1, he describes jazz as a "hybrid form of musical expression"?

    (A) it was a new and original form of music
    (B) it was improvised
    (C) it began as an underground musical movement
    (D) it drew upon many musical forms
    (E) it was a form of music as foreign as it was American

5. According to this passage, early jazz was primarily played on which of the following?

    (A) player-piano rolls
    (B) banjo
    (C) brass and reed instruments
    (D) instruments made from farm tools
    (E) voice

6. The main theme of this passage is

    (A) the influence of Negro folk music
    (B) comparisons between rag, the blues, and jazz
    (C) the development of early American music
    (D) the limitations of Negro music
    (E) the origins of jazz

7. According to the author, what was the ultimate effect of "the border beyond which the Negro could not go"?

    (A) The limitations white men imposed on the early Negro musicians actually enabled these musicians to develop their own great form of music.
    (B) By shutting obviously talented Negro jazz musicians out of the mainstream musical culture, American music suffered an inestimable loss.
    (C) The racial border allowed Negro musicians great musical freedom within their boundaries.

(D) We will never know how far black musicians could have progressed were they never shunned by white institutions.

(E) The jazz audience was enthusiastic but its size sadly limited by reasons of race.

8. What effects did European instruments have on the blues?

   I. The music gained a much wider following among the white audience.

  II. Their influence on the blues paved the way to jazz.

 III. Brass and reed began to take prominence over voice.

 IV. Blues musicians adapted their music to the timbres of European instruments.

  V. European instruments killed the blues; with the integration of brass and reed instruments, the blues became jazz.

    (A) I, II, III (B) I, II, V (C) II, III, IV, V
    (D) II, III, IV (E) all of the above

9. Why can't one say with certainty when and where jazz began?

(A) Numerous musicians claimed to have been the first to play jazz; there is no way to verify or discredit these claims.

(B) There is disagreement as to the actual definition of jazz; therefore the time and location of the birth of jazz is also up for debate.

(C) Jazz was largely ignored by critics and music historians when it first appeared on the music scene.

(D) The mass migration of Negroes after the Civil War makes it difficult to determine where and when jazz originated.

(E) The "birthplace of jazz" is a distinction many cities, including New Orleans and Chicago, share.

10. Which of the following is *not* true of classic blues?

(A) Classic blues and ragtime appeared on the American musical scene about the same time.

(B) Classic blues was often solely instrumental as well as vocal.

(C) Classic blues had more diverse musical influences than the blues.

(D) Classic blues was influenced by the popular music of the time.

(E) Classic blues became a form of professional entertainment.

11. The author suggests that all but one of the following elements were involved in the development of jazz:

(A) ragtime

(B) pseudo folk music

(C) European music

(D) church music

(E) blues

12. The author uses the word *legitimate* in the first sentence of the passage to imply that Negro folk music

(A) easily adapted to Western European harmonies

(B) is characterized by unique elements which are indigenous to the Negro community

(C) easily resisted attempts to dilute its complex musical forms

(D) established its authenticity in the years following World War I

(E) evolved from both European and neo-African traditions

ANSWERS AND EXPLANATIONS, PASSAGES 1-3

Passage 1

1. (D)	2. (C)	3. (D)	4. (A)	5. (C)	6. (D)
7. (A)	8. (E)	9. (A)	10. (B)	11. (C)	12. (D)

Passage 2

1. (C)	2. (B)	3. (C)	4. (B)	5. (C)	6. (A)
7. (E)	8. (B)	9. (D)	10. (D)	11. (C)	12. (D)

Passage 3

1. (D)	2. (A)	3. (B)	4. (D)	5. (C)	6. (E)
7. (A)	8. (D)	9. (D)	10. (B)	11. (D)	12. (B)

PASSAGE 1

The first European ever to sail across the wide Pacific was curious about the hidden worlds beneath his ship. Between the two coral islands of St. Paul and Los Tiburones in the Tuamotu Archipelago, Magellan ordered his sounding line to be lowered. It was the conventional line used by explorers of the day, no more than 200 fathoms long. It did not touch bottom, and Magellan declared that he was over the deepest part of the ocean. Of course, he was completely mistaken, but the occasion was nonetheless historic. It was the first time in the history of the world that a navigator had attempted to sound the depths of the open ocean.

Now hundreds of vessels are equipped with sonic sounding instruments that trace a continuous profile of the bottom beneath the moving ship. Soundings are accumulating much faster than they can be plotted on the charts. Little by little, like the details of a huge map being filled in by an artist, the hidden contours of the ocean are emerging. But, even with this recent progress, it will be years before an accurate and detailed relief map of the ocean basins can be constructed.

The general topography is, however, well established. Once we have passed the tide lines, the three great geographic provinces of ocean are the continental shelves, the continental slopes, and the floor of the deep sea. Each of these regions is as different from the others as an arctic tundra from a range of the Rocky Mountains.

The continental shelf is of the sea, yet of all the regions of the ocean it is most like the land. Sunlight penetrates to all but its deepest parts. Plants drift in the waters above it; seaweeds cling to its rocks and sway to the passage of the waves. Familiar fishes—unlike the weird monsters of the abyss—move over its plains like herds of cattle. Much of its substance is derived from the land—the sand and the rock fragments and the rich topsoil carried by running water to the sea and gently deposited on the shelf. Its submerged valleys and hills, in appropriate parts of the world, have been carved by glaciers into a topography much like the northern landscapes we know, and the terrain is strewn with rocks and gravel deposited by the moving ice sheets. Indeed many parts (or perhaps all) of the shelf have been dry land in the geologic past, for a comparatively slight fall of sea level has sufficed, time and again, to expose it to wind and sun and rain. The Grand Banks of Newfoundland rose above the ancient seas and were submerged again. The Dogger Bank of the North Sea shelf was once a forested land inhabited by prehistoric beasts; now its forests are seaweeds and its "beasts" are fishes.

Of all parts of the sea, the continental shelves are perhaps most directly important to man as a source of material things. The great fisheries of the world, with only a few exceptions, are confined to the relatively shallow waters over the continental shelves. Seaweeds are gathered from their submerged plains to make scores of substances used in foods, drugs, and articles of commerce. As the petroleum reserves left on continental areas by ancient seas become depleted, petroleum geologists look more and more to the oil that may lie, as yet unmapped and unexploited, under these bordering lands of the sea.

The shelves begin at the tide lines and extend seaward as gently sloping plains. The 100-fathom contour used to be taken as the boundary between the continental shelf and the slope; now it is customary to place the division wherever the gentle declivity of the shelf changes abruptly to a steeper descent toward abyssal depths. The world over, the average depth at which this change occurs is about 72 fathoms; the greatest depth of any shelf is probably 299 to 300 fathoms.

Nowhere off the Pacific coast of the United States is the continental shelf much more than 20 miles wide—a narrowness characteristic of coasts bordered by young mountains perhaps still in the process of formation. On the American east coast, however, north of Cape Hatteras the shelf is as much as 150 miles wide. But at Hatteras and off southern Florida it is merely the narrowest of thresholds to the sea. Here its scant development seems to be related to the press of that great and rapidly flowing river-in-the-sea, the Gulf Stream, which at these places swings close inshore.

The widest shelves in all the world are those bordering the Arctic. The Barents Sea shelf is 750 miles across. It is also relatively deep, lying for the most part 100 to 200 fathoms below the surface, as though its floor had sagged and been downwarped—further evidence of the work of the ice. The deepest shelves surround the Antarctic continent, where soundings in many areas show depths of several hundred fathoms near the coast and continuing out across the shelf.

Once beyond the edge of the shelf, as we visualize the steeper declivities of the continental slope, we begin to feel the mystery and the alien quality of the deep sea—the gathering darkness, the growing pressure, the starkness of a seascape in which all plant life has been left behind and there are only the unrelieved contours of rock and clay, of mud and sand.

1. (D) Choice (A) is incorrect because the passage does not say that *all* fishing grounds are confined to the continental shelves; in the second sentence it says there are *a few exceptions.* (B) is incorrect because although the passage does mention both fishing grounds and seaweed, it does not say that there is any connection between the two. (C) is incorrect because the author merely gives three examples of the importance of continental shelves—fisheries, seaweed, and oil—but does not say which is the most important. (D) is explicitly stated in the fifth paragraph. (E) is incorrect because it is not the fishing grounds that are becoming scarcer as we dig for oil but the "petroleum reserves" in the last sentence of the fifth paragraph.

2. (C) Choice (A) is incorrect because in the second sentence of the sixth paragraph, the author says that the 100-fathom contour *used to be taken as the boundary,* not now. (B) and (E) are clearly wrong because in the sixth and seventh paragraphs the writer points out at some length that both the width and depth of the continental shelves vary from place to place. (D) at first looks as if it could be true, but the actual words in the passage are *on the American east coast . . . north of Cape Hatteras the shelf is as much as 150 miles wide,* and farther south the shelf is much narrower. (C) is correct; the words in the passage are *wherever the gentle declivity of the shelf changes abruptly to a steeper descent.* This is simply another way of saying *where the shelf begins to descend abruptly.*

3. (D)   The discussion concerning the narrowness of the shelves is in the seventh paragraph. Choice (A) is incorrect because the Gulf Stream has nothing to do with the Pacific Coast, which is what the question is asking about. (B) is incorrect because the depth and width of the shelves are never related; they are discussed in separate paragraphs. (C) is similarly incorrect; the first sentence of the sixth paragraph implies that all shelves decline gradually, not just narrow ones. (D) is stated in the first sentence of the seventh paragraph. (E) is incorrect for the same reason as (C); no connection is ever made between the slope of the continental shelves and their width.

4. (A)   You could have backed into choice (A) by a process of elimination. However, the answer is found in the fifth and seventh paragraphs. In the fifth paragraph the passage points out the importance of the continental shelves, and in the seventh paragraph it states that the shelf north of Cape Hatteras is very wide and the shelf south of Cape Hatteras very narrow. It seems safe to assume that the wide shelf is more important than the narrow one. (B) says just the opposite, in that the author states in the fifth paragraph that petroleum geologists look to the oil that might lie under the continental shelves and that the shelf north of Cape Hatteras is a particularly wide one. (C) is irrelevant, in that the depth of the continental shelf north of Cape Hatteras is never related to its width. (D) is incorrect because the mention of the Gulf Stream in the seventh paragraph does not apply to the continental shelf on the east coast north of Cape Hatteras, but to the area off southern Florida. (E) is incorrect for a similar reason; the mention of *young mountains* applies to the *Pacific Coast,* not the continental shelf on the east coast north of Cape Hatteras.

5. (C)   Statement (I) is made in the seventh paragraph. Statement (II) is made in the fifth paragraph: *petroleum geologists look more and more to the oil that may lie under* the continental shelves. Statement (III) is contradicted in the seventh paragraph: *at Hatteras and off southern Florida it is merely the narrowest of thresholds to the sea* (or narrower than along the Pacific Coast). Statement (IV) can be found in the fifth paragraph: *Seaweeds are gathered from their submerged plains to make scores of substances used in foods, drugs, and articles of commerce.* Statement (V) would be correct if only it read *south* of Cape Hatteras instead of *north.* If you were not alert you probably were fooled into choice (B).

6. (D)   Choice (A) is incorrect because in the third sentence of the first paragraph the author says the sounding line was *no more* than 200 fathoms long. (B) is incorrect because although the author does mention St. Paul, he never says Magellan was the first European to sail to the island. (C) is similarly incorrect; the author says that it was in the Tuamotu Archipelago that Magellan sounded the ocean's depths; it never says that he discovered it. (D) is explicitly stated in the last sentence of the paragraph. (E) is incorrect because although Magellan thought he had discovered the deepest part of the ocean, the author says *he was completely mistaken.*

7. (A)   You could have backed into the correct answer because it is built into the question. You probably realized that a *comparison* is a *simile,* but even if you did not know that the definition of a *simile* is a comparison using *like* or *as,* you could have backed into the correct answer; it can be found in the fourth paragraph.

8. (E)   Choice (A) is incorrect. In the eighth paragraph, the author states that the *widest* shelves border the Arctic, not the *deepest.* Choice (B) is incorrect; in the seventh paragraph, the author specifically states that nowhere off the Pacific Coast of the United States is the continental shelf much more than 20 miles wide. He never discusses the depth. (C) is incorrect because the only reference to Los Tiburones is in the first paragraph of the passage; the author never discusses the continental shelves. (D) is incorrect because the only reference to Cape Hatteras and the continental

shelves is in the third paragraph from the end in the context of *width,* not *depth.* (E) is correct; the answer is explicitly stated in the last sentence in the next-to-last paragraph: *The deepest shelves surround the Antarctic continent.*

9. (A)   You could have backed into choice (A) by a process of elimination. In the last sentence of the second paragraph, the author says, *it will be years before an accurate and detailed relief map of the ocean basins can be constructed.* Chances are you eliminated (B), (C), and (E) because none of these choices has to do with an extended length of time. Your remaining choices, (A) and (D), might have presented some difficulty if you did not know that *protracted* means "drawn out" or "lengthened in time" and that *discursive* means "rambling" or "passing rapidly from one subject to another." But if you carefully considered both words, you might have recognized the prefix *dis-,* which means "apart" or "away," and the prefix *pro-,* which means "advancing or projecting forward"; in that case, you would have settled on (A) as the correct answer.

10. (B)   Choice (A) looks good at first, but the question asks you what caused the topographical features of the continental shelf. In the fourth paragraph, *rock fragments* describes the *substance* of the continental shelf, not its topographical features. (B) is the answer; it is directly stated in the fourth paragraph: *its submerged valleys . . . have been carved by glaciers into a topography.* (C) is irrelevant. (D) is incorrect; the author discusses prehistoric beasts in the fourth paragraph as examples of inhabitants of a time when the seas were forested land. (E) is an interesting choice because in the fourth paragraph the author discusses how the Grand Banks of Newfoundland rose above the seas and then submerged again, but it has nothing to do with the topography of the continental shelf.

11. (C)   Even if you did not know that the word *stark* means "harsh" or "desolate," you could have backed into the correct answer by a process of elimination. If you look at the last paragraph, the author says, *the starkness of a seascape in which all plant life has been left behind . . . only unrelieved contours of rock and clay, of mud and sand.* Choice (C), *severe,* is the perfect choice.

12. (D)   Remember that even though the question asks you to determine the author's attitude or tone, you need to prove your answer by some statement in the passage. Choice (A) is irrelevant; the author never says he is determined to explore the continental slopes. (B) is also irrelevant; there is no evidence to prove that the author is amused; if anything, his mood is just the opposite. (C) is totally wrong. There is no mention of sea creatures. (D) is the correct answer; the author states in the last paragraph, *we visualize the declivities of the continental slope . . . we feel the mystery of the deep sea.* (E) is both incorrect and irrelevant; the author has simply taken the word *declivities* out of context.

PASSAGE 2

From our present vantage point it now appears that what Freud was trying to accomplish during the thirty years between 1890 and 1920, when the unconscious mind reigned as the sovereign concept in his psychological system, was to discover those determining forces in personality that are not directly known to the observer. //

EX. 1

Just as physics and chemistry make known that which is unknown about the nature of matter by means of experiment and demonstration, // so the task of psychology for Freud was to seek out those factors in personality of which we are ignorant. This

EX. 1

seems to be the meaning of Freud's statement that "our scientific work in psychology will consist in translating unconscious processes into conscious ones, and thus filling in the gaps in conscious perceptions." // Freud is merely acknowledging the well-known fact that the goal of all the sciences is to substitute knowledge for ignorance

EX. 1

For example, man is not directly aware of the process of digestion. This knowledge does not enable him to perceive (be directly aware of) his own digestive processes as they are occurring; // nevertheless, he knows understands what is taking place. // In a similar manner, one is not aware of unconscious mental processes, but psychology can teach him about what is going on below the level of awareness.

// For example, a person who has an accident is usually not aware that the accident

EX. 1

may represent a desire to hurt himself. Yet this is precisely what a number of studies

EX. 2

have shown. Or a person who has an abnormal craving for food or liquor is ordinarily not conscious of the fact that the craving may grow out of a frustrated desire for love.

EX. 3

Yet this is often the case. Even when a person learns that there is a relationship between accident proneness and feelings of guilt or between alcoholism and frustrated love, he probably does not become directly conscious of this relationship as it exists in him.

The First World War opened the eyes of official medicine to the value of the psychoanalytic idea. While the medical profession still was careful to keep its distance, it came at last, through the observation of war neurosis, to a recognition of the significance of psychic factors in producing neurotic disturbances. Some of the psy-

EX. 1

choanalytic conceptions, such as "the advantage of being ill" and the "flight into illness" suddenly became popular. By the end of the war it was evident even to medical diehards that "shell-shock," so-called, was not necessarily caused by physical concussion, and that the many arms, legs, and trigger fingers were rooted not so much in the conscious desire to malinger as in the unconscious mechanisms which Freud first described. // The last psychoanalytic congress, held in Budapest in 1918, before the German collapse, was attended by official representatives of the allied governments of the Central European powers, and they agreed to the establishment of psychoanalytic stations for the treatment of war neurosis. Although the war ended before this could be put into effect, a psychoanalytic institute and clinic for veterans was established in Berlin in 1920, and Ferenczi, during the Bolshevist rule in Hungary, conducted a successful course of psychoanalytic instruction at the University of Budapest.

By the early 1930s the psychoanalytic approach to human problems had tinctured the thinking of the world. Whether people completely understood what they were saying or not, Freudian terms such as *complex, libido, sublimation,* and *fixation* had crept into their everyday language. // In the 1920s, awareness of Freud and his discoveries had been limited to the avant-garde and to the so-called intelligentsia. // By the next decade the Freudian word had seeped down to pulp magazines, comic strips, musical comedies, and advertising copy. Learned journals and technical articles designed for scientists referred to his doctrines.

// Whether or not people agreed with Freud's concept of the Oedipus complex, they were prone to trace their current difficulties back to their childhood situations. Whether they preferred the age of innocence to the era of infantile sexuality, Freud's doctrines had so far revolutionized the field of child psychology that they were beginning to rear their children in a spirit diametrically opposed to the rigid authority which characterized Freud's own childhood. //Where their sex life had been a subject neither for conscious consideration nor discussion, where it had been blanketed under centures of traditionally imposed reticence and guilt, people were emerging from an era of sexual licence (which had been their first understanding of what Freud was saying) into a more sane, more balanced recognition of their fundamental natures.

★

These attitudes and these points of view came to them not from a study of Freud's work but indirectly, through novels, plays, magazines, and newspapers. Revolutionary as Freud's concepts proved to be in the field of normal and abnormal psychology, his

★

EX. 1

influence in the arts was greater. And of all artists the writer (because his preoccupation, like Freud's, is with men's motivation) was most influenced by Freudian concepts. Whether it be the novel or poetry, drama or biography, historical literature or surrealist outpourings, detective fiction or movie scripts which are examined, there is apparent not only in the content but increasingly in the form an overwhelming concern with those unconscious emotional forces in human behavior and society which Freud first charted for his era.

★

//Art and literature, which has been primarily concerned with a depiction of the surface world of reality, began to penetrate below the surface in order to expose the hidden motives and drives which Freud had uncovered. The working of the unconscious mind began to take precedence, as a matter of concern to artists, over the description of the conscious mind.

★

Freud believed that if psychology were to justify itself as a science it would have to discover the unknown causes of behavior. That is why he made so much of unconscious causation or motivation in the early years of psychoanalysis. For Freud, what is unconscious is what is unknown.

★

1. (C)   This question is another form of the "title" question. You are looking for an answer that deals with most of the sentences in the passage. (A) is too narrow; some of Freud's theories are briefly mentioned in the passage, but the author's primary concern is the development of the psychoanalytic approach to human behavior. (B) is too narrow; furthermore, Freud's interest was not only in the causes of neurotic behavior but discovering the determining forces underlying human behavior in general. (C) is correct because almost every paragraph in the passage has to do with some aspect of the development and acceptance of the psychoanalytic approach to human problems advanced by Freud. (D) is irrelevant; the author never discusses the reasons why psychology remains an inexact science. (E) is not correct because the author never deals with Freud's methodology.

2. (B)   This question is asking you what the goal of *science* is, not the goal of Freud. Choice (A) is incorrect because in the first paragraph the author states that it is the task of *psychology, not science,* to translate *unconscious processes into conscious ones.* (B) is explicitly stated in the third to last sentence of the first paragraph: *the goal of all the sciences is to substitute knowledge for ignorance.* (C) is incorrect; that is the goal of the psychologist. The idea is presented in the last sentence of the first paragraph. (D) is irrelevant; the author never says that the goal of science is to create systematic bodies of knowledge. (E) is absolutely wrong; any discussion of the unconscious in this passage remains in the psychological domain, which the author clearly distinguishes from the scientific.

3. (C)   Choice (A) is dead wrong; it contradicts the major theme of the passage, which is the working of the unconscious mind. (B) is an appealing choice but it is also incorrect because it never answers the question, which is to state the most important *concept* in Freud's theory. (C) is correct; the idea is reiterated throughout the entire

passage, but particularly in the final paragraph, which focuses the unconscious as the "sovereign concept" (these words are taken from the first paragraph) in his psychoanalytic theory. (D) is simply not true. In the final paragraph, the author indicates that Freud understood what he would have to do in order to justify psychology as a science, but such validation does not constitute a theory. (E) is incorrect; the author mentions *war neurosis* in the third paragraph, but he never says that curing neurosis was Freud's most important theoretical concept.

4. (B)   Choice (A) is incorrect; although the answer is appealing, the author never states this in the passage. (B) is the correct answer and is clearly stated in the second sentence of the first paragraph: *physics and chemistry make known that which is unknown about the nature of matter.* (C) is totally irrelevant; the author never says this in the passage. (D) is irrelevant; the primary goal of chemistry and physics is to study the nature of matter, not the physical processes in man. (E) is irrelevant; the author relates Freud's statement concerning scientific work in psychology, but nowhere does the author say that helping individuals understand their physiology is a goal of chemistry and physics.

5. (C)   The question is telling you that four of the five choices are true; that is, they can be located somewhere in the passage. The one that is not stated in the passage is the correct answer. (A) is expressed in a variety of ways throughout the passage, including the last sentence in the final paragraph. (B) is clearly expressed in the first two paragraphs. (C) is correct; it not only contradicts the essence of Freud's theory—which is rooted in psychology, not biology—but nowhere in the passage does the author say this. (D) is stated throughout. It is most clearly expressed in the first sentence, in which the author talks about the *determining forces in personality.* (E) is nicely expressed in the first paragraph, in which the author quotes Freud: *"our scientific work in psychology will consist in . . . filling in the gaps in conscious perceptions."*

6. (A)   The best approach in answering this type of reading-comprehension question is to systematically narrow down your choices. Statement (I) can be found in the last sentence of the second paragraph, in which the author says that there is an unconscious relationship between accident proneness and feelings of guilt; therefore, you can eliminate (B) and (C) because either choice has (I) as a part of the answer. Statement (II) might be true, but it is never stated in the passage, so you could have eliminated (D) and (E); they both have (II) as part of the answer. (A) is the best choice. Statement (IV) can be found in the last sentence of the second paragraph: *Even when a person learns that there is a relationship between accident proneness and feelings of guilt . . . he probably does not become directly conscious of this relationship as it exists in him.*

7. (E)   The answer to this question can be found in the third paragraph of the passage. (A) is incorrect; the author says that the psychoanalytic stations were never actually established. (B) is incorrect; in fact, the author states just the opposite, that the war ended before the psychoanalytic stations could be put into effect. (C) is irrelevant; this answer is another example of words taken out of context; in this case, "official representatives" for the purpose of confusing you. (D) is also irrelevant; the author never states this in the passage. (E) is the answer; it can be found in the first sentence of the third paragraph.

8. (B)   Choice (A) is incorrect; this answer is never stated in the passage. (B) is correct; the answer is clearly stated in the fourth paragraph of the passage. (C) is irrelevant; there is no mention of private psychiatric offices. (D) is also irrelevant; the author never says this. (E) is incorrect; the author states just the opposite idea in the fifth paragraph: *people were emerging from an era of sexual licence (which had been their first understanding of what Freud was saying) into a sane, more balanced recognition of their fundamental natures.*

9. (D)   It is clear that the mention of *avante-garde* and *intelligentsia* in the first part of the paragraph contrasts with the second half, which discusses the popular influence of Freudian psychology. (A) is irrelevant; the author never mentions trained psychologists. (B) is also irrelevant; it is never mentioned in the passage. Although (C) is an appealing choice, because the word *intelligentsia* does seem to refer to intelligence, it actually means "the intellectual" or "a class or group of people having a special claim in views or principles." Besides, the author never refers to their level of intelligence. (D) is correct. Aside from the fact that intellectual is a better description, the word *Avant* is from the French, meaning "before," which suggests a person who is ahead of his time or "on the cutting edge."

10. (D)   Choice (A) is irrelevant; the author never says this in the passage. Although (B) might be true, it does not answer the question as to why Freud's theories had such a great influence on the arts, particularly literature. (C) is an interesting answer, in that the author says in the first paragraph that the goal of both science and psychology are to *make known that which is unknown,* but he never states that the arts and science have many similarities. In fact, in the last paragraph, the author discusses what psychology would have to do to *justify* it as a science. (E) is completely irrelevant; the author never makes the link between Freud's theory of the Oedipus complex and its relationship between art and literature.

11. (C)   This question is telling you that four of the five answer choices can be located in the passage. The one that is not in the passage is the correct answer. You probably realized that (C) is correct, in that all of the remaining choices are clearly stated in the passage. Statements (I) and (II) can be found in the fifth paragraph. Statements (III) and (IV) are clearly stated in paragraphs four and six.

12. (D)   You might recall from the sections on Sentence Completions and Part II of the Reading Comprehension, Words in Context, that one of the important clues in this sentence is the word *and,* which implies that whatever is on one side of the word—in this case, the word *guilt*—there should be a word of similar import on the other side. Yet, looking over your choices, you might find you still need more information in order to narrow down your choices. If you examined the sentence further, you might have discovered from your diagramming that there are several important clues in this sentence, including the words *subject, neither, consideration, nor discussion,* and *blanketed under.* Even if you did not know that *celibacy* means "an unmarried state," the best answer is (D), in that *silence* conveys the idea expressed in the sentence; in fact, *reticence* means "keeping silent."

PASSAGE 3

  Legitimate Negro folk music lived through the various efforts to water it down and became one of the decisive elements in that most American of musical styles, jazz. || Yet Jazz itself is a hybrid form of musical expression; it has evolved through many stages, from a variety of traditions, both European and neo-African.   ★

  During the 1870s and 1880s, various elements of Negro folk music and pseudo-folk music came together in ragtime, the earliest ancestor of jazz that we know about.   ★
EX. 1

Ragtime, or rag, combined the cakewalk, march rhythms, and the idiom of the banjo. In its heyday (1895–1915), rag was written out in full rather than improvised and was published in great quantity for the piano. It became so respectable that it actually moved toward the outer fringes of classical music. Moreover, many of the early rags were recorded on player-piano rolls, so it is possible to hear exactly how someone like the black composer-pianist Scott Joplin (1868–1917), the "King of Ragtime," actually performed his music. Rag is the earliest American music of which this can be said.

What has been called "classic blues" was the result of more diverse sociological

EX. 2

and musical influences than any other kind of American Negro music called the blues. Musically, classic blues showed the Negro singer's appropriation of a great many elements of popular American music, notably the music associated with popular theater or vaudeville. The instrumental music that accompanied classic blues also reflected this development, as it did the Negro musician's maturing awareness of more instrumental style, possibly as a foil to be used with his naturally vocal style. Classic blues appeared in America at about the same time as ragtime, the most instrumental or nonvocal music to issue from Negro inspiration. Ragtime is also a music that is closely associated with the popular theater of the late nineteenth and early twentieth centuries. Although ragtime must be considered as a separate kind of music, borrowing more European elements than any other music commonly associated with Negroes, it contributed greatly to the development of Negro music from an almost vocal tradition to one that could begin to include the melodic and harmonic complexities of instrumental music.

Socially, classic blues and the instrumental styles that went with it represented the Negro's entrance into the world of professional entertainment and the assumption of the psychological imperatives that must accompany such a phenomenon. Blues was a music that arose from the needs of a group, although it was assumed that each man had his *own* blues and that he would sing them. As such, the music was private and personal, although the wandering country blues singers of earlier times had from time to time casual audiences who would sometimes respond with gifts of food, clothes, or even money. But again it was assumed that anybody could sing the blues. If someone had lived in this world into manhood, it was taken for granted that he had been given the content of his verses.

Given the deeply personal quality of blues singing, there could be no particular method for learning blues. As a verse form it was the lyrics which were most important, and they issued from life. But classic blues took on a certain degree of professionalism. It was no longer strictly the group singing to ease their labors or the casual expression of personal deliberations on the world. It became a music that could be used to entertain others formally. The artisan, the professional blues singer, appeared; blues singing no longer had to be merely a passionately felt avocation, it could now become a way of making a living. An external and sophisticated idea of performance had come to the blues, moving it past the casualness of the "folk" to the conditioned emotional gesture of the "public."

The blues, a type and style of vocal music that grew out of the field hollers and work songs of the rural South coexisted with and fertilized the early jazz style. The blues entered the consciousness of the general public only in the years immediately following World War I, through singers like Ma Rainey (1886–1939) and Bessie Smith (about 1900–1937). The early jazz musicians took over the blues form as well as the vocal style of blues singing, with its great flexibility of pitch, rhythm, and tone color.

The primitive blues was still very much a vocal music; the singers relied on the unpredictability and mobility of the human voice for their imaginative catalysts. But the growing use of European instruments such as brass and reeds almost precluded song, except as accompaniment or as an interlude. When Negroes began to master more and more "European" instruments and began to think musically in terms of their timbres, as opposed to, or in conjunction with, the voice, blues began to change, and the era of jazz was at hand.

"Jazz began in New Orleans and worked its way up the river to Chicago" is the ★ announcement most investigators of mainstream popular culture are apt to make when dealing with the vague subject of jazz and its origins. And while that is certainly a rational explanation, charmingly simple, it is more than likely untrue. Jazz, or purely instrumental blues, could no more have begun in one area of the country than could blues. The mass migrations of Negroes throughout the South and the general liberating effect of the Emancipation make it extremely difficult to say just exactly where and when jazz, or purely instrumental blues (with European instruments), originated. It is easy to point out that jazz is a music that could not have existed without blues and its various antecedents. // However, jazz should not be thought of as a successor to blues, but as a very original music that developed out of, and was concomitant with, blues and moved off into its own path of development. One interesting point is that although jazz developed out of a kind of blues, blues in its later popular connotation came to mean a way of playing jazz, and by the swing era the widespread popularity of the blues singer had already been replaced by the jazz player's. By then, ★ blues was for a great many people no longer a separate music.

There was always a border beyond which the Negro could not go, whether musically ★ or socially. There was always a possible limitation to any dilution or excession of cultural or spiritual references. The Negro could not ever become white and that was his strength; at some point, always, he could not participate in the dominant tenor of the white man's culture. It was at this juncture that he had to make use of other resources, whether African, subcultural, or hermetic. And it was this boundary, this no man's ★ land, that provided the logic and beauty of his music.

1. (D)   Statement (I) is directly contradicted in the second paragraph; the author specifically states that *rag was written out in full rather than improvised.* Therefore, you could have eliminated (A), (B), and (C), in that statement (I) is a part of each answer choice. If you look at your two remaining choices, the only variable that will enable you to zero in on the correct answer is whether or not statement (III) is in the passage. In the last sentence of the third paragraph, the author says that ragtime has borrowed *more European elements than any other music associated with Negroes;* he never mentions African folk songs. The answer, of course, is (D).

2. (A)   Most students know that the word *appropriate* as an adjective means "suitable or fitting for a particular purpose," but might not know the verb form of the word as it is used in this context. If you examined your diagramming of this passage you would have probably noticed some important clues that could have helped you narrow down your choices. The author tells you in the first sentence of the third paragraph that classic blues is *the result of* many cultural influences. He expands on this idea in the following sentence when he says that *classic blues showed the Negro singer's appropriation of a great many elements of American music.* If you substituted your own word in place of *appropriation* (in the same way as you substitute your own word in the blank in the sentence-completion question), you would have arrived at some variation of the words *taking on* or *adopting*—practically synonyms for the word *appropriation,* which means "to take possession of." Besides, it continues the author's discussion in the previous paragraph, in which he talks about the elements that have come together to create ragtime. (A) is the perfect choice.

3. (B)   This question is telling you that only one of the five choices can be located in the passage. (A) is incorrect; the author clearly contradicts this statement in the next to last paragraph, in which he says *jazz should not be thought of as a successor to blues.* (B) is correct because the author says in the next to last paragraph that it is extremely difficult to say *just exactly where and when jazz or purely instrumental blues originated.* (C) is incorrect; in the sixth paragraph, the author speaks of Ma Rainey

and Bessie Smith as early blues singers, not jazz singers. (D) is not true; in the second paragraph of the passage, the author states that in the 1870s and 1880s various music elements came together to form ragtime, not jazz. (E) is an appealing possibility because the author does make such a statement in the first sentence in the next to last paragraph, but it is only for the purpose of proving it false, which the author goes on to do in the rest of the paragraph. This is an answer that was obviously designed to catch the unsuspecting student off guard.

4. (D)   This question should have presented few problems, even if you did not know the meaning of the word *hybrid.* There are ample clues in the first paragraph to help you arrive at the correct answer. Looking over your choices, you could have easily eliminated (A), in that the author says that jazz *evolved through many stages* and *from a variety of traditions;* therefore, it is the exact opposite of an original form of music. (B) is irrelevant; the question is asking for the definition of *hybrid;* besides, the author never says that it was improvised. (C) is incorrect; this idea is never stated in the passage. (D) is correct. In speaking of jazz as a hybrid form, the author goes on to explain the various elements that came together to create this style of music; *hybrid* means "anything derived from sources or elements of different kinds." (E) is irrelevant; it has nothing to do with the question.

5. (C)   Choice (A) is incorrect; in the second paragraph the author says that "early rags" were created on player-piano rolls, not early jazz. (B) is incorrect; the author refers to the banjo only in relation to its musical style or rhythm, not as an instrument that was played on; besides, the banjo reference is in the context of ragtime, not early jazz. (C) is correct. In the third paragraph from the end, the author says that with *the growing use of European instruments such as brass and reeds . . . the era of jazz was at hand.* (D) is irrelevant; it is never mentioned in the passage. (E) is incorrect; in the third paragraph from the end, the author speaks of voice as essential to blues, not jazz.

6. (E)   This question is another form of the "title" question. The answer you are looking for refers to most of the sentences in the passage. (A) is too narrow; it is briefly mentioned in this passage as one of the influences in the creation of ragtime, the earliest ancestor of jazz. (B) is irrelevant; the author never makes distinct comparisons. Besides, throughout the passage he illustrates how these forms of music evolved from and influenced one another. (C) is irrelevant; although the author says in the first paragraph that jazz is the most American of musical styles, he never discusses the development of early American music in the passage or even how it might be characterized. (D) is irrelevant. In the last paragraph the author mentions the musical and cultural parameters that bound the Negro, but only as it relates to his creative innovations in music, particularly jazz.

7. (A)   The answer is clearly stated in the last paragraph. The author says *it was this boundary . . . that provided the logic and beauty of his music.* (B) is incorrect; the author states just the opposite in the final sentence of the passage. (C) is irrelevant; it is never stated in the passage. (D) is incorrect; in fact, the author suggests just the opposite idea, that while the black musician might have been shunned by white institutions, it was this boundary that enabled him to progress. (E) is irrelevant; this answer is never stated in the passage.

8. (D)   Statement (I) is never expressed in the passage; therefore, you could have eliminated (A) and (B). In that statements (II), (III), and (IV) are part of every remaining choice, the only thing left to decide is whether statement (V) can be located in the passage. The author never says that European instruments killed the blues, nor

does he say that the blues became jazz; he says that the *blues began to change and the era of jazz was at hand.* Choice (D) is the correct answer.

9. (D) The answer to this question can be found in the next to last paragraph. Choice (D) is irrelevant; the author never refers to any musicians who claim to have been the first to play jazz. (B) is incorrect; the author says *it is extremely difficult to say just exactly where and when jazz originated.* (C) is irrelevant; the author never says this in the passage. (D) is correct. The author says *The mass migrations of Negroes throughout the South and the general liberating effect of the Emancipation make it extremely difficult to say where and when jazz originated.* (E) is incorrect; the author contradicts this; in fact, he says that *it is untrue.*

10. (B) This question is telling you that four of the five answer choices are true and can be found in the passage. The one that is not in the passage is the correct answer. (A) is true; it is stated in the third paragraph of the passage. (B) is the correct answer; the author never says that classic blues was often solely instrumental as well as vocal. He says that the primitive blues was a *vocal music* and that when Negroes began to *master more instruments, blues began to change.* (C) is true; the answer can be found in the first sentence of the second paragraph. (D) is also true; in the second paragraph the author says that classic blues reflected *many elements of popular American music.* (E) is true; this statement can be found in the first sentence of the fourth paragraph.

11. (D) This question is similar to the previous one. The author is telling you that of the five choices, the one that is *not* stated in the passage is the correct answer. You probably had no difficulty narrowing your choices down to (D); the author never says that church music was one of the elements involved in the development of *jazz.* Choices (A) and (B) can be found in the second paragraph. (C) is presented in the third paragraph from the end, and (E) is clearly expressed in the next to last paragraph in the passage.

12. (B) Remember that even though the question asks you what the author implies, you need to prove your answer by some statement in the passage. Even if you did not know that the word *legitimate* means genuine or authentic, you could have backed into the right answer by a process of elimination. Choice (A) is irrelevant; there is no evidence to prove this. Choice (B) is correct. Since the author clearly states that Negro folk music resisted all attempts to "water" it down, the author is telling the reader that Negro folk music maintained its integrity; in other words, it remained true to its unique characteristics. (C) is true but it does not answer the question. (D) is irrelevant; this answer is specifically referring to the blues in paragraph six. (E) is incorrect; when the author says in the first paragraph that "it has evolved from a variety of traditions both European and neo-African," he is specifically referring to jazz, of which Negro folk music is only "one of the decisive elements."

Part IV
Practice Reading Comprehension for Related Passages

In this section of the Reading Comprehension, the emphasis is on your ability to reason and make critical judgments based on related passages. If you have mastered the reading techniques presented in Parts I and III, and the vocabulary techniques explained in Part II, reading these passages and answering the questions should not pose a problem for you. The reason for this is because just like all of the Reading Comprehension questions, including this section on related passages, *every answer you need to find will be built into the passage.*

Techniques for Reading Related Passages

Step 1: Diagram Passage A and Passage B

The best approach for handling this section is to read passages A and B using the same diagramming techniques you learned in Parts I and III. However, in this section there are two important questions to keep in mind as you read each passage. The first question is *What position does the author take toward his subject; is he positive, negative, or objective?* The second question to ask yourself is *What arguments does the author advance to support his point of view?* Since you will be using the information from one passage to interpret the information in the other, you need to be very clear as to how the passages complement one another.

Step 2: Identify the Main Idea in Each Paragraph

In order to facilitate your reading and understanding of each passage, there are two techniques you have already learned that will prove to be the most valuable. The first technique is to put an asterisk (*) before the main ideas in each paragraph. Since you may be looking for ideas expressed in one passage that may or may not be expressed in the other, you will find yourself frequently looking back over your passages to check out information in order to narrow down your choices. So putting an asterisk before the main ideas in each paragraph will help you understand the author's point of view.

Step 3: Identify the Supporting Arguments in Each Paragraph

The third important technique is to number all of the arguments the author uses to support his ideas. This technique will enable you to glance quickly over the key points the author makes without having to reread each paragraph in detail.

Step 4: Answer the Questions by Passage

One approach you might use to ease your way through the questions in this section is to answer all of the questions that relate to passage A first; then answer all of the questions that relate to passage B. This will help you stay focused on the main points in each passage.

PRACTICE EXERCISES

Here are three reading comprehension exercises on related passages for you to practice on. The answers and explanations will follow. Handle them exactly as you handled passages in the earlier parts of this section. The first step, remember, begins with understanding the key words in the questions following the passage. Also keep in mind that except for the title question, you must be able to locate the answer within the passage. That does not mean your answer choice will be stated word for word in the passage, but it will be the only answer choice that can be proved by information in the passage.

PASSAGE 1

The next two passages are followed by questions based on their content and the relationship between them. Answer the questions on the basis of what is *stated* or *implied* in the passages, and in any introductory material that might be provided.

The following passages present contrasting views on euthanasia or mercy killing.

Passage A

Mercy for the suffering patient has been the primary reason given by those who advocate euthanasia. It is cruel to prolong intense suffering on the part of someone who is mortally ill and desires to die. Mercy dictates intervention. Furthermore, a person has a right to decide whether he should continue to live or not, and such a decision can be reached after rationally weighing the benefits of continued living against the suffering involved. If a person has such a right, it cannot be wrong for him to ask another to help him carry out his desire, nor can it be wrong for another to do so.

Proposals to legalize euthanasia would permit both acts of omission and commission resulting in death, given certain safeguards. Furthermore, there are a number of additional requirements, beyond mere consent or request, that are present in most legislative proposals: the patient must be over the age of twenty-one; the agent must be a physician who should have consulted with another physician or with some specified authority; and sometimes a period of time is required between the request for euthanasia and the act itself, during which the patient's possible change of mind must be heeded.

More important, those not competent to give consent, even if they are over the age of twenty-one, would not fit the requirements. Those who are legally incompetent, such as great numbers of retarded, have not been held capable of initiating procedures to resist medical treatment, nor have their guardians been held so capable. Much less, then, would they be able to re-

quest euthanasia. Those who are physically unable to communicate, such as the patients who are in coma, would likewise be excluded from consideration by euthanasia legislation requiring consent, in spite of the fact that much public concern with euthanasia stems from an awareness of the conditions under which their lives are prolonged.

Considering these safeguards, even if euthanasia does not always represent the most beneficial act for patients, and even if there are possibilities of cures, those few patients who would request euthanasia ought to have the right to decide whether or not they wish to take such odds and continue to suffer, or choose to die. Even if helping someone to die differs from other forms of help in that it involves destruction, and even if administered euthanasia differs from suicide, given that the act is lawful and the agent willing, those who want to perform such acts should be empowered to do so. And even if very few would actually request euthanasia, their small number does not in itself bar providing them with relief. All of these factors, as they are considered purely on an individual basis, fail to make a sufficient case against euthanasia.

Passage B

In considering a case for euthanasia, it should be kept in mind that nowhere in the long history of disagreement among doctors about the certainty of the prognosis of death has the question been resolved as to where one draws the line and determines that the patient is actually dying. A patient who is seriously ill may or may not be dying. Consequently, the proviso, that the patient be dying for euthanasia to be performed, is fraught with ambiguity. Furthermore, since mercy for the suffering patient has been the primary argument for legalizing euthanasia, it raises the question as to why only patients who are actually dying should be shown mercy, whereas those who face interminable periods of suffering must continue without relief.

Furthermore, the distinction between acts of omission and commission are central to the issue of euthanasia in regard to whether one considers euthanasia an intentional act on the part of another, or through suicide assisted or unassisted, or through omitting acts to prolong life. The question remains whether there is any difference between killing a person and letting him die through omitting a remedy. It is the ambiguous area of intentional omission which begs our greatest concern. There are no clear lines of distinction between some acts of omission and of commission.

There are other, more serious, risks involved in legalizing euthanasia. It might not always be merciful. There is the real possibility that a patient might die as a result of an error in the prognosis of their disease. Others might die who could have recovered as a result of a new approach to their illness. Still others might die who did not really wish to die, even though the request seemed genuine.

Furthermore, where dying would be merciful, and even if patients have the right to determine whether they want to continue to live or not, it might justify suicide and the refusal of life-prolonging treatment but not for another to engage in an act of killing. There seems to be a fundamental difference between helping a person end his life and engaging in an act of commission.

Furthermore, there are a very limited number of patients who suffer and are near death who are willing and able to express a desire to die in a manner that would be acceptable to courts and physicians. There are probably only a very few cases that would fall under the rubric of euthanasia that would fit the requirements of the legislative proposals suggested.

What all of this suggests is that the most serious risk to legalizing voluntary euthanasia is the fear of the abuses and errors which might result, specifically the danger to those individuals who have not requested euthanasia. Rules may be misapplied, and distinctions blurred.

1. What does the author of passage A mean by "odds" in the statement: ". . . those few patients who would request euthanasia ought to have the right to decide whether or not they wish to take such odds . . ."

   (A) decision
   (B) chance
   (C) jeopardy
   (D) intention
   (E) destiny

2. According to passage A, most legislative proposals concerning euthanasia require all of the following except

   (A) the patient must request euthanasia
   (B) the patient must be over 21 years of age
   (C) the agent must be a physician
   (D) a period of time may be mandated between the request and the act
   (E) the act must involve both commission and omission

3. The author of passage B describes the requirement that a patient be dying in order for euthanasia to be performed as

   (A) narrow
   (B) abstract
   (C) comprehensive
   (D) vague
   (E) viable

4. According to each author, what role does mercy play in decisions concerning euthanasia?

   I. Author A argues that mercy mandates intervention.
   II. Each author implies a different concept of mercy in these situations.
   III. Author B argues that mercy clarifies situations in which suffering is ambiguous.
   IV. Author B argues that mercy does not justify a person's engagement in an act of killing.
   V. Author A argues that mercy prohibits any intervention.

   (A) I and IV only
   (B) II and III only
   (C) I, II, and IV only
   (D) II and V only
   (E) II, III, and V only

5. The irony of author B's reference to "interminably" ill patients is that it implies that

   (A) suffering, nonterminal patients deserve the option of euthanasia
   (B) a patient who is ill might not be dying
   (C) legalizing euthanasia will benefit all patients
   (D) doctors cause their patients to suffer
   (E) all patients suffer for interminable periods of time

6. How does author A distinguish between "helping someone to die" and other forms of help?

   (A) helping someone to die is the same as suicide
   (B) other forms of help involve only acts of commission
   (C) helping someone to die involves destruction

(D) helping someone to die involves acts of commission, but not acts of omission
(E) other forms of help have no safeguards

7. According to passage A, which of the following groups of people is not excluded from requesting euthanasia?

(A) patients who are in a coma
(B) patients who are mentally sound and over age 21
(C) patients who are brain-dead
(D) patients who are legally incompetent
(E) patients who are mentally retarded

8. If author B were to replace the word *rubric* with a synonym, which suggested word would be most appropriate?

(A) accumulation
(B) confirmation
(C) completeness
(D) heading
(E) succession

9. Both authors are most likely to agree with which of the following statements?

(A) All patients have a right to request euthanasia.
(B) Euthanasia is always a merciful act.
(C) The determination that a patient is dying is generally clear cut.
(D) Comatose patients do not suffer and should not be allowed to experience euthanasia.
(E) Euthanasia is a very controversial and delicate issue.

10. What does author A mean when he suggests that willing agents should be "empowered"?

(A) agents should be powerful
(B) patients should be dying
(C) doctors should be impartial
(D) agents should be authorized
(E) patients should be powerless

11. By an "act of omission," author B means

(A) intentionally withholding a remedy or treatment from a patient
(B) committing a patient to an aggressive treatment program
(C) encouraging a patient to request euthanasia
(D) discharging a patient from the hospital
(E) providing a patient with additional medicines

12. When author A states "their small number does not in itself bar providing them with relief," what is he saying about minority/majority rights?

(A) The rights of the few should be determined by the majority.
(B) Despite their small numbers, the needs of the minority should be met.
(C) It is impossible to provide everyone with relief.
(D) The needs of the minority should be met if they resemble those of the majority.
(E) The minority is best able to judge the needs of the majority.

13. Which title best reflects the essence of the debate over euthanasia?

(A) Intervention
(B) Euthanasia: Mercy or Murder?
(C) Genuine Suffering
(D) Euthanasia Equals Suicide
(E) Affirmative Euthanasia

PASSAGE 2

The next two passages are followed by questions based on their content and the relationship between them. Answer the questions on the basis of what is *stated* or *implied* in the passages, and in any introductory material that might be provided.

The following passages present contrasting views on abortion.

Passage A

Pro-life supporters believe that men and women are not only intrinsically different but they have different roles to play; most pro-life activists believe that motherhood, with all that entails, is the most fulfilling role that women can have. They adhere to the traditional belief that women should be wives and mothers first. They argue that for a woman to shift gears from her emotional role in the home to a competitive role in the office is damaging to both men and women, and to their children.

Therefore, abortion is intrinsically wrong because it takes a human life and what makes women special is their ability to nourish life. Second, it is wrong because by giving women control over their fertility, it breaks up an intricate set of social relationships between men and women that has traditionally surrounded women and children. They believe, therefore, that abortion is wrong because it shifts the balance in the relationship between men and women, one which they feel is appropriate and natural. They see tenderness, morality, caring, emotionality, and self-sacrifice as the exclusive province of women; and if women cease to be traditional women, who will do the caring?

These views about the intrinsic nature of men and women also shape their views about sex. Many pro-life people see sex as sacred and values that define sexuality as a wholesome physical activity challenge everything they believe. Sex is sacred because in their view it has the capacity to be something transcendent, to bring into existence another human life; recreational sex is seen as a form of desecration.

Because pro-life people believe that the purpose of sexuality is to have children, they also believe that one should not plan the exact number and timing of children too carefully, for it is both wrong and foolish to make detailed life plans that depend upon exact control of fertility. That is not to say that pro-life people do not approve of planning. But because of their world view and their religious faith they see human planning as a matter of priorities: if individuals want fame, money, and worldly success, then they have every right to pursue them. But if they are sexually active (and married, as they should be if they are sexually active), they have an obligation to subordinate other parts of life to the responsibilities they have taken on by virtue of that activity.

More than anything else, pro-life people subscribe to a strict moral code. Morality is a straightforward set of rules that specify what is moral behavior. Thus, abortion offends the deepest moral conviction that they live by: it breaks a divine law. The Commandment says "Thou shalt not kill." For pro-life adherents, the moral status of the fetus is not a matter of personal definition; for them, it is a "human life," and taking that life clearly violates the Commandment.

Passage B

Abortion, choice, family planning, a woman's reproductive rights are not the business of government. These are essentially rooted in one's belief system, in one's personal theology, in what one believes, not only about when life begins, but also about what life means, and what life is worth. We need to be free from the harassment of crazed fundamentalists, religious and secular, and free from the pseudo-moralistic pronouncements of government. In religion, these beliefs get codified and sometimes calcified in the structures of beliefs. Thankfully, the majority of these structures believe still that choice is a theologically valid way of looking at life.

Organized religious bodies are not always the strongest, gutsiest, most courageous structures in the American social galaxy, but somewhere deep in their residual beings, something is on their books that asserts their commitment to choice, and, which after a struggle, more or less, reaffirms it. Most see choice as affirming life. They do not see it as its denial. If terminating a fetus is chosen, the majority of these systems say there are justifiable reasons for that decision and they are acceptable before God. There is no reason to feel guilty for the choice being made. These decisions are highly personal decisions and they ought not to be inhibited or prohibited by government. Government should stay out of our bedrooms, our churches, our synagogues, and our wombs.

I need no senator, no judge, no president, no assembly person to guide me in these matters, even as I need no faith-filled fundamentalist telling me what I ought to do with my own sexuality. I am infuriated by their presumptive hubris when they dare to try. I am angry for myself and for my society. But beneath the anger lies a great sadness, that America should be brought to the brink of a major tragedy; the tragedy of too many unwanted children, the tragedy of blighted lives. We see what it brings, a reoccurring cycle of poverty and frustration.

How hatefully ironic that in the name of sanctity some would force birth and then tolerate life's debasement. There is nothing sacred about conception or gestation, that is only a corridor to living. But there is something enormously sacred about the cultivation of born life. Here "compulsory pregnancy people" are most cruelly and crucially deficient. Here their concerns are conspicuously absent. In all of society's efforts to underwrite, protect, and defend the needs of the neediest, "compulsory pregnancy people" are deafeningly silent and notoriously absent. I am fed up with their pious babbling on street corners, and their absence when someone is needed to pick up the fallen and give physical succor to the sore, the sick, and the starving. Ours, then, is a two-front battle; the struggle to retain the right to choose and the struggle to obtain dignity for life once chosen.

1. According to the author of passage A, what do pro-life supporters fear will be the major consequence of a woman abandoning her role in the home?

   (A) Men will feel threatened by domineering women.
   (B) Women will hurt themselves if they switch gears to competitive jobs.
   (C) Women will have more power than men in society.

(D) Children will be brought up by men.
(E) Society will lose much of its caring, morality, and tenderness.

2. The author's tone in passage A suggests that he would most likely agree with which of the following statements?

   (A) Abortion is an acceptable alternative if individuals want fame, money, and worldly success.
   (B) Abortion might be necessary if people are sexually active and unmarried.
   (C) Abortion is inherently wrong because it takes a human life.
   (D) Abortion preserves the sacredness of sex by preventing unwanted children.
   (E) Abortion allows women to escape from their traditional, constricted roles as mothers.

3. From the words *presumptive hubris* we can infer that author B

   (A) is offended by the haughtiness of pro-life supporters
   (B) is very angry with society
   (C) respects the determination of pro-life supporters
   (D) feels that pro-life senators are upstanding citizens
   (E) finds all pro-choice people to be very arrogant

4. Passage A implies that the moral code to which pro-life people subscribe is fundamentally founded on

   (A) the assumption that all people have the responsibility to bear children
   (B) a biblical prohibition of killing
   (C) a belief in the benefits of family planning
   (D) the desire to maintain traditional male-female relationships
   (E) a conviction that women are blessed because of their ability to nourish life

5. How does each author view the concept of choice?

   I. Author A believes that people who are married and sexually active should subjugate any desires to control fertility to their obligations to procreate.
   II. Author B believes that the government should have the right to control a woman's reproductive freedoms.
   III. Author A believes that choice is sacred because sex has the potential to create human life, and is therefore transcendental.

IV. Author B believes that choice is a private, personal decision that values and affirms born life, and that does not recognize the sanctity of conception.
V. Both authors believe that choice is an intrinsic part of a democratic society.

   (A) I and II only
   (B) II and III only
   (C) V only
   (D) I and IV only
   (E) III and IV only

6. According to passage B, the fate of many unwanted children is

   (A) ironic
   (B) complex
   (C) tragic
   (D) ingenuous
   (E) antagonistic

7. In passage B, "poverty and frustration" are cited as

   (A) part of a transient cycle of breakdown and renewal
   (B) examples of America's economic problems
   (C) the main causes of childhood tragedies
   (D) the consequences of many unplanned, unwanted children
   (E) the result of the disregard for the sanctity of human life

8. How would the author of passage B describe the "strictly moral, traditional, devotional" people portrayed in passage A?

   (A) earnest, cooperative, austere
   (B) eloquent, magnanimous, emotional
   (C) dangerous, exasperating, irrational
   (D) apprehensive, opinionated, pedantic
   (E) sanctimonious, fundamentalist, presumptuous

9. The author's tone in passage B is best described as

   (A) apathetic
   (B) indignant
   (C) indifferent
   (D) conciliatory
   (E) intolerant

10. Passage A suggests that pro-life people believe that the innate character of men and women

   (A) influences views of sexuality
   (B) dictates that men are strong, whereas women are powerless

(C) ensures a belief in the virtues of recreational sex

(D) guarantees a desire to procreate

(E) leads to the embrace of a strict moral code

11. When the author of passage B states that the decisions surrounding abortion are "highly personal decisions," he implies that

(A) the government has a moral responsibility to become involved in the personal matters of its citizens

(B) people considering abortion should seek help at local church, synagogue, and governmental offices

(C) these decisions are difficult because they affect the fate of a potential, unborn person

(D) the individual should have the right to make a private decision, free from governmental interference

(E) an individual's private, personal theology does not influence his/her decision to consider abortion

12. Which of the following best expresses the central meaning of passage A?

(A) obligations and responsibilities

(B) motherhood

(C) transcendent sexuality

(D) life is sacred

(E) the natural order of things

13. Which author would most likely agree with the statement: "We must first and foremost protect the dignity and welfare of the living"?

(A) A only

(B) Both A and B

(C) B only

(D) Neither A nor B

(E) This statement is unrelated to either passage

PASSAGE 3

The two passages below are followed by questions based on their content and the relationship between them. Answer the questions on the basis of what is *stated* or *implied* in the passages, and in any introductory material that might be provided.

The following passages contain contrasting views on animal conservation.

Passage A

In every part of the world the natural balance between predators and their prey is an extremely important factor in maintaining the status quo. The consequences of any significant interference with the balance of nature can be serious. Leopards, for example, prey mainly upon baboons and bush pigs, both of which can cause great devastation of crops if their numbers are allowed to increase dramatically. And this is just what happened. The virtual elimination of the leopards has enabled these two species to increase to plague proportions, necessitating special measures to protect crops from excessive devastation. One important threat to animal populations arises from the increase in human populations all over the world and the attempts to improve their standards of living. Conservationists recognize that as more land is brought under cultivation to meet these needs, so less remains available for wildlife, which in consequence must accept a reduction in numbers. What they are anxious to ensure is that sufficient of each species shall remain to guarantee its continued existence. To demand that no such diminuation should be tolerated would be to fly in the face of the facts of twentieth-century realities.

The capture and export of excessive numbers of certain species of animals is another important factor leading to dangerous reductions in numbers. Live animals are exported in large numbers for several reasons: to maintain supplies to zoos, to supply the large demands for certain species used in medical research, and to supply the pet trade. Various species of monkeys have become extremely important in medical research and in the preparation of vaccines, particularly polio vaccine. It has been calculated that the annual turnover in monkeys by the medical profession is something like 25,000. The demand falls mainly upon a few species and it is questionable for how long these species can meet such demands without becoming in danger of extinction.

However alert conservation bodies may be, it seems almost inevitable that certain threatened species will in the end suffer extinction in the wild. The numbers of some animal species may already have fallen below the minimum necessary to guarantee their survival even with complete protection; or the authorities of the countries in which they live may give no heed to the warnings and pleas of the conservationists. Even if a species is finally doomed to extinction as a wild species, preservation is still not impossible provided measures to build up breeding stocks in captivity are taken in time.

Zoos throughout the world today realize that their most important role is saving threatened animals from extinction, and they can only do this by learning how to breed these animals in sufficient numbers in captivity. But their efforts so far have shown that conditions which will enable a particular animal to survive and live to a ripe old age may not allow it to breed satisfactorily. The conditions needed for successful breeding are undoubtedly more critical than those needed for successful survival.

Passage B

To convince people and government that the destruction of species will upset the natural balance of the communities of which they form a part is not such an easy task. But the need to conserve animals which are economically valuable will be obvious to any businessman, who will appreciate the possible consequences of extinction to his own or others' pockets. Even so he may well be prepared to risk destroying a species provided that in doing so he can make a quick profit for himself. Some of the larger species of whales are facing extinction today because the international whaling fraternity is not prepared to settle for a somewhat lower profit in order to ensure the continued existence of animals upon which their prosperity depends. Even the fur trade, while it understands quite clearly the inevitable consequences of its illicit trading in leopard skins, for example, continues its large-scale poaching and smuggling operations.

By 1964 it was estimated that the annual export of leopard skins from East Africa alone had reached something like 50,000. Illicit trading in leopard skins had become the most profitable and skillfully organized racket in East Africa. And as leopard skins become scarce, the price goes up, and as the price goes up, so poaching becomes more worthwhile because the rewards are greater.

Hunting for what might be described as pleasure, as distinct from hunting commercially valuable animals, has also played a part in reducing animals' numbers in the past, though today the big game hunter is, himself, facing extinction, partly because of the prohibitive cost of organizing safaris and partly through restrictions which have been increasingly imposed upon his activities in recent decades by governments anxious to conserve their dwindling wildlife. Such are the dangers which these so-called "sportsmen" brought to the continued existence of the Kodiak bear during the latter part of the nineteenth century. The giant brown bears of Alaska and Kodiak Island have no commercial or economic value to the native populations, nor do they interfere with agriculture or any other human activity. Yet, they, too, have been facing considerable

danger of ultimate extinction since before the end of the nineteenth century through the utter selfishness of the big game hunter.

To shoot a Kodiak bear became the proof that the hunter was in the premier class. This might not have mattered if he had been content to secure his trophy and return home with it. But having arrived at great personal expense, he regarded it as a great pity to leave without having slaughtered the largest number of bears, regardless of the fact that apart from his one trophy, the remainder would be of little or no use to him. Such was the mentality of the so-called sportsmen of the nineteenth and early twentieth centuries.

Undoubtedly the most effective method of preserving any animal threatened with extinction is for the country in which it lives to grant it absolute protection, which means that no one may kill specimens or capture them and send them abroad. There are three ways in which this can be achieved. A general prohibition order forbidding killing or capture can be effective if the animal is generally distributed in the country. If it is confined to a restricted area, then this area can be declared a sanctuary for the animal. Where there is a need to protect not only the one species but a number of other native species as well, this can best be achieved by setting up a national park, where all killing is forbidden. Many animals are migratory, living in different areas in the winter and summer. Therefore, to be effective, reserves and national parks must include both habitats as well as the migration routes between them, otherwise the protection given is only partial.

The value of natural predators to the animals on which they prey has been confirmed on Isle Royale, an island national park in Lake Superior where moose have always been abundant. Their numbers fluctuated, however. They would reach a peak of two or three thousand and then decline rapidly, because they had so outstripped the available grazing area that large numbers of them died of starvation. After these mass deaths even those which survived were in poor condition, and they remained in a weak state until the grazing had had a chance to recover.

During this period of population fluctuation the moose had no natural enemies. During the winter of 1949, however, following one of the periodic starvation cycles, a pack of timber wolves crossed the fifteen miles of ice from the Canadian shore. Today both the moose and the grazing are always in good condition. The wolves prevent the moose population growing sufficiently to outstrip its food supply. Their culling, however, is selective, the vast majority of those killed being either old or sick, thus leaving the strongest and healthiest to provide the next generation. As a result Isle Royale now has one of the most flourishing moose populations in the whole of North America.

1. Passage A suggests that an indirect result of a decreased leopard population would be

    (A) greater safety for humans
    (B) a decrease in bush pig populations
    (C) an increase in human populations
    (D) excessive crop devastation
    (E) a decrease in plague proportions

2. A possible reason given by author B for the "virtual elimination of leopards" mentioned in passage A is

    (A) leopards are killed by Kodiak bears
    (B) leopard skins are economic assets
    (C) pleasure hunters kill leopards
    (D) leopards have difficulty breeding
    (E) leopards are hosts to various plagues

3. What does author A mean by "absolute" protection?

    (A) unqualified
    (B) indomitable
    (C) partial
    (D) elaborate
    (E) incomplete

4. The organized trading racket described in passage B could alternately be described as a(n)

    (A) unauthorized free trade agreement
    (B) illegal trade organization
    (C) chartered trade association
    (D) legitimate business establishment
    (E) legal speculation

5. Why does author A fear that some species might become extinct despite conservation efforts?

    (A) Some conservation efforts are too extreme.
    (B) Many sanctuaries provide hostile environments.
    (C) Migration routes might be disrupted.
    (D) Some species might escape from national parks.
    (E) The numbers of some species might be too low to support survival.

6. According to passages A and B, all of the following are threats to animal populations except

    (A) humans' increased standard of living
    (B) increased land cultivation

    (C) increased breeding of animal stocks in captivity
    (D) increased economic value of animal skins
    (E) increased human populations

7. From passage B one can conclude that the shooting of a Kodiak bear

    (A) established a hunter's reputation as an expert
    (B) helped keep the bear population under control
    (C) was economically beneficial to the hunters
    (D) was required to protect agricultural investments
    (E) was the selfless act of a game hunter

8. Author A implies that, compared to the conditions needed for captured animals to survive, those needed to ensure successful breeding are

    (A) more trivial
    (B) less profuse
    (C) equal in significance
    (D) more critical
    (E) more equivocal

9. According to passage A, why must a national park be large?

    (A) Some animals are confined to a restricted area.
    (B) It must contain both migration routes and seasonal habitats.
    (C) Certain species propagate better in large areas.
    (D) It is more difficult to capture wild animals in a large area.
    (E) Some native species are generally distributed throughout a country.

10. Passage B implies that which of the following reasons will convince communities to conserve animals?

    (A) People have a humanitarian responsibility to respect animal life.
    (B) Trade in animal parts is not profitable.
    (C) Animals have economic value.
    (D) Governments restrict the killing of certain species.
    (E) Capture of some animals is an arduous task.

11. The attitude of author B toward pleasure hunters is best described as

    (A) judgmental
    (B) ambivalent

(C) satirical

(D) didactic

(E) indiscriminate

12. Authors A and B would most likely agree that

  (A) governments make too many animal conservation restrictions

  (B) there is no economic profit to be gained in killing animals

  (C) the number of national parks should be greatly reduced

  (D) the severity of animal conservation regulations should be increased

  (E) some authorities and traders pay no attention to conservation warnings

13. From passage B it can be inferred that the mentality of nineteenth- and early twentieth-century sportsmen was

  (A) environmentally conscious, restrained, attentive

  (B) abstracted, heedless, absorbed

  (C) communal, self-sacrificing, excessive

  (D) careless, imprudent, inconsiderate

  (E) expedient, innocuous, profitable

ANSWERS AND EXPLANATIONS, PASSAGES 1–3

Passage 1
  1. (B) 2. (E) 3. (D) 4. (D) 5. (A) 6. (C)
  7. (B) 8. (D) 9. (E) 10. (D) 11. (A) 12. (B)
  13. (B)

Passage 2
  1. (E) 2. (C) 3. (A) 4. (B) 5. (D) 6. (C)
  7. (D) 8. (E) 9. (B) 10. (A) 11. (D) 12. (D)
  13. (C)

Passage 3
  1. (D) 2. (B) 3. (A) 4. (B) 5. (E) 6. (C)
  7. (A) 8. (D) 9. (B) 10. (C) 11. (A) 12. (E)
  13. (D)

PASSAGE 1

Passage A

Mercy for the suffering patient has been the primary reason given by those who advocate euthanasia. It is cruel to prolong intense suffering on the part of someone who is mortally ill and desires to die. Mercy dictates intervention. Furthermore, a person has a right to decide whether he should continue to live or not, and such a decision can be reached after rationally weighing the benefits of continued living against the suffering involved. If a person has such a right, it cannot be wrong for him to ask another to help him carry out his desire, nor can it be wrong for another to do so.

Proposals to legalize euthanasia would permit both acts of omission and commission resulting in death, given certain safeguards. Furthermore, there are a number of additional requirements, beyond mere consent or request, that are present in most legislative proposals: the patient must be over the age of twenty-one; the agent must be a physician who should have consulted with another physician or with some specified authority; sometimes a period of time is required between the request for euthanasia and the act itself, during which the patient's possible change of mind must be heeded.

More important, those not competent to give consent, even if they are over the age of twenty-one, would not fit the requirements. Those who are legally incompetent, such as great numbers of retarded, have not been held capable of initiating procedures to resist medical treatment, nor have their guardians been held so capable. Much less, then, would they be able to request euthanasia. Those who are physically unable to communicate, such as the patients who are in coma, would likewise be excluded from consideration by euthanasia legislation requiring consent, in spite of the fact that much public concern with euthanasia stems from an awareness of the conditions under which their lives are prolonged.

Considering these safeguards, even if euthanasia does not always represent the most beneficial act for patients, and even if there are possibilities of cures, those few patients who would request euthanasia ought to have the right to decide whether or not they wish to take such odds and continue to suffer, or choose to die. Even if helping someone to die differs from other forms of help in that it involves destruction, and even if administered euthanasia differs from suicide, given that the act is lawful and the agent willing, those who want to perform such acts should be empowered to do so. And even if very few would actually request euthanasia, their small number does not in itself bar providing them with relief. All of these factors, as they are considered purely on an individual basis, fail to make a sufficient case against euthanasia.

Passage B

In considering a case for euthanasia, it should be kept in mind that nowhere in the long history of disagreement among doctors about the certainty of the prognosis of death has the question been resolved as to where one draws the line and determines that the patient is actually dying. A patient who is seriously ill, may or may not be dying. Consequently, the proviso, that the patient be dying for euthanasia to be performed, is fraught with ambiguity. Furthermore, since mercy for the suffering patient has been the primary argument for legalizing euthanasia, it raises the question as to why only patients who are actually dying should be shown mercy, whereas those who face interminable periods of suffering must continue without relief.

Furthermore, the distinction between acts of omission and commission are central to the issue of euthanasia in regard to whether one considers euthanasia an intentional act on the part of another, or through suicide assisted or unassisted, or through omitting acts to prolong life. The question remains whether there is any difference between killing a person and letting him die through omitting a remedy. It is the ambiguous area of intentional omission which begs our greatest concern. There are no clear lines of distinction between some acts of omission and of commission.

There are other, more serious, risks involved in legalizing euthanasia. It might not always be merciful. There is the real possibility that a patient might die as a result of an error in the prognosis of their disease. Others might die who could have recovered as a result of a new approach to their illness. Still others might die who did not really wish to die; even though the request seemed genuine.

Furthermore, where dying would be merciful, and even if patients have the right to determine whether they want to continue to live or not, it might justify suicide and the refusal of life-prolonging treatment but not for another to engage in an act of killing. There seems to be a fundamental difference between helping a person end his life and engaging in an act of commission.

Furthermore, there are a very limited number of patients who suffer and are near death who are willing and able to express a desire to die in a manner that would be acceptable to courts and physicians. There are probably only a very few cases that would fall under the rubric of euthanasia that would fit the requirements of the legislative proposals suggested.

What all of this suggests is that the most serious risk to legalizing voluntary euthanasia is the fear of the abuses and errors which might result, specifically the danger ★
① to those individuals who have not requested euthanasia. Rules may be misapplied, and
② distinctions blurred.

1. (B)   If you look at the first sentence in the final paragraph of the passage, you probably realize that the word *odds* means "the balance of probability in favor of something occurring." With that definition in mind, you might have interpreted the sentence to mean that a patient should have the right to decide whether or not he desires to undergo prolonged suffering on the "outside chance" that there might be a cure for his disease or to request euthanasia. *Possibilities of cures* does not mean "certainty." Therefore, in that the patient cannot know if, in fact, a cure will be found, it is up to him to "take a *chance*," to make a decision, one way or another, based solely on probability. (B) is the perfect choice.

2. (E)   This question is telling you that four of the five answer choices can be found in the passage. The one that is not is the correct answer. You could have backed into choice (E), in that all of the other answer choices are explicitly stated in the second paragraph of the passage.

3. (D)   The answer can be found in the third sentence of passage (B); in fact, it is the main idea of the paragraph. The author states that *the proviso, that the patient be dying for euthanasia to be performed, is fraught with ambiguity.* If you were not certain as to the meaning of the word *ambiguity,* you should know from the prefix *ambi-* that the word has the meaning of "both." If you look at the preceding sentence, the author says that even though a person is seriously ill, he *may or may not be dying.* Therefore, you know that the word *ambiguity* has something to do with mixed or double messages. Your most important clue, however, is in the first sentence of the passage in which the author explicitly states *Nowhere has the question been resolved as to where one draws the line and determines that the patient is actually dying.* The best answer is choice (D); *ambiguity* means "doubtfulness" or "uncertainty."

4. (C)   This question clearly demonstrates the importance of diagramming main ideas and supporting evidence, in that you need to quickly identify the points of comparison in both passages, as well as to pinpoint the differences. In this type of question it is especially important to back into the answer by a process of elimination. You probably realized that statement (I) is true. It is stated word for word in the second sentence of the passage. Besides, you probably noted that this was the author's main point, which he expressed in the very first sentence. The following step is very important. In that you now know that statement (I) is true, you can easily eliminate (B), (D), and (E) because it is obvious that statement (I) is not included as part of these answers. Left with choices (A) and (C), you probably realized that statement (IV) is true because it is included in both of the remaining answers. The final step in narrowing down your choices is to decide whether statement (II) is true or not. Looking back over both passages, you will see that the author in passage A defines mercy as an act of intervention required to end suffering because it is *cruel to prolong it.* In passage B, the author suggests that the most merciful choice might mean not risking someone's life. There are too many possibilities for error.

5. (A)   The correct answer can be found in the last sentence of the first paragraph. Choice (B) is incorrect because the irony in question does not refer to the idea that the patient who is ill might not be dying but, rather, why euthanasia should be performed on only those patients who are dying and not on those who face prolonged periods of suffering. Choices (C), (D), and (E) are never mentioned in the passage.

6. (C)   Choice (A) is incorrect because the author states just the opposite in the last paragraph: *euthanasia differs from suicide, given that the act is lawful and the agent willing.* (B) is incorrect because the author never says that; in fact, in talking about euthanasia in the first sentence of the second paragraph, the author says that *proposals to legalize euthanasia would permit both acts of omission and commission.* (C) is stated clearly in the second sentence of the last paragraph. (D) is incorrect for the same reason as choice (B). (E) is never mentioned in the passage.

7. (B)   This question is telling you that four of the five choices are stated in the passage. Only one answer is not. You could have backed into the right answer, in that (A), (D), and (E) are explicitly stated in the second paragraph. Although the author never uses the word *brain-dead,* we can assume that these are the patients who are "not competent to give consent" or "physically unable to communicate." The answer, therefore, is (B).

8. (D)   This question should have presented few problems even if you did not know the meaning of the word *rubric.* In diagramming the two sentences that make up this paragraph there are ample clues to help you arrive at the correct answer. You might have realized that the second sentence is a reiteration of the first. The first sentence describes the physical and psychological requirements for patients who would be *acceptable* by *courts* and *physicians* to be considered for euthanasia. In the following sentence, if you substitute for the word *rubric* each of the available choices, chances are you came up with (D) as your answer. The word *rubric* means a "title" or "heading."

9. (E)   Choice (A) is irrelevant; neither passage is concerned with whether or not a patient has a right to *request* euthanasia; a person has a right to *request* anything he wants. These passages are concerned with one specific issue: whether given certain safeguards, agents who are willing to administer euthanasia should be allowed to do so. (B) is incorrect because in both passages the authors contradict the statement. (Be careful of answers that make sweeping generalizations such as *all* or *always;* often on the basis of one such word the entire answer can be eliminated.) In passage A, in the first sentence of the last paragraph, the author says, *even if euthanasia does not always represent the most beneficial act for patients,* and in passage B, the author explicitly states in the third paragraph, *It might not always be merciful.*

10. (D)   If you read the second sentence in the last paragraph, in which the author states, *given that the act is lawful and the agent willing, those who want to perform such acts should be empowered to do so,* chances are the word that came to mind in place of *empowered* was something like *allowed.* You probably realized that you were looking for a positive word. That would eliminate (B) and (E) because both answers are negative. In that most students know that *impartial* means "unbiased," or free from prejudice, you would have realized that (C) is irrelevant. Left with (A) and (D), it should be obvious that you are not looking for a word that means "to be strong physically"; it simply doesn't fit. The answer, of course is (D); the word *empowered* means "authorized to" or "permitted to."

11. (A)   Choice (A) is correct because the answer is presented in the second paragraph. In the first two sentences, the author distinguishes between acts of commission, "intentional acts on the part of another," and acts of omission, "omitting acts to prolong life." You could have eliminated (B) and (E) because both answers are acts of commission, the exact opposite meaning we are looking for. (C) and (D) are both irrelevant; they have no relationship to acts of omission.

12. (B)   Choice (A) is incorrect because the author never says that; in fact, he says just the opposite. (B) is correct; the answer to this question can be found in the next to last

sentence in the passage. The important clue is in the words *even if* in the first part of the sentence. (You can easily substitute the words *in spite of* for *even if.*) These words usually signal that whatever idea is expressed in the first part of this sentence, it will be contradicted in the second part; that is, in the *event* or *outside chance* something unforeseen happens, plans should be carried out as originally intended. The second important clue is the word *few,* referring to the number of patients that would request euthanasia. You probably realize that your sentence means that even though a small number of patients request euthanasia, it should be performed anyway; it should not *bar* or prevent them from getting relief. Choice (C) is irrelevant; *relief* is mentioned in the sentence but it does not answer the question. Choices (D) and (E) are never mentioned in the passage, but would mean just the opposite even if they were.

13. (B)   Remember, because this is the "title" question, you are looking for an answer that deals with most of the lines in the passage. Choice (A) is too narrow; the idea of intervention is considered in both passages, but it is directly out of context. (B) is clearly the main concern of both passages, especially in that one of the key words in the question is the word *debate,* which is expressed in the words *mercy or murder.* (C) is incorrect; it is too narrow. It bears no relevance to the issue of euthanasia. (D) is also irrelevant. Although the idea of suicide is expressed in the controversy of whether or not to legalize euthanasia, the author explicitly states in passage A that *administered euthanasia differs from suicide.* A similar idea is expressed in the next to last paragraph in passage B, in which the author states that *even if patients have the right to determine whether they want to continue to live or not, it might justify suicide . . . but not for another to engage in an act of killing.* (E) is an intriguing idea because a part of the controversy is a consideration of euthanasia as a merciful act, but it is far too narrow to be considered as the main idea of both passages. Besides, it bypasses the central theme, which focuses primarily on the controversial aspects of euthanasia.

PASSAGE 2

Passage A

Pro-life supporters believe that men and women are not only intrinsically different but they have different roles to play; most pro-life activists believe that motherhood, with all that entails, is the most fulfilling role that women can have. They adhere to the traditional belief that women should be wives and mothers first. They argue that for a woman to shift gears from her emotional role in the home to a competitive role in the office is damaging to both men and women, and to their children.

Therefore, abortion is intrinsically wrong because it takes a human life and what makes women special is their ability to nourish life. Second, it is wrong because by giving women control over their fertility, it breaks up an intricate set of social relationships between men and women that has traditionally surrounded women and children. They believe, therefore, that abortion is wrong because it shifts the balance in the relationship between men and women, one which they feel is appropriate and natural. They see tenderness, morality, caring, emotionality, and self-sacrifice as the exclusive province of women; and if women cease to be traditional women, who will do the caring?

These views about the intrinsic nature of men and women also shape their views about sex. Many pro-life people see sex as sacred and values that define sexuality as a wholesome physical activity challenge everything they believe. Sex is sacred because in their view it has the capacity to be something transcendent, to bring into existence another human life; recreational sex is seen as a form of desecration.

Because pro-life people believe that the purpose of sexuality is to have children, they also believe that one should not plan the exact number and timing of children too carefully, for it is both wrong and foolish to make detailed life plans that depend upon exact control of fertility. // That is not to say that pro-life people do not approve of planning. // But because of their world view and their religious faith they see human planning as a matter of priorities: if individuals want fame, money, and worldly success, then they have every right to pursue them. // But if they are sexually active (and married, as they should be if they are sexually active), they have an obligation to subordinate other parts of life to the responsibilities they have taken on by virtue of that activity.

More than anything else, pro-life people subscribe to a strict moral code. Morality is a straightforward set of rules that specify what is moral behavior. Thus, abortion offends the deepest moral convictions that they live by: it breaks a divine law. The Commandment says "Thou shalt not kill." For pro-life adherents, the moral status of the fetus is not a matter of personal definition. For them it is a "human life," and taking that life clearly violates the Commandment. ★

Passage B

Abortion, choice, family planning, a woman's reproductive rights are not the business of government. These are essentially rooted in one's belief system, in one's ★ personal theology, in what one believes, not only about when life begins, but also about what life means, and what life is worth. We need to be free from the harassment of crazed fundamentalists, religious and secular, and free from the pseudo moralistic pronouncements of government. In religion, these beliefs get codified and sometimes calcified in the structures of beliefs. Thankfully, the majority of these structures believe still that choice is a theologically valid way of looking at life.

// Organized religious bodies are not always the strongest, gutsiest, most courageous structures in the American social galaxy, // but somewhere deep in their residual beings, something is on their books that asserts their commitment to choice ★ and, which after a struggle, more or less, reaffirms it. Most see choice as affirming life. // They do not see it as its denial. // If terminating a fetus is chosen, the majority of ① these systems say there are justifiable reasons for that decision and they are acceptable before God. There is no reason to feel guilty for the choice being made. These decisions are highly personal decisions and they ought not to be inhibited or prohibited by government. Government should stay out of our bedrooms, our churches, our ② synagogues, and our wombs.

I need no senator, no judge, no president, no assembly person to guide me in these matters, even as I need no faith-filled fundamentalist telling me what I ought to do with my own sexuality. I am infuriated by their presumptive hubris when they dare to ★ try. I am angry for myself and for my society. // But beneath the anger lies a great sadness that America should be brought to the brink of a major tragedy; the tragedy of too many unwanted children, the tragedy of blighted lives. We see what it brings, a reoccurring cycle of poverty and frustration.

★ // How hatefully ironic that in the name of sanctity some would force birth and then ① tolerate life's debasement. There is nothing sacred about conception or gestation, that ② is only a corridor to living. // But, there is something enormously sacred about the cultivation of born life. Here "compulsory pregnancy people" are most cruelly and crucially deficient. Here their concerns are conspicuously absent. In all of society's efforts to underwrite, protect, and defend the needs of the neediest, "compulsory pregnancy people" are deafeningly silent and notoriously absent. // I am fed up with their pious babbling on street corners, and their absence when someone is needed to ③ pick up the fallen and give physical succor to the sore, the sick, and the starving. // ① Ours then is a two-front battle, the struggle to retain the right to choose and the ★ struggle to obtain dignity for life once chosen. ②

1. **(E)** Choice (A) is incorrect because the author says that the major consequence of a woman abandoning her role in the home is to shift the balance between men and women; he never says that "men will feel threatened by domineering women." (B) might be misleading for some students. The author never says that women will hurt themselves if they switch gears to competitive jobs, but he does say that a shift to competitive jobs will be damaging to both men and women; furthermore, in the next paragraph he says that it is the *relationship* that will suffer. (C) is incorrect because in the second paragraph the only idea of power the author discusses is giving women control over their fertility; it has nothing to do with having more power than men. (D) is irrelevant; the author never suggests that children will be raised by men. (E) can be found in the last sentence of the second paragraph. It is summed up in the words *if women cease to be traditional women, who will do the caring?*

2. **(C)** Remember that even though the question asks what the author's *tone* or *attitude* is, you must be able to prove the answer by some statement in the passage. (A) is incorrect; the author emphatically contradicts this statement. In the next to last paragraph, the words *fame, money,* and *worldly success* are taken directly out of context, but the author is discussing *family planning,* not abortion. (B) is dead wrong; throughout the entire passage, the author takes the pro-life position that abortion is wrong. His reference to being *sexually active* in the next to last paragraph refers to *family planning as a matter of priorities.* (C) is the right answer. It can be found in the last paragraph. (D) is incorrect; the entire passage, especially the last paragraph, stresses the idea that abortion is wrong and violates divine law. (E) is irrelevant; it is never stated in the passage.

3. **(A)** The correct answer can be found in the next to last paragraph. It should be clear from your diagramming that there are several important clues to help you narrow down your choices. The important clue in the second sentence is the word *infuriated* because it suggests that you are looking for a negative answer. Looking over your choices, it would be possible to eliminate (C) and (D) because both answers are obviously positive. (B) has a certain appeal because the author does say *I am angry . . . for my society* but he is referring to a very specific part of society, the anti-choice people. (E) is dead wrong; it is the anti-choice people he finds to be arrogant, not the pro-choice. But the author clearly states in the first sentence of this paragraph that he is *infuriated* with people such as the *faith-filled fundamentalist telling me what to do.* (A) is the perfect choice; *presumptive hubris* implies an "arrogant assumption of one's own superiority."

4. **(B)** Choice (A) is incorrect because the passage does not say that the moral code to which pro-life people subscribe is that all people have the "responsibility" to bear children. Rather, in the last paragraph of the passage it says that the moral code prohibits abortion because it breaks a divine law. (B) is the right answer. It can be found in the last two sentences of the passage. (C) is incorrect; in fact, the author states just the opposite idea in the first sentence of the fourth paragraph: *it is both wrong and foolish to make detailed life plans that depend upon exact control of fertility.* (D) is incorrect; although the author states in the opening paragraph that pro-life people *adhere to the traditional belief that women should be wives and mothers first,* he never states that this is the moral code on which their position is founded. (E) is incorrect for a similar reason as (D); although in the first sentence of the second paragraph the author says that a woman's ability to nourish life is what makes them special, he never states that this is their moral code.

5. **(D)** Statement (I) is explicitly stated in the next to last paragraph in the passage. You could have immediately eliminated choices (B), (C), and (E) because statement (I) is not a part of these answers. With choices (A) and (D) remaining, you would eas-

ily have eliminated (A), in that statement (II) totally contradicts the point of the entire passage. You could have backed into choice (D), the correct answer. Statement (IV) is found in the first paragraph, in which the author stresses the idea that choice *is not the business of government,* and in the second sentence of the final paragraph, in which he says *There is nothing sacred about conception.*

6. (C) Choice (A) is incorrect; the only mention of irony is in the first sentence of the last paragraph, but in this context, irony refers to the author's attitude toward the position of pro-life people; it never refers to the fate of unwanted children. (B) is irrelevant; it is never stated in the passage. Choices (D) and (E) are also irrelevant; ingenuous means "frank" or "candid," and *antagonistic* means "in opposition to something." Choice (C) is correct; in the third paragraph the author explicitly states that the fate of unwanted children is a "major tragedy," specifically "the tragedy of blighted lives."

7. (D) Choice (A) is irrelevant; it is never stated in the passage. (D) is the correct answer and is clearly stated in the third paragraph. The author says it is the tragedy of unwanted children that brings *a reoccurring cycle of poverty and frustration.* (B) is irrelevant; the author never cites "poverty and frustration" as examples of Americans' economic problems. (C) is incorrect; poverty and frustration are not cited as the main causes of childhood tragedy; they are presented as the result of the tragedy of unwanted children.

8. (E) The question asks you to state the attitude of author B toward the pro-life supporters described in passage A. You could have easily backed into the correct answer. In that you know that the attitude of author B is negative, you could have eliminated (A) and (B) because at least two out of the three adjectives in each answer are positive. (C) is irrelevant; nowhere in the passage does the author use these words to describe the compulsory pregnancy people. (D) is incorrect; although pro-life supporters could be considered opinionated and pedantic, which means "to be excessively firm in one's beliefs," they exhibit no "apprehension" or "anxiety." Remember that even though an answer seems possible, you must be able to locate it in the passage. The answer, of course, is (E); the words *fundamentalist* and *presumptuous* can be found in the first sentence of the third paragraph, and the word *sanctimonious,* which means "making a show of" or "pretense of holiness," is evident in the first sentence of the final paragraph.

9. (B) The way to recognize the author's tone is to ask how the author intends for us to feel about the subject and then to locate the answer in the passage. You could have easily backed into the correct answer. The author's attitude toward pro-life supporters is clearly expressed in the next to last paragraph, in which he says *I am infuriated . . . when they dare to try,* and in the next to last line in the passage: *I am fed up with their pious babbling.* The only word that reflects the author's attitude and the tone of his remarks is *indignant,* choice (B), which means "displeasure at something deemed unworthy."

10. (A) The correct answer can be found in the first sentence of the third paragraph. (B) is irrelevant; although the author discusses the idea of giving women control over their fertility, he never says that men are strong and women are powerless. (C) is totally wrong; in fact, the author states just the opposite, that there is nothing virtuous in recreational sex. He says: *recreational sex is seen as a form of desecration.* (D) is irrelevant; it is never stated in the passage. (E) is incorrect; the author never says that the innate character of men and women leads to a *strict moral code.* He says it shapes their views that *sex is sacred.*

11. (D)   Remember that even though the question asks you what the author *implies,* you must be able to prove the answer by some statement in the passage. Choice (A) is incorrect; the author states just the opposite idea in the first sentence of the passage. (B) is irrelevant. The question is referring to the relationship of government to decisions regarding abortion; it has nothing to do with where one should go to seek help. (C) is incorrect because the question has nothing to do with the difficulty or ease of making a decision regarding abortion. (D) is correct; the answer is found in the next to last sentence of the second paragraph: *These decisions . . . ought not to be inhibited or prohibited by government.* (E) is untrue; the author takes the exact opposite position. In the first paragraph he states *Abortion, choice . . . are essentially rooted in one's belief system, in one's personal theology.*

12. (D)   This question is another form of the "title" question. You are looking for an answer that deals with most of the lines in the passage. Choice (A) is too broad; the answer never identifies to what or to whom these obligations and responsibilities refer. (B) is too narrow; the author's discussion of motherhood is only one aspect of the larger concern of this passage, which is why pro-life supporters believe that abortion is wrong. (C) is too narrow; the idea of sexuality as transcendent is mentioned only in the third paragraph. (D) is correct because almost every paragraph in this passage deals with some aspect of the idea that pro-life supporters believe that human life is sacred. (E) is irrelevant; it is an idea suggested by the discussion of birth control in the fourth paragraph, but only amounts to words taken out of context.

13. (C)   Remember that you must be able to locate the answer to this question in one of the two passages. Choice (A) is incorrect; the author never states his concern for the dignity and welfare of the living. His arguments only concern those of the unborn fetus. Therefore, you can easily eliminate (B) and (D). (C) can be found in more than one place in the passage, particularly in the last sentence: *ours then is a two-front battle . . . the struggle to obtain dignity for life once chosen.* (E) is incorrect because the author of passage B does support this idea.

PASSAGE 3

Passage A

In every part of the world the natural balance between predators and their prey is an extremely important factor in maintaining the status quo. The consequences of any significant interference with the balance of nature can be serious. Leopards, for example, prey mainly upon baboons and bush pigs, both of which can cause great devastation of crops if their numbers are allowed to increase dramatically. And this is just what happened. The virtual elimination of the leopards has enabled these two species to increase to plague proportions, necessitating special measures to protect crops from excessive devastation. One important threat to animal populations arises from the increase in human populations all over the world and the attempts to improve their standards of living. // Conservationists recognize that as more land is brought under cultivation to meet these needs, so less remains available for wildlife, which in consequence must accept a reduction in numbers. What they are anxious to ensure is that sufficient of each species shall remain to guarantee its continued existence. To demand that no such diminuation should be tolerated would be to fly in the face of the facts of twentieth-century realities.

The capture and export of excessive numbers of certain species of animals is another important factor leading to dangerous reductions in numbers. Live animals are exported in large numbers for several reasons: to maintain supplies to zoos, to supply the large demands for certain species used in medical research, and to supply the pet trade. Various species of monkeys have become extremely important in medical research and in the preparation of vaccines, particularly polio vaccine. It has been calculated that the annual turnover in monkeys by the medical profession is something like 25,000. The demand falls mainly upon a few species and it is questionable for how long these species can meet such demands without becoming in danger of extinction.

However alert conservation bodies may be, it seems almost inevitable that certain threatened species will in the end suffer extinction in the wild. The numbers of some animal species may already have fallen below the minimum necessary to guarantee their survival even with complete protection; or the authorities of the countries in which they live may give no heed to the warnings and pleas of the conservationists. Even if a species is finally doomed to extinction as a wild species, preservation is still not impossible provided measures to build up breeding stocks in captivity are taken in time.

Zoos throughout the world today realize that their most important role is saving threatened animals from extinction, and they can only do this by learning how to breed these animals in sufficient numbers in captivity. But their efforts so far have shown that conditions which will enable a particular animal to survive and live to a ripe old age may not allow it to breed satisfactorily. The conditions needed for successful breeding are undoubtedly more critical than those needed for successful survival.

Passage B

To convince people and government that the destruction of species will upset the natural balance of the communities of which they form a part is not such an easy task. But the need to conserve animals which are economically valuable will be obvious to any businessman, who will appreciate the possible consequences of extinction to his own or others' pockets. Even so he may well be prepared to risk destroying a species provided that in doing so he can make a quick profit for himself. Some of the larger species of whales are facing extinction today because the international whaling fraternity is not prepared to settle for a somewhat lower profit in order to ensure the continued existence of animals upon which their prosperity depends. Even the fur trade, while it understands quite clearly the inevitable consequences of its illicit trading in leopard skins, for example, continues its large-scale poaching and smuggling operations.

By 1964 it was estimated that the annual export of leopard skins from East Africa alone had reached something like 50,000. Illicit trading in leopard skins had become the most profitable and skillfully organized racket in East Africa. And as leopard skins become scarce, the price goes up, and as the price goes up, so poaching becomes more worthwhile because the rewards are greater.

Hunting for what might be described as pleasure, as distinct from hunting commercially valuable animals, has also played a part in reducing animals' numbers in the past, though today the big game hunter is, himself, facing extinction, partly because of the prohibitive cost of organizing safaris and partly through restrictions which have been increasingly imposed upon his activities in recent decades by governments anxious to conserve their dwindling wildlife. Such are the dangers which these so-called "sportsmen" brought to the continued existence of the Kodiak bear during the latter part of the nineteenth century. The giant brown bears of Alaska and Kodiak Island have no commercial or economic value to the native populations, nor do they interfere with agriculture or any other human activity. Yet, they, too, have been facing considerable danger of ultimate extinction since before the end of the nineteenth century through the utter selfishness of the big game hunter.

To shoot a Kodiak bear became the proof that the hunter was in the premier class.

This <u>might not have mattered</u> if he had been <u>content</u> to <u>secure</u> his <u>trophy</u> and <u>return home</u> with it. // But <u>having arrived</u> at <u>great personal expense</u>, he <u>regarded</u> it as a great <u>pity</u> to <u>leave without</u> having <u>slaughtered</u> the <u>largest number</u> of <u>bears</u>, regardless of the fact that apart from his one trophy the remainder would be of little or no use to him. Such was the <u>mentality</u> of the so-called <u>sportsmen</u> of the <u>nineteenth</u> and <u>early twentieth</u> <u>centuries</u>.

// Undoubtedly the most effective method of preserving any animal threatened with extinction is for the country in which it lives to grant it absolute protection, which ★ means that no one may kill specimens or capture them and send them abroad. There are three ways in which this can be achieved. A general <u>prohibition order forbidding</u> ① <u>killing</u> or capture can be effective <u>if</u> the <u>animal</u> is generally <u>distributed</u> in the <u>country</u>. If it is <u>confined</u> to a <u>restricted area</u>, then this area can be <u>declared</u> a <u>sanctuary for</u> the ② <u>animal</u>. Where there is a need to protect not only the one species but a number of other native species as well, this can best be achieved by <u>setting up</u> a <u>national park</u>, ③ where <u>all killing is forbidden. Many animals</u> are <u>migratory</u>, living in different areas in the winter and summer. Therefore, <u>to be effective, reserves</u> and national parks <u>must</u> ④ <u>include</u> both <u>habitats as well as</u> the <u>migration routes between them</u>, otherwise the protection given is only partial.

// The value of natural predators to the animals on which they prey has been confirmed on Isle Royale, an island national park in Lake Superior where moose have ① always been abundant. Their <u>numbers fluctuated</u>, however. They <u>would reach</u> a <u>peak</u> of <u>two</u> or <u>three thousand</u> and then <u>decline rapidly</u>, because they <u>had</u> so <u>outstripped</u> the <u>available grazing</u> area that <u>large numbers</u> of them <u>died</u> of <u>starvation</u>. After these mass deaths even <u>those</u> which <u>survived</u> were in <u>poor condition</u>, and they remained in a weak state until the grazing had had a chance to recover.

<u>During this period</u> of <u>population fluctuation</u> the <u>moose</u> had <u>no natural enemies</u>. <u>During</u> the <u>winter</u> of <u>1949</u>, however, following one of the periodic starvation cycles, a <u>pack</u> of <u>timber wolves crossed</u> the <u>fifteen miles</u> of <u>ice</u> from <u>the Canadian</u> shore. <u>Today both</u> the <u>moose</u> and the <u>grazing</u> are <u>always</u> in <u>good condition</u>. The <u>wolves prevent</u> the <u>moose population growing sufficiently</u> to <u>outstrip its food supply</u>. Their culling, however, is <u>selective</u>, the vast <u>majority</u> of those <u>killed</u> being <u>either</u> old or <u>sick</u>, thus <u>leaving</u> the <u>strongest</u> and <u>healthiest</u> to <u>provide</u> the next <u>generation</u>. As a <u>result</u> Isle <u>Royale</u> now <u>has</u> one of the most <u>flourishing moose populations</u> in the whole of North America.

1. (D)   Choice (A) is irrelevant; the author never says that decreased leopard populations would result in greater safety for humans. (B) is incorrect because the author states just the opposite in the first paragraph. (C) is also irrelevant; the author never says this. Besides, any correlation between a decrease in the leopard populations and an increase in human populations is ludicrous. (D) is explicitly stated in the first paragraph. The author says that an indirect result of a decreased leopard population would necessitate the use of *special measures to protect crops from excessive devastation*. (E) is irrelevant; the idea of plague proportions in the opening paragraph refers to the increase in number of baboons and bush pigs. The author never says that the leopard population reached plague proportions in the first place.

2. (B)   Choice (A) is irrelevant; nowhere in the passage does the author state that leopards are killed by Kodiak bears. (B) is correct because the answer is clearly stated in the second paragraph: *Illicit trading in leopard skins had become the most profitable . . . racket in East Africa.* (C) is incorrect; the author uses the term *pleasure hunters* to distinguish between the so-called big game hunters and those who are hunting commercially valuable animals. He never says that pleasure hunters kill leopards. (D) is irrelevant; there is no reference in the passage to the breeding habits of leopards. (E) is also irrelevant; it is never stated in the passage.

3. (A) If you look at the first sentence of the fifth paragraph, you probably realize that the word *absolute* means "complete" or "perfect." Furthermore, the words *no one* in the statement *no one may kill specimens or capture them* indicates that there are to be no modifications or conditions to this rule. Therefore, you could have eliminated (C) and (E) because both *partial* and *incomplete* are opposite in meaning to the word you are looking for. If you do not know that *indomitable,* choice (B), means "that cannot be subdued or overcome," you probably recognized the prefix *in-,* which means "not." You might also have realized that the first few letters of the root begin the word *dominate.* These clues should have reinforced your feeling that (B) is not the answer you are looking for. Left with (A) and (D), you might have had some difficulty in narrowing your choices because you might have not realized that *unqualified,* choice (A), which means "not qualified" or "fitted," has more than one meaning. (D) is an appealing choice because you know that *elaborate* means "worked out with great care and nicety of detail," and that answer lends itself to a sense of the quality of protection the animals would receive. However, the major clue for you to pay attention to are the words *no one;* in this context, *unqualified* means "absolute," "not limited or modified in any way." (A) is the best choice; it is the perfect synonym for the word we are looking for.

4. (B) Even though (A) is incorrect, it is an amusing choice. Organized trading rackets are certainly contingent on unauthorized (in that they are illegal) trade agreements, freely made between parties, but nowhere does the author state this in the passage. (B) is correct; the answer is presented in the second paragraph: *Illicit trading . . . had become the most profitable . . . organized racket.* (C), (D), and (E) are obviously wrong because all three answers stress the legality of these organized trading rackets, which totally contradicts the way they are described by the author.

5. (E) Choice (A) is irrelevant; the author never says that some conservation efforts are extreme; on the contrary, he implies throughout the passage that in many instances they are not extreme enough. Even if (B) were not irrelevant, in that nowhere does the author present this idea, the answer is illogical. A sanctuary, by definition, is a place of refuge and safety; the idea that it would be hostile is contradictory and absurd. (C) is incorrect; the only reference the author makes to migration routes is in discussing effective ways to protect those animals that live in different areas in winter and summer; he makes no reference to any disruption of migration routes. (D) is irrelevant; it is never stated in the passage. (E) is clearly stated in the second sentence in the next to last paragraph: *The numbers of some animal species may already have fallen below the minimum necessary to guarantee their survival even with complete protection.*

6. (C) This question is telling you that four of the five choices are *true;* only one answer will be false. Remember that this means you should be able to locate every answer choice but one in either passage A or B. Here, choice (A) is true. The author says that humans' increased standard of living is a threat to animal populations. He supports this idea in passage A, six sentences into the first paragraph. (B) is true. In the third sentence from the end of the first paragraph in passage A, the author says *as more land is brought under cultivation . . . less remains available for wildlife, which in consequence must accept a reduction in numbers.* (C) is untrue. The author says just the opposite. In the first sentence of the second paragraph, the author says that the capture and export of numbers of certain species is an important factor in reductions in the animal population. (D) is true. In the second paragraph of passage B, the author states that as skins become scarce, the price goes up, and as the price goes up, poaching becomes more worthwhile. (E) is true. The answer can be found in the fifth sentence in the opening paragraph of passage A: *One important threat to animal populations arises from the increase in human populations.*

7. (A) Choice (A) is clearly stated in the passage. In the first sentence of the fourth paragraph, the author says: *To shoot a Kodiak bear became the proof that the hunter was in the premier class.* (B) is incorrect; in fact, the opposite is stated. In the fourth paragraph, the author says that bears have been facing danger of extinction through the selfishness of the big game hunters. (C) is incorrect; the author totally contradicts this statement. In the fourth paragraph he says that the bears have no commercial or economic value. (D) is incorrect. The author specifically states: *nor do they interfere with agriculture.* (E) is dead wrong; in the last sentence of the fourth paragraph, the author specifically cites the *selfishness,* not the *selflessness,* of the game hunter that has motivated his desire to kill such large numbers of Kodiak bear.

8. (D) Remember that even though the question asks what the author implies, you must still be able to locate the answer in the passage. You should have been able to tell from the question that all of the information you need to find the correct answer is in the last sentence of the passage: *The conditions needed for successful breeding are undoubtedly more critical than those needed for successful survival.* Although as often as not words lifted directly out of context are used by the test makers as deliberate traps for students, in this instance you might have taken a chance on (D), which is the correct answer, even if you did not know that *trivial,* choice (A), means "insignificant," *profuse,* choice (B), means "extravagant" or "abundant," and, *equivocal,* choice (E), means "questionable" or "doubtful."

9. (B) Choice (A) is incorrect. The author never says this. The only discussion of animals confined to a restricted area is in the fifth paragraph, in which the author says that a restricted area will make a prohibition order forbidding killing or capture effective. (B) is the correct answer. In the last sentence of this paragraph, the author states that in order to be effective, reserves and national parks *must include both habitats as well as the migration routes between them.* (C) is incorrect; the only discussion of propagation is in passage A in the last paragraph, in which the author says that zoos need to learn how to breed animals in captivity. (D) is incorrect; there is nothing in the passage to support this statement. (E) is irrelevant, even though the statement is true. It doesn't answer the question. The author only says that a large national park is necessary because *many animals are migratory and the park must include migration routes;* it is not because some species of animals are distributed throughout a country.

10. (C) Choice (A) is incorrect. In fact, the author states that people *may well be prepared to risk destroying a species provided that in doing so he can make a quick profit for himself.* (B) is completely wrong; the entire passage testifies to just the opposite. Almost every paragraph is concerned with some aspect of illicit trading. (C) is the correct answer. The author states in the first paragraph that the need to conserve animals that are economically valuable *will be obvious to any businessman.* (D) is irrelevant; the question is asking what reasons would convince a community to voluntarily conserve animals. Whether or not governments restrict the killing of certain species of animals is not a reason. No one has to be convinced to follow a law; he is only required to obey it. (E) is incorrect. The answer is never supported in the passage. Besides, even though the capture of some animals might prove difficult, this would hardly be considered an adequate deterrent.

11. (A) Even if you are totally unfamiliar with the meaning of several of the words in the answers, there are still techniques you can use to narrow down your choices. You should have been able to tell from the question that all of the information you will need to find the correct answer can be found in the third and fourth paragraphs of the passage. It should be obvious from your reading that the author's attitude toward pleasure hunters is decidedly negative. He specifically refers to their *utter selfishness.* Therefore, you could have eliminated (B), in that *ambivalent* means "the coexistence

of opposite and conflicting feelings about the same person or object." Even if you did not know the meaning of the word, you might have realized that the prefix *ambi-* means "both" because most students are familiar with the word *ambidextrous,* which means "skillful with both hands." You probably decided this was not the correct answer. You would have eliminated (E) for the same reason; you would have known that the prefix *in-* means "not" and that the word *discriminate* means "to distinguish between." You would have realized that in this context the author is not able to form an opinion, not the word you are looking for. You might have eliminated (C) because you probably know that satire is a style of writing that uses sarcasm or ridicule to expose the truth about something. In this passage, the author is forthright and explicit in his portrayal of the hunters. Left with (A) and (D), you were probably able to back into the correct answer, (A), even though you might not have known that *didactic* means "instructive" or "inclined to lecture others too much;" *judgmental* seems to fit perfectly.

12. (E) Remember that you must be able to locate the answer to this question in both passages. (A) is incorrect; if anything, both passages indicate the urgent need for animal conservation restrictions. (B) is incorrect; in fact, most of passage B is concerned with the businessman and the illicit traders who risk destroying entire species of animals just to ensure their own prosperity. (C) is irrelevant; the author never discusses the numbers of national parks in existence. (D) is also irrelevant; in passage B, the author details methods of preserving animals threatened with extinction. There is no reference to the need for the *severity of animal conservation regulations to be increased* in either passage A or B. (E) is the best answer because both authors refer to the wanton disregard of warnings by conservationists of the need to preserve animal populations.

13. (D) The most important method in dealing with this type of question is to decide whether the answer you are looking for is positive or negative and then to narrow down your choices. In the third and fourth paragraphs, the author says that these sportsmen demonstrated *utter selfishness* and killed large numbers of bears even though *apart from his one trophy the remainder would be of little use to him.* You should have been able to eliminate (A) and (C) because both choices include positive, not negative, words. To further narrow down your answers, you might try to identify any words in the remaining choices that cannot be supported by the information given in the text. The important thing to know is that if one word in any of the choices is incorrect, the entire answer can be eliminated. Left with (B), (D), and (E), you could have gotten rid of (B) because the word *abstracted,* which means "lost in thought" or "preoccupied," is totally irrelevant. It is likely that choices (D) and (E) proved difficult because of the vocabulary. You might not have known that *imprudent* means "lacking discretion or good judgment," or that *expedient* means "advantageous" or "profitable" and *innocuous* means "harmless," but you could have backed into the correct answer if you realized that the word *profitable* is not supported in the text; in fact, the author says that *the giant brown bears of Alaska and Kodiak Island have no commercial or economic value.* This answer totally contradicts the qualities of the nineteenth- and twentieth-century sportsmen described in the passage. The perfect choice is (D).

SAMPLE TESTS

Verbal Assessment Test 1

Each sentence below has one or two blanks, each blank indicating that something has been omitted. Beneath the sentence are five lettered words or sets of words. Choose the word or set of words that *best* fits the meaning of the sentence as a whole.

1. "When you send your delegate to the conference," suggested the adviser, "make sure he is not a mere _____ of your district but the very _____ of all you stand for."

   (A) ambassador . . embodiment
   (B) representative . . epitome
   (C) mentor . . consummation
   (D) composition . . symbol
   (E) emissary . . fledgling

2. Whereas Jack often presents the facts with the hardly honorable intention of _____, his amoral cohort Stephen dispenses with the partial deception and _____ outright.

   (A) equivocation . . lies
   (B) litigation . . prosecutes
   (C) objectivity . . panders
   (D) fabrication . . investigates
   (E) fabricating . . comments

3. Only when properly tuned can a piano produce _____ sound.

   (A) redolent (B) luxuriant
   (C) euphonious (D) discordant
   (E) ceremonious

4. I find it difficult to understand how Karen, who speaks with such _____ in public lectures, can show such _____ at home.

   (A) consequence . . harmony
   (B) grace . . elegance
   (C) zeal . . apathy
   (D) rapidity . . swiftness
   (E) animation . . euphoria

5. That long-winded writer does not realize that his audience would much prefer _____ to flowery, bombastic _____ .

   (A) succinctness . . verbosity
   (B) temerity . . impetuosity
   (C) elegance . . perfection
   (D) inspiration . . neutrality
   (E) ambiguity . . modulation

6. The meaning of the law was in no way _____ ; it was clear, precise, and _____ .

   (A) impractical . . legal
   (B) compatible . . amenable
   (C) temporary . . modern
   (D) concise . . terse
   (E) ambiguous . . definitive

7. "The reasoned approach would be _____ ," explained the mediator. "But it is all too apparent that with typical irrationality, the other side will choose _____ ."

   (A) castigation . . clemency
   (B) acquiescence . . neutrality
   (C) circumspection . . prudence
   (D) conciliation . . defiance
   (E) deference . . submission

8. The magnificence of man's achievements in the past is cause for _____ in facing the future; but the future, unknown and imponderable, still _____ us.

(A) agony . . castigates
(B) consolation . . perplexes
(C) uncertainty . . assures
(D) mourning . . enlightens
(E) austerity . . ingratiates

9. The minister was wont to _____ and _____ sinful conduct.

(A) approve . . encourage
(B) deprecate . . decry
(C) examine . . laud
(D) admonish . . vindicate
(E) vilify . . compliment

Each question below consists of a related pair of words or phrases, followed by five lettered pairs of words or phrases. Select the lettered pair that *best* expresses a relationship similar to that expressed in the original pair.

10. AUDIBLE:STRIDENT: : (A) benign:harmless
(B) beatific:blissful (C) balmy:fragrant
(D) stout:athletic (E) bright:glaring

11. FRICTION:HEAT: : (A) denotation:connotation (B) earnest:pledge (C) summons:danger
(D) surge:collision (E) death:grief

12. COLD:GELID: : (A) enthusiastic:zealous
(B) fortuitous:accidental (C) forward:obstinate
(D) germane:pertinent (E) gnarled:twisted

13. BOTHER:PERSECUTE: :
(A) extricate:disentangle (B) eschew:avoid
(C) extol:honor (D) flaccid:flabby
(E) esteem:worship

14. DISSEMINATION:KNOWLEDGE: :
(A) gazette:newspaper
(B) corroboration:evidence
(C) imagination:overused
(D) contractor:building
(E) circulation:magazine

15. SHEEP:FLOCK: : (A) crop:produce
(B) student:fraternity (C) aviary:bird
(D) fruit:vegetable (E) expedition:explorer

The next two passages are followed by questions based on their content. Answer the questions following each passage on the basis of what is *stated* or *implied* in the passage, and in any introductory material that might be provided. Questions 16 through 21 are based on the following passage.

In this passage, the author discusses various aspects on the origin of life.

Scientific research on the origin of life is in an exploratory phase, and all its conclusions are tentative. We know that the organisms that lived on earth 2 billion or more years ago were simple microbial forms. There is even some evidence that life might already have existed when the first known solid crust formed on earth, almost 4 billion years ago. The geological record indicates that liquid water, other chemicals, and a suitable atmosphere for prebiotic chemical activity were present on earth more than 3.8 billion years ago. Earliest life was unicellular or noncellular, existed in the absence of oxygen, and may have been incapable of producing its own nutrients from solar or chemical energy. Experimental results and astronomical observations are consistent with the idea that the steps required to link and set into operation the essential components of a living cell could have occurred under conditions prevailing on the primitive earth. They could not occur now because of the destructive effects on today's abundant molecular oxygen, not only on simple unprotected living systems but also on the intermediate products that might have generated the component molecules of such systems.

Experiments conducted under plausible primitive-earth conditions have resulted in the production of amino acids, the nucleotide components of DNA, and DNA-like chains of these nucleotides. Many biologically interesting molecules have also been detected by astronomers using radio-telescopes. We can, therefore, explain how the early oxygen-free earth provided a hospital site for the accumulation of molecules suitable for the construction of living systems. Such molecules could have been formed as a result of chemical reactions on the earth's surface, or they could have arrived in carbonaceous meteorites. Perhaps both sources are responsible for their presence.

For those who are studying aspects of the origin of life, the question no longer seems to be whether life could have originated by chemical processes. Prebiological chemical evolution is seen as a trial-and-error process leading to the success of one or more systems built from the many possible chemical components. The system that evolved with the capability of self-replication and mutation led to what we now define as a living system.

16. The main concern of this passage is

(A) the processes by which life could have evolved on earth
(B) the question of when life evolved on earth
(C) prebiological evolution
(D) the conditions on primitive earth

(E) a description of early unicellular or noncellular life

17. According to the writer, all but one of the following conditions were needed for the development
of earliest life:

(A) liquid water
(B) molecular oxygen
(C) necessary chemicals
(D) suitable atmosphere
(E) nonbiological components

18. In the last sentence of the passage, the author uses
the word *mutation* to mean

(A) duplication
(B) transformation
(C) reproduction
(D) immobility
(E) repetitiousness

19. Which of the following statements is best supported by the article?

(A) Earliest life used solar energy to produce
nutrients.
(B) Earliest life could not have existed 3.8
billion years ago.
(C) The molecules necessary for the development
of life could have come from outer space.
(D) Earliest life could not have existed without
the presence of molecular oxygen.
(E) Scientists now know exactly how life
developed on earth.

20. Select the statement that, according to the author,
is true:

(A) Life began over 4 billion years ago.
(B) Evolution began as a trial-and-error process.
(C) Scientists question whether life could have
originated by processes involving
nonbiological components.
(D) Earliest life was dependent on solar and
chemical energy for nutrients.
(E) DNA is one of the components of amino acids.

21. According to the writer, astronomers using radio-
telescopes have found

(A) life in space
(B) carbonaceous meteorites
(C) prebiological chemical evolution in space
(D) evidence that life evolved in space
(E) molecules suitable for constructing life in
space

Questions 22 through 30 are based on the following
passage.

*The author of this passage gives his views on the caste
system in India.*

Centuries ago, castes and the thousands of sub-
divisions within each caste were professional, heredi-
tary guilds. Thus Gandhi belonged to the Vaisya caste
and to the ModhBania subcaste. Banias are traders,
and the Gandhis, far back, were grocers. Gandhi
means grocer. Tradition as well as the local authorities kept all adults within their own guilds so that
higher castes could not lose caste by being flooded
with members of lower castes and low castes were not
invaded by unemployed from above. This arrangement presumably gave each group the advantage of
economic security, but it also subjected the individual
to economic regimentation.

Though caste often performed this stabilizing economic function, its origin was political and its sanc-
tion religious. The Aryans, who came south from their
Central Asian homelands thousands of years ago during the long, unchronicled night before the dawn of
history, gradually conquered India from the Indus
River and the Himalaya Mountains down to the southern tip of the peninsula at Cape Comorin, and as they
proceeded they tolerantly merged their own customs
and ideas with the indigenous cultures—the product is
the composite now known as Hinduism. Yet they
made the native inhabitants their economic tools, re-
taining for themselves the profitable and glamorous
tasks of governing and fighting. So great was the power
of religion, however, that the Brahmans established
themselves as the highest caste, higher than the rulers
and warriors, and this chiefly because they were able to
give the caste gradations a guarantee of stability by hal-
lowing them with a mantle of religion. They clothed
caste in a sacred formula of immutable fate. You are a
Brahman or a Sudra or untouchable because of your
conduct in a previous incarnation. Caste rank is thus
preordained for this life and everyone must submit.

But the darkest aspect of the caste system stems
from the very root of segregation itself: the fear of
pollution, of spiritual defilement, particularly on the
part of the Brahman leaders of Indian society. Fed
over thousands of years by the sacred literature and
over countless generations by traditions and law, this
fear led to enormous inequalities among the members
of the various castes.

In the hierarchy of the caste system, every caste
was considered either more or less pure than every
other caste, and a man's social status and relationships
were determined by his caste's degree of purity. Some
castes were so bereft of purity that the sight of them
defiled all other castes. Members of the Chandala

caste, for example, could not leave their isolated quarters or villages without striking a wooden clapper to warn of their contaminating approach. On the other end of the same spectrum, some Brahman castes held themselves so pure that contact with a member of almost any other caste could make them spiritually unclean. Such Brahmans sometimes dined in wringing wet clothes that they had washed themselves, because permitting the garments they wore at meals to dry on a clothesline invited pollution from the shadow of a passerby.

Obviously, attitudes as extreme as these were damaging to the members of all castes, the high as well as the low. But it was among the so-called outcastes or exterior castes—"once-born" castes so low in status that they were held to be outside the pale of human society—that the caste system did its greatest harm. For the members of such castes, who were often forbidden even to use the public roads lest their shadows defile their "twice-born" superiors, life was one long humiliation—a humiliation no less degrading for the fact that most outcastes acquiesced in it. Subservient, almost always illiterate, usually poverty-stricken, these "untouchables" exhibited the effects of the caste system at its worst.

22. The main theme of this passage is

    (A) the development of Hinduism in India
    (B) the historical development of the governing class system in India
    (C) a description of the various castes in Hindu India
    (D) the origins of the caste system in India
    (E) the contrast between the Aryan caste and the Brahman caste

23. According to this writer, the caste that had the most power and influence in India was the

    (A) Aryan caste
    (B) Brahman caste
    (C) ruling caste
    (D) Vaisya caste
    (E) merchant and trader caste

24. Hinduism, according to this writer, is

    (A) the native culture of India
    (B) the native religion of India
    (C) totally brought into India by the early Aryan invaders
    (D) a mixture of Aryan and native Indian cultures
    (E) a creation of the Brahman caste

25. The writer implies that the Brahman caste had influence in India because of their

    (A) wealth
    (B) political power
    (C) alliance with the Aryans
    (D) great fighting strength
    (E) control of religious power

26. According to this writer, all but one of the following was characteristic of the caste system in India:

    (A) totally indigenous
    (B) rigid: one couldn't move from one caste to another
    (C) inherited from father to son
    (D) thought to be decreed by inimitable fate
    (E) preordained

27. According to the passage, which of the following is most critical to the implementation of segregation in a society?

    (A) longstanding laws
    (B) time-honored traditions
    (C) fear of spiritual defilement
    (D) sacred literature
    (E) ancient religious codes of morality

28. Some Brahman castes avoided contact with members of other castes because they believed such contact could

    (A) promote members of lower castes into higher castes
    (B) cause the Brahman to go blind
    (C) encourage civil disobedience
    (D) weaken the political independence of each caste
    (E) taint the spiritual purity of the Brahman

29. Within the caste system, castes were ordered in terms of

    (A) purity
    (B) wealth
    (C) humility
    (D) subservience
    (E) pride

30. The author implies that the greatest disadvantage faced by the once-born outcastes was

    (A) they were forced to strike wooden clappers
    (B) they had to dine in wet clothing
    (C) they had no place in human society
    (D) they had unclean shadows
    (E) they were forbidden to use all roads

SECTION 2

Time—30 Minutes
35 Questions

Each sentence that follows has one or two blanks, each blank indicating that something has been omitted. Beneath the sentence are five lettered words or sets of words. Choose the word or set of words that *best* fits the meaning of the sentence as a whole.

1. "It is through persistent _____ and not carefree _____ that success is achieved," remarked the English professor.

   (A) covetousness . . culpability
   (B) assiduity . . indolence
   (C) decadence . . defamation
   (D) discipline . . rigidity
   (E) belligerence . . indulgence

2. Unlike the _____ and magnificent heroes of the old legends, we felt _____ in the face of danger.

   (A) intrepid . . fearful
   (B) cowardly . . fearless
   (C) notorious . . exalted
   (D) temperate . . inconsequential
   (E) noble . . challenged

3. If you cannot settle the dispute, we will submit it to _____ , with full legal procedures to be followed exactly and equitably.

   (A) introspection (B) admonition
   (C) adjudication (D) scrutiny
   (E) addendum

4. I warned him not to drive too fast, but knowing how _____ he is, he must have.

   (A) temperate (B) temerarious
   (C) gluttonous (D) sober (E) indulgent

5. "The _____ poverty of my subjects," mused the regretful king, "makes me ashamed of my noble and _____ domain."

   (A) sportive . . stringent
   (B) retrospective . . introspective
   (C) abject . . exalted
   (D) rampant . . ignominious
   (E) inconsequential . . incontrovertible

6. Unlike the huge and disobedient dog, the little kitten was gentle and _____ .

   (A) touchy (B) titanic (C) thermal
   (D) tractable (E) testy

7. The unfortunate lot of the prisoners of war proved to be _____ most of the time and often _____ .

   (A) waggish . . wizened
   (B) eulogistic . . extemporaneous
   (C) propitious . . beneficial
   (D) difficult . . unbearable
   (E) dormant . . hilarious

8. Their petty arguments are always a combination of _____ and _____ .

   (A) extirpation . . implantation
   (B) denunciation . . introspection
   (C) reflection . . frenzy
   (D) bickering . . squabbling
   (E) intellect . . reason

9. During the Second World War, _____ was tantamount to _____ .

   (A) infamy . . glory
   (B) expulsion . . immigration
   (C) annihilation . . rejuvenation
   (D) collaboration . . cooperation
   (E) resistance . . sympathy

10. Although our agreements on most matters show a simple _____ , our opinions were so similar this time that they _____ .

    (A) discord . . diverged
    (B) concurrence . . coincided
    (C) collusion . . ramified
    (D) accord . . exploded
    (E) assent . . opprobrium

Each question that follows consists of a related pair of words or phrases, followed by five lettered pairs of words or phrases. Select the lettered pair that *best* expresses a relationship similar to that expressed in the original pair.

11. WANTING:DEFICIENT: :
    (A) tousled:disheveled (B) lovable:repugnant
    (C) vapid:tasty (D) noxious:innocuous
    (E) cowardly:heroic

12. PUGILIST:GLOVE: : (A) boat:fisherman
    (B) artist:palette (C) weaver:type
    (D) hunter:game (F) contractor:building

13. LITHOGRAPHER:ENGRAVING: :
    (A) deity:prayer (B) poet:poem
    (C) artisan:craft (D) draft:soldier
    (E) bibliophile:library

14. DRAFTSMAN:COMPASS: : (A) writer:book
    (B) angler:rod (C) sand:glazier
    (D) hammer:carpenter (E) planter:produce

15. DIFFIDENT:TIMOROUS: :
    (A) beholden:independent (B) callow:ripe
    (C) colloquial:formal (D) crude:elegant
    (E) perspicacious:discerning

16. SOLDIER:ARMY: : (A) pilot:airplane
    (B) messenger:courier (C) shield:lampshade
    (D) nail:hook (E) cow:herd

17. ENERVATING:DEBILITATING: :
    (A) eon:moment (B) sadness:despair
    (C) transparent:opaque (D) dormant:active
    (E) heartfelt:insincere

18. VACILLATING:STEADFAST: :
    (A) sebaceous:oily (B) sinuous: winding
    (C) sheepish:diffident (D) sonorous:resonant
    (E) presumptuous:unassuming

19. EAGER:RELUCTANT: : (A) pacific:tranquil
    (B) mediatory:intercessory
    (C) property:landed (D) ripe:mature
    (E) bogus: authentic

20. WALK:LIMP: : (A) hop:leap
    (B) clash:sound (C) memory:lapse
    (D) negligence:character
    (E) speech:stutter

21. ACCELERATE:SPEED: : (A) velocity:wind
    (B) motion:propel (C) crescendo:sound
    (D) tide:ebb (E) din:noise

22. PRESSURE:VALVE: : (A) rays:filter
    (B) tourniquet:arm (C) handcuffs:criminal
    (D) injection:hypodermic
    (E) circulate:newspaper

23. GERM:DISEASE: : (A) explosion:debris
    (B) intensity:madness (C) microbe:experiment
    (D) seek:find (E) accident:carelessness

The passage below is followed by questions based on its content. Answer the questions on the basis of what is *stated* or *implied* in the passage, and in any introductory material that might be provided. Questions 24 through 35 are based on the following passage.

The following passage examines the character and influence of Marxism.

Critics of Marx have frequently argued that the logic of Marx's theory is not impeccable. As a necessitarian, so it is said, he leaves no room for freedom, and thus deprives ideological exhortation itself of any point. In this matter, his critics have failed to see that the term *inevitable,* as used by Marx, is primarily a term of encouragement for some and of doom for others. It belongs not to the language of scientific description, but to that of ideological conflict. Its function is the prophetic one of awakening the workingmen of the world to a sense of their own historic mission as deliverers of mankind.

Despite the failures of Marxism we must not forget the pioneer character of this grand attempt to unite all the philosophical, scientific, and moral strands of the Victorian age into one vast system with almost universal scope. The low degree of scientific accuracy which marks numerous aspects of Marxism, the fuzziness and ambiguity of many of its concepts, cannot detract from the impressive majesty of its thought structure, just as the incomparable vision of Freud cannot appear less brilliant by the countless corrections to which his ideas have been subjected.

It is precisely this attempt at an overall synthesis of nineteenth-century moral and scientific thought which has given Marxism such a powerful influence over intellectuals and vast social movements throughout the world and has made it one of the most significant rallying cries of our century. To explain the attractiveness of Marxism as an ideology is the task of the student of contemporary history. One of the secrets of this success is the close tie of Marxist analysis to a value orientation: radical criticism of bourgeois society, of America, of colonialism, of every system of exploitation and inequality.

Marxism further expresses the yearning of backward societies for a place in the sun, of underprivileged minorities for equal treatment, of manual workers for a place of respect in their social system. It proclaims the cause of progress in areas and in social strata where this word has not yet acquired a hollow sound. It brings to the underprivileged the hope and the conviction that they will catch up with, and overtake, those who are on top today; that the last shall be the first, and not in a paradise beyond but on this earth and in the near future. Moreover, Marxism boasts that it extends to social processes that scientific technology which has so impressively changed the material aspects of life of proletarians and backward nations. It can all the more easily lay an exclusive claim to scientific validity in social thought because it has often been the first or only one to tackle problems which are crucial to the strata on which it relies.

For troubled intellectuals everywhere, its chief attraction lies in the proclaimed unity of theory and practice, in the attempt to find a broad synthesis of radical criticism, sober science, and a belief in progress. However much its proponents may denounce religion, Marxism as an ideology endeavors to satisfy all the religious urges in men, and the claim to be scientific can be seen as a necessary prerequisite in the modern age, without which men would not even be religious. Marxism is a doctrine of salvation and damnation, and some of the same fears and hopes which drew men into the fold of religions in the past now cause them to join this movement.

We have spoken of the disintegration of this ideology. The grand synthesis fell apart, not only because of its inherent logical inconsistencies, but also because the psychological dispositions which made it seem plausible disappeared with the deceptive harmony of the Victorian age. It must be clearly understood that this falling apart of Marxism does not by any means indicate its disappearance or even its decay. On the contrary, many heirs of Marx and Engels have been and are still doing extremely fruitful work as social scientists. In that sense, the disintegration of Marxism can be seen as a blossoming and flourishing of Marx's ideas in many different directions. And yet, the unity of the essential elements which we have singled out as the basic components of Marxism has been destroyed. The very ruins of this imposing intellectual edifice, however, confront us with one of the thorniest and most painful questions of all: the problem of our attitude to contemporary events, and its relationship to social science. The concept of the unity of theory and practice makes us aware of the inseparable connection between social science, political attitude, and action. The social scientist cannot help being a citizen, and the question is whether the citizen and the scientist can dwell in the same individual without influencing each other, whether part of the citizen can encapsulate itself into scientific detachment without either the citizen's decisions or the scientist's findings being affected. This indicates the end of the notion that there can be any detached, dispassionate, pure social science: everything turns into ideology.

For Marx, developments in religious, philosophical, or political thought are essentially by-products of modifications in the modes of material production and organization. What he proposed, in effect, was to invert Hegel's idealistic interpretation of history so that the ideational "superstructure" could be correctly understood for the first time as an effect rather than as a determining cause of basic changes in the social system. The consequence of this inversion is that Marx construed progress not in terms of spiritual self-development or "freedom," but, rather, in terms of the improvement of the underlying economic conditions of social life. The amelioration of man's lot, for Marx, thus begins, even if it does not end, with a solution to the problem of poverty. And the salvation of man, the cure for his loneliness as well as for his misery, lies, at bottom, in a collective attack upon this problem. "The anatomy of civil society," said Marx, "is to be sought in political economy." So, also, he might have added, with the anatomy of human progress.

24. The word *impeccable* in the first sentence most nearly means

(A) pragmatic
(B) effete
(C) perfect
(D) effective
(E) ideological

25. The critics of Marx cite as his failure

  I. the admission of a basic underlying inevitability by which man's actions are determined
  II. his concept of inevitability, which lacks scientific description
  III. his definition of progress as improvement of economic conditions
  IV. a closed ideological theory that admits no freedom
  V. the fact that he viewed material production as a by-product of political thought

(A) I only (B) II only (C) II and III only
(D) I and IV only (E) III, IV, and V

26. According to the author,

(A) Hegel considered the ideational "superstructure" an effect rather than a determining cause of basic changes in the social system
(B) Marx believed that the improvement of man's condition begins with an understanding of the anatomy of human progress.
(C) the solution to the problem of man's misery

rests in a collective attack upon the social system

(D) the mass of men treat the idea of inevitability as a term of doom

(E) Marx considered the solution to the problem of poverty the first step toward the salvation of man

27. According to the author, which of the following observations are true concerning Marx's interpretation of history?

(A) Ideological conflict is the basis for sound political theory.

(B) Workingmen will inevitably awaken to a sense of their own historic mission as deliverers of mankind.

(C) Changes in man's thinking result from changes in modes of material production and organization.

(D) Determining the cause of basic changes in the social system will lead to the amerlioration of man's lot.

(E) The composition of civil society lies in an understanding of the conditions of the social environment.

28. The author's development of the passage suggests that, if continued, the passage would next

(A) discuss Marx's views on collectivism

(B) further develop Hegel's idealistic interpretation of history

(C) further discuss arguments propounded by the critics of Marx

(D) defend the workingman as prophet and deliverer

(E) discuss the logic of Marx's theory

29. What is the author's general assessment of Marx's theories?

(A) Marx, for all his fuzzy logic and ambiguity, was undoubtedly one of the greatest visionaries of the twentieth century.

(B) Marx was the savior of the underprivileged working class, but also interested in the state more than the individuals living under the state.

(C) Marx's theories were then and will continue to be the basic foundation from which all political philosophy will stem.

(D) Marx's logic is often faulty, and thus jeopardizes any value we might be tempted to attribute to his ideas.

(E) The author did not allow any of his own opinions to intrude upon his essay.

30. Which of the following is a criticism of Marx's theories *not* mentioned by the author?

(A) ambiguity of certain concepts

(B) necessarianism

(C) faulty economic foundations

(D) inconsistent logic

(E) troubled relationship to current events

31. Which of the following did Marx *not* champion?

(A) equal treatment for underprivileged minorities

(B) the economic and social rise of manual workers

(C) redistribution of wealth

(D) the economic and social rise of the bourgeoisie

(E) criticism of colonialism

32. According to the author, why should a student of history be able to explain the appeal of Marxist thought?

(A) Marx was the first philosopher to apply scientific methods to economic analysis.

(B) Marx rejected religion in favor of politics.

(C) Marxism decisively influenced many social movements of the twentieth century.

(D) Marx and Engels were responsible for the Cold War of the twentieth century.

(E) The history of Marxism and the growth of Marxist states is in many ways the history of Europe itself.

33. What effect did the passing of the Victorian age have on Marxian ideology?

(A) Marxian ideology suffered; after the Victorian period, the psychological dispositions on which it had depended were no longer so uniform.

(B) Marxian ideology benefitted from the diversification of opinions and ideas due to the growth of cities in the modern age.

(C) Marxian ideology suffered due to the notable decline in European intellectual life with the passing of the Victorian age.

(D) Marxian ideology was in many ways fulfilled; the modern age shared Marx's high hopes for progress and science.

(E) Marxian sympathizers drastically increased in number in response to the widening

economic and social gaps of modern-day
Europe.

34. What was Marx's relationship to the theories of
Hegel?

(A) Marx was the first to seriously consider the
economic and social implications of Hegel's
writings; Marxian theory preserves Hegel's
basic concepts but expands upon them.
(B) Marx's theories were considered very
radical for their time, as they were largely
refutations of Hegel, who at that time was
generally considered the preeminent
political philosopher of the era.
(C) Marx shunned Hegel's writings, as they
were very hostile toward even mildly
Communistic thought.

(D) Marx maintained Hegel's basic ideological
structure but substituted economics as the
real basis of a social system.
(E) Marx twisted Hegel's ideational "superstructure" into a system for more effectively
organizing the different social groups of a
society.

35. According to the author, which of the following
would Marx consider a first step toward progress?

I. spiritual self-development
II. a solution to poverty
III. improvement of economic conditions for the
proletariat

(A) I (B) II, III (C) I, II
(D) all of the above (E) II, III

SECTION 3

Time—15 Minutes
13 Questions

The next two passages are followed by questions based
on their content and the relationship between them.
Answer the questions on the basis of what is *started*
or *implied* in the passages, and in any introductory
material that might be provided. Questions 1 through
13 are based on the following passages.

*The following passages present contrasting views on
gun control.*

Passage A

It is only when we learn that a crime involving a handgun is committed every two minutes—with a death occurring more than once an hour—that we can begin to
understand the deep and passionate responses of those
who support some kind of national gun control legislation. In view of the need to stem the increasing volume
of handgun-related violence, the pro-control supporters
argue that the reduction of the criminal use of firearms
by controlling the access of all citizens to firearms will
result in fewer crimes and less human destruction.

Every commission or major study of crime and violence has advocated much stricter gun-control laws.
The only reason that this pressure has failed to produce much tighter controls of firearms is a powerful
and well-organized lobby of gun owners, most notably the National Rifle Association. The debate be-

tween the "gun controllers" and the "gun lobby" has
been incredibly virulent. In addition to the political
charges of self-interest, participants in the gun-control
struggle have even resorted to such accusations as
mental illness and sedition.

The gun-control position rests on the self-evident
proposition that if there were no guns, there would be
no crimes committed with the guns. But few are hopeful about achieving that situation. Instead, their argument is that if there were fewer guns or if gun
ownership were better controlled by the government,
there would be fewer crimes with guns. Furthermore,
it is their contention that the mere possession of
weapons is a threat to public safety and order and that
gun ownership must be tightly regulated by the government, that gun owners can only keep and bear arms
by permission of the state, thus requiring that they
secure permits and pay fees and taxes.

The preferred program of most gun-control advocates contains a number of elements such as continuing and tightening all existing laws; permissive
licensing for long guns; restrictive licensing for all
handguns and the prohibition of cheap handguns, the
so-called "Saturday night specials." The great majority of gun crimes are committed with handguns, and it
is their belief that such legislation would drastically
curtail domestic violence. Control of the handguns
also has political implications since relatively few are

used for recreation, thereby rendering the objection of sportsmen to such restrictions highly ineffective.

Passage B

In the gun-control debate, the most outlandishly paranoid theories of gun ownership have appeared. Some people seem to believe that private arsenals exist primarily for political purposes—to kill blacks, whites, or liberals. But the majority of firearms in this country are rifles which are used primarily for hunting. A secondary purpose of these "long guns" is target and skeet shooting. Millions of gun owners are also collectors, gaining satisfaction from the mere possession of firearms, but even the serious collectors who hold them as historical or aesthetic artifacts number in the hundreds of thousands.

Most gun owners care little about their firearms per se, considering them as mere tools, to be properly cared for and, because they are potentially deadly, to be handled with caution. Yet within the ranks of the gun owners is a hard core of gun fanatics for whom firearms are an all-consuming hobby. To them, the possession, handling, and use of guns are a central part of life. They not only accumulate guns, but also read books and magazines about firearms and socialize with kindred spirits in gun clubs and gun stores. Many such people combine business with pleasure as gun dealers, gunsmiths, soldiers, policemen, and officials of gun owners' organizations. These enthusiasts have political importance because they are the core of the organized gun owners, easily aroused and mobilized to thwart the enemies of their passion.

It appears that at least one half of all American households are armed. They own guns for recreation or self-protection. The principal form of recreation, hunting, has deep cultural roots. In rural areas and small towns, a boy's introduction to guns and hunting is an important rite of passage. Possession of a gun for self-protection is based upon a perception of a real or potential threat to personal, family, or home security that is beyond the control of the police. Very rarely is there criminal or seditious intent. Yet these gun owners are told that their possession of weapons is a threat to public safety and order and that they can keep their weapons only with permission of the state.

In defense, they have organized themselves into an effective lobby by publicizing that the legislative attempts to restrict gun ownership is only the first step toward liquidating the private ownership and use of firearms in America. They claim that such legislation will have no effect on crime but will merely strip away the rights and privileges of Americans. The gun lobbyist takes the position that handgun confiscation would bring the federal government into a confronta-

tion with millions of responsible citizens to enforce a program that would have no effect upon violence; hence, the lack of evidence to justify confiscation requires that this remain a matter of individual choice rather than government fiat. In a free country the burden is upon those who wish to restrict freedom of choice to show good reason for doing it. And when the freedom is as deeply valued by as many as handgun ownership, the evidence for infringing upon it must be very strong indeed.

1. In modifying their goals in legislating gun control, the gun control supporters are implying that

    (A) they realize many gun owners use their guns for legitimate purposes, such as hunting, target shooting, and defense of private property
    (B) they do not want to appear too extremely radical and seditious to the rest of the country
    (C) they realize it is futile to fight for a complete ban of gun ownership
    (D) they have other, nonlegislative strategies to limit the ownership of guns in the United States
    (E) they are as determined as ever to limit the ownership of, and eventually bring about the banning of guns in the United States

2. What is the effect of the author's phrase "paranoid theories" (paragraph 1 of passage B) on the passage?

    I. The author thus associates gun control advocates with the mentally imbalanced.
    II. The author displays his refusal to take such theories with any seriousness.
    III. The author implies that gun owners are more fearful and suspicious than other people.

    (A) all of the above (B) I (C) II
    (D) II, III (E) I, II

3. According to the author of passage A, the most vital elements of gun control legislation are all but which of the following:

    (A) maintaining all existing gun control laws
    (B) banning of the most widely accessible, inexpensive guns
    (C) mandatory licensing of all guns; both long guns and handguns
    (D) banning all handguns, with the exception of those licensed for hunting and sport shooting
    (E) rewriting existing gun control laws to make them more stringent

4. Which of the following statements would a gun owner most likely *disagree* with?

   (A) There is an inverse relationship between the number of guns in circulation and the public safety.
   (B) Most guns are not shot at humans; they are either used to hunt animals or they are collector's items.
   (C) Guns have value beyond utility; they are also of anthropological interest as artifacts.
   (D) The government ought to respect its citizens' sense of judgment and responsibility.
   (E) In general, the more distant the government's control over its citizens, the better.

5. The basic argument of those who favor gun control is

   (A) Americans are guaranteed the right to bear arms by the Constitution.
   (B) Fewer guns in circulation means fewer crimes committed with guns.
   (C) The victims of gun-related crimes are all too often valuable citizens and innocent individuals.
   (D) For the protection of its citizens, the government should be able to effectively keep track of guns and their owners; currently this is impossible, due to the United States' relaxed gun legislation.
   (E) Gun owners are all too frequently unequipped with the proper wisdom and sense of responsibility that the possessor of such a dangerous weapon should have.

6. Why is the handgun the weapon that most gun control advocates wish to prohibit?

   (A) It is the most potentially lethal weapon.
   (B) It is used by very few hunters.
   (C) It is easiest for an individual to use.
   (D) It is the easiest to obtain and used most widely.
   (E) It is not protected by the National Rifle Association.

7. According to the author of passage B, which of the following fits the typical profile of a gun owner?

   (A) He enjoys reading about firearms and associating with others who share his interest through gun clubs and the like.
   (B) He has a largely independent spirit; he cares little for society's rules or opinions.
   (C) He considers his ownership of guns a

political statement and will fight for his rights with ceaseless passion.
   (D). He cares about his guns mainly for their utilitarian purposes; hunting or self-defense.
   (E) He is a gun dealer, gunsmith, soldier, or policeman who was probably introduced to guns at a young age.

8. With which of the following criticisms of passage B would the author of passage A most likely agree?

   (A) Passage B refuses to acknowledge the link between widespread ownership of guns and the high rate of domestic violence.
   (B) Passage B includes a sophisticated and critical assessment of the relationship between hunting and American culture.
   (C) Passage B employs an excessively radical tone, thus jeopardizing an argument that is otherwise not unreasonable.
   (D) Passage B expresses an attitude that is overly concerned with the preservation of order at the expense of individual freedom.
   (E) Passage B should have included the argument that it is people and not guns that take lives.

9. Which of the following criticisms of passage A is most valid *and* most likely to be expressed by the author of passage B?

   (A) Passage A wholly refuses to acknowledge the existence of hunters and sportsmen in its bid to restrict gun ownership.
   (B) Passage A characterizes gun control advocates as motivated by concern for the welfare of their society.
   (C) Passage A is based on an uneven sympathy for individuals in non-urban environments.
   (D) Passage A refers to the gun ownership advocates as a "lobby" but does not use this loaded term to characterize the gun control advocates.
   (E) Passage A expresses an extremely conservative, right-wing attitude not shared by most Americans.

10. Which of the following statements is true?

   I. Both of the authors all but openly admit their own loyalties to one side or the other; though they pose as disinterested third-party reporters, their sympathies are obvious.
   II. Both of the authors employ numbers or statistics to in some way buttress their arguments.

III. Both of the authors agree that crime must be controlled.

(A) I (B) I, II, III (C) III (D) I, II, III
(E) I, III

11. The word *fiat* in the last paragraph of passage B most nearly means

(A) failure
(B) public announcement
(C) punishment
(D) decree
(E) guardianship

12. The most interesting paradox concerning gun owners is

(A) statistics show that gun owners are most often criminals
(B) at least one-half of American households are armed
(C) most gun owners consider their weapons as mere tools
(D) gun owners tend to be more politically active than gun control advocates
(E) gun owners and gun control advocates often *agree* on other political issues

13. Which group of gun owners constitutes the strongest political lobby?

(A) hunters
(B) home and property owners
(C) the middle class
(D) gun enthusiasts
(E) gun dealers

ANSWERS

Verbal Assessment Test 1

Section 1	Section 2	Section 3
1. (A)	1. (B)	1. (C)
2. (A)	2. (A)	2. (E)
3. (C)	3. (C)	3. (D)
4. (C)	4. (E)	4. (A)
5. (A)	5. (C)	5. (B)
6. (E)	6. (D)	6. (D)
7. (D)	7. (D)	7. (D)
8. (B)	8. (D)	8. (A)
9. (B)	9. (D)	9. (D)
10. (E)	10. (B)	10. (B)
11. (E)	11. (A)	11. (D)
12. (A)	12. (B)	12. (C)
13. (E)	13. (B)	13. (D)
14. (E)	14. (A)	
15. (B)	15. (E)	
16. (A)	16. (E)	
17. (B)	17. (B)	
18. (B)	18. (E)	
19. (C)	19. (E)	
20. (B)	20. (E)	
21. (E)	21. (C)	
22. (D)	22. (A)	
23. (B)	23. (A)	
24. (D)	24. (C)	
25. (E)	25. (D)	
26. (E)	26. (E)	
27. (D)	27. (C)	
28. (E)	28. (E)	
29. (A)	29. (A)	
30. (C)	30. (C)	
	31. (D)	
	32. (C)	
	33. (A)	
	34. (D)	
	35. (E)	

Verbal Assessment Test 2

SECTION 1

Time—30 Minutes
30 Questions

Each sentence that follows has one or two blanks, each blank indicating that something has been omitted. Beneath the sentence are five lettered words or sets of words. Choose the word or set of words that *best* fits the meaning of the sentence as a whole.

1. The new _____ prohibits _____ and other trespassing.

   (A) assignment . . reporting
   (B) statute . . assault
   (C) dictate . . demonstrations
   (D) code . . surveying
   (E) ordinance . . poaching

2. To _____ our fears, the prudent guide took us on a different route, with _____ difficulties than normal.

   (A) increase . . smaller
   (B) allay . . fewer
   (C) excite . . ghastlier
   (D) diminish . . greater
   (E) terminate . . more

3. " _____ our salaries," said the workers, "and we'll _____ our productivity."

   (A) augment . . increase
   (B) recind . . escalate
   (C) create . . destroy
   (D) impeach . . praise
   (E) enlarge . . entangle

4. The _____ war criminal was sentenced to death for the atrocities he committed.

   (A) ominous (B) nonchalant
   (C) nominal (D) noisome (E) nefarious

5. While talk of antiballistic missiles would surely have been _____ in the days of the Ancient Greeks, references to law and culture would have been as _____ then as they are today.

   (A) likely . . unusual
   (B) current . . rare

   (C) anachronistic . . relevant
   (D) mundane . . spiritual
   (E) holy . . blasphemous

6. The valiantly defiant little country refuses to be _____ by superior foreign _____ .

   (A) coerced . . force
   (B) persuaded . . zealousness
   (C) assuaged . . aggression
   (D) destroyed . . aid
   (E) esteemed . . flattery

7. The mother warned her children: "Do not involve yourselves with _____ youngsters; they tend to be _____ ."

   (A) aggressive . . pugnacious
   (B) benevolent . . kind
   (C) generous . . parsimonious
   (D) gluttonous . . thin
   (E) intimidating . . reactionary

8. When the bottle of molasses broke, the viscous liquid began to _____ along the floor and _____ through the cracks.

   (A) squirt . . filter
   (B) ooze . . seep
   (C) soak . . squeeze
   (D) vegetate . . spurt
   (E) gush . . freeze

9. _____ speech is not generally found in _____ works.

   (A) archaic . . contemporary
   (B) understandable . . superb
   (C) rational . . exaggerated
   (D) objective . . reliable
   (E) overt . . published

Each question that follows consists of a related pair of words or phrases, followed by five lettered pairs of words or phrases. Select the lettered pair that *best* ex-

157

presses a relationship similar to that expressed in the original pair.

10. FROWN:SNEER: : (A) sugar:honey
    (B) admonition:curse (C) hallucination: fantasy
    (D) battle: fight (E) height:giant

11. DICTIONARY:WORDS: : (A) periodical:title
    (B) Bible:prayer (C) catalogue:item
    (D) treatise:volume (E) thesis:professor

12. BENIGN:MALIGNANT: : (A) bland:pungent
    (B) contractual:covenantal
    (C) supplicant:solicitous (D) salutary:beneficial
    (E) adverse:contrary

13. BRIGHT:BRILLIANT: : (A) genius:wisdom
    (B) stairs:elevator (C) simmer:boil
    (D) justice:equality (E) courtesy:politeness

14. NEEDLE:EMBROIDERY: :
    (A) hammer:carpenter (B) automobile:aviation
    (C) book:entymologist (D) lobster:cuisine
    (E) scalpel:surgery

15. SCRAWL:CALLIGRAPHY: : (A) light:prism
    (B) infirmity:debility
    (C) incongruity:disharmony
    (D) transgression:law (E) splatter:painting

The next two passages are followed by questions based on its content. Answer the questions following each passage on the basis of what is *stated* or *implied* in the passage, and in any introductory material that might be provided. Questions 16 through 21 are based on the following passage.

The following passage, which is about industrial society, is mainly concerned with modern corporations.

The household as an economic unity was supplemented by small business enterprise—by the merchant who was in command of his own capital, who employed his own servants and agents, and who assumed personally the risks of buying and selling household products. Household manufacture itself gave way to the relatively small factory. Its owner or his immediate agent directed the labor force, identified himself with the product, assumed the risks of the business, and took the profits. He was a simple and comprehensible figure, and he had a straightforward role to perform. It would have been surprising had he not also become the object of social nostalgia, and he has. He is the small businessman.

There is no more distinctive feature of the modern industrial society than the great corporation. These have no single owner; management, direction, and achievement are identified not with any individual but with an organization. Perhaps these corporations suffer from a kind of social elephantiasis. Size brings rewards in executive prestige, and growth *qua* growth is the most obvious measure of executive achievement. The distinction of heading the largest corporation far exceeds that of heading the most profitable corporation. Yet we also owe the more distinctive achievements of modern capitalism to the large corporation. Certainly we are indebted to it for most of the goods by which we set such store. Automobiles, their gasoline, the electric marvels, washing machines, refrigerators, the food that goes into them, bathtubs and the steel, copper, nickel and aluminum from which or by which they are fabricated, all come from the vast organization. The reason is simple. Instead of genius, the large corporation makes use of the combined efforts of many men of specialized but not remarkable ability. It substitutes organization for exceptional individual qualifications. This is highly efficient and something the small firm, by definition, cannot do. In addition the large corporation can command capital, can minimize risk, and is a good vehicle for routine customers' goods innovation.

16. The main idea of this section is best expressed as

    (A) the debt we owe the large corporation
    (B) modern capitalism and the profit motive
    (C) modern industrial society
    (D) characteristics of the large corporation
    (E) nostalgia and the small businessman

17. Which one of the following statements is not true?

    (A) Corporations suffer from the social stigma of hugeness.
    (B) Achievement on the executive level is measured in growth.
    (C) Heading a corporation that is distinctive in terms of its profits is less advantageous than heading a corporation that is distinctive in terms of its size.
    (D) The large corporations capitalize on the combined mediocrity of many rather than the exceptional qualified few.
    (E) One of the primary differences between the small business and the large corporation is that achievement in the former is identified with an individual and achievement in the latter is identified with an organization.

18. According to the author, to the modern corporate executive, the small businessman has come to represent

(A) a remarkable object lesson in risk-taking
(B) a longing for a way of doing business that no longer exists
(C) our abiding indebtedness to his economic resourcefulness
(D) a way to gauge success in business
(E) a noteworthy example of economic mediocrity

19. In his discussion of the large corporation, the author's tone can be described as

(A) tolerant
(B) caustic
(C) sympathetic
(D) ironic
(E) sarcastic

20. In this passage, the writer implies that

(A) one could do worse than operating a small business
(B) the benefits derived from modern capitalism are largely produced by the giant corporations
(C) the large corporation suffers from insufficiency
(D) the original economic unit was the small business enterprise
(E) the large corporation is an excellent vehicle for capital risk

21. The word *elephantiasis* in the second paragraph most probably means

(A) toughness
(B) animalism
(C) hugeness
(D) disease
(E) clumsiness

Questions 22 through 30 are based on the following passage.

The following passage discusses tribal cultures and patterns of behavior in British Columbia.

The three cultures of Zuni, of Dobu, and of the Kwakiutl are not merely heterogeneous assortments of acts and beliefs. They have each certain goals toward which their behavior is directed and which their institutions further. They differ from one another not only because one trait is present here and absent there, and because another trait is found in two regions in two different forms. They differ still more because they are oriented as wholes in different directions. They are traveling along different roads in pursuit of different ends, and these ends and these means in one

society cannot be judged in terms of another society, because essentially they are incommensurable.

All cultures, of course, have not shaped their thousand items of behavior to a balanced and rhythmic pattern. Like certain individuals, certain social orders do not subordinate activities to a ruling motivation. They scatter. If at one moment they seem to be pursuing certain ends, at another they are off on some tangent apparently inconsistent with all that has gone before, which gives no clue to activity that will come after.

This lack of integration seems to be as characteristic of certain cultures as extreme integration is of others. It is not everywhere due to the same circumstances. Tribes like those of the interior of British Columbia have incorporated traits from all the surrounding civilizations. They have taken their patterns from the manipulation of wealth from one culture area, parts of their religious practices from another, contradictory bits from still another. Their mythology is a hodgepodge of uncoordinated accounts of culture heroes out of three different myth cycles represented in areas around them.

Yet in spite of such extreme hospitality to the institutions of others, their culture gives an impression of extreme poverty. Nothing is carried far enough to give body to the culture. Their social organization is little elaborated, their ceremonial is poorer than that in almost any other region of the world, their basketry and beading techniques give only a limited scope for activity in plastic arts. Like certain individuals who have been indiscriminately influenced in many different directions. Their tribal patterns of behavior are uncoordinated and casual.

In these tribes of British Columbia, the lack of integration appears to be more than a mere simultaneous presence of traits collected from different surrounding peoples. It seems to go deeper than that. Each facet of life has its own organization, but it does not spread to any other. At puberty great attention is paid to the magical education of children for the various professions and the acquisition of guardian spirits. On the western plains this vision practice saturates the whole complex of adult life, and the professions of hunting and warfare are dominated by correlated beliefs. But in British Columbia the vision quest is one organized activity and warfare is quite another. Similarly feasts and dances in British Columbia are strictly social. They are festive occasions at which the performers mimic animals for the amusement of the spectators. But it is strictly tabu to imitate animals who are counted as possible guardian spirits. The feasts do not have religious significance, nor do they serve as opportunities for economic exchange. Every activity is segregated, as it were. It forms a complex of its own, and its motivations and goals are proper to its own limited field and are not extended to the whole life of the people. Nor does any characteristic psychological response appear to have arisen to dominate the culture as a whole.

22. The title that best expresses the idea of this passage is

    (A) Tribal Patterns of Behavior
    (B) The Zuni, Dobu, and Kwakiutl Cultures as Examples of the Way Tribes Develop Distinct Social Patterns
    (C) The Lack of a Ruling Motivation in Certain British Columbian Tribes
    (D) The Place of Myth and Ceremonial Practices in British Columbia
    (E) Economic and Religious Patterns Among the Zuni, Dobu, and Kwakiutl Tribes

23. According to this writer, the main difference between the Zuni, Dobu, and Kwakiutl tribes is

    (A) they are located in different geographical areas
    (B) they pursue different ends
    (C) the circumstances of their development are different
    (D) they differ in the extreme poverty of one of the tribes
    (E) they differ in behavior and attitude

24. This writer implies that the tribes of the interior of British Columbia have primarily the following characteristics in common:

    (A) their pattern of the manipulation of wealth
    (B) their mythology
    (C) their religious practices
    (D) their culture is made up of traits from surrounding cultures
    (E) their myth cycles are uncoordinated

25. According to this writer, the primary unfortunate result of a tribe's adopting the institutions of others is

    (A) lack of creativity on their own
    (B) social disorganization
    (C) uncoordinated patterns of behavior
    (D) extreme poverty of religious ceremony
    (E) undifferentiated mythology

26. According to the writer, all but one of the following characteristics is true of the tribes of the interior of British Columbia:

    (A) no "body" to their culture
    (B) simple social organization
    (C) limited art and crafts creativity
    (D) uncoordinated mythology
    (E) inhospitable to other cultures

27. The passage implies that the overall society of the tribes of British Columbia is structured in such a way that

    (A) some feasts incorporate elements of both social and religious observance
    (B) no one activity derives its organization from another
    (C) certain integral beliefs tie all activities together
    (D) no activity has any substantive organization
    (E) the whole of adult life is connected by beliefs related to the vision practice

28. According to the passage, the guardian spirits of the British Columbian tribes belong to the realm of the

    (A) military
    (B) artistic
    (C) social
    (D) spiritual
    (E) economic

29. What does this author think about evaluating one culture in terms of another?

    (A) Comparative evaluation reveals the different goals of each society.
    (B) Examination of the infrastructures of both societies allows identification of the essential truths of each society.
    (C) Comparative judgment often proves that two cultures are oriented in the same direction.
    (D) Judging one culture in terms of another often reveals the superior qualities of one culture.
    (E) Societies are intrinsically unique and should only be evaluated individually.

30. One could best describe the organization of the activities of the British Columbian tribes as

    (A) hierarchical
    (B) segregated
    (C) elaborate
    (D) rigid
    (E) integrated

SECTION 2

Time—30 Minutes
35 Questions

Each sentence that follows has one or two blanks, each blank indicating that something has been omitted. Beneath the sentence are five lettered words or sets of words. Select the word or group of words that *best* fits the meaning of the sentence as a whole.

1. Seeing that the theft hurt the victim, Henry returned the loot, proving he was _____ .

   (A) copious (B) contrite (C) irreverent
   (D) dejected (E) corrupt

2. That reserved man is so _____ that surely he leads a _____ life.

   (A) unreliable . . persuasive
   (B) effete . . promiscuous
   (C) banal . . exciting
   (D) ascetic . . monastic
   (E) auspicious . . negative

3. The thieves, although criminals, _____ violence and _____ murder.

   (A) loved . . detested
   (B) destressed . . appeased
   (C) abhorred . . abominated
   (D) revenged . . enjoyed
   (E) opposed . . contemplated

4. Unlike the tract that Uncle Bob lives on, Cousin Sam's land is fertile and _____ .

   (A) artificial (B) eroded (C) arable
   (D) debauched (E) sterile

5. The common image is that business decision-making is very logical and rational; however, one authority in the field suggests that the process is more _____ than most people think.

   (A) circumscribed (B) methodical
   (C) structured (D) intuitive (E) certain

6. In _____ her child, the mother expressed her _____ .

   (A) harassing . . affection
   (B) rebuking . . disapprobation
   (C) injuring . . ambivalence

   (D) seizing . . discouragement
   (E) teasing . . thoughtlessness

7. Surprisingly, it often appears that people who are opposites have an _____ for each other.

   (A) abhorrence (B) antipathy (C) affinity
   (D) indifference (E) antagonism

8. With new evidence brought to light, the judge _____ the man once thought to be guilty.

   (A) exonerated (B) exhumed (C) effaced
   (D) engaged (E) exiled

9. It is a (an) _____ matter to converse with someone who is _____ .

   (A) impossible . . convivial
   (B) important . . indigent
   (C) precarious . . benevolent
   (D) simple . . obdurate
   (E) easy . . affable

10. If one desires to gain the respect of others, it is inadvisable to _____ and _____ against others in so hostile a manner.

    (A) slander . . deify
    (B) inveigh . . rail
    (C) castigate . . laud
    (D) demonstrate . . resist
    (E) stigmatize . . rant

Each question that follows consists of a related pair of words or phrases, followed by five lettered pairs of words or phrases. Select the lettered pair that *best* expresses a relationship similar to that expressed in the original pair.

11. INTERPRETER:THEORY: : (A) text:translation
    (B) translator:language
    (C) doctor:prescription
    (D) architect:blueprint
    (E) equation:mathematics

12. BRANCHES:TREE: : (A) duck:feathers
    (B) petticoat:skirt (C) tines:fork
    (D) man:limbs (E) tools:carpenter

13. PLUMBER:WRENCH: : (A) sculptor:marble
(B) voice:singer (C) carpenter:hammer
(D) book:cover (E) mandible:bird

14. SOMBRERO:HAT: : (A) gloves:hand
(B) ruler:measurement (C) shoes:boots
(D) paw:bear (E) shawl:wrap

15. PIPES:SINK: : (A) intestines:person
(B) grain:silo (C) wires:car (D) clouds:sky
(E) hands:clock

16. CROWD:PEOPLE: : (A) crackers:box
(B) girls:women (C) opera:singers
(D) group:individuals (E) sugar:grains

17. TRUNK:CAR: : (A) elephant:horse
(B) foot:shoe (C) house:window
(D) ferry:sailboat (E) weight:barbell

18. SEISMOLOGIST:EARTHQUAKE: :
(A) architect:building (B) microbiologist:slide
(C) cosmologist:skin (D) anthropologist:tribe
(E) priest:sinner

19. CLOTHES:WASHING MACHINE: :
(A) birds:aviary (B) gas:engine
(C) books:library (D) cake:oven
(E) bees:hive

20. EMERALD:JEWEL: : (A) cedar:wood
(B) loaf:bread (C) disease:symptom
(D) pebble:rock (E) design:blueprint

21. PUDDLE:LAKE: : (A) bridge:river
(B) shack:house (C) river:stream
(D) vein:artery (E) ravine:moat

22. DISCOMFORT:AGONY: :
(A) simper:scowl (B) warn:threaten
(C) extol:disparage (D) praise:honor
(E) humiliate:ignore

23. MOUND:MOUNTAIN: : (A) forest:tree
(B) arrow:spear (C) wail:weep
(D) limp:hobble (E) joke:quip

The passage below is followed by questions based on its content. Answer the questions on the basis of what is *stated* or *implied* in the passage, and in any introductory material that might be provided. Questions 24 through 35 are based on the following passage.

The following passage discusses the importance of ocean current systems and their effect on climate.

Whether any place will know the harsh extremes of a continental climate or the moderating effect of the sea depends less on its nearness to the ocean than on the pattern of currents and winds and the relief of the continents. The east coast of North America receives little benefit from the sea, because the prevailing winds are from the west. The Pacific coast, on the other hand, lies in the path of the westerly winds that have blown across thousands of miles of ocean. The moist breath of the Pacific brings climatic mildness and creates the dense rain forests of British Columbia, Washington, and Oregon; but its full influence is largely restricted to a narrow strip by the coast ranges that follow a course parallel to the sea. Europe, in contrast, is wide open to the sea, and "Atlantic weather" carries hundreds of miles into the interior.

By a seeming paradox, there are parts of the world that owe their desert dryness to their nearness to the ocean. The aridity of the Atacama and Kalahari deserts is curiously related to the sea. Wherever such marine deserts occur, there is found this combination of circumstances: a western coast in the lee of the prevailing winds, and a cold coastwise current. So on the west coast of South America the cold Humboldt streams northward off the shores of Chile and Peru—the great return flow of Pacific waters seeking the equator. The Humboldt, it will be remembered, is cold because it is continuously being reinforced by the upwelling of deeper water. The presence of this cold water offshore helps create the aridity of the region. The onshore breezes that push in toward the hot land in the afternoons are formed of cool air that has lain over a cool sea. As they reach the land they are forced to rise into the high coastal mountains—the ascent cooling them more than the land can warm them. So there is little condensation of water vapor, and although the cloud banks and the fogs forever seem to promise rain, the promise is not fulfilled so long as the Humboldt rolls on its accustomed course along these shores. On the stretch from Africa to Caldera there is normally less than an inch of rain in a year. It is a beautifully balanced system—as long as it remains in balance. What happens when the Humboldt is temporarily displaced is nothing short of catastrophic.

At irregular intervals the Humboldt is deflected away from the South American continent by a warm current of tropical water that comes down from the north. These are years of disaster. The whole economy of the area is adjusted to the normal aridity of climate. In the years of El Niño, as the warm current is called, torrential rains fall—the downpouring rains of the equitorial regions let loose upon the dust-dry hillsides of the Peruvian coast. The soil washes away, the mud huts literally dissolve and collapse, crops are destroyed. Even worse things happen at sea. The cold-water fauna of the Humboldt sickens and dies in the warm water, and the birds that fish the cold sea for a living must either migrate or starve.

The vast current systems, which flow through the oceans like rivers, lie for the most part offshore and one might suppose their influence in intertidal matters to be slight. Yet the currents have far-reaching effects, for they transport immense volumes of water over long distances—water that holds its original temperature through thousands of miles of its journey. In this way tropical warmth is carried northward and arctic cold brought far down toward the equator. The currents, probably more than any other single factor, are the creators of the marine climate.

The importance of climate lies in the fact that life, even as broadly defined to include all living things of every sort, exists with a relatively narrow range of temperature, roughly between 32°F. and 210°F. The planet Earth is particularly favorable for life because it has a fairly stable temperature. Especially in the sea, temperature changes are moderate and gradual, and many animals are so delicately adjusted to the accustomed water climate that an abrupt or drastic change is fatal. Animals living on the shore and exposed to air temperatures at low tide are necessarily a little more hardy, but even these have their preferred range of heat and cold beyond which they seldom stray.

Most tropical animals are more sensitive to change—especially toward higher temperatures—than northern ones, and this is probably because the water in which they live normally varies by only a few degrees throughout the year. Some tropical sea urchins, keyhole limpets, and brittle stars die when the shallow waters heat to about 99°F. The arctic jellyfish Cyanea, on the other hand, is so hardy that it continues to pulsate when half its bell is imprisoned in ice, and may revive even after being solidly frozen for hours. The horseshoe crab is an example of an animal that is very tolerant of temperature change. It has a wide range as a species, and its northern forms can survive being frozen into ice in New England, while its southern representatives thrive in tropical waters off Florida and southward to Yucatán. Shore animals for the most part endure the seasonal changes of temperate coasts, but some find it necessary to escape the extreme cold of winter.

Ocean temperatures vary from about 28°F. in polar seas to 96°F in the Persian Gulf, which contains the hottest ocean water in the world. To creatures of the sea, which with few exceptions must match in their own bodies the temperature of the surrounding water, this range is tremendous, and change of temperature is probably the most important single condition that controls the distribution of marine animals.

24. The main idea of this selection is best expressed as

   (A) temperature ranges
   (B) ocean currents and their effect on marine life
   (C) current systems
   (D) the importance of climate and animal adaptation
   (E) arctic cold and tropical warmth

25. According to this passage, ocean current systems

   (A) are given to abrupt changes in temperature
   (B) prevent tropical warmth from being carried northward
   (C) determine marine climate
   (D) have little influence in intertidal matters
   (E) bear little resemblance to those found in rivers

26. The author implies that

   (A) animals have a high degree of adaptability
   (B) most tropical animals are highly sensitive to sudden drops in temperature
   (C) sea animals are less hardy than animals living on shore
   (D) most living things cannot tolerate sudden shifts in temperature
   (E) animals learn to adapt within a broad range of temperatures

27. The word *temperate* in the last sentence of the next to the last paragraph most probably refers to

   (A) marine climate
   (B) a well-protected shoreline
   (C) a moderate climate
   (D) an area where temperatures remain stable
   (E) an area where there are sudden shifts in temperature

28. Which of the following statements is *not* true?

   (A) The water, which ocean currents transport long distances, retains its original temperature.
   (B) The horseshoe crab has a very limited range as a species.
   (C) Shore animals exposed to air temperatures at low tide are tough.
   (D) Keyhole limpets are sensitive to changes toward higher temperatures.
   (E) The Cyanea is able to survive being solidly frozen for hours.

29. What explanation does the author give for the occasional catastrophic rains of Peru?

(A) The water of the Humboldt over-condenses, thus causing excess precipitation.

(B) Peru's topography, both mountainous and flat, throws an element of unpredictability into the climate of Peru.

(C) Peru, as well as Chile, is near the equator.

(D) The usual cold current that streams from the south is overtaken by a tropical current.

(E) Scientists have put forth various theories; one definitive explanation has never been agreed on.

30. Which of the following statements is true about the sea?

(A) Temperature changes in the sea are usually moderate.

(B) The temperature of the sea has little effect on most of its inhabitants.

(C) It is only with the introduction of recent technology that scientists can now predict the pattern of currents.

(D) All land by the sea is moist and mild in climate.

(E) Temperatures never vary more than 28 degrees from ocean to ocean.

31. According to the author, why is Earth favorable for the propagation of life?

(A) Earth's pattern of currents and winds is unique.

(B) The varying temperatures of Earth's many oceans can support a diversity of plant and animal life.

(C) The ratio of ocean to desert is greatly in favor of the life-producing ocean.

(D) The temperature of Earth is relatively stable and narrow in range.

(E) The Earth offers a wide range of nutrients and habitats for its creatures.

32. What reason(s) does the author give for the dryness of the region of Chile?

I. Chile's mountainous topography

II. Chile's location on the western coast of South America

III. the presence of a cold current off Chile's coast

(A) I (B) III (C) II, III
(D) all of the above
(E) none of the above

33. The usual climate of Peru is

I. tropical
II. dry
III. cloudy
IV. wet

(A) I, IV (B) II, III (C) II
(D) I, III, IV (E) IV

34. What occurs when the Humbolt is deflected by tropical northern currents?

I. The water's fauna freezes and dies.
II. Flooding on the coasts of Peru.
III. The usual ecological balance of the water is disturbed.
IV. The Atacama desert becomes even hotter.
V. The Humbolt is reinforced by the upswelling of deeper water.

(A) I (B) I, II (C) II, III, V
(D) V (E) I, II, III, IV

35. Which of the following statements about marine life is true?

(A) Tropical animals are less sensitive to temperature change than northern ones.

(B) Northern animals are less sensitive to higher temperature change.

(C) Throughout the year, tropical animals experience greater change in temperature than northern animals.

(D) In most cases, shore animals will migrate to escape the cold of winter.

(E) The body temperature of both tropical and northern animals tends to match the temperature of their environments.

SECTION 3

Time—15 Minutes
13 Questions

The next two passages are followed by questions based on their content and the relationship between them. Answer the questions on the basis of what is *stated* or *implied* in the passages, and in any introductory material that might be provided. Questions 1 through 13 are based on the following passages.

The following passages present contrasting views on adoption procedures.

Passage A

Closed adoption procedures were born in the late nineteenth century. At the time, a strong social reform movement sought protection and help for unwed pregnant women and their illegitimate children through the founding of state-licensed adoption agencies. Right from the beginning there were questions concerning how these programs would be administered and who determined who adopted which baby. In the democratic tradition, biological parents have certain fundamental rights concerning their children. But, in the eyes of nineteenth-century society, the birthmother forfeited that right because of her presumed promiscuity. The founders of the first adoption agencies felt compassion for the plight of unwed mothers but still considered them sinners and social outcasts. The other party to the adoption, the adopting parents, might have been consulted about the placement of the children, but they, too, were considered social pariahs; their infertility was seen as the result of being cursed by God. The children themselves were too young to have any say. Only the agency's own social workers had the legitimacy and social standing to make the critical decisions in each adoption. Given the social milieu of the day, adoption agencies met little resistance establishing their almost total power over the adoption process.

With closed adoption, neither birthparents nor adopting parents were permitted access to any information about each other. Information on their biological origins was kept from adopted children even when they reached adulthood. While such clandestine procedures seem shocking today, they served an important function in their day. The secrecy protected the birthmother from facing a lifetime of social ostracism. Adoption shielded the child from being branded ille-

gitimate. In many states, hospitals routinely stamped the birth certificate of a child born to an unwed mother with the word *illegitimate* printed in large red letters. But once the child was adopted, the court replaced this stigmatized birth certificate with a more conventional version that made no reference to the child's biological parents, married or unmarried.

For all of these reasons, "closed adoption" became synonymous with "adoption" by the middle of the twentieth century. Regulations forbade any exchange of information between adopting parents and birthparents and all adoption records were sealed. All control over the adoption process was taken from birthparents and entrusted solely to licensed agencies.

Passage B

Traditionally in this country, adoption has been an all-or-nothing proposition, irrevocably ending all contact with the birthparents. But that is slowly changing, both because of the increasing popularity of open adoptions, in which the birth and adoptive parents may meet and maintain a relationship, and the emerging industry of support groups, businesses and nonprofit organizations that help adoptees and birthparents contact each other. At the same time, the growing adoption-reform movement, which since the 1970s has fought for giving adult adoptees access to their birth records, has begun to frame its cause as a civil rights movement.

As a democratic country, the United States has had a tradition of being distrustful of any type of governmental secrecy. This has been the case from the Founding Fathers and the Bill of Rights to the Watergate scandal. Because of this opposition, some laws requiring secrecy in adoption were not approved until the 1940s. But soon they were part of every state's regulations concerning adoption.

The American Adoption Congress and other groups argue that every person has a fundamental right to information about his or her identity. Keeping that information hidden, they say, is an unacceptable and wounding form of discrimination, even in cases where there is no special medical need for adoptees to learn about their backgrounds. Adoptive parents complain that they are discriminated against in many contexts. For example, until the Family and Medical Leave Act went into effect, few employers offered adoptive parents the same maternity and paternity leaves available to biological parents. And in most states, insurance companies that provide immediate coverage for most newborns delay coverage for adopted children until the placement is finalized—a process that can take two years. And even then they may not cover the baby's pre-existing medical problems.

Open adoption does not mean shared parenthood. Legally there is only one formal set of parents—the adoptive parents—with the right to make decisions for their child. But the matter goes far beyond legalities. While there is no single, universally agreed on standard for what constitutes open adoption, it usually means that the important decisions in the adoption are left strictly up to the adoptive parents and birthparents. Moreover, usually the adoptive parents and birthparents are not restricted from using their names, exchanging information, or maintaining ongoing contact. In what is called semi-open adoption, there are usually limitations imposed on the decision-making power of all the parties, on the sharing of information, and on contact before and after birth. These restrictions can often undermine the benefits of complete involvement of all parties in all critical decisions which creates the sense of respect and cooperation that is generated through the adoption process.

1. In passage A the author contends that prior to the twentieth century, society's overriding attitude toward an unwed mother was that

   (A) she be involved in all the critical decisions affecting her
   (B) she make herself available to the adoptive parents
   (C) she automatically gave up all her rights
   (D) she assist the administrators of the agency in working out the process of adoption
   (E) she relinquish control to the adoptive parents

2. According to passage A, the state adoption agency was concerned with all of the following except

   (A) preventing the adopted children from learning about their birthparents
   (B) protecting the birthmother from prejudice
   (C) protecting and helping unwed mothers
   (D) protecting the children from discrimination
   (E) giving the birthmother unlimited control over her child in the adoption procedures

3. Prior to the twentieth century, society's attitude toward an unwed mother was that she was

   (A) too young to have any say in adoption procedures

(B) unfairly discriminated against
(C) promiscuous in her social behavior
(D) entitled to the same maternity rights as the adoptive parents
(E) entitled to certain fundamental rights concerning her child

4. According to each author, what role does secrecy play in the adoption process?

   I. Author A justifies secrecy as a procedure that offers protection to the biological mother.
   II. Each author implies that the traditional position on adoption has consistently advocated procedures that forbid the open exchange of information.
   III. Author B implies that adoption restrictions are essential for fostering respect and cooperation.
   IV. Author B argues that open adoption does not mean that adoptive parents are denied the legal right to make decisions.
   V. Author B supports the idea that adoption shields the child from being branded illegitimate.

   (A) I and IV only (B) II and III only
   (C) I, II, and IV only (D) II and V only
   (E) II, III, and V

5. What does the author of passage B mean by the statement "Traditionally in this country, adoption has been an all-or-nothing proposition, irrevocably ending all contact with the birthparents"?

   (A) that for the most part, the adoption process consistently maintained closed procedures
   (B) that trust is essential for a successful adoption
   (C) that the adoption agencies need to function within the framework of democratic ideals
   (D) that the founders of the first adoption agencies were mainly interested in the total welfare of the children born to unwed mothers.
   (E) that since the late nineteenth century, social reform movements have dominated the administration of adoption agencies

6. If author A were to replace the word *pariahs* in the first paragraph of passage A, which suggested word would be most appropriate?

   (A) sinners
   (B) rejects
   (C) adoptees
   (D) rebels
   (E) dissenters

7. The most interesting paradox of author A's reference to the founders of the first adoption agencies is that

   (A) they were able to gain total control over the adoption process even though they met with great resistance
   (B) even though they were committed to social reform they stigmatized the children of unwed mothers
   (C) even though they considered unwed mothers sinners, they had great sympathy for them
   (D) even though they were interested in protecting the illegitimate children, the children themselves were denied their fundamental rights
   (E) even though they were individuals interested in social justice, they took away the rights of the unwed mother

8. The word *clandestine* in the second paragraph of passage A most nearly means

   (A) protective
   (B) legitimate
   (C) conventional
   (D) hidden
   (E) limited

9. The author of passage B is critical of secrecy of adoption because

   (A) without access to medical records, most insurance companies restrict coverage for the adopted child
   (B) it means that all of the important decisions concerning the child are made by the adoptive parents
   (C) it is a serious form of prejudice
   (D) it runs counter to the all-or-nothing position of traditional adoption procedures
   (E) the adoption reform movement has revoked the idea that children are too young to have a say in adoption procedures

10. How would the author of passage A respond to the author of passage B's position that "every person has a right to information about his or her identity"?

    (A) The unwed mother forfeited that right because of her presumed promiscuity.
    (B) Adopting parents should have free access to an exchange of information with the birth parents.
    (C) Once the child is adopted he should be privileged to any information as to his biological parents.
    (D) The agency's own social workers should

gradually diminish control over the critical decisions made in adoption procedures.
    (E) Hospitals proved the necessity for secrecy because they routinely stamped the birth certificate with the word *illegitimate*.

11. According to author B, open adoption means all of the following except that

    I. the adoptive parents and the biological parents are not restricted from using their names
    II. all of the important decisions are made by the adoptive parents
    III. the standard for what constitutes open adoption is open to interpretation
    IV. legally open adoption means shared parenthood

    (A) I and IV only
    (B) II and III only
    (C) I, II, and IV only
    (D) II and IV only
    (E) I, II, and III only

12. According to the author of passage B, adoptive parents contend that the most serious discriminating practice against them centers around

    (A) the fact that they are considered social outcasts
    (B) the stigma on their baby's birth certificate prior to his official adoption
    (C) the inability of their adopted child to make contact with his birthparents
    (D) insurance coverage for their newborn child
    (E) their inability to use their own names

13. Semi-open adoption differs from open adoption in every way but which of the following:

    (A) unlike open adoption, semi-open adoption can diminish the good will between the birthparents and the adoptive parents
    (B) there are limitations placed on the sharing of information between the biological parents and the adoptive parents
    (C) the really important decisions in the adoption are shared between the birthparents and the adoptive parents
    (D) restrictions on the decision-making power of all parties undermines the benefits throughout the adoption process
    (E) there are restrictions placed on contact between the adoptive parents and the biological parents before and after the birth of the baby

ANSWERS

Verbal Assessment Test 2

Section I	Section 2	Section 3
1. (E)	1. (B)	1. (C)
2. (B)	2. (D)	2. (E)
3. (A)	3. (C)	3. (C)
4. (E)	4. (C)	4. (C)
5. (C)	5. (D)	5. (A)
6. (A)	6. (B)	6. (B)
7. (A)	7. (C)	7. (C)
8. (B)	8. (A)	8. (D)
9. (A)	9. (E)	9. (C)
10. (B)	10. (B)	10. (A)
11. (C)	11. (D)	11. (E)
12. (A)	12. (C)	12. (D)
13. (C)	13. (C)	13. (C)
14. (E)	14. (A)	
15. (E)	15. (A)	
16. (D)	16. (D)	
17. (A)	17. (B)	
18. (B)	18. (D)	
19. (C)	19. (D)	
20. (B)	20. (A)	
21. (C)	21. (E)	
22. (B)	22. (B)	
23. (B)	23. (B)	
24. (D)	24. (B)	
25. (B)	25. (C)	
26. (E)	26. (C)	
27. (B)	27. (C)	
28. (C)	28. (B)	
29. (E)	29. (D)	
30. (B)	30. (A)	
	31. (D)	
	32. (D)	
	33. (B)	
	34. (C)	
	35. (E)	

Verbal Assessment Test 3

Section 1

Time—30 Minutes
30 Questions

Each sentence that follows has one or two blanks, each blank indicating that something has been omitted. Beneath the sentence are five lettered words or sets of words. Choose the word or set of words that *best* fits the meaning of the sentence as a whole.

1. Offensive jokes about national origin are both _____ and _____.

   (A) admirable . . advantageous
   (B) propitious . . pejorative
   (C) destructive . . salutary
   (D) derogatory . . disparaging
   (E) beatific . . unpleasant

2. The dissolution of two-parent families, though it may _____ the adults involved, is _____ to many children.

   (A) excuse . . painful
   (B) benefit . . harmful
   (C) entangle . . damaging
   (D) restrict . . liberating
   (E) free . . confusing

3. Some people believe that the dramatic changes in family structure, though regrettable, are impossible to reverse, that family breakup is a(n) _____ feature of American life. Furthermore, anyone who thinks otherwise is indulging in _____ or trying to turn back the clock.

   (A) established . . fantasy
   (B) undeniable . . disillusionment
   (C) conditional . . self-deception
   (D) inevitable . . nostalgia
   (E) gratuitous . . denial

4. Although Tom usually exhibits _____ , he was so excited by the last remark that he retorted in complete and unbridled _____.

   (A) participation . . exposure
   (B) happiness . . instigation
   (C) complacency . . restraint

   (D) resurgence . . resilience
   (E) composure . . fury

5. The experts wanted to determine whether the painting was _____ or merely a(n) _____ imitation.

   (A) radical . . reactionary
   (B) authentic . . bogus
   (C) lustrous . . incendiary
   (D) illusionary . . essential
   (E) sleazy . . flawless

6. His _____ habits result in his _____ work.

   (A) indolent . . inferior
   (B) impeccable . . objectionable
   (C) slothful . . praiseworthy
   (D) pleasant . . offensive
   (E) concise . . shameful

7. The acrobat's _____ maneuvers, if performed by an untrained amateur, could prove _____.

   (A) sinful . . blissful
   (B) daring . . disastrous
   (C) engaging . . annoying
   (D) chaotic . . edifying
   (E) dramatic . . callous

8. The hypocrite loves to _____ others for wrongdoing even though he is as guilty as they.

   (A) conciliate (B) commandeer
   (C) pacify (D) laud (E) chide

9. The manufacturer's plan was designed to _____ energy wastefulness without appreciably _____ profits.

   (A) curtail . . diminishing
   (B) augment . . increasing
   (C) amplify . . dilating
   (D) animate . . degenerating
   (E) enrich . . benefiting

169

Each question that follows consists of a related pair of words or phrases, followed by five lettered pairs of words or phrases. Select the lettered pair that *best* expresses a relationship similar to that expressed in the original pair.

10. FILM:IMAGE: : (A) palette:brush
    (B) canvas:painting (C) smock:easel
    (D) filter:light (E) darkness:luminescence

11. PHYSICIAN:X-RAY: :
    (A) chronometer:timekeeper
    (B) whistle:referee (C) actuary:statistics
    (D) quilt:bedspread (E) composer:symphony

12. IRRIGATION:GROWTH: : (A) weeds:grass
    (B) trees:birds (C) sunlight:photosynthesis
    (D) approval:approbation (E) guilt:forgiveness

13. TRICKLE:DELUGE: : (A) breeze:gale
    (B) storm:drizzle (C) peony:flower
    (D) book:journal (E) painting:poster

14. PARRY:BLOW: : (A) fly:bird
    (B) evade:arrest (C) extinguish:ashes
    (D) demonstrate:annoyance (E) engage:interest

15. DEFECTION:COUNTRY: : (A) excavation:dig
    (B) desertion:army (C) restitution:compensation
    (C) indigence:poverty (D) recuperation:illness

The next two passages are followed by questions based on their content. Answer the questions following each passage on the basis of what is *stated* or *implied* in the passage, and in any introductory material that might be provided. Questions 16 through 21 are based on the following passage.

The following passage is about A Tale of Two Cities *by Charles Dickens.*

Throughout the nineteenth century, Europe was haunted by the specter of revolution. The flaming holocaust that had been born in France and poured its fiery floods over nearly all the rest of the Continent troubled the nightmares of the dominant classes with shuddering visions of an infuriated Jacquerie burning down chateaux, ferocious mobs tearing through the streets, howling tribunals, the rumbling of tumbrils, the hiss and thud of the guillotine, the bloodbaths of the Napoleonic Wars. The rulers of the nations had put back—or almost put back—the clock but they had not solved the problems of social injustice and suffering. The Terror might rise again.

A Tale of Two Cities was born amid such social conflicts. Dickens wrote it not in a time of peace, prosper-

ity, and stability but of mass protest and imminent revolution. He first conceived of the story shortly after a hundred people had been killed or wounded by the bomb with which Orsini attempted to assassinate Napoleon III. Even as the novel was being published, revolutions deposed the rulers of Parma, Modena, and Romagna, and there were insurrections in the Papal States. Only a year later, in four swift months, Garibaldi's Redshirts swarmed over all Sicily and triumphantly captured Naples. Everywhere the old tyrannies and injustices were crashing. Unless England's landowners, merchants, and industrialists took warning, might not their turn come next?

A Tale of Two Cities was thus not only a work of art, it was also a tract for the times, a conditional prophecy. The French Revolution had been the decisive upheaval that had destroyed the eighteenth-century world and shattered the power of the aristocracy in France, had shaken it even in the rest of Europe. It was the convulsive womb out of which the modern world had been born. Readers of the novel have not always realized the degree to which Dickens was appealing to troubled social conscience and a fear of social turmoil.

16. The author is primarily concerned with

    (A) political conditions in Europe in the nineteenth century
    (B) the social and political climate that gave birth to *A Tale of Two Cities*
    (C) social injustice and suffering that resulted from the Napoleonic Wars
    (D) protest and revolution in the nineteenth century
    (E) the prophetic value of *A Tale of Two Cities*

17. As a consequence of Orsini's attempt to assassinate Napoleon,

    (A) revolution broke out in Parma, Modena, and Romagna
    (B) English landowners and industrialists realized they were in danger
    (C) Dickens conceived of *A Tale of Two Cities*
    (D) the old tyrannies and injustices were destroyed
    (E) the Jacquerie began a series of insurrections in the Papal States

18. The author implies that the French Revolution

    (A) fostered insurrection in the Papal States
    (B) destroyed the power of the French aristocracy
    (C) infuriated the Jacquerie
    (D) inspired fear of social upheaval
    (E) troubled the dominant classes in Europe

19. In the first sentence of the last paragraph, the author uses the phrase "conditional prophecy" to mean that

    (A) social injustice and concern over suffering needed to result in action
    (B) the inevitable consequence of revolution would result from the circumstances of the time
    (C) protest and revolution were the consequences of a troubled social conscience
    (D) peace and stability were the proving ground for revolution
    (E) mass protest would result from a disgruntled aristocracy

20. The author suggests that the vision of all but one of the following troubled the ruling classes in nineteenth-century Europe:

    (A) mobs tearing through the streets
    (B) the burning down of chateaux
    (C) the specter of fiery floods
    (D) the bloodbaths of the Napoleonic Wars
    (E) nightmare sounds of the tumbrils

21. Dickens's main purpose in writing *A Tale of Two Cities* was to

    (A) shatter the power of the aristocracy
    (B) restore peace, prosperity, and stability to France
    (C) prod the social conscience of those who feared social upheaval
    (E) assuage the fury of Garibaldi and the Jacquerie

Questions 22 through 30 are based on the following passage.

The following passage examines the nature of witchcraft in seventeenth-century New England.

It was not simply as Puritans that New Englanders drew on witchcraft beliefs in the seventeenth century. Their need for witches also grew out of their experience as settlers. New England may have been a religious commonwealth, but its people were nevertheless colonizing a land and creating a society—an enterprise as much individual and secular as collective and spiritual. It was an endeavor that generated contradictions of its own.

To locate witchcraft in its structural as well as its ideological context is to raise issues that concern the witch and her accusers. For though the witch was a creation of Puritan belief, she was also the creation of the neighbors who denounced her, and the story of witchcraft is as much theirs as hers.

The relationships between accuser and accused were so complex that sorting them out completely is an impossible task. Where community consensus concerning a woman's witchcraft was strongest, as many as twenty, thirty, or forty people might come into court to explain how their suspicions had been aroused. They might relate incidents that had taken place weeks, even decades before, and their testimony left much that was ambiguous, often including the source of the original complaint. The impression one carries away after reading thousands of these depositions is that over the years, individuals who had been involved in minor confrontations with the accused shared their concerns with their neighbors, some of whom in turn saw her shape in their own difficulties and shared this with their neighbors, and so on until the community's leaders responded to the danger at hand. The individual who filed the official complaint, if a complaint was filed, was only one and perhaps only the most recent of many accusers.

Moreover, to acknowledge only those people who named names as accusers overlooks the ministers, magistrates, juries, and other members of the community who validated some accusations and invalidated others; the community was as much an accuser as any individual within it.

When a community looks only for evidence of guilt and ignores or suppresses all contradictory evidence, the result is a witch hunt. And a witch hunt was developing in Salem as the community felt itself to be so beset by evil that it was no longer capable of perceiving the good.

The primary causes should now be clear. There was an outbreak of epidemic hysteria in Salem Village which originated in experiments with the occult. And the hysterical hallucinations of the afflicted persons were confirmed by some concrete evidence of actual witchcraft and by many confessions, the majority of them also hysterical. A number of other explanations have been offered, but most of them are more or less unconvincing. It has been argued that the outbreak was the result of the malice accumulated during a long series of village quarrels, and it is true that there had been no scarcity of petty quarrelling in Salem Village. But many small towns have such a history, and few of them have witch hunts. It has also been argued that the outbreak was due to Puritanism. Puritans, we have all been taught, were repressive. But the degree of repressiveness in Puritan society is open to debate. The demonstrably hysterical behavior at Salem was the result of fear rather than repression. It has also been argued that the outbreak owed much to the fact that Massachusetts at this time felt itself gravely threatened. There is much to be said for this argument. What more likely time would Massachusetts' arch enemy, the Devil, choose for his attack than precisely that time when she was beset by all her other enemies? The Salem witchcraft hysteria occurred at a time when the very existence of the colony had been threatened for more than a generation.

22. According to the author, all but one of the following can be considered a cause of the Salem witch hunts:

(A) many of the accused confessed to their guilt
(B) people were experimenting in witchcraft
(C) hallucinations of the afflicted were all confirmed by concrete evidence
(D) the existence of the Massachusetts colony had been threatened for some time
(E) fear

23. With which of the following statements would the author probably agree?

(A) Witch hunts are always the result of bitter and long-standing grievances between neighbors.
(B) One of the primary causes for the outbreak of hysteria in Salem was the severe repression of the Puritan community.
(C) Witch hunts are the result of a dispassionate and critical examination of the evidence.
(D) Epidemic hysteria is the direct result of witchcraft and hallucination.
(E) The presence of fear in a community is one of the factors that could produce hysteria.

24. In developing the passage, the author does all but one of the following:

(A) attempt to suggest causes for the epidemic hysteria in the Salem community
(B) refute certain beliefs about the causes for the hysteria in Salem
(C) examine the conditions under which hysteria is likely to emerge in a community
(D) defend an individual's right to experiment in witchcraft
(E) suggest that there is some question as to how repressive the Puritan society was

25. Which of the following best expresses the main idea of the passage?

(A) the Salem witch hunts
(B) repression and fear in Salem

(C) some thoughts about the origins of hysteria in the Salem community
(D) the significance of long-standing quarrels as a contributing factor to community hysteria
(E) hallucinations and the occult in Salem Village

26. All of the following can be ascribed to the Salem community except for

(A) Puritanism
(B) petty quarreling
(C) devil worship
(D) suppression of evidence
(E) repression

27. The author traces the development of an accusation to show that

(A) accusations were always based on concrete proof
(B) many accusations had no clear basis
(C) all accusations were identical
(D) witches deserved the accusations made against them
(E) people only accused their neighbors of witchcraft

28. The first paragraph of the passage suggests that the process of colonization is primarily

(A) secular
(B) personal
(C) spiritual
(D) communal
(E) all of the above

29. The "ideological context" cited in the second paragraph most likely refers to the Puritans'

(A) social structure
(B) economic practices
(C) government policy
(D) farming techniques
(E) religious beliefs

30. The tone of this passage is best described as

(A) remorseful
(B) apathetic
(C) rhetorical
(D) speculative
(E) caustic

SECTION 2

Time—30 Minutes
35 Questions

Each sentence below has one or two blanks, each blank indicating that something has been omitted. Beneath the sentence are five lettered words or sets of words. Choose the word or set of words that *best* fits the meaning of the sentence as a whole.

1. The deterioration in father-child bonds is most severe among children who experience divorce at an early age. The father-child bond is _____ , often _____ damaged in disrupted families.

   (A) severely . . irreparably
   (B) earnestly . . casually
   (C) seriously . . decidedly
   (D) eagerly . . impatiently
   (E) objectionably . . vehemently

2. The death of a father is not likely to disrupt the authority structure in any radical way. When a father dies, he is no longer physically present, but death does not _____ him as (an) authority figure in the child's life. On the contrary, his authority may be _____ through death.

   (A) debase . . aggravated
   (B) dethrone . . limited
   (C) diminish . . enhanced
   (D) ruin . . magnified
   (E) elevate . . intensified

3. The great educational tragedy of our time is that many American children are failing in school not because they are intellectually or physically _____ but because they are emotionally _____.

   (A) damaged . . motivated
   (B) limited . . apathetic
   (C) indifferent . . disillusioned
   (D) impaired . . incapacitated
   (E) stimulated . . discouraged

4. Martin is widely recognized as one of the most knowledgeable and accomplished snake hunters in the Appalachians. Snake finding is not only Martin's _____ , he has refined it into a(n) _____ , mapping and counting rattlers on a daily basis, year after year.

   (A) passion . . obsession
   (B) interest . . existence

   (C) preoccupation . . life
   (D) preference . . hobby
   (E) profession . . business

5. Unlike bald eagles or grizzly bears, snakes are maddeningly difficult to count. They do not mark territories, leave distinctive signs, or even show themselves with any frequency, so a patch of woods where snakes are _____ may be practically _____ from one where they are absent.

   (A) infrequent . . synonymous
   (B) plentiful . . indistinguishable
   (C) swarming . . irreconcilable
   (D) rare . . indeterminate
   (E) invisible . . unintelligible

6. Some primates, such as orangutans, lead _____ lives, meeting only for the occasional mating. But the average group of primates is supremely _____ , whether it is a family of a dozen gorillas living in a mountain rain forest, or a troop of 100 baboons in the African grasslands.

   (A) gregarious . . communicative
   (B) disgruntled . . driven
   (C) secluded . . reclusive
   (D) solitary . . social
   (E) desolate . . withdrawn

7. In 1982 only 5 percent of gunshot victims at Chicago's Cook County Hospital had been hit by more than one bullet. By 1991, with the _____ of easy-to-buy assault weapons, that rate had quintupled.

   (A) promise (B) insurgence (C) recall
   (D) discharge (E) proliferation

8. Given that people do differ in language, religion, and ethnicity, the only alternative to tyranny or genocide is for people to learn to live together in mutual respect and _____ . That is not an idle hope. Despite all the past wars over religion, people of different religions do _____ peacefully in many countries.

   (A) tolerance . . coexist
   (B) dignity . . relate
   (C) tranquility . . cooperate

(D) amicability . . synchronize
(E) enmity . . exist

9. Another constant in Japan reportage by American journalists over the decades has been that the Japanese financial system is a "house of cards," perennially _____ on the brink of _____.

(A) teetering . . recovery
(B) tilting . . solvency
(C) hovering . . collapse
(D) consolidating . . disaster
(B) stabilizing . . exhaustion

10. Disease is a _____ experience. You see people with tremendous fame or wealth or political power or achievement, and there are times when all of these material attributes don't change things. It teaches you what's substantial in life, like family relationships and friends.

(A) demeaning (B) common (C) humbling
(D) bewildering (E) mortifying

Each question below consists of a related pair of words or phrases, followed by five lettered pairs of words or phrases. Select the lettered pair that *best* expresses a relationship similar to that expressed in the original pair.

11. HONE:KNIFE: : (A) dull:edge
(B) focus:microscope (C) grate:cheese
(D) drive:wedge (E) shatter:glass

12. WHET:APPETITE: : (A) deepen:thought
(B) stimulate:interest (C) dull:sensitivity
(D) lose:consciousness (E) lower:threshold

13. DISEASE:PLAGUE: : (A) depression:sadness
(B) secret:lie (C) loyalty:nationalism
(D) boredom:apathy (E) peninsula:island

14. INFILTRATE:ORGANIZATION: :
(A) decipher:message (B) covert:operation
(C) trespass:property (D) access:code
(E) interpret:signal

15. COURAGE:FOOLHARDINESS: :
(A) self-opinionated:dogmatic
(B) obsequiousness:respect
(C) slackness:neglect (D) pride:arrogance
(E) frank:forthrightness

16. TIME:SCYTHE: : (A) freedom:mountain top
(B) ignorance:chains (C) justice:scales
(C) peace:eagle (E) liberty:sickle

17. MUSEUM:PAINTING: : (A) theater:audience
(B) auction:merchandise (C) flock:sheep
(D) zoo:animal (E) hangar:airplane

18. REITERATE:STATEMENT: : (A) revise:plans
(B) duplicate:efforts (C) rescind:order
(D) expunge:information
(E) restate:questions

19. SOOTHE:PACIFY: : (A) cruel:pitiless
(B) crooked:loyal (C) skillful:awkward
(D) prejudiced:impartial
(E) retribution:forgiveness

20. TINGE:COLOR: : (A) indelicate:remark
(B) increased:advantage
(C) peerless:example (D) nuance:meaning
(E) subordinated:idea

21. STAR:CONSTELLATION: : (A) rim:wheel
(B) chair:table (C) pulpit:church
(D) cow:herd (E) remedy:cure

22. EMBEZZLEMENT:THIEVERY: :
(A) housebreaking:shoplifting
(B) hijacking:plagerism
(C) abducting:plundering
(D) extortion:looting
(E) bootlegging:smuggling

23. FISH:SCALES: : (A) x-rays:surgeon
(B) man:epidermis (C) bird:feathers
(D) tree:limbs (E) zebra:stripes

Questions 24 through 35 are based on the following passage.

The following passage discusses the nature of culture in society.

Because of man's great capacity for adaptability and his remarkable ingenuity, he can improve in a great variety of ways upon the manner in which the lower animals meet their needs. Within every society there are particular ways in which needs are met. The origins of these ways are usually "lost in the mists of antiquity" or, as the Australian aborigines say, they "belong in the dream time." In fact, one of the hardest things in anthropology is to trace the origin of custom. There is usually no one old enough to remember its origin because as a rule it came into being a very long time ago, long before written history. Culture represents man's response to his basic needs. Culture is man's way of making himself comfortable in the world. It is the behavior he had learned as a member of society. We may define culture as the way of life of a people, the environment which a group of human beings occupying a common territory have created in the form of ideas, institutions, pots and pans, language, tools, services, and sentiments.

It is this man-made environment, culture, that all human societies impose upon the physical environment and in which all human beings are trained. Culture becomes so identified with life itself that it may be fairly said that it is not so much superimposed on life as it is a substitute for it. Just as a tool substitutes for and extends the capacities of the hand, so culture substitutes for and extends the capacities of life.

The criteria by which culture may be recognized are: (1) it must be invented; (2) it must be transmitted from generation to generation; and (3) it must be perpetuated in its original or in modified form. While some lower animals are capable of very limited cultural behavior, man alone seems to be virtually unlimited in his capacity for culture. The process of creating, transmitting, and maintaining the past in the present is culture—the capacity which the American semanticist Alfred Korzybski called "time-binding." Plants bind chemicals, animals bind space, but man alone binds time.

Not one item of his tribal social organization, of his language, of his local religion, is carried in his germ-cell. Culture is not a biologically transmitted complex. What is lost in Nature's guaranty of safety is made up in the advantage of greater plasticity. The human animal does not, like the bear, grow himself a polar coat in order to adapt himself, after many generations, to the Arctic. He learns to sew himself a coat and put up a snow house. From all we can learn of the history of intelligence in pre-human as well as human societies, this plasticity has been the soil in which human progress began and in which it has maintained itself. In the ages of the mammoths, species after species without plasticity arose, overreached itself, and died out, undone by the development of the very traits it had biologically produced in order to cope with its environment. The beasts of prey and finally the higher apes came slowly to rely upon other than biological adaptations, and upon the consequent increased plasticity the foundations were laid, bit by bit, for the development of intelligence.

Perhaps, as is often suggested, man will destroy himself by this very development of intelligence. But no one has suggested any means by which we can return to the biological mechanisms of the social insect, and we are left no alternative. The human cultural heritage, for better or for worse, is not biologically transmitted. We must accept all the implications of our human inheritance, one of the most important of which is the small scope of biologically transmitted behavior, and the enormous role of the cultural process of the transmission of tradition.

22. The main idea of this passage is best expressed as

   (A) man's capacity for adaptability
   (B) the origin of custom
   (C) culture and the physical environment
   (D) criteria of culture
   (E) why culture develops and what it is

25. The author implies that

   (A) within every society there are standardized ways to meet the needs of its members
   (B) the main business of anthropology is to trace the origin of custom
   (C) every human being is subjected to the teachings of his culture
   (D) because of man's creative mind, he is superior to the lower animals in meeting his needs
   (E) life is a substitute for culture

26. The criteria by which culture can be recognized include all of the following except that

   (A) it must be maintained in its original form or a modified form
   (B) it must have a highly developed capacity for symbolic thought
   (C) it must be invented
   (D) it must be passed on through succeeding generations
   (E) it may be perpetuated in some form

27. The author suggests that a characteristic that distinguishes man from some animals is

   (A) a lower animal can extend his capacity for life to a greater extent than man
   (B) some lower animals are capable of extended cultural behavior
   (C) man is unlimited in his capacity for culture
   (D) man is able to interact with his environment
   (E) man is able to bind space

28. Man's "time-binding" ability permits him to

   (A) substitute a tool for his hand
   (B) recognize and define culture
   (C) modify his culture
   (D) preserve the past
   (E) discover the origin of culture

29. Which of the following does the author suggest?

   I. Men's continued reliance on their intelligence might prove dangerous.
   II. The significance of men's cultural inheritance.

III. Both animals and humans have adapted in ways other than biological.
IV. Animals also have developed something that can be justly termed *culture*.

   (A) I and II only
   (B) I and IV only
   (C) II, III, and IV only
   (D) I, II, and III only (E) all

30. The word *ingenuity* in the first paragraph most nearly means

   (A) dexterity
   (B) intelligence
   (C) productivity
   (D) flexibility
   (E) creativity

31. Which of the following topics was *not* discussed by the author?

   (A) evolution
   (B) intelligence
   (C) differences between men and animals
   (D) inheritance of traits
   (E) the meaning of culture

32. According to the author, why did humans survive while many other species became extinct?

   (A) Animals relied too much on brute strength.
   (B) Men were able to remember and record their history.
   (C) Men had relatively fewer "needs" than the others.
   (D) Men developed plasticity whereas animals adapted biologically.
   (E) Few animal species developed a sophisticated language.

33. According to the author, why is the origin of custom the most difficult thing in anthropology to trace?

   (A) It grew out of an instinctive response to life, with no rational basis.

(B) Man only remembers those things he needs to aid him in his survival.
(C) There is no one left to bear witness to its origin.
(D) Customs are so indigenous to man's nature that he saw no reason for writing them down.
(E) Man lacked the foresight to imagine that there might come a time when society would have wished they had been written down.

34. The interesting paradox illustrated by the author's reference to the ages of the mammoths is

   (A) that although man's intelligence has enabled him to survive, he is still dependent on biological forces that could overtake him at any time
   (B) that although man's intelligence has ensured his survival, it is this characteristic that will finally destroy him
   (C) that an animal's biological adaptability often carries with it the seeds of its own destruction
   (D) that it is not the physical environment that is instrumental in shaping man's culture but, rather, that man imposes culture on his physical environment
   (E) according to the author, although culture is not "superimposed" on life, neither is it a natural expression or outgrowth of life.

35. The author implies that which of the following is a characteristic of man in relation to the concept of "time-binding"?

   (A) It is a biologically transmitted phenomenon.
   (B) It is spatial in nature and relies on familiar environmental constants from generation to generation.
   (C) It must be reinvented in each successive generation.
   (D) It is a psychological phenomenon transmitted and maintained through human intelligence.
   (E) In order for customs to be perpetuated, their foundations must be continually modified.

SECTION 3

Time - 15 minutes
13 Questions

The next two passages are followed by questions based on their content and the relationship between them. Answer the questions on the basis of what is *stated* or *implied* in the passages, and in any introductory material that might be provided. Questions 1 through 13 are based on the following passages.

The following passages present contrasting views on the link between television violence and aggressive behavior in the TV viewer.

Passage A

Intrigued by the question of whether there is a link between television violence and the conduct of TV viewers in real life, researchers have published a number of studies and position papers over the past four decades. Most say the evidence is undeniable, that TV makes the nation a more dangerous place and has a pernicious influence on the young people it tends to addict.

Researchers suggest that television is sending the message to young people that violence is not only exciting and powerful but solves problems. TV is implicated in half the violent crimes committed annually in the United States, and while researchers do not believe that TV violence prompts instant reactions, they say that over time, a cumulative effect desensitizes certain TV watchers and heightens their aggressive instinct. Some conclude that television has brought subtle changes in attitude that, while imperceptible to the individual, have produced tragic results. According to one research in the 1950s, statistics show that about one in 20,000 Americans committed murder in a single year. Now that probability has doubled. Many experts believe surveys implicating TV violence are incontrovertible. While they acknowledge that even the most sophisticated research cannot identify beforehand which individual will be trouble-prone because of TV watching, investigators have determined that TV violence accounts for an increase of aggressive behavior in the range of 3 percent to 15 percent and that some of that hostility translates into crime.

The issue is particularly troubling to feminists, who feel that depictions of women which are degrading and dehumanizing elicit violent and aggressive behavior toward them. Social-science research evidence speaks to these concerns about the harms following exposure to certain images of women. At this point the evidence for the effects of exposure to violent pornography seems most compelling. Research shows that pornographic depictions of violence toward women and depictions of subordination of women tend to perpetuate subordination, which may lead to lower pay at work, insult and injury at home, or even battery on the streets.

The legal position likens pornography to violent programming on TV and other forms of speech that promote hatred and bigotry. But the courts conclude that the materials are all protected by the First Amendment, and that while racial bigotry, anti-Semitism, and violence on television all influence cultural and social behavior, it is all protected speech. Furthermore, any other response to these issues could well put the government in control of all the institutions of culture, effectively monitoring and censoring our thoughts. From the courts' point of view, the harm done to society as a whole by restricting certain forms of speech is greater than the harms to the individual groups of persons who are suffering from the discrimination.

Passage B

Those who challenge the idea that TV violence promotes aggressive behavior say that researchers have been too eager to see a cause-and-effect relationship between television shows and behavior. They say that the root problem is the aggressive personality and a violent American society that is unable to contain such behavior. Rather than singling out television as a factor promoting violence, they cite social dislocation, economic constraints, and family disruption as the primary causes. TV is but one of many factors underlying social dysfunction, and violent programming likely accounts for only a slight upward swing in the measure of aggression. Some critics claim that a host of politically correct investigators are diverting attention from the vexing social problems that are the true causes of violence in America while advancing their own cultural agenda. The reason is obvious. Executives in the television industry have found that some of the most violent programs also happen to be the most commercial, desirable, and popular. Furthermore, producers voice concern that efforts to reduce violence would make television bland. Consequently, the industry's consistent position is that there is no conclusive evidence that violence on television causes viewers to behave violently; the industry itself will sponsor the research to determine the relationship between viewing violence and violent behavior; and they are going to reduce the amount of violence.

While there is a fairly broad consensus among academics who have studied the issue that television violence, while not necessarily causing real-life violence, does tend to make children less sensitive to its effects. It is also their belief that television violence should be viewed in the same way as video-game violence, movie violence, or rock-lyric violence, noting, for example, that video games are often more explicit in their depictions of violence.

In this context, some researchers list Saturday morning cartoons among the most socially destructive programs. But most television executives argue that parents should be the ones to determine what their children watch. What is needed is more parental responsibility. They point to the adventures of Wile E. Coyote and Daffy Duck as too violent for children to watch. But one political analyst pointed out that Wile E. Coyote's suffering is just a consequence of his evil plans. In fact, the researchers' credibility goes out the window when they equate cartoons with graphic depictions of violence.

An idea that is not often debated among the issues concerning TV violence and its effects is whether in a nation saturated with violence a portrayal of violence is valuable because it is therapeutic. One academic suggests that the answer may be yes if the portrayal is so realistic that it nearly sickens viewers and strengthens their resolve to enforce domestic tranquility.

1. Both author A and author B would be most likely to agree with which of the following statements:

(A) There is incontrovertible evidence to prove that TV violence influences violent behavior.
(B) Portrayals of women on TV that are violent and degrading elicit violent and aggressive behavior toward women.
(C) Violent programming on TV is one factor that accounts for an increase in aggressive behavior.
(D) Although violent programming on television influences violent behavior, family disruption must be considered a significant contributing factor.
(E) Movie violence and rock-lyric violence weigh more heavily in the increase of violent behavior than violence on television.

2. Which title best reflects the essence of the debate in both passage A and passage B?

(A) Examining the Causes of Violence in America
(B) The Effect of the Media on Behavior
(C) The Dehumanizing Effect of TV Violence on Women
(D) Violence and the Television Industry
(E) The Relationship Between Television Violence and Violent Behavior

3. By the word *pernicious* in the first paragraph of passage A, the author means

(A) persuasive
(B) addictive
(C) benign
(D) harmful
(E) deadly

4. According to the author of passage A, the major legal conflict surrounding the question of whether or not TV violence influences violent behavior relates directly to the issue of

(A) feminists who express concern about the harm engendered by graphic depictions of violence toward women
(B) the studies and position papers on TV and violence researched over the past four decades
(C) the position of the television industry that there is no conclusive cause-and-effect relationship between violence on television and the increase in violent behavior
(D) government control of cultural and social behavior
(E) First Amendment rights

5. According to the author of passage A, even where it has been proven that violence is one of the primary causes of the increase in violent behavior, any interference in TV programming could result in

(A) the need for increased parental responsibility and active involvement in their children's television viewing
(B) total government control and regulation of society
(C) the need for a more realistic portrayal of violence as a therapeutic measure
(D) the removal of socially destructive cartoons from TV programming
(E) certain governmental restrictions on freedom of speech

6. The author of passage B infers that all of the following are contributing factors to the increase in violence except

 (A) individuals who are suffering from enormous economic restraints
 (B) violent programming on television
 (C) the upheavals in family life
 (D) the graphic depictions of violence in cartoons
 (E) the social disorder in people's lives

7. Both author A and author B would agree that

 (A) television violence tends to make children less sensitive to its effects
 (B) whenever there is an increase in aggressive behavior there is also an increase in crime
 (C) television violence should be viewed in the same way as video games, which have even more explicit violence
 (D) if violence were reduced on TV, it would make television uninteresting and less commercially viable
 (E) sophisticated research can identify beforehand which individuals will be "trouble-prone" because of TV watching

8. In the first paragraph of passage A, in which the author states that "TV has a pernicious influence on the young people it tends to addict," he is implying that

 (A) it is possible that some young people overdose on TV violence in the same way as a drug addict who ends up injuring others or himself
 (B) for some young viewers, TV violence can be described as a type of drug dependency
 (C) for some viewers, watching too many violent TV programs can result in a loss of sensitivity
 (D) whatever negative effects result from watching violent programs on TV, it can in no way compare to the seriousness of a major drug addiction
 (E) there is a direct cause-and-effect relationship between TV violence and drug addiction

9. When the author of passage A says, in the second paragraph, that over time a cumulative effect desensitizes certain TV watchers, what does he imply when he says that it also "heightens their aggressive instincts"?

 (A) that it brings their aggressive instincts under control

 (B) that they become more aware of their own aggressive feelings
 (C) that at the same time as their response to programs of violence on TV diminishes in intensity, just the opposite happens in their real life; they become more aggressive
 (D) that the more shows of TV violence they watch, the more sensitive they become
 (E) that exposure to TV violence sensitizes the viewer to a need for more violence

10. The one factor experts on TV violence are unable to identify is

 (A) which cartoons are likely to influence the young viewer who is prone to violence
 (B) which is more likely to create aggressive acting out in the young viewer: video game violence, movie violence, TV violence, or rock-lyric violence
 (C) which TV viewer is likely to exhibit aggressive behavior because of violent programming on TV
 (D) whether investigators are diverting attention from social problems that might be the real causes of violence and blaming it on TV because of a vested self-interest.
 (E) what role the family plays in influencing and encouraging aggressive behavior

11. According to the author of passage A, television violence influences the young viewer in all of the following ways except

 (A) showing him that violence is an efficient way to solve problems
 (B) causing him to feel that aggressive behavior contributes to a feeling of power
 (C) creating in him a feeling that violence is an exciting way of life
 (D) opening him up to a life of crime as a possible consequence of his aggressive behavior
 (E) creating in him feelings of subordination

12. According to each author, what are the crucial issues revolving around TV violence and its relationship to aggressive behavior?

 I. Author A argues that TV programs that promote violence are preferable to the damage that might result to society by restricting certain freedoms.
 II. Each author stresses different factors that contribute to violence in America.
 III. Author B singles out television as a major factor promoting violence.

IV. Author B argues that cartoons that portray suffering, such as Wile E. Coyote, should not be used as examples of the type of graphic descriptions of violence that promote aggressive behavior.

(A) I and IV only
(B) II and III only
(C) I, II, and IV only
(D) II and IV only
(E) II, III, and IV

13. According to author B, the real cause of violence in America is rooted in

(A) the portrayal of violence on television
(B) vexing problems in society
(C) the lack of parental responsibility in supervising their children's television viewing
(D) exposure to violent pornographic depictions on TV
(E) the uncontrollable and aggressive nature of man

ANSWERS

Verbal Assessment Test 3

Section 1	Section 2	Section 3
1. (D)	1. (A)	1. (C)
2. (B)	2. (C)	2. (E)
3. (D)	3. (B)	3. (D)
4. (E)	4. (A)	4. (E)
5. (B)	5. (B)	5. (E)
6. (A)	6. (D)	6. (D)
7. (B)	7. (E)	7. (A)
8. (E)	8. (A)	8. (B)
9. (A)	9. (C)	9. (C)
10. (D)	10. (C)	10. (C)
11. (C)	11. (B)	11. (C)
12. (C)	12. (B)	12. (C)
13. (A)	13. (D)	13. (E)
14. (B)	14. (C)	
15. (B)	15. (D)	
16. (B)	16. (C)	
17. (C)	17. (D)	
18. (B)	18. (B)	
19. (B)	19. (A)	
20. (C)	20. (D)	
21. (D)	20. (D)	
22. (E)	22. (E)	
23. (C)	23. (B)	
24. (D)	24. (E)	
25. (C)	25. (C)	
26. (C)	26. (B)	
27. (B)	27. (C)	
28. (E)	28. (C)	
29. (E)	29. (D)	
30. (D)	30. (E)	
	31. (A)	
	32. (D)	
	33. (C)	
	34. (C)	
	35. (D)	

PART TWO

The Mathematical
Assessment Test

INTRODUCTION

The SAT has a new look and a new name. It is now called SAT I: Reasoning Tests. The mathematics portion of the SAT I: Reasoning Tests consists of three types of questions: multiple choice, quantitative comparisons, and "grid-ins." The grid-in questions have not been used before and require that the student construct an answer and "bubble" it in on a special grid.

A total of 60 questions taken from these three types (multiple choice, quantitative comparisons, and grid-ins) will make up the mathematics portion of SAT I. One 30-minute section will probably contain 25 multiple choice questions and will therefore be identical to the type of math section that has always appeared on previous editions of the SAT. Another 30-minute section will probably consist of 15 quantitative comparison questions and 10 grid-in questions. (Grid-in questions are also called student-produced response questions.) A third 15-minute section will most likely contain an additional 10 multiple choice questions that will be similar to the multiple choice questions that appear in the first section. We can't say what the exact order of these sections will be when you take your SAT I, but your math score will be based on your performance on these 60 questions. Your total math testing time will be 75 minutes.

This new format represents the first major changes made to the SAT in about 20 years. It is likely that you are wondering, why now? Perhaps you are nervously thinking, why did this have to happen to me? The changes have been made by the College Board to create a test that better resembles the type of work you do each day in your math classes. You should actually welcome these changes and not be fearful of them.

As you can see, for example, SAT I now contains 10 questions for which you must produce your own answers. This might be a new type of SAT question, but it is certainly not a new type of question for you. Most of your regular math tests, quizzes, and homework is student-produced work! So you see, you already have much experience to rely on. Furthermore, the content of these student-produced questions is no different from the content used to develop other questions on the test. Also, you will be allowed but not required to use a calculator when you take the test. Again, this is something that most high school math students have grown accustomed to, and so with the guided preparation contained in this book, your transition to the new SAT I should be a smooth one.

Although the format of SAT I is different, as you begin your preparation we should point out that much of the exam remains the same. In fact, a recent brochure published by the College Board to describe the redesigned tests states, "The content of the SAT I Mathematical Reasoning Test will remain fundamentally the same as the current SAT Mathematics Test, but with increased emphasis on the student's ability to apply mathematical concepts and interpret data." All of the problems contained in the mathematics portion of this book have been specifically designed to help you develop these very skills.

The math questions contained on the SAT I are taken from three general content areas: basic arithmetic, elementary algebra, and geometry. Basic arithmetic questions might involve using the operations of addition, subtraction, multiplication, and division with whole numbers, fractions, and decimals. Questions might also be based on the properties of odd and even integers, averages, and percents. The algebra questions will test your ability to work with linear equations, simple quadratic equations, factoring, and exponents. However, algebra topics such as the quadratic formula, logarithms, or fractional and negative exponents are not tested. Geometry questions might test your knowledge of area, volume, and perimeter of simple shapes, as well as your understanding of the relationships that exist in parallel lines, isosceles triangles, and equilateral triangles. Some questions are based on the Pythagorean Theorem and the special relationships that exist in 30-60-90 triangles and 45-45-90 triangles. In the mathematics part of this book, all of these topics are reviewed for you in the sections of the Review Guide. In addition, all of the SAT I–type questions contained in the sample tests are taken from these content areas.

A Note on Calculators

Students are permitted but not required to bring a calculator when they take SAT I. You may use any four-function, scientific, or graphing calculator, but you are not allowed to use a calculator with paper tape or printer, hand-held minicomputers, pocket organizers, or lap-top computers.

None of the questions of SAT I absolutely require a calculator for their solution, but some might be solved more quickly with one. Used appropriately, a calculator can decrease your chances of making a computational error. However, for some questions, it would be a mistake to even try to use a calculator. These questions are simply "calculator irrelevant."

We strongly recommend that you bring a calculator with you when you take SAT I, but make sure you are familiar with it. Being comfortable with your calculator is part of your preparation for this exam. We suggest that as you work through the Review Guide questions and sample test questions in this book, you do so with your chosen calculator at your side. As you attempt to use it, you will find that sometimes it helps a great deal, sometimes it only helps a little, and sometimes it doesn't help at all. Your continued attempts to use your calculator on the problems in this book will help you gradually develop your own personal "feel" for where and when to use its power most effectively. Remember, however, that the calculator is only a tool and it is only as "powerful" as the person using it.

Grid-In Answers

SAT I contains 10 grid-in, or student-response, questions. For these questions, students must construct their answers and not just select them from printed multiple choices. Students must then enter their answers correctly on grids provided on their answer sheets. The grid looks like this:

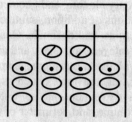

Notice that there are spaces above the bubbles to write in your answer. These spaces are provided to help you correctly grid your answer. Also note that the grid includes places to include a decimal point or a fraction line. Please note that *only grid-*

ded answers can be scored. If you write in an answer without gridding in the bubbles below it, the answer will not be scored. It will be as if you had skipped that question. Gridding in mathematical answers can be confusing, so let's go over how it should be done. Suppose you arrive at an answer of 526. It can be gridded as either $\boxed{|5|2|6}$ or $\boxed{5|2|6|}$. If you grid it as $\boxed{5|2|6|}$, do *not* add a zero in the fourth box because that would change the answer to 5260.

A decimal answer of 8.1 can be gridded as either $\boxed{|8|.|1}$ or $\boxed{8|.|1|}$. The decimal .25 could then be gridded as either $\boxed{|.|2|5}$ or $\boxed{.|2|5|}$. In addition, .25 could be gridded as its fractional equivalent, 1/4 $\boxed{|1|/|4}$.

This method of gridding answers is fairly easy except when you want to grid a mixed number such as 4½. If you simply grid $|4|1|/|2|$, it will be wrong! This response will be "read" by the scoring machine as 41/2. To avoid this problem, convert your original answer of 4½ into either an improper fraction, %, or a decimal, 4.5. Either of these forms are correct and can be gridded easily.

Format of the Mathematics
Part of This Book

On the following pages are comprehensive materials to provide you with the review and practice necessary to do your best on the mathematics portion of SAT I. Included in these materials are the following:

• A sample 25-question Mathematics Assessment Test, which you should attempt even before you read the Review Guide. This test includes 10 grid-in questions so that you can become familiar with this feature of SAT I.

• The answers to the aforementioned assessment test, along with detailed explanations of each answer. You should read all of the explanations, even if you answered the question correctly. These explanations might contain a faster way of solving the problem, or describe a problem-solving technique you might use in another problem. Some explanations include mistakes commonly made. These mistakes are labeled *ERROR* and are included because we feel that by reading them you can only decrease your chances of making them. Many questions are chosen for SAT I simply because they can trap an unsuspecting test taker into using faulty logic that appears obvious and correct at first glance. Reading our *ERROR* descriptions can help you become a more savvy test taker.

• A Review Guide in 12 sections, containing information on elementary geometry, elementary algebra, and arithmetic. Read and digest the 12 Review Guide sections, studying only one or two of them at a time. The Review Guide contains background information on the topics we feel are the most important for solving the problems you will confront on SAT I. All topics and concepts that have frequently been used as the basis of SAT questions are contained in this handy guide.

• 120 sample SAT-type questions (10 in each of the 12 Review Guide sections). These questions range in difficulty from easy to hard and reflect the manner in which the questions of SAT I might test your understanding of a particular concept. Be sure to read the detailed explanations given with the answers to all 120 review questions.

• 11 Mathematical Assessment Tests, including several in each of the three formats you can expect to see on SAT I. These tests contain over 200 SAT I-type problems, including 30 student-response questions and 45 quantitative-comparison questions.

Each of these tests presents its problems in order of difficulty, exactly the way they are presented on SAT I. Work these sections keeping careful track of the allotted time for each section. (Remember, have your calculator at hand.) You will notice as you progress through the sample tests that certain topics keep reoccurring. This is as it would be if you had the opportunity to take four complete actual SAT I's. Note these topics well and refer back to the Review Guide to continually strengthen your understanding of them.

• Answers and detailed explanations of all of the questions contained in the 11 Mathematical Assessment Tests. The explanations of these answers are an integral part of the book. They contain problem-solving techniques that can help you learn to work more quickly and accurately and to "reframe" more difficult questions.

As You Begin

You have already set an important goal for yourself: to earn the highest score you possibly can on SAT I. This is why you bought this book. However, this is only the first step to a higher score. The book contains what we feel is a comprehensive and effective program to prepare you for SAT I. But it can only be effective if you stay actively involved with the material it contains. It is truly a workbook. So underline or highlight the concepts in the Review Guide you wish to return to for additional review. Be sure to work out each problem and *then* check the answers and read the answer explanations. (Do all of your scratch work in the book because you will not have scrap paper when you take SAT I.)

If you work in this way, you will find the detailed explanations more helpful and interesting. They should sound logical and natural, and give you the feeling that you are not working alone. Good luck!

SAMPLE TEST

Mathematical Assessment Test 1

Time—30 Minutes
25 Questions

Notes: 1. The use of a calculator is permitted. All numbers used are real numbers.
2. Figures that accompany problems in this test are intended to provide information useful in solving the problems. They are drawn as accurately as possible, *except* when it is stated in a specific problem that a figure is not drawn to scale. All figures lie in a plane unless otherwise indicated.

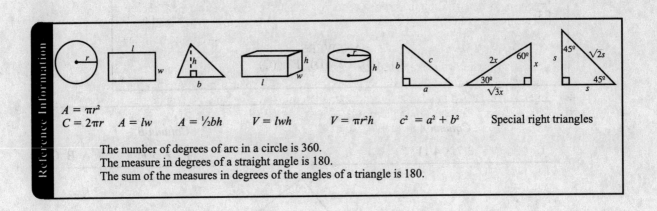

$A = \pi r^2$
$C = 2\pi r$ $A = lw$ $A = \frac{1}{2}bh$ $V = lwh$ $V = \pi r^2 h$ $c^2 = a^2 + b^2$ Special right triangles

The number of degrees of arc in a circle is 360.
The measure in degrees of a straight angle is 180.
The sum of the measures in degrees of the angles of a triangle is 180.

189

DIRECTIONS FOR QUANTITATIVE COMPARISON QUESTIONS

Questions 1 through 15 each consist of two quantities, one in column A and one in column B. You are to compare the two quantities and on the answer sheet fill in:

A   if the quantity in column A is greater
B   if the quantity in column B is greater
C   if the two quantities are equal
D   if the relationship cannot be determined from the information given

Notes: 1. In certain questions, information concerning one or both of the quantities to be compared is centered above the two columns.
2. A symbol that appears in both columns represents the same thing in column A as it does in column B.
3. Letters such as *x, y,* and *n* stand for real numbers.
4. Since there are only four choices, *never mark (E).*

EXAMPLES

	Column A	Column B
E1.	The average of 3, 5, and 10	9
E2.	$x - y$	$y - x$
E3.	6% of 8	8% of 6

ANSWERS
E1. (B), E2. (D), E3. (C)

	Column A	Column B	
1.	$3/7 \times 4/11$	$4/7 \times 3/11$	A B C D

2. x

$$x \quad \triangle \quad 90 \quad 40$$

40   A B C D

3. $1/x = 4$

x 4   A B C D

4.   The remainder when 843,273 is divided by 2   The remainder when 843,275 is divided by 5   A B C D

5. $l_1 \parallel l_2$

$\overline{PL}$ $\overline{PQ}$ A B C D

| 6. | 60% of 40   24 | 40% of 60   24 | A B Ⓒ D |

The average of x and y is 4

| 7. | x | 2 | A B C D |

$$3k - 4 < 17$$

| 8. | k | 7 | A B C D |

| 9. | x | 60 | A Ⓑ C D |

$$abc = 0$$
$$a > b$$

| 10. | ac | bc | Ⓐ B C D |

| 11. | $\dfrac{1}{\sqrt{5}}$ $\frac{1}{2}$ $\frac{5}{10}$ $\frac{4}{10}$ | $\dfrac{\sqrt{5}}{5}$ $\frac{2}{5}$ | Ⓐ B C D |

Note: Figure not drawn to scale

| 12. | m | n | A Ⓑ C D |

$$x = 1$$
N is an integer ≥ 0

| 13. | X^{N+1} | $(X+1)^N$ | A B C D |

An item costs x dollars

| 14. | Amount of money after a discount of 30% | Amount of money paid after successive discounts of 10% and 20% | A B C D |

$$R > S$$

| 15. | t | $R - S$ | A B C D |

DIRECTIONS FOR STUDENT-PRODUCED RESPONSE QUESTIONS

Each of the remaining ten questions (16–25) requires you to solve the problem and enter your answer by marking the special grid, as shown in the examples below.

Answer: $\frac{5}{14}$ or 5/14   Answer: 2.5

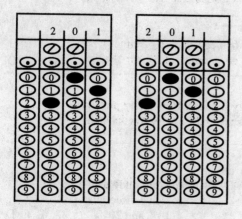

Answer: 201

Either position is correct.

• *Decimal Accuracy:* If you obtain a decimal answer, **enter the most accurate value the grid will accommodate.** For example, if you obtain an answer such as 0.666 . . . , you should record the result as .666 or .667. **Less accurate values such as .66 or .67 are not acceptable.**

Acceptable ways to grid $\frac{2}{3}$ = .6666 . . .

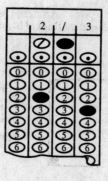
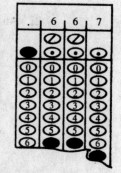

- Mark no more than one oval in any column.
- Because the answer sheet will be machine-scored, **you will receive credit only if the ovals are filled in correctly.**
- Although not required, it is suggested that you write your answer in the boxes at the top of the columns to help you fill in the ovals accurately.
- Some problems may have more than one correct answer. In such cases, grid only one answer.
- No question has a negative answer.
- **Mixed numbers** such as 2½ must be gridded as 2.5 or 5/2.

    (If 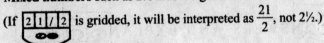 is gridded, it will be interpreted as $\frac{21}{2}$, not 2½.)

16. How many 2½-inch sections can be cut from a rope that is 25 inches long?

17. 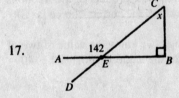 In the figure at the left, find the value of x.

18. A dress which usually sells for $80.00 is on sale at a 15% discount. What is the sale price of the dress?

19. Janet received grades of 72, 82, 89, and 97 on her first four biology exams. What grade does she need on her next exam to have an average of 87 for the five exams?

20. Water drips into a bathtub at a rate of 1 pint every 8 hours. How many pints of water will drip into the tub between 9 A.M. on Tuesday and 9 P.M. on Wednesday?

21. If $L*A = L/A$, find 8[4*2].

22. An 800-page report is 1.25 inches thick. How many inches thick will 70 pages of the report be?

23. 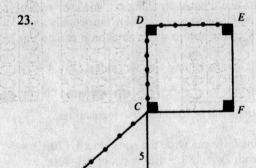 In the accompanying figure, the area of square *CDEF* is 36, the area of right triangle *ABC* is 30, and *CA* = 5. Find the total length of the dotted path *ABCDE*.

24. A bag contains 4 blue chips, 5 green chips, and 6 yellow chips. What is the least number of chips a blindfolded person should withdraw to be sure that he has 3 of the same color?

25. The gas gauge of a truck shows that it is 1/4 full. After 9.5 gallons are added, the gauge shows that the tank is 7/9 full. What is the full capacity of the tank?

ANSWERS AND EXPLANATIONS

1. (C)	6. (C)	11. (C)	16. (10)	21. (64)
2. (A)	7. (D)	12. (D)	17. (52)	22. (.105)
3. (B)	8. (B)	13. (D)	18. (68)	23. (37)
4. (A)	9. (B)	14. (B)	19. (95)	24. (7)
5. (A)	10. (D)	15. (A)	20. (4.5)	25. (18)

1. (C) The product of the fractions in column A equals the product of the fractions in column B, $3/7 \times 4/11 = 12/77 = 4/7 \times 3/11$; therefore, the correct choice is (C).

2. (A) There are 180° in every triangle. In this triangle we know the value of two of the angles, 90° and 40°. This leaves $180 - 90 - 40$ for the angle x. $180 - 90 - 40 = 50$.

3. (B) Solve the equation $1/x = 4$ by multiplying each side by x. $\cancel{x} \cdot 1/\cancel{x} = 4 \cdot x$, or $1 = 4x$. Now, divide each side of the new equation by 4: $1/4 = 4x/4$, or $1/4 = x$.

4. (A) Dividing an odd number such as 843,273 by 2 leaves a remainder of 1. Dividing a number that ends in 5 such as 843,275 by 5 leaves a zero remainder.

5. (A) The shortest distance between two parallel lines is a line perpendicular to the parallel lines. Since PQ makes a 67° angle with l_2 and PL makes a 43° angle with l_2, PQ is closer to a perpendicular line (90°) and is therefore shorter than PL.

6. (C) Calculate 60% of 40. This equals $.6 \times 40 = 24$. Calculate 40% of 60. This equals $.4 \times 60 = 24$. The quantities are equal.

7. (D) The average of x and y is 4. This means that $\frac{x+y}{2} = 4$ or $x + y = 8$. In one case, x could equal 2 if y equals 6, but x could equal anything provided the sum of $x + y = 8$. For example, x could equal 1 and y could equal 7. There are actually an infinite number of solutions to $x + y = 8$ and therefore we must choose choice (D).

8. (B) Solve the inequality $3k - 4 < 17$ by first adding 4 to both sides: $3k - 4 + 4 < 17 + 4$, or $3k < 21$. Now, divide each side by 3: $\frac{3k}{3} < \frac{21}{3}$, $k < 7$. We choose column B. Notice that the rules for solving equations can be used to solve inequalities.

9. (B) Since we have 180° along the line l, we can write the equation $x + 120 + x = 180$, or $2x + 120 = 180$. This leaves us with $2x = 180 - 120 = 60$, or $1x = 30$.

10. (D) Let's substitute some values for a, b, and c, remembering that $abc = 0$ and $a > b$. If $abc = 0$, then at least one of the variables must be 0, so:

a	b	c
3	2	0
0	−2	5

$ac = 3 \times 0 = 0, bc = 2 \times 0 = 0; ac = bc$

$ac = 0 \times 5 = 0, bc = -2 \times 5 = -10; ac \neq bc$

Since *ac could* be equal to *bc,* and *ac could* be more than *bc,* this one example shows that not enough information is given to determine whether or not any relationship exists.

11. (C)   The value of a fraction remains unchanged when it is multiplied by a form of the number 1. $\frac{1}{\sqrt{5}} \times \frac{\sqrt{5}}{\sqrt{5}} = \frac{1\sqrt{5}}{\sqrt{5}\sqrt{5}} = \frac{\sqrt{5}}{\sqrt{25}} = \frac{\sqrt{5}}{5}$. Therefore, the quantities in both columns are equivalent, or choice (C). Another way to test if two fractions are equal or not (and perhaps somewhat quicker in a problem such as this) is to compare their "cross-products." That is, if $\frac{a}{b} = \frac{c}{d}$ then $ad = bc$, and inversely, if $\frac{a}{b} \neq \frac{c}{d}$, then $ad \neq bc$. So, in this problem, since $1 \times 5 = \sqrt{5} \times \sqrt{5} = \sqrt{25} = 5$, the fractions are equivalent.

ERROR   Not knowing the method for "rationalizing" the denominator of a fraction; that is, converting an irrational denominator into a rational one.

12. (D)   Since no units are given on the *x* and *y* axes, it is impossible to tell if $m > n$, $m = n$, or $m < n$. Remember, if you are told that the figure is *not* drawn to scale, you should not infer any information by measurement.

ERROR   "It looks as if *m* and *n* are equal."

13. (D)   1 "raised" to any power is still 1. $1^0 = 1$, $1^5 = 1$, $1^{100} = 1$. In column B, if $x = 1$, then $(x + 1) = 2$. Since *n* is an integer greater than *or equal to* 0, $(x + 1)^n$ could be 2^0, 2^1, 2^5, and so on. Since $2^0 = 1$, the quantity in column B is greater than *or* equal to the quantity in column A. Therefore, no relationship can be determined.

ERROR   Forgetting that *n* could be 0 in column B leads to the *wrong* conclusion that the quantity in column B is always greater than the quantity in column A.

14. (B)   What's better? A discount of 30% on the price of an item, or successive discounts (one after the other) of 10% and then 20%? Suppose the item costs $100.00 (that's a nice number to work with when dealing with % problems). After the one-time discount of 30%, the item will cost $100 - .30(100) = 100 - 30 = \$70.00$. Start with $100.00 again. After the first discount of 10%, the item will cost $100 - .10(100) = 100 - 10 = \$90.00$. After the second discount of 20%, the item will cost $90 - .20(90) = 90 - 18 = \$72.00$. Therefore, the quantity in column B is greater. Since no value was given to the original price, a one-time discount of *n*% is better than multiple discounts that add up to *n*.

ERROR   Not knowing how to figure a discount when given a % rate.

15. (A)   In any triangle, each side is less than the sum of the two other sides and greater than the difference of the two other sides. So, in this case, $r - s < t < r + s$. Therefore $t > r - s$, or choice (A). Let's suppose for a moment that $r = 7$, and $s = 4$. If $t = 11$, then no triangle can be "built" because the two sides, *r* and *s*, would "fall down" and just fit on "top" of *t*. So *t* must be less than $r + s = 11$. If *t* were less than $r - s = 3$, say $t = 2$, then the sides of the triangle would be 7, 4, and 2. If you "turned" the triangle around so that 7 was now the base, the other two legs, 4 and 2,

would "fall down" on 7 and leave a gap of 1, since $4 + 2 = 6$. Thus the intuitive theorem above.

ERROR   There are many students who draw triangles and label the sides with any lengths they wish. For example, can a triangle with sides of 3, 5, and 86 really exist?

16. Divide the total length of 25 inches by 2½:

$$25 \div 2\frac{1}{2} = \overset{5}{\cancel{25}} \times \frac{2}{\underset{1}{\cancel{5}}} = 5 \times \frac{2}{1} = \frac{10}{1} = 10$$

17. An exterior angle of a triangle is equal to the sum of the "remote" angles. (Remote angles are those that do not "touch" the exterior angle.) $142 = x + 90$. Solving for x, we get $142 - 90 = x = 52$.
   If you do not remember this theorem, then find the angle next to 142 on the line *AB*. $142 + \angle CEB = 180$ (straight line). $\angle CEB = 180 - 142 = 38$. Since *BCE* contains $180°$ and we know two of its angles (90 and 38), we can find x. $180 = 90 + 38 + x$ or $180 = 128 + x$. x will be $180 - 128 = 52$.

18. Here we need to find 15% of 80. $.15 \times 80$ on your calculator will tell you that 15% of 80 is 12. Subtract the $12 discount and the sale price is $68.

19. If Janet is to average 87 on 5 exams, she must accumulate a total of 87×5 points ($87 \times 5 = 435$ points). By adding her first four scores (72, 82, 89, 97) we find she has already earned 340 points. She therefore needs to get $435 - 340 = 95$ points on the fifth test.

Technique: In problems where you know the final average, you can quickly arrive at the missing score by comparing each score to the desired average. In this way, we can think of the first score of 72 as being $72 - 87$ (the final average) $= -15$, or 15 points below the average. Likewise, the second score is $82 - 87 = -5$, or 5 points below the average. The first four scores will look like this:

$$72 - 87 = -15$$
$$82 - 87 = -5$$
$$89 - 87 = +2$$
$$97 - 87 = +10$$

By adding these positive and negative numbers, we arrive at -8. This means that right before the fifth exam, Janet is 8 points below her goal of an 87 average. On the fifth test she must earn 87, *plus* make up those 8 points! She must therefore earn $87 + 8 = 95$ on that exam.

20. There are 36 hours between 9 A.M. Tuesday and 9 P.M. Wednesday. Divide 36 by 8 to see how many pints of water will drip in this time. $36 \div 8 = 4.5$ pints.

21. First evaluate what's inside the bracket. $[4*2] = 4^2/2 = 16/2 = 8$. The final answer will be 8 times the value of the bracket, or $8 \times 8 = 64$.

22. You could begin by finding the thickness of one page by dividing 800 into 1.25. $1.25 \div 800 = .0015$. Seventy times this number ($70 \times .0015$) is our answer. $70 \times .0015 = .1050$ inch.

23. To solve this problem, we must know the dimensions of both the square and the triangle. Since the area of the square is 36, then each of its sides is 6 (6 × 6 = 36). So far, so good. The triangle is a bit trickier. Start again with what you know. The area is 30 and the height is 5. Since we know that the area of a triangle is ½ B × H, we can make the following equation:

$$30 = \frac{1}{2}B \times 5$$
$$^{30}/_5 = \frac{1}{2}B = 6$$
$$B = 12$$

Now that we know two sides of the right triangle, we can use the Pythagorean Theorem (or knowledge of the triples) to find the hypoteneuse, BC.

$$5^2 + 12^2 = BC^2$$
$$25 + 144 = BC^2$$
$$\sqrt{169} = BC = 13$$

(This is the 5-12-13 triple worth remembering.) The total distance $ABCDE$ is 12 + 13 + 6 + 6 = 37.

24. Use the "worst case" to solve this problem. The blindfolded person selects a blue, a green, and a yellow chip on his first three tries. Then he selects another blue, green, and yellow on his next three tries. (We are up to 6 chips.) The seventh pick, no matter which color, will be the third of one of the colors. Yes, you could pick three chips of the same color in less than 7 tries, maybe even in only 3 tries, but you can't be sure that will happen.

25. With the addition of 9½ gallons, the tank's gauge moved from 1/9 to 7/9. This is equal to 7/9 − 1/4 = (28 − 9)/36 = 19/36 of the tank. Therefore, 9½ = 19/36 tankful.

$$\frac{19}{2} = \frac{19}{36}T \text{ or } T = \frac{\cancel{19}}{2} \times \frac{36}{\cancel{19}} = \frac{36}{2} = 18 \text{ gallons}$$

REVIEW GUIDE

Section 1: Angle Relationships

Note: Unless otherwise stated, all lines are straight lines that lie in the same plane.

When two lines intersect, pairs of vertical angles are equal.

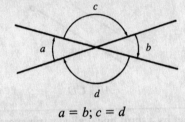

$$a = b; c = d$$

The sum of the angles about a point on one side of a line is 180.

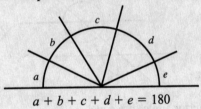

$$a + b + c + d + e = 180$$

Two angles are complementary if their sum is a right angle, or 90.

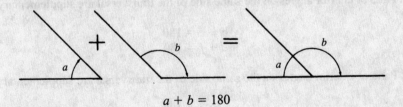

$$a + b = 90$$

Two angles are supplementary if their sum is a straight angle, or 180.

$$a + b = 180$$

If two lines intersect and form right angles, they are perpendicular. $AB \perp CD$ means that line AB is perpendicular to line CD.

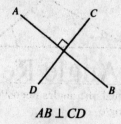

$$AB \perp CD$$

If two lines do not intersect, they are parallel. (Remember that a line extends infinitely in both directions.) $AB \parallel CD$ means that line AB is parallel to line CD.

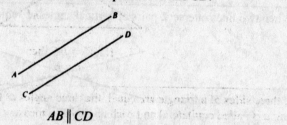

$$AB \parallel CD$$

If two parallel lines are cut by a third line (called a transversal), then:

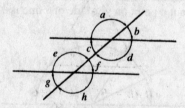

1. Pairs of alternate interior angles are equal.

$$c = f; d = e$$

2. Pairs of alternate exterior angles are equal.

$$a = h; b = g$$

3. Pairs of corresponding angles are equal.

$$a = e; c = g$$
$$b = f; d = h$$

4. Pairs of interior angles on the same side of the transversal are supplementary.

$$c + e = 180$$
$$d + f = 180$$

5. Pairs of exterior angles on the same side of the transversal are supplementary.

$$a + g = 180$$
$$b + h = 180$$

The sum of the measures of the angles of any triangle is 180.

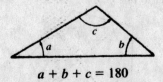

$$a + b + c = 180$$

If two sides of a triangle are equal, the angles opposite those sides are equal. The triangle is called an isosceles triangle.

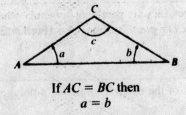

If $AC = BC$ then
$$a = b$$

If three sides of a triangle are equal, the three angles of the triangle are equal. The triangle is called equilateral and each angle has a measure of 60.

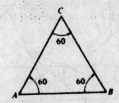

If $AB = BC = CA$ then
$$a = b = c = 60$$

An exterior angle of a triangle is equal to the sum of the two nonadjacent interior angles.

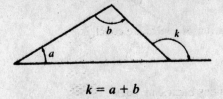

$$k = a + b$$

An exterior angle of a triangle is greater than either of the nonadjacent interior angles.

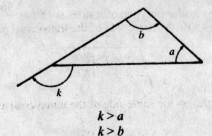

$$k > a$$
$$k > b$$

The sum of the measures of the interior angles of a polygon with *n* sides is $180(n - 2)$.

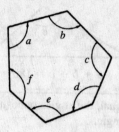

$$n = 6$$
$$a + b + c + d + e + f = 180(6 - 2)$$
$$= 180(4)$$
$$= 720$$

The sum of the measures of the exterior angles of a polygon with *n* sides is always 360.

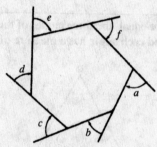

$$a + b + c + d + e + f = 360$$

Each exterior angle of a *regular* polygon of *n* sides is $\frac{360}{n}$.

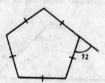

$$\frac{360}{5} = 72$$

Each interior angle of a *regular* polygon of *n* sides is $180 - \frac{360}{n}$.

$$k = 180 - \frac{360}{5} = 180 - 72 = 108$$

As the number of sides of a *regular* polygon increases, each exterior angle of the polygon decreases.

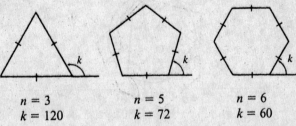

$$n = 3 \qquad n = 5 \qquad n = 6$$
$$k = 120 \qquad k = 72 \qquad k = 60$$

As the number of sides of a *regular* polygon increases, each interior angle of the polygon increases.

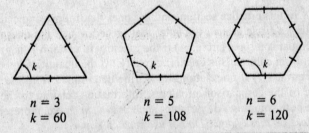

$$n = 3 \qquad n = 5 \qquad n = 6$$
$$k = 60 \qquad k = 108 \qquad k = 120$$

In a circle, the measure of a central angle is equal to the measure of its intercepted arc.

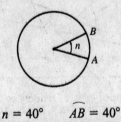

$$n = 40° \qquad \overset{\frown}{AB} = 40°$$

In a circle, the measure of an inscribed angle is equal to ½ its intercepted arc.

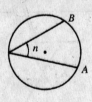

$$n = 40° \qquad \overset{\frown}{AB} = 80°$$

An angle inscribed in a semicircle is a right angle.

$$k = 90°$$

In a circle, the opposite angles of an inscribed quadrilateral are supplementary.

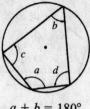

$$a + b = 180°$$
$$c + d = 180°$$

PRACTICE PROBLEMS

DIRECTIONS: In this practice section, and the ones that follow, indicate the correct answer by putting a circle around the letter that precedes it. If the question is of the quantitative-comparison type, circle (A) if the quantity in column A is greater; circle (B) if the quantity in column B is greater; circle (C) if the quantities in both columns are equal; and circle (D) if no relationship can be determined from the information given. In some of the comparison problems, information relating to the problem is centered above both columns. All variables such as *x, y, m, k*, etc. represent real numbers. (*Do all work on these pages. Do not use scratch paper.*)

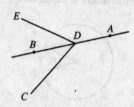

1.1   In the figure above, the measure of ∡ *CDE* is 70 and line *AB* divides that angle into two equal angles. What is the measure of ∡ *ADC*?

(A) 35   (B) 55   (C) 75   (D) 110   (E) 145

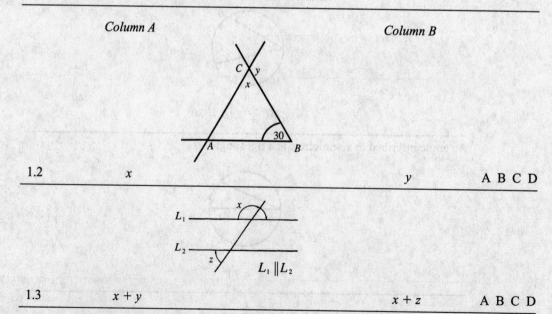

Column A		*Column B*
1.2 x		y A B C D
1.3 $x + y$		$x + z$ A B C D

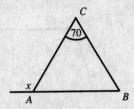

1.4   Triangle *ABC* is isosceles, with *AC = CB*. Find *x*.

(A) 110   (B) 115   (C) 55   (D) 70   (E) 125

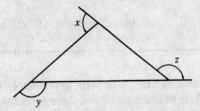

1.5   In the figure above, the *sum* of the angles marked *X, Y,* and *Z* is

(A) 180°   (B) 360°   (C) 540°   (D) 720°   (E) It cannot be determined
from the information given

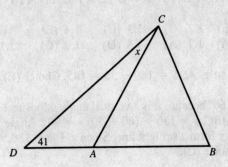

1.6   Triangle *ABC* is equilateral. Find *x*.

(A) 19   (B) 41   (C) 60   (D) 79   (E) 120

	Column A		Column B	
	Column A		*Column B*	

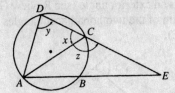

	Column A	Column B	
1.7	z	y	A B C D
1.8	x	y	A B C D
1.9	2	$\overset{\frown}{ABC}$	A B C D

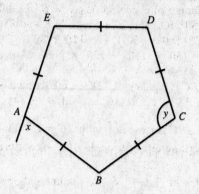

All sides of polygon *ABCDE* are equal.

1.10   *x*   *y*   A B C D

Note: In comparison problems like 1.7 to 1.10, *never mark choice* (*E*) (on the actual SAT answer sheet). In these practice problems, there *is* no choice (E), so that you will get used to the idea.

ANSWERS AND EXPLANATIONS

1.1 (E)   1.2 (C)   1.3 (C)   1.4 (E)   1.5 (B)
1.6 (A)   1.7 (A)   1.8 (D)   1.9 (C)   1.10 (B)

1.1 $\angle CDB = 35$, so $\angle ADC = 180 - 35 = 145$. Choice (E).

1.2   Angle *CAB* = 60° because it is a vertical angle opposite a 60° angle. Since there are 180° in triangle *ABC*, $x = 180 - (60 + 30)$ $x = 90°$. Angle *y* is the supplement of *x* since together $x + y$ form a straight line. Since $x + y = 180$, $y = 180 - x$ or $180 - 90 = 90$. $y = 90$. Choice (C).

1.3 $x + y = 180$; $y = z$ (alternate exterior angles). By substitution, $x + z = 180$. Therefore $x + y = x + z$. Choice (C).

1.4   The base angles of an isosceles triangle are equal. Since there are 110° (180 − 70) to be split evenly between $\angle A$ and $\angle B$, $\angle A$ will be $110/2 = 55$. Now, *x* can be determined in two ways. First, *x* is the supplement of 55 so it would equal $180 - 55 = 125$. Also, *x* is an exterior angle (see Review Guide) of triangle *ABC* and is therefore equal to the sum of the two nonadjacent angles ($B + C$). $X = B + C = 55 + 70 = 125$. Choice (E).

1.5

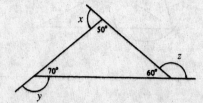

If you remember that the sum of the exterior angles of any polygon is 360°, this is an easy question. Otherwise, since the angles of a triangle add up to 180° (see the directions at the beginning of each section of the SAT), substitute numbers for the interior angles (such as 50°, 60°, and 70°). Since X, Y, and Z are supplements of these interior angles, $X = 130°$ ($180° - 50°$), $Y = 110°$ ($180° - 70°$), and $Z = 120°$ ($180° - 60°$). So $X + Y + Z = 130° + 110° + 120° = 360°$. Choice (B).

1.6   Since $\triangle ABC$ is equilateral, $CAB = 60$. Its supplement, $CAD = 180 - 60 = 120$. Since there are 180° in $\triangle DAC$, $x = 180 - (41 + 120) = 180 - 161 = 19$. Choice (A).

1.7 z is an exterior angle of triangle ADC. Therefore $z > y$. Choice (A).

1.8 $x = \frac{1}{2} \overarc{AD}$; $y = \frac{1}{2} \overarc{ABC}$. We do not know the relationship between the two arcs. (Which one is greater? *Do not* assume that the one which *looks* greater *is* indeed greater.) Therefore, we cannot say what relationship exists between x and y. If arcs AD and ABC were equal, then x would indeed equal y because inscribed angles of the same circle that intercept equal arcs are equal. *However,* we must mark choice (D).

1.9 $y = \frac{1}{2}\overarc{ABC}$ (inscribed angle $= \frac{1}{2}$ its intercepted arc. Therefore, $2y = \overarc{ABC}$). Choice (C).

1.10   Since $ABCDE$ has 5 equal sides, the measure of one of its exterior angles (such as x) is $360/5 = 72$. The measure of all the interior angles of a 5-sided polygon is given by the formula $(N - 2)180$, where $N = 5$. Therefore, all the interior angles of $ABCDE = (5 - 2)180 = 540$. Since all the sides of $ABCDE$ are equal, then all the angles are equal. So any one of these angles (such as y) will equal $540/5 = 108$. Choice (B).

Section 2: Right Triangle Relationships

In a right triangle, (hypotenuse)² = (leg)² + (leg)². The hypotenuse is opposite the right angle (it is the longest side of the triangle) and "stands alone" in the equation above.

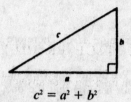

$$c^2 = a^2 + b^2$$

In a 45°-45°-90° right triangle, the hypotenuse is equal to the product of a leg (the legs are equal in this isosceles triangle) and $\sqrt{2}$.

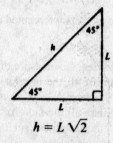

$$h = L\sqrt{2}$$

In a 30°-60°-90° right triangle, the leg opposite the 30° angle is one-half the length of the hypotenuse, and the leg opposite the 60° angle is equal to the product of one-half the hypotenuse and $\sqrt{3}$.

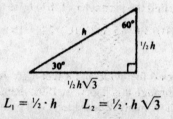

$$L_1 = \tfrac{1}{2} \cdot h \qquad L_2 = \tfrac{1}{2} \cdot h\sqrt{3}$$

An equilateral triangle can be divided into two 30°-60°-90° right triangles by an altitude drawn from any angle. The altitude is then equal to the product of one-half one of the sides of the equilateral triangle and $\sqrt{3}$.

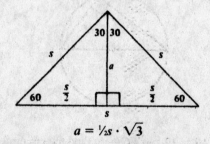

$$a = \tfrac{1}{2}s \cdot \sqrt{3}$$

Certain "triplets" of integers occur frequently on the SAT in dealing with the Pythagorean Theorem, $a^2 + b^2 = c^2$. Some of the basic ones are 3-4-5; 5-12-13; 8-15-17; 7-24-25 (and their multiples).

Example: $8^2 + 15^2 = 17^2$
(64 + 225 = 289. Remember, the largest number is the hypotenuse.)

PRACTICE PROBLEMS

See page 204 for instructions on marking your answers.

2.1 In a certain rectangle, the length is 2 more than twice the width. If the perimeter of the rectangle is 34, find the length of a diagonal.

(A) 13 (B) 14 (C) 15 (D) 16 (E) 17

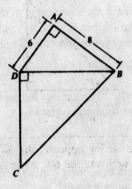

2.2 In the figure above, find the perimeter of *ABCD*, if *CD = DB*.

(A) $34 + 5\sqrt{3}$ (B) $30 + 5\sqrt{2}$ (C) $24 + 10\sqrt{3}$ (D) $34 + 10\sqrt{2}$
(E) $24 + 10\sqrt{2}$

2.3 A doorway measures 4 feet wide and 8 feet high. A man wants to carry some circular table tops through this doorway. If the diameters of these tops are 7, 8, 9, 10, and 11 feet, how many of these tops will he be able to carry through the doorway?

(A) 1 (B) 2 (C) 3 (D) 4 (E) 0

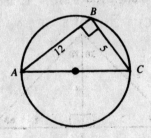

2.4 In triangle *ABC*, *AB* = 12 and *BC* = 5. Find the circumference of the circle.

(A) 42.25π (B) 169π (C) 6.5π (D) 13π (E) 26π

2.5   A rectangular flashing sign consists of 7 rows of lights. Each row contains 24 individual light bulbs. How many bulbs are on when only the diagonal is lit?

(A) 31   (B) 25   (C) 24   (D) 18   (E) 56

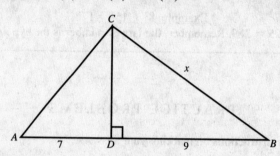

2.6   The area of triangle $ABC = 96$. Find CB.

(A) 16   (B) 12   (C) 15   (D) 8   (E) 10

2.7   A runner and a cyclist leave the same point at the same time. The runner travels directly south at 8 miles per hour. The cyclist travels directly west at 15 miles per hour. How many miles apart are they in two hours?

(A) 17   (B) 7   (C) 46   (D) 34   (E) 23

2.8   The area of a square is $4a^2$. The area of the square formed by connecting the midpoints of the original square in order is

(A) $a^2 \sqrt{2}$ (B) $2a^2$ (C) $3a^2$ (D) $\dfrac{\sqrt{2}}{2} a^2$ (E) $\dfrac{a^2}{\sqrt{3}}$

2.9   A man walks 3 miles due east, then 4 miles due north, then 5 miles due east. How far is he from his starting point?

(A) 12 miles   (B) $18 \sqrt{2}$ miles   (C) $4 \sqrt{5}$ miles   (D) 15 miles
(E) $\sqrt{42.5}$ miles

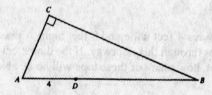

2.10   In right triangle ABC above, $\overline{AC} = 5$, $\overline{BC} = 12$ and $\overline{AD} = 4$. $\overline{DB} = ?$

(A) $\sqrt{53}$ (B) 9   (C) $\sqrt{20}$ (D) 8   (E) $6 \sqrt{2}$

ANSWERS AND EXPLANATIONS

2.1 (A) 2.2 (E) 2.3 (B) 2.4 (D) 2.5 (B)
2.6 (C) 2.7 (D) 2.8 (B) 2.9 (C) 2.10 (B)

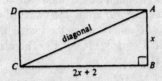

2.1. In the figure above, if the width is represented by x, the length is $2x + 2$. The *perimeter* is the distance "around" the rectangle, or $x + 2x + 2 + x + 2x + 2 = 34$; $6x + 4 = 34$; $6x = 30$; $x = 5$. The width is 5 and the length is $2(5) + 2 = 12$. Since triangle ABC is a right triangle (all the angles of a rectangle are right angles), $AC^2 = AB^2 + BC^2$; $AC^2 = 5^2 + 12^2 = 25 + 144 = 169$. Taking the square root of both sides of the equation, $AB = \sqrt{169} = 13$ (169 is a "perfect square"). *Or,* since 5-12-13 is a special triplet of Pythagorean numbers, the answer could have been obtained more quickly simply by inspection. Choice (A).

2.2 The perimeter of $ABCD = AB + BC + CD + DA$. We do not know the lengths of CD and BC. In right triangle DAB, $DB^2 = AD^2 + AB^2$; $DB^2 = 6^2 + 8^2 = 36 + 64 = 100$; $DB = \sqrt{100} = 10$. (6-8-10 is a multiple of 3-4-5.) Because $CD = DB$, $CD = 10$. Therefore, right triangle CDB is an *isosceles* right triangle.

So, $CB = 10\sqrt{2}$. The perimeter of $ABCD$ is therefore $8 + 10\sqrt{2} + 10 + 6 = 24 + 10\sqrt{2}$. Choice (E).

Note: Even if you forgot the special relationship in an isosceles right triangle you could have taken a few seconds more and done the problem as follows: $BC^2 = 10^2 + 10^2 = 100 + 100 = 200$; $BC = \sqrt{200} = \sqrt{100 \cdot 2} = \sqrt{100} \cdot \sqrt{2} = 10\sqrt{2}$, etc. It is then extremely important to know how to *simplify* square roots in order to "recognize" the answer. We shall do this in the next Review Guide section.

2.3 The largest table top that can be carried through the doorway is the one that can be carried through on a slant, as in the diagram. The diagonal of the doorway is found by the Pythagorean Theorem: $AC^2 = AB^2 + BC^2 = 4^2 + 8^2 = 16 + 64 = 80$; $AC = \sqrt{80}$. Now, because $9 > \sqrt{80}$, only two tops can be carried through. They have diameters of 7 and 8. $7^2 = 49$ and $8^2 = 64$. 9^2, 10^2, and 11^2 are all greater than 80. Choice (B).

2.4   The circumference of a circle is obtained by the formula $C = \pi D$ or $2\pi R$. This information is listed at the beginning of each math section of the SAT. To find the circumference of this circle, we need to know the value of the diameter AC. AC is the hypotenuse of right triangle ABC and by using the Pythagorean Theorem, $(AC)^2 = 5^2 + 12^2$; $(AC)^2 = 25 + 144$; $(AC)^2 = 169$; $AC = 13$. The circumference of the circle is therefore $C = 13\pi$. Choice (D).

Note: Choice (A) is the area of the circle, obtained from the formula $A = \pi R^2$, where R equals one-half the diameter [in this case, $R = 13/2 = 6.5$ and $\pi(6.5)^2 = 42.25\pi$]. Be sure you answer the question asked. Students often mix up area and circumference because the formulas look a little alike.

2.5   In order to answer this question, you need to find the number of bulbs along the diagonal. Since the sign is rectangular, the diagonal is the hypotenuse of a right triangle with sides equal to 7 and 24. By the Pythagorean Theorem we get $7^2 + 24^2 = (AB)^2$; $49 + 576 = 625$; $(AB)^2 = 625$, so $AB = 25$. If you knew the 7-24-25 triplet, you could find the answer by inspection. Choice (B).

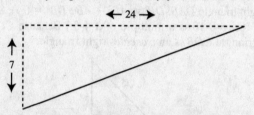

2.6   Since the area of triangle ABC is 96, you can make an equation using the formula for the area of a triangle, which appears in the instructions at the beginning of each SAT. Area $= \frac{1}{2} B \times H$; $96 = \frac{1}{2}(9 + 7)(CD)$; $96 = \frac{1}{2}(16)CD = 8CD$ or $CD = \frac{96}{8}$, which equals 12. Now x can be determined by using the Pythagorean Theorem: $12^2 + 9^2 = x^2$; $144 + 81 = x^2$; $225 = x^2$; $x = 15$.

Note that the 9-12-15 triangle is a multiple of the 3-4-5 triplet, which is often used on the SAT. By multiplying the 3-4-5 triplet by 3, you obtain 9 and 12 for the first two sides. These correspond to the sides of our triangle, and therefore the answer will simply be $3 \times 5 = 15$. Choice (C).

2.7   Notice that because the runner moves directly south and the cyclist moves directly west, the angle at P is 90 degrees. The distance between them is the hypotenuse AB. The triangle uses the triplet 8-15-17, so the hypotenuse AB is 17, but (A) is *not* the correct answer. Because they each travel for 2 hours, the runner goes $2 \times 8 = 16$ miles and the cyclist goes $2 \times 17 = 34$ miles. Choice (D). Recognizing the 8-15-17 triplet in this problem is only part of the solution. You must not forget to use this information correctly to answer the question asked! Of course the test makers know that many students have simply memorized the "triples," and so they have choice (A) to trap them.

The diagram for this problem looks like this:

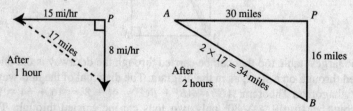

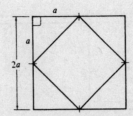

2.8   In that the area of a square is (side)², each side of the original square can be found by applying the formula $4a^2 = \text{side}^2$, so each side $= \sqrt{4a^2} = 2a$. Therefore we have four isosceles right triangles formed, each with legs of length a and hypotenuse $a\sqrt{2}$. The hypotenuse of any of these isosceles right triangles is a side of the smaller square (which we can use to find *its* area). To find the area of the smaller square, area $= (a\sqrt{2})^2 = (a\sqrt{2})(a\sqrt{2}) = a^2\sqrt{4} = a^2 \cdot 2 = 2a^2$. Choice (B).

Note: You can also find the area of the smaller square by subtracting the areas of the four isosceles right triangles from the area of the larger square. The area of any isosceles right triangle $= \frac{1}{2}$ (leg)². Because a base and height have to be perpendicular, and because the two legs of a right triangle are perpendicular, either one could be called the base and either one could be called the height. So, in this case, the area of one of the isosceles right triangles is just $\frac{1}{2}a^2$. In that there are four of these triangles, the total area of the four triangles is $(4)(\frac{1}{2}a^2)$ or $2a^2$. The area of the large, square areas of the four triangles $= 4a^2 - 2a^2 = 2a^2$. Choice (B).

Note: Do *not* get the impression that if you join the midpoints of *any* geometric figure, you get $\frac{1}{2}$ the area. Let's look at the equilateral triangle again. We will join the midpoints of each of its sides. Then, by a theorem you learned in Geometry, each of these smaller line segments is parallel to a side of the original triangle and is $\frac{1}{2}$ its length. If the sides of the original equilateral triangle are each 10, let's say, then the sides of the smaller equilateral triangle are each 5. The area of the large triangle is $\frac{10^2}{4}\sqrt{3}$ or $\frac{100}{4}\sqrt{3} = 25\sqrt{3}$, whereas the area of the smaller triangle is $\frac{5^2}{4}\sqrt{3} = \frac{25}{4}\sqrt{3}$!

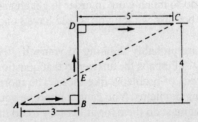

2.9   After drawing the foregoing diagram (as most of you have done), the first inclination is to find BE and DE so you can use the Pythagorean Theorem in triangles ABE and CDE. Unfortunately, all you know is $\frac{3}{AE} = \frac{5}{DE}$ by similar triangles. This *one* equation is not enough to help you find BE and DE. But what if AC were the hypotenuse of a right triangle AFC? (See p. 214.) Then the problem is easy, isn't it? $AC^2 = AF^2 + FC^2$. $AF = 4$ (it is parallel to BD) and $FD = 3$ (it is parallel to AB), making $FC = 8$ (i.e., $3 + 5$). So, $AC^2 = 4^2 + 8^2 = 16 + 64 = 80$, and $AC = \sqrt{80} = \sqrt{16 \cdot 5} = \sqrt{16} \cdot \sqrt{5} = 4\sqrt{5}$. Choice (C).

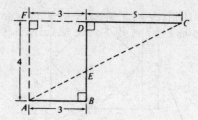

Perhaps you wondered why we stressed the word *one* in the preceding paragraph. Well, the problem *can* be done if you use *two* equations. See the diagram below.

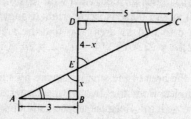

If you let $BE = x$, then $DE = 4 - x$, since $DB = 4$. Since $\angle B = \angle D$ and $\angle BEA = \angle DEC$ (vertical angles are equal), the triangles are similar by A.A. ($\angle A = \angle C$, also, since they are alternate interior angles. But two angles are enough. In fact, if two angles of one triangle are equal, respectively, to two angles of another triangle, then the third angles are equal.) Since the triangles are similar, their corresponding sides are in proportion: $\dfrac{AB}{BE} = \dfrac{DC}{DE}$; $\dfrac{3}{x} = \dfrac{5}{4 - x}$. Now, "cross-multiplying," $5x = 3(4 - x)$; $5x = 12 - 3x$; $8x = 12$; $x = 1.5$. So, $BE = 1.5$ and $DE = 4 - 1.5 = 2.5$. Now, use the Pythagorean Theorem on both triangles to get AE and EC (which you will add later to get the answer, AC). In right triangle ABE, $AE^2 = AB^2 + BE^2 = 3^2 + 1.5^2 = 9 + 2.25 = 11.25$. So, $AE = \sqrt{11.25}$. In right triangle CDE, $EC^2 = DC^2 + DE^2 = 5^2 + 2.5^2 = 25 + 6.25 = 31.25$. So, $CE = \sqrt{31.25}$. Therefore, $AC = AE + EC = \sqrt{11.25} + \sqrt{31.25}$. Since $3 < \sqrt{11.25} < 4$ and $5 < \sqrt{31.25} < 6$, then $8 < \sqrt{11.25} + \sqrt{31.25} < 10$. Thus we can eliminate choices (A), (B), (D), and (E), since the answer must be between 8 and 10.

Remember, though, very few problems should take more than a minute or two. You are not supposed to do so much work in order to get an answer. But it does work! We avoided this method because we felt you would have gone bananas had you seen this explanation first.

At this moment, you are probably thinking to yourself, "How was I supposed to know to draw AF and FD?" Perhaps the answer to that question can only be found after you have done hundreds of problems like these. The more problems you do, the better you become at doing problems! You cannot improve your score in mathematics by reading problems. You must do them, or at least try to do them. You must agonize over them and stick with them until you have convinced yourself that you have given them your best try. Unfortunately, too many students give up after one or two minutes, turn to the answers, and persuade themselves that they are studying.

Technique: Let's do this problem by *estimation*—assuming you couldn't do it any other way. Since the longest side of a right triangle is the hypotenuse, AE must be greater than 3 and CE must be greater than 5. That means that AC (what you are looking for) must be greater than 8. Also, since a straight line segment is the shortest distance between two points, AC must be less than $AB + BD + DC$, so AC must be less than 12. Using the inequality symbols, $8 < AC < 12$. Now, look at the answers. Choice (A) is 12. That's out! Choice (B) is $18\sqrt{2}$. That's certainly out! Choice (D) is 15.

Out! And finally, choice (E) is $\sqrt{42.5}$. Well, $\sqrt{42.5}$ must be somewhere between 6 and 7, since $6 \times 6 = 36$ and $7 \times 7 = 49$. So that lets choice (E) out. Everything is out except for Choice (C).

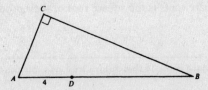

2.10 Using the Pythagorean relationship, $\overline{AC}^2 + \overline{BC}^2 = \overline{AB}^2$, so $5^2 + 12^2 = \overline{AB}^2$. $25 + 144 = \overline{AB}^2$. $\sqrt{169} = \overline{AB}^2$. $\sqrt{169} = \overline{AB}$. So, $\overline{AB} = 13$. Since $\overline{AD} = 4$, $\overline{DB} = \overline{AB} - \overline{AD} = 13 - 4 = 9$. Choice (B).

Should You Guess?

Note: To make the explanation simpler, we shall assume that $\frac{1}{4}$ of a credit is taken off for each wrong answer and *no* credit is taken off for an answer that is omitted. On the quantitative-comparison questions, $\frac{1}{3}$ of a credit is taken off for each wrong answer because there are only four choices instead of five.

Let's suppose, on a test with 75 questions, you answered 40 correctly and 20 incorrectly and left out 15. Your raw score (your score before it is "scaled" into a range of 200 to 800) is then $40 - \frac{1}{4}(20) = 40 - 5 = 35$. If you had guessed at all 75 answers, statistically you would have gotten $\frac{1}{5}$ (since there are five choices for each question) of the answers correct. Your raw score would be 15! This is therefore not a good habit. If you just marked the 40 answers you *knew* to be correct, your raw score would be 40. So, obviously, it is a good idea to guess only when you can lower the odds against you. That is, you *should* guess, but only after you have definitely eliminated one or more of the obvious wrong answers. If you can eliminate three wrong answers, therefore, the odds of getting the right answer rise from 20 percent to 50 percent. If you do not fill in an answer blank you lose no credit, nor do you gain. If you get the answer right, you gain one credit. If you get it wrong, you lose only $\frac{1}{4}$ of a credit. The odds are excellent in a 50 percent situation that you can improve your score by guessing.

An educated guess is one in which you must decide between two or three answers rather than four or five. Try to keep your guessing to a minimum unless you are in that range.

In problem 2.10, there is no room for an educated guess.

In problem 2.9, choice (E) was $\sqrt{42.5}$. Now, why do you suppose that was there? If you had done the problem by similar triangles, you would have had for your answer that $AC = \sqrt{11.25} + \sqrt{31.25}$. Now, in the rush for time, you could have easily added these two square roots to get $\sqrt{42.50}$. Choice (E). Perhaps one example will convince you that you can't always add two square roots like that:

ERROR $\quad \sqrt{9} + \sqrt{16} = \sqrt{9 + 16} = \sqrt{25} = 5$

$\qquad\qquad \downarrow \qquad \downarrow$

$\qquad\qquad 3 \ + \ \ 4 \qquad\qquad\qquad\qquad = 7$

So, obviously, $\sqrt{a} + \sqrt{b} \neq \sqrt{a + b}$. In *certain* cases, such as when $a = b = 0$, it is true. But be careful!

In the next section, you will review the rules for working with square roots.

Section 3: Arithmetic of Square Roots

The product of two square roots is the square root of their product.

$$(\sqrt{x})(\sqrt{y}) = \sqrt{xy}$$

The quotient of two square roots is the square root of their quotients.

$$\frac{\sqrt{x}}{\sqrt{y}} = \sqrt{\frac{x}{y}}$$

The sum or the difference of two square roots can only be found when their radicands are equal. (The radicand is the number that appears under the square root symbol.)

Addition

$$\sqrt{32} + \sqrt{50} =$$
$$\sqrt{16 \cdot 2} + \sqrt{25 \cdot 2} =$$
$$\sqrt{16} \cdot \sqrt{2} + \sqrt{25} \cdot \sqrt{2} =$$
$$4\sqrt{2} + 5\sqrt{2} =$$
$$9\sqrt{2}$$

Subtraction

$$\tfrac{1}{2}\sqrt{300} - 2\sqrt{48} =$$
$$\tfrac{1}{2}\sqrt{100 \cdot 3} - 2\sqrt{16 \cdot 3} =$$
$$\tfrac{1}{2}\sqrt{100} \cdot \sqrt{3} - 2\sqrt{16} \cdot \sqrt{3} =$$
$$\tfrac{1}{2} \cdot 10\sqrt{3} - 2 \cdot 4\sqrt{3} =$$
$$5\sqrt{3} - 8\sqrt{3} =$$
$$-3\sqrt{3}$$

Multiplication

$$\sqrt{18} \cdot \sqrt{32} =$$
$$\sqrt{576} =$$
$$24$$

Sometimes it is easier to multiply two square roots if you *simplify* the radicand first.

$$\sqrt{18} \cdot \sqrt{32} =$$
$$\sqrt{9 \cdot 2} \cdot \sqrt{16 \cdot 2} =$$
$$3\sqrt{2} \cdot 4\sqrt{2} =$$
$$3 \cdot 4 \cdot \sqrt{2} \cdot \sqrt{2} =$$
$$12\sqrt{4} =$$
$$12 \cdot 2 =$$
$$24$$

To simplify a radicand, as you have seen in the previous examples, means to write the radicand as a product of two factors, one of which is the largest perfect square less than the radicand. Then, using the rule $\sqrt{xy} = \sqrt{x}\,\sqrt{y}$, the radicand is "reduced" to such an extent that it does not contain any perfect squares.

$$\sqrt{32} =$$
$$\sqrt{4 \cdot 8} =$$
$$\sqrt{4} \cdot \sqrt{8} =$$
$$2 \sqrt{8}$$

But 8 can be simplified or reduced *further,* since $\sqrt{8} = \sqrt{4 \cdot 2} = \sqrt{4} \sqrt{2} = 2 \sqrt{2}$. Therefore, $\sqrt{32}$ should have been written as $\sqrt{16 \cdot 2}$. Then, $\sqrt{16} \sqrt{2} = 4 \sqrt{2}$. You will get to the same point eventually—it is just quicker to use the biggest perfect square in the beginning.

Division

$$\frac{\sqrt{175}}{\sqrt{112}} =$$

$$\sqrt{\frac{175}{112}} =$$

$$\sqrt{\dfrac{\dfrac{7}{7} \cdot \dfrac{25}{1}}{\dfrac{7}{7} \cdot \dfrac{16}{1}}} =$$

$$\sqrt{\frac{25}{16}} =$$

$$\frac{5}{4}$$

Sometimes it is easier to simplify before dividing the square roots.

$$\frac{\sqrt{175}}{\sqrt{112}} =$$

$$\frac{\sqrt{25 \cdot 7}}{\sqrt{16 \cdot 7}} =$$

$$\frac{\sqrt{25} \sqrt{7}}{\sqrt{16} \sqrt{7}} =$$

$$\frac{5 \sqrt{7}}{4 \sqrt{7}} =$$

$$\frac{5}{4} \cdot \frac{\sqrt{7}}{\sqrt{7}} =$$

$$\frac{5}{4} \cdot 1 =$$

$$\frac{5}{4}$$

Perfect Squares

Memorize the following; it will save you time when working with square roots. The numbers under the square root symbols are the first 20 perfect squares.

$$\sqrt{1} = 1 \qquad \sqrt{121} = 11$$
$$\sqrt{4} = 2 \qquad \sqrt{144} = 12$$
$$\sqrt{9} = 3 \qquad \sqrt{169} = 13$$
$$\sqrt{16} = 4 \qquad \sqrt{196} = 14$$
$$\sqrt{25} = 5 \qquad \sqrt{225} = 15$$
$$\sqrt{36} = 6 \qquad \sqrt{256} = 16$$
$$\sqrt{49} = 7 \qquad \sqrt{289} = 17$$
$$\sqrt{64} = 8 \qquad \sqrt{324} = 18$$
$$\sqrt{81} = 9 \qquad \sqrt{361} = 19$$
$$\sqrt{100} = 10 \qquad \sqrt{400} = 20$$

Approximate Square Roots of Whole Numbers

It would also be helpful to know the approximate values of some square roots should you ever need them in using the technique of *estimation*. (The symbol $\approx$ means "approximately equals.")

$$\sqrt{2} \approx 1.4$$
$$\sqrt{3} \approx 1.7$$
$$\sqrt{5} \approx 2.2$$
$$\sqrt{7} \approx 2.6$$

If you forget these values, you can use the square root key on your calculator to get them. Try finding the $\sqrt{2}$ by pressing the square root key ($\sqrt{\ }$) and the 2 on your calculator. You get 1.414213, which is approximately equal to 1.4.

PRACTICE PROBLEMS

See page 204 for instructions on marking your answers.

3.1 $\sqrt{112} + 8\sqrt{7} =$

(A) $8\sqrt{119}$ (B) $24\sqrt{7}$ (C) $12\sqrt{7}$ (D) $\sqrt{127}$ (E) none of these

3.2 $\sqrt{16x^{16}} =$

(A) $8x^8$ (B) $4x^8$ (C) $4x^4$ (D) $8x^4$ (E) none of these

3.3 $\sqrt{200}\sqrt{500} =$

(A) $100\sqrt{10}$ (B) $10\sqrt{10}$ (C) 100 (D) $20\sqrt{7}$ (E) $100\sqrt{7}$

3.4 $\sqrt{162} - \sqrt{32} =$

(A) $\sqrt{130}$ (B) $5\sqrt{2}$ (C) $13\sqrt{2}$ (D) 5 (E) $65\sqrt{2}$

3.5 $\dfrac{\sqrt{116}}{\sqrt{29}} =$

(A) 4 (B) 2 (C) $4\sqrt{2}$ (D) $6\sqrt{3}$ (E) 18

3.6 $\dfrac{\sqrt{50} + \sqrt{32}}{\sqrt{2}} =$

(A) $\sqrt{41}$ (B) $5 + 4\sqrt{2}$ (C) $4 + 5\sqrt{2}$ (D) $9\sqrt{2}$ (E) 9

3.7 $(\sqrt{2} - 1)(\sqrt{2} + 1) =$

(A) $\sqrt{2} - 1$ (B) 1 (C) $\sqrt{2} + 1$ (D) 2 (E) 0

3.8 $\dfrac{1}{\sqrt{5}} =$

(A) $\dfrac{\sqrt{5}}{5}$ (B) $\dfrac{2\sqrt{5}}{5}$ (C) $5\sqrt{5}$ (D) 5 (E) $\sqrt{5}$

3.9 Of the following, the one that is an *irrational* number is:

(A) $\sqrt{169}$ (B) $9\sqrt{9}$ (C) $\sqrt{32} \cdot \sqrt{2}$ (D) $\sqrt{50}$ (E) $\dfrac{\sqrt{18}}{\sqrt{2}}$

3.10 If $\sqrt{x^2 + y^2} = x + y$, then which of the following must be true?

(A) $x = y$ (B) $x = 0$ (C) $x - y \neq 0$ (D) $x + y = 0$ (E) $xy = 0$

ANSWERS AND EXPLANATIONS

3.1 (C)	3.2 (B)	3.3 (A)	3.4 (B)	3.5 (B)
3.6 (E)	3.7 (B)	3.8 (A)	3.9 (D)	3.10 (E)

3.1 Remember, the only time you can add two square roots is when their radicands are equal. The *clue* here is the 7 under the square root sign in the second summand. Obviously, 112 can be written as a product of two factors, one of which is 7. Divide 7 into 112 to get 16. $\sqrt{112} = \sqrt{16 \cdot 7} = \sqrt{16}\sqrt{7} = 4\sqrt{7}$. So, $\sqrt{112} + 8\sqrt{7} = 4\sqrt{7} + 8\sqrt{7} = 12\sqrt{7}$. Choice (C).

3.2 About 80 to 90 percent of average students get this problem wrong. It *is* true that $\sqrt{16} = 4$, *but* $\sqrt{x^{16}} = x^8$, *not* x^4. Choice (B). Remember, $4 \times 4 = 16$, but $x^4 \times x^4 = x^8$, *not* x^{16}. We shall review the operations and exponents in the next section.

3.3 You can use estimation and your calculator to answer this question. Exact values are obtained by pressing the square root key, followed by the number whose square root you want. By pressing $\sqrt{}$ and 200 you get $\sqrt{200}$, which is 14.142135. Likewise, pressing $\sqrt{}$ and 500 gives you 22.360679. By estimation, $\sqrt{200} \cdot \sqrt{500}$ is 14×22. Again, your calculator tells you $14 \times 22 = 308$. In choice (A), use the $\sqrt{}$ key to find $\sqrt{10}$, which is 3.162277. By approximating 3.162277 as 3, we get a value for choice (A) of $100 \times 3 = 300$. This is close to 308, so it could be the answer. In choice (B), $10\sqrt{10}$ is approximately $10 \times 3 = 30$. Out! Choice (C) is also out of the ballpark completely. In choice (D), 7 is approximately 2.6, and $20\sqrt{7}$ is not even close to 308. As for choice (E), $100\sqrt{7} = 100(2.6) = 260$. Closer than the others but still out! So, the choice must be (A).

3.4 You can use a calculator here too. But let's do it in the straightforward way. $\sqrt{162} - \sqrt{32} = ?$ First simplify $\sqrt{32}$. The factors of 32 will give you a clue as to how to simplify 162. (32 is a smaller number to work with.) $\sqrt{32} = \sqrt{16 \cdot 2} = \sqrt{16}\sqrt{2} = 4\sqrt{2}$. So, in order to subtract, $\sqrt{162}$ must also have a factor of $\sqrt{2}$. $\sqrt{162} = \sqrt{81 \cdot 2} = \sqrt{81}\sqrt{2} = 9\sqrt{2}$. So, $\sqrt{162} - \sqrt{32} = 9\sqrt{2} - 4\sqrt{2} = 5\sqrt{2}$. Choice (B).

3.5 You can divide first to get $\dfrac{\sqrt{116}}{\sqrt{29}} = \sqrt{\dfrac{116}{29}} = \sqrt{4} = 2$. Choice (B).

Or, you can simplify where you can to get, $\dfrac{\sqrt{116}}{\sqrt{29}} = \dfrac{\sqrt{4 \cdot 29}}{\sqrt{29}} = \dfrac{\sqrt{4}}{1} \cdot \dfrac{\sqrt{29}}{\sqrt{29}} = \dfrac{2}{1} \cdot 1 = 2$.

3.6 Many students get this problem wrong because they are unsure of themselves when it comes to "canceling" in fractions. We shall review the operations on fractions in a later section. You can divide first to get $\dfrac{\sqrt{50} + \sqrt{32}}{\sqrt{2}} = \sqrt{25} + \sqrt{16} = 5 + 4 = 9$. Choice (E).

Or, you can simplify first to get $\dfrac{\sqrt{50} + \sqrt{32}}{\sqrt{2}} = \dfrac{\sqrt{25 \cdot 2} + \sqrt{16 \cdot 2}}{\sqrt{2}} =$

$\dfrac{5\sqrt{2} + 4\sqrt{2}}{\sqrt{2}} = \dfrac{\sqrt{2}(5 + 4)}{\sqrt{2}} = \dfrac{\sqrt{2}}{\sqrt{2}}(5 + 4) = 1 \cdot 9 = 9$.

3.7 It is necessary to know how to multiply two binomials in order to solve this problem. We shall review this in Section 10. But, for now, $(a + b)(a - b) = a^2 - b^2$ (the difference of two squares). So, in this problem, $(\sqrt{2} - 1)(\sqrt{2} + 1) = \sqrt{2}^2 - 1^2 = \sqrt{2}\sqrt{2} - 1 = \sqrt{4} - 1 = 2 - 1 = 1$. Choice (B).

3.8 This problem could be solved using a calculator but, ironically, it will take longer that way. It would be best if you recognized that $\dfrac{1}{\sqrt{5}}$ can be transformed into $\dfrac{\sqrt{5}}{5}$ [choice (A)] in one very tricky step. I'm sure you agree with the simple fact that any value multiplied by 1 leaves the value unchanged. So, let's multiply $\dfrac{1}{\sqrt{5}}$ by 1. But let's give the 1 a special form, namely $\dfrac{\sqrt{5}}{\sqrt{5}}$. Any fraction that has the same numerator and denominator must equal 1.) So, in our tricky multiplication by 1 we get $\dfrac{1}{\sqrt{5}} \times \dfrac{\sqrt{5}}{\sqrt{5}}$. The new numerator is $1 \times \sqrt{5}$, which is $\sqrt{5}$. The denominator is $\sqrt{5} \times \sqrt{5}$, which is simply 5. Remember, multiplying a square root by itself "undoes" the square root. The new denominator is 5 and the entire new fraction, which is equivalent to the original fraction, is $\dfrac{\sqrt{5}}{5}$. Choice (A).

3.9 An irrational number (when working with square roots) is a square root of a nonperfect square. $\sqrt{169} = 13$; $9\sqrt{9} = 9 \times 3 = 27$; $\sqrt{32}\sqrt{2} = \sqrt{64} = 8$; $\sqrt{18}/\sqrt{2} = \sqrt{9} = 3$; so these are all rational numbers. $\sqrt{50} = \sqrt{25 \cdot 2} = \sqrt{25}\sqrt{2} = 5\sqrt{2} = 5 \cdot (1.414213562 \ldots)$. This product is an irrational number. The square root of 2 is a decimal that never repeats. So, the answer is choice (D).

3.10 Here is another bugaboo among students. So many of them believe that $\sqrt{x^2 + y^2} = x + y$. What about this one? $\sqrt{3^2 + 4^2}$. Is it $3 + 4$? Well, $3^2 + 4^2 = 9 + 16 = 25$. So, $\sqrt{3^2 + 4^2} = \sqrt{25} = 5$. Since $5 \neq 7$, something must be wrong. That something is the fact that $\sqrt{x^2 + y^2} \neq x + y$ for all values of x and y. However, what if either *x or y* or both *x and y* are 0? Then, if $x = 0$, $\sqrt{0^2 + y^2} = \sqrt{0^2 + y^2} = \sqrt{y^2} = y$. Because *y* can be written as $0 + y$, then it *is* true that $x^2 + y^2 = x + y$. Likewise, letting $y = 0$, you will come up with the result that $\sqrt{x^2 + y^2} = x + y$. Letting both *x* and *y* be 0, $\sqrt{0^2 + 0^2} = 0 + 0$, so it *is* true when both *x* and *y* are 0. Now, let's look at the choices.

(A) $x = y$. What if $x = 1$ and $y = 1$? Then $\sqrt{1^2 + 1^2} = \sqrt{1 + 1} = \sqrt{2}$. $\sqrt{2} \neq 2$ (so $\sqrt{1^2 + 1^2} \neq 1 + 1$).

(B) $x = 0$. Yes, that works, *but,* read the directions carefully. The problem states, "which of the following *must* be true?" Watch out for that word *must.* We have found out that *x* could be 0, but then again, it doesn't have to be. (*y could* be 0 *only* and $\sqrt{x^2 + y^2} = x + y$.)

(C) *Must* it be true that $x - y$ can't be 0? What if both *x* and *y* were 0? Then $x - y$ does equal 0 and $\sqrt{x^2 + y^2} = x + y$.

(D) *Must* it be that $x + y = 0$? That only happens if *x* and *y* have opposite signs, such as 3 and -3. Let's try this one: $\sqrt{3^2 + (-3)^2} = \sqrt{9 + 9} = \sqrt{18}$. So, does $\sqrt{18} = 3 + (-3)$? No.

(E) If $xy = 0$, then either *x* or *y*, or *x* and *y*, are 0. This *must* be the case if $x^2 + y^2 = x + y$. Choice (E).

Choices (B) and (E) look somewhat alike. Choice (B), however, is not inclusive enough. Also, why just $x = 0$? That is the giveaway. From the symmetry of the problem, why should only *x* have to be 0?

When you see "catchwords" such as *must, never,* or *always,* be on your guard for that *one* case that "blows apart" the theory. For example, "All prime numbers are odd." Well, 3, 5, 7, 11, 13, 17, 19, 23, 29, and so on are all prime numbers (divisible only by themselves and 1), and in fact there are an infinite number of prime numbers, all odd. However, there is *one* even prime number, 2!

Square Roots of Exponents

The square root of a variable raised to a power is the variable raised to one-half that power.

$$\sqrt{X^{36}} = X^{18}$$
$$\sqrt{X^{10}} = X^5$$

When the radicand contains a number and a variable raised to a power, take the square root of the number and divide the power by 2.

$$\sqrt{16X^6} = 4X^3$$
$$\sqrt{36X^{16}} = 6X^8$$

Section 4: Exponents

In general:

1. $(a^x)(a^y) = a^{x+y}$ 4. $a^0 = 1$
2. $(a^x)^y = a^{xy}$ 5. if $a^x = a^y$, then $x = y$
3. $a^x \div a^y = a^{x-y}$

Let's see some examples of the above rules.

1. $2^4 \times 2^2 = (2 \times 2 \times 2 \times 2)(2 \times 2) = 2 \times 2 \times 2 \times 2 \times 2 \times 2 = 2^{4+2} = 2^6$

Note: Be careful! 2^4 does *not* mean $2 \times 4 = 8$. It means 2 is multiplied by itself 4 times; $2^4 = 16$. Likewise, $2^3 = 8$, *not* 6. Many students seem to make this careless error.

2. $(2^4)^2 = (2 \times 2 \times 2 \times 2)(2 \times 2 \times 2 \times 2) = 2 \times 2 \times 2 \times 2 \times 2 \times 2 \times 2 \times 2 = 2^8$.

Note: There seems to be much confusion over examples 1 and 2. In example 1, $2^4 \times 2^2$ means $16 \times 4 = 64$. In example 2, $(2^4)^2$ means 16^2 or 256.

3. $2^5 \div 2^3 = \dfrac{2 \times 2 \times 2 \times 2 \times 2}{2 \times 2 \times 2} = 2 \times 2 = 2^2 = 2^{5-3}$

$32 \div 8 = \qquad\qquad\qquad\qquad\qquad 4$

$2^5 \div 2^5 = \dfrac{2 \times 2 \times 2 \times 2 \times 2}{2 \times 2 \times 2 \times 2 \times 2} = 1 = 2^{5-5} = 2^0$

4. (See above example) $2^0 = 1$.
5. If $2^5 = 2^x$, then obviously $x = 5$.

PRACTICE PROBLEMS

See page 204 for instructions on marking your answers.

	Column A	Column B	
4.1	9^2	3^4	A B C D
4.2	2^{5-1}	$2^5 - 1$	A B C D
4.3	$x \geq 0$		
	$(x^{10})^2$	x^{100}	A B C D
4.4	$8^{2x} = 4^{3y}$		
	x	y	A B C D

4.5 If $n = 1$, then $3^n + 3^{n+1} =$

   (A) 216 (B) 81 (C) 27 (D) 18 (E) 12

4.6 $7 \times 7 \times 7 \times 7 =$

    (A) 4^7 (B) 7^4 (C) 14^2 (D) 4^3 (E) 49^4

4.7 $(2^0)(9^1) =$

    (A) 9   (B) 18   (C) 2   (D) 1   (E) 0

	Column A		*Column B*	
4.8	Value of x when $N = 1$	$X = \dfrac{3N}{N}$	Value of x when $N = 3$	A B C D

N is a positive integer

4.9	$(2)^N$	$(-2)^{N+1}$	A B C D

$0 \leq x \leq 4$

4.10	$(1/2)^x$	$1/32$	A B C D

ANSWERS AND EXPLANATIONS

    4.1 (C)   4.2 (B)   4.3 (D)   4.4 (C)   4.5 (E)
    4.6 (B)   4.7 (A)   4.8 (B)   4.9 (D)   4.10 (A)

4.1 $9^2 = (3^2)^2 = 3^4$, so the quantities in column A and column B are equal. Choice (C). Since the exponents are small, you can get each value ($9^2 = 81$; $3^4 = 81$) either by multiplying ($9 \times 9 = 81$; $3 \times 3 \times 3 \times 3 = 81$) or using your calculator.

4.2 $2^{5-1} = 2^4 = 16$. $2^5 - 1 = 32 - 1 = 31$. So, the quantity in column B is greater. Choice (B).

4.3 $(x^{10})^2 = (x^{10})(x^{10}) = x^{20}$. So, it *seems* that x^{100} is the greater quantity. *However,* we do not know what number x is! We shall use the technique of *substitution.* You must be careful using this technique. You must make *several* substitutions rather than one; otherwise, you will be led to an incorrect conclusion. If $x = 1$, $x^{20} = 1^{20} = 1$. Likewise, $1^{100} = 1$. So the quantities *could* be equal. If $x = 2$, $2^{20} < 2^{100}$. If $x = \frac{1}{2}$, then $(\frac{1}{2})^{20} > (\frac{1}{2})^{100}$. (The value of a fraction that is between 0 and 1 *decreases* as it is raised to higher and higher powers. Examples: $(\frac{1}{3})^2 = \frac{1}{9}$; $(\frac{1}{3})^3 = \frac{1}{27}$. Therefore, because *no decision* can be made concerning the relationship of the quantities, we must mark choice (D).

4.4   We could do this problem by trying some numbers for x and y. Let $x = y = 1$. $8^{2 \cdot 1} \stackrel{?}{=} 4^{3 \cdot 1}$. Does $8^2 \stackrel{?}{=} 4^3$? $8 \times 8 \stackrel{?}{=} 4 \times 4 \times 4$. $64 = 64$. Yes! So, x *must* equal y. *But,* this was very lucky! Suppose we had a problem where it turned out that x was equal to $\dfrac{2y}{3}$. Then it is doubtful that you would have been so lucky when substituting your numbers. Do this problem in a straightforward manner: Given $8^{2x} = 4^{3y}$; $(2^3)^{2x} = (2^2)^{3y}$; $2^{6x} = 2^{6y}$; so, $x = y$. Choice (C).

4.5 $3^1 + 3^{1+1} = 3^1 + 3^2 = 3 + 9 = 12$. Choice (E). Why those other particular answers? Perhaps you thought (*ERROR*) $3^1 + 3^2 = (3 + 3)^3 = 6^3 = 216$. Or perhaps you thought (*ERROR*) $3^1 + 3^2 = 3^3 = 27$.

4.6   By definition, $A \times A \times A \times A$ means A^4. $7 \times 7 \times 7 \times 7 = 7^4$. Choice (B).

4.7 $(2^0)(9^1) = (1)(9) = 9$. Choice (A). Once again, it is very easy to be careless. Always raise to powers first, then multiply. Also remember $2^0 = 1$, not 2, or 0.

4.8   The value of column A (when $N = 1$) is $3^1/1 = 3$. The value of column B (when $N = 3$) is $3^3/3 = 27/3 = 9$. Choice (B).

4.9   You can solve this problem as you solved the last problem, by substitution. But be careful of the -2 in column B. It complicates things. N must be a positive integer, so starting with $N = 1$, we get column A to be $(2)^1 = 2$ and column B to be $(-2)^{1+1} = (-2)^2 = +4$. Now, for safe measure, try $N = 2$. Column A becomes $(2)^2 = 4$, but column B becomes $(-2)^{2+1} = (-2)^3 = -8$! Because our first two substitutions produced contradictory results, we choose choice (D). The rules for signed numbers are reviewed in another section of the Review Guide.

4.10   Column A is the only quantity that changes in this problem. As X increases from 0 to 4, the fraction $(1/2)^x$ will decrease from $(1/2)^0 = 1$ to $(1/2)^4 = 1/16$. But even the smallest value of $(1/2)^x$, which is $(1/2)^4 = 1/16$, is still *larger* than 1/32. Choice (A).

Section 5: Fractions

$$\frac{N \text{ (numerator)}}{D \text{ (denominator)}}$$

Addition: Like Denominators

$$\frac{a}{c} + \frac{b}{c} = \frac{a+b}{c}$$

Examples: $\quad \dfrac{2}{3} + \dfrac{5}{3} = \dfrac{2+5}{3} = \dfrac{7}{3}$

$$\frac{x}{y} + \frac{3x}{y} = \frac{x+3x}{y} = \frac{4x}{y}$$

Subtraction: Like Denominators

$$\frac{a}{c} - \frac{b}{c} = \frac{a-b}{c}$$

Examples: $\quad \dfrac{4}{7} - \dfrac{1}{7} = \dfrac{4-1}{7} = \dfrac{3}{7}$

$$\frac{x}{3} - \frac{1-x}{3} = \frac{x-(1-x)}{3} = \frac{x-1+x}{3} = \frac{2x-1}{3}$$

Addition: Unlike Denominators

$$\frac{a}{m} + \frac{b}{n} = \frac{an+bm}{mn}$$

Examples: $\quad \dfrac{2}{3} + \dfrac{4}{5} = \dfrac{(2)(5)+(3)(4)}{15} = \dfrac{10+12}{15} = \dfrac{22}{15}$

$$\frac{3}{4} + \frac{7}{12} = \frac{(3)(12)+(4)(7)}{48} = \frac{36+28}{48} = \frac{64}{48} = \frac{4}{3}$$

Or the more familiar way: $\quad \dfrac{3}{4} = \dfrac{9}{12}$

$$+ \quad \frac{\dfrac{7}{12} = \dfrac{7}{12}}{}$$

so,

$$\frac{9}{12}$$
$$+\frac{7}{12}$$
$$\overline{\frac{16}{12}=\frac{4}{3}}$$

(So, even with the lowest common denominator, you can *still* reduce.)

With only two fractions, using the formula $\dfrac{a}{m}+\dfrac{b}{n}=\dfrac{an+bm}{mn}$ is much quicker than seeking the "lowest common denominator," as taught in elementary school. Actually, the formula is derived from the more familiar method: If you have to add $\dfrac{a}{m}+\dfrac{c}{n}$, multiply the left fraction by $\dfrac{n}{n}$ and the right fraction by $\dfrac{m}{m}$ to get $\dfrac{a}{m}\cdot\dfrac{n}{n}+\dfrac{b}{n}\cdot\dfrac{m}{m}=\dfrac{an}{mn}+\dfrac{bm}{mn}=\dfrac{an+bm}{mn}$. A "quickie" way to add two fractions, then, is to use the following diagram:

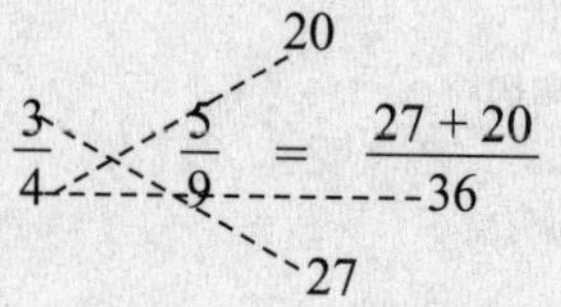

$$\frac{3}{4}\diagdown\!\!\!\diagup\frac{5}{9}=\frac{27+20}{36}$$

Subtraction: Unlike Denominators

$$\frac{a}{m}-\frac{b}{n}=\frac{an-bm}{mn}$$

Example: $\dfrac{2}{3}-\dfrac{5}{7}=\dfrac{(2)(7)-(5)(3)}{21}=\dfrac{14-15}{21}=\dfrac{-1}{21}$

Adding and Subtracting Mixed Numbers

A mixed number is an integer together with a fraction, such as $2\frac{1}{4}$ or $3\frac{1}{2}$. To add or subtract mixed numbers, change them first to fractions, and then use the previous methods.

Examples: $3\frac{1}{2}+4\frac{1}{4}=\dfrac{7}{2}+\dfrac{17}{4}=\dfrac{28+34}{8}=\dfrac{62}{8}=\dfrac{31}{4}$

$2\frac{3}{4}-6\frac{2}{5}=\dfrac{11}{4}-\dfrac{32}{5}=\dfrac{55-128}{20}=-\dfrac{73}{20}$

Of course, by the more familiar way:

$$2\frac{3}{4} = \frac{15}{20}$$

$$-\ 6\frac{2}{5} = \frac{8}{20}$$

$$-4 \qquad \frac{7}{20} \quad \text{which means} \quad -4 + \frac{7}{20} = \frac{-80}{20} + \frac{7}{20}$$

$$= \frac{-73}{20}$$

Remember, though, $-4\frac{7}{20}$ is *wrong*. $-4\frac{7}{20}$ means $\frac{-87}{20}$ (that "pesky" negative sign makes the entire mixed number negative!)

Multiplication: Like and Unlike Denominators

$$\left(\frac{a}{m}\right)\left(\frac{b}{n}\right) = \frac{ab}{mn}$$

$$\left(\frac{a}{c}\right)\left(\frac{b}{c}\right) = \frac{ab}{cc}$$

Examples: $\left(\dfrac{2}{3}\right)\left(\dfrac{5}{7}\right) = \dfrac{10}{21}$

$$\left(\frac{3}{4}\right)\left(\frac{5}{4}\right) = \frac{15}{16}$$

Division

$$\frac{a}{m} \div \frac{b}{n} = \frac{a}{m} \cdot \frac{n}{b} = \frac{an}{mb}$$

Examples: $\dfrac{2}{3} \div \dfrac{4}{5} = \dfrac{2}{3} \cdot \dfrac{5}{4} = \dfrac{10}{12} = \dfrac{5}{6}$

$$2\frac{1}{2} \div 3\frac{1}{4} = \frac{5}{2} \cdot \frac{4}{13} = \frac{20}{26} = \frac{10}{13}$$

Rules of Addition and Subtraction

1. To add two fractions with the same denominator, add the numerators *only,* and keep the common denominator.
2. To subtract two fractions with the same denominator, subtract the numerators *only,* and keep the common denominator.
3. To add two fractions with different denominators, change the fractions to equivalent forms in which they have the same denominator and then proceed as in rule 1. (Or use the faster symbolic method.)

4. To subtract two fractions with different denominators, change the fractions to equivalent forms in which they have the same denominator and then proceed as in rule 2. (Or use the faster symbolic method.)

Since the rules for adding and subtracting fractions seem so logical, we shall not dwell on them here. Only one silly error needs explaining. Some students add (or subtract, as the case may be) the denominators as well as the numerators. For example: $^3/_4 + ^1/_4 = ^4/_8$. *ERROR!*

"Listen" to the problem. "Three-fourths plus one-fourth equals?" Yes, it equals four-fourths or 1, *not* $^4/_8$ or $^1/_2$.

Rules of Multiplication Explained

The rules for multiplication and division of fractions do not seem logical to many students, so we will attempt to show their logic. In most verbal problems, the word *of* denotes multiplication. For example, $^1/_3$ of $^1/_7$ means $^1/_3 \times ^1/_7$. But what is $^1/_3$ of $^1/_7$? What does it "look like"? Each vertical strip below represents $^1/_7$ of the original region.

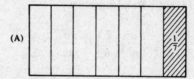

Each horizontal strip below represents $^1/_3$ of the original region.

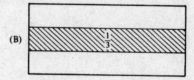

Now, if you superimpose (A) onto (B), you will get 21 equal regions.

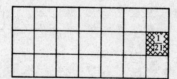

That crosshatched region represents $^1/_3$ of a $^1/_7$ strip, or, as you can see, $^1/_{21}$ of the entire region. It also represents $^1/_7$ of $^1/_3$ of the region. So $^1/_3$ of $^1/_7$ is the same thing as $^1/_7$ of $^1/_3$. They both are equivalent to $^1/_{21}$. Using the same pictorial argument, $^2/_3$ of $^4/_7$ would be $^8/_{21}$.

Intuitively, then, $\dfrac{2}{3}$ of $\dfrac{4}{7}$ means $\left(\dfrac{2}{3}\right) \cdot \left(\dfrac{4}{7}\right) = \dfrac{(2)(4)}{(3)(7)} = \dfrac{8}{21}$. So, we have the multiplication postulate, $\left(\dfrac{a}{m}\right) \cdot \left(\dfrac{b}{n}\right) = \dfrac{ab}{mn}$.

Rules of Division Explained

It is probably the rule for division of fractions that remains most mysterious for generations of students: When you *divide* two fractions, you *invert* the divisor and *multiply*.

1. If you multiply the numerator and the denominator of a fraction by the same number, nothing happens; that is, the value of the fraction remains unchanged. Example: $(^3/_4)(^5/_5) = {}^{15}/_{20}$, which is precisely $^3/_4$ again. Any number (and a fraction is certainly a number) multiplied by the number 1 is the same number. When you multiply the numerator and the denominator by the same number, such as in $^5/_5$, you are really multiplying by a form of the number 1. That is why $^3/_4 = {}^{15}/_{20}$. $^3/_4$ is also equal to $^{21}/_{28}$, if you multiply by $^7/_7$.

2. Now, what is the value of $^3/_4 \div {}^7/_8$? Using a parallel example, $6 \div 2$ can be written as $^6/_2$. Likewise, $^3/_4 \div {}^7/_8$ can be written as $\dfrac{^3/_4}{^7/_8}$. In other words, we have a fraction whose numerator and denominator are both fractions.

3. We can multiply the numerator and the denominator of $\dfrac{^3/_4}{^7/_8}$ by any number we choose and it will still give us back the original value of $\dfrac{^3/_4}{^7/_8}$. So, let's multiply by $\dfrac{^8/_7}{^8/_7}$ (which is still 1). Why $\dfrac{^8/_7}{^8/_7}$? Well, let's see what happens.

$$\dfrac{^3/_4}{^7/_8} \cdot \dfrac{^8/_7}{^8/_7} = \dfrac{^{24}/_{28}}{^{56}/_{56}} = \dfrac{^{24}/_{28}}{1} = {}^{24}/_{28}$$

(Because any number divided by 1 is that number again.) So, the rule, invert and multiply, makes sense if you remember that what is really happening is that you are multiplying the numerator *and* the denominator by the inverted divisor!

Repeating the rule once again, $\dfrac{a}{b} \div \dfrac{c}{d} = \dfrac{a}{b} \cdot \dfrac{d}{c} = \dfrac{ad}{bc}$, $^3/_4 \div {}^7/_8 = (^3/_4)(^8/_7) = {}^{24}/_{28}$.

"Reducing" Fractions

$^{24}/_{28} = (^2/_2)(^{12}/_{14}) = (1)(^{12}/_{14}) = {}^{12}/_{14}$. But, $^{12}/_{14} = (^2/_2)(^6/_7) = (1)(^6/_7) = {}^6/_7$. So, $^{24}/_{28}$ has been "reduced" to a form equivalent to $^{24}/_{28}$. It would have been faster to divide the numerator and the denominator of $^{24}/_{28}$ by 4 $[^{24}/_{28} = (^4/_4)(^6/_7) = (1)(^6/_7) = {}^6/_7]$ rather than dividing by 2 and then by 2 again. So, the idea in reducing fractions is to try to find the *largest* divisor of the numerator and the denominator of the fraction that is to be reduced.

Perhaps you realized that all we are doing here is using the rule for multiplication, $\dfrac{ac}{bc} = \left(\dfrac{a}{b}\right)\left(\dfrac{c}{c}\right) = \left(\dfrac{a}{b}\right)(1) = \dfrac{a}{b}$.

When adding fractions or subtracting fractions with unlike denominators we had to change to equivalent forms. Perhaps we could call that process "gaining" rather than "reducing." For example, $3/4 = 27/36$. That is, $(3/4)(9/9) = 27/36$. $3/4$ is also equal to $63/84$, since $(3/4)(21/21) = 63/84$. In fact, any fraction can be written in an infinite number of equivalent forms. So, when confronted with $3/4 + 5/6 + 1/3 - 5/8$, it is obvious we have to change all denominators to some number divisible by 4, 6, 3, and 8. Well,

$$4 = 2 \times 2$$
$$6 = 2 \times 3$$
$$3 = 3$$
$$8 = 2 \times 2 \times 2$$

What number contains these prime factors (without duplication)? In order for 4 to divide into our number we will need at least 2×2. In order for 6 to divide into our number we will need a 2 and a 3 as factors. But we *already* have a 2 (from the factors of 4). So, our number has to have at least $2 \times 2 \times 3$ in order to be divisible by 4 and 6. Do we need another 3 in order for our third number, 3, to divide into our number? No, we have one already. Now, how about 8? 8 will not divide into $2 \times 2 \times 3$ unless we "tack on" another 2. So, our final common denominator will be $2 \times 2 \times 3 \times 2$, or 24.

$$\frac{3}{4} = \frac{?}{24} \qquad \frac{5}{6} = \frac{?}{24} \qquad \frac{1}{3} = \frac{?}{24} \qquad \frac{5}{8} = \frac{?}{24}$$

We must have multiplied 4 by 6 in order to get 24 in our first fraction. So, we have to multiply 3 by that same 6 to write $3/4$ in its equivalent form: $(3/4)(6/6) = 18/24$. Instead of wasting our time thinking "What did we multiply 4 by in order to get 24?" we could have asked the equivalent question, "24 divided by 4 is what?" In fact, this is what most students do. They say, "4 into 24 is 6.   6 times $3 = 18$." So, $3/4 = 18/24$. That's why it is so important to be able to find a common denominator—one that is *divisible* by all of the others. Therefore,

$$\frac{3}{4} + \frac{5}{6} + \frac{1}{3} - \frac{5}{8} = \frac{18}{24} + \frac{20}{24} + \frac{8}{24} - \frac{15}{24} = \frac{18 + 20 + 8 - 15}{24} = \frac{31}{24}$$

"Canceling"

Canceling and reducing are synonymous. Remember, though, that you are really using the multiplication rule $\dfrac{ac}{bc} = \left(\dfrac{a}{b}\right)\left(\dfrac{c}{c}\right)$. Many careless errors are made because students forget this fact.

Examples: $\dfrac{2x + 6y}{2} = \left(\dfrac{2}{2}\right)\left(\dfrac{x + 3y}{1}\right) = (1)\left(\dfrac{x + 3y}{1}\right) = x + 3y$

ERROR   So many students are overenthusiastic cancelers. That is, they slash out things as long as they are on both top and bottom. That, in fact, is exactly how they explain what they are doing: "If you see a number on top and bottom of a fraction, just cross it out." So, in the very same problem, they do the following: $\dfrac{\cancel{2}x + 6y}{\cancel{2}} = x + 6y$.

The important thing to remember is that you can only cancel when you have a *product* in the numerator and a *product* in the denominator, *both* of which contain the same factor(s). You *can* cancel in the situation above, but only after changing the numerator to a product:

$$\frac{2x + 6y}{2} = \frac{\cancel{2}(x + 3y)}{\cancel{2}} = x + 3y$$

Here is another example, showing how a quadratic expression can be simplified so that you end up with factors you can cancel (see Section 10 for the formulas for simplifying quadratics):

$$\frac{x^2 - 5x + 6}{x - 3} = \frac{\cancel{(x-3)}(x-2)}{\cancel{(x-3)}(1)} = \frac{x-2}{1} = x - 2$$

PRACTICE PROBLEMS

See page 204 for instructions on marking your answers.

5.1 Of the following fractions, which is the greatest?

(A) $^3/_4$ (B) $^7/_8$ (C) $^7/_{12}$ (D) $^2/_3$ (E) $^{19}/_{24}$

5.2 If $J = \dfrac{1}{\dfrac{1}{p} + \dfrac{1}{q}}$ when $p = 1$ and $q = \frac{1}{3}$, then $J =$

(A) $^1/_4$ (B) $^1/_2$ (C) $^3/_4$ (D) 2 (E) $^4/_3$

5.3 If $\dfrac{1}{1 + \dfrac{t}{1 + t}} = 1$, then $t =$

(A) 0 (B) -1 (C) -2 (D) 1 (E) 2

5.4 If $p = 3q/8$, $q = 2n/3$, then $p =$

(A) $\dfrac{n}{4}$ (B) $\dfrac{9n}{16}$ (C) $4n$ (D) $\dfrac{25n}{24}$ (E) $2n$

5.5 $\dfrac{3^1/_4 + 3^1/_4 + 3^1/_4 + 3^1/_4}{4} =$

(A) $3^1/_4$ (B) $4^1/_2$ (C) $6^1/_2$ (D) $8^1/_4$ (E) 3

5.6 At North High School, 9 out of 10 seniors enter college. 4 out of 5 of these get their degrees, and 1 out of 4 of these go on to postgraduate work. What fraction of North High School's seniors go on to postgraduate work?

(A) $^3/_{10}$ (B) $^{17}/_{30}$ (C) $^{20}/_{39}$ (D) $^9/_{50}$ (E) $^1/_6$

	Column A	Column B	
		$\dfrac{1}{x} < 1$	
5.7	0	x	A B C D
		$y \neq 0$	
5.8	$1 - \dfrac{x}{y}$	$\dfrac{y - x}{y}$	A B C D

5.9 $\dfrac{x^2y^2 - 1}{xy} - 1 =$

    (A) $xy + 1$ (B) $xy - 1$ (C) xy (D) 1 (E) $1 - xy$

5.10 If $^2/_3$ of $^3/_5$ of x is equal to 6, then $^1/_3$ of x is equal to

    (A) 2   (B) 5   (C) 9   (D) 12   (E) 15

ANSWERS AND EXPLANATIONS

    5.1 (B)   5.2 (A)   5.3 (A)   5.4 (A)   5.5 (A)
    5.6 (D)   5.7 (D)   5.8 (C)   5.9 (A)   5.10 (B)

5.1 Change all of the fractions to equivalent forms with the same denominator. $^3/_4 = {}^{18}/_{24}$; $^7/_8 = {}^{21}/_{24}$; $^7/_{12} = {}^{14}/_{24}$; $^2/_3 = {}^{16}/_{24}$; $^{19}/_{24} = {}^{19}/_{24}$. If fractions have the same denominator, then the one with the greatest numerator is the greatest fraction. Therefore, choice (B).

5.2 Substitute $p = 1$ and $q = {}^1/_3$: $J = \dfrac{1}{\dfrac{1}{1} + \dfrac{1}{^1/_3}}$.

$\dfrac{1}{^1/_3} = \left(\dfrac{1}{1}\right)\left(\dfrac{3}{1}\right) = 3.$ (In fact, 1 "over" any fraction is that fraction "inverted.")
So, $J = \dfrac{1}{1 + 3} = \dfrac{1}{4}$. Choice (A).

5.3 The easiest way to this problem is to substitute each answer choice until a true statement occurs. Trying (A)—that is, substituting 0 for t—we get $\dfrac{1}{1 + \dfrac{0}{1 + 0}} = \dfrac{1}{1 + \dfrac{0}{1}} =$

$\dfrac{1}{1 + 0} = \dfrac{1}{1} = 1.$ We were lucky in that our first substitution produced the correct answer. Choice (A).

    If you wish to do the problem algebraically; $\dfrac{1}{1 + \dfrac{t}{1 + t}} = \dfrac{1}{\dfrac{1}{1} + \dfrac{t}{1 + t}}$. In order to

add the two fractions in the denominator, you need a common denominator. What will (1) and $(1 + t)$ divide into? $(1)(1 + t)$, or just $1 + t$. So, $\dfrac{1}{1} = \left(\dfrac{1}{1}\right)\left(\dfrac{1 + t}{1 + t}\right) = \dfrac{1 + t}{1 + t}$.

So, we are down to $\dfrac{1}{\dfrac{1 + t}{1 + t} + \dfrac{t}{1 + t}} = \dfrac{1}{\dfrac{1 + t + t}{1 + t}} = \dfrac{1}{\dfrac{1 + 2t}{1 + t}}$. Because we are told that

this fraction $= 1$, we can set up the equation $\dfrac{1}{\dfrac{1 + 2t}{1 + t}} = \dfrac{1}{1}$, cross-multiplying

$(1)(1) = \left(\dfrac{1 + 2t}{1 + t}\right)(1)$ or $\dfrac{1 + 2t}{1 + t} = 1 = \dfrac{1}{1}$. Cross-multiplying once again, $(1 + 2t)(1) = $

$(1 + t)(1)$; therefore, $1 + 2t = 1 + t$. Subtracting t from both sides of the equation, $1 + t = 1$. Subtracting 1 from both sides of the equation, $t = 0$.

    If there were no answers given to this problem, you would have had to do this problem algebraically. (And what if the answer weren't as simple?) Nevertheless, if the answers are given, sometimes the best way to approach the problem is by simple substitution of the answers until one works.

5.4 If $p = {}^3/_8(q)$, then $p = ({}^3/_8)({}^2/_3)(n)$. So, $p = ({}^6/_{24})(n)$ or $({}^1/_4)(n)$. Choice (A).

Note: It is easier to multiply two fractions *after* "canceling," as the numbers are smaller to work with: $\left(\dfrac{3}{8}\right)\left(\dfrac{2}{3}\right)(n) = \dfrac{\cancel{3} \times \overset{1}{\cancel{2}}}{\underset{4}{\cancel{8}} \times \cancel{3}}\, n = \dfrac{1}{4}\, n.$

How about "making up" some of your own numbers for this problem? Let $q = 8$. Then $p = \left(\dfrac{3}{8}\right)(8)$, which is just 3. Then $8 = \dfrac{2}{3}(n)$. Well, $\dfrac{8}{1} = \dfrac{2(n)}{3}$; cross-multiply; $(8)(3) = (1)(2n)$, so $24 = 2n$ and $n = 12$. So, because $q = 8$, we are led to the fact that $p = 3$ and $n = 12$. The question asks, $p = ?$ Well, trying all of the answers once again (remembering your "made-up" numbers), $3 = ?$ Look at choice (A), $\dfrac{n}{4} \cdot \dfrac{n}{4} = \dfrac{12}{4}$ using your numbers! So, choice (A) is the correct choice.

5.5 You *can* add $3^1/_4 + 3^1/_4 + 3^1/_4 + 3^1/_4$ to get 12 and $^4/_4$ or $12 + 1$ or 13. Then you must divide 13 by 4 in order to get the correct answer, $3^1/_4$ ($3^1/_4 = {}^{13}/_4$)! *However,* if you know the distributive postulate, $a(b + c + d + e) = ab + ac + ad + ae$, you would realize that $3^1/_4 + 3^1/_4 + 3^1/_4 + 3^1/_4 = 3^1/_4(1 + 1 + 1 + 1) = 3^1/_4(4)$. Therefore, $\dfrac{3^1/_4 + 3^1/_4 + 3^1/_4 + 3^1/_4}{4} = \dfrac{4(3^1/_4)}{4} = 3^1/_4$. Choice (A).

5.6 "9 out of 10" means $\dfrac{9}{10}$, likewise for the other fractions. And *of* means "multiply." So, $\left(\dfrac{1}{4}\right)\left(\dfrac{4}{5}\right)\left(\dfrac{9}{10}\right) = \dfrac{1 \times 4 \times 9}{4 \times 5 \times 10} = \dfrac{9}{50}$. Choice (D).

5.7 If $\dfrac{1}{x} < 1$, what *could* x be? Try *several* numbers. If $x = 3$, the statement is true. So, it would seem that x could be any positive integer: $\dfrac{1}{3} < 1$, $\dfrac{1}{8} < 1$, and so on. Therefore, the quantity in column B *would* be the greater quantity. *However,* perhaps we did not try enough numbers. What if $x = -5$? Then $\dfrac{1}{x} = \dfrac{1}{-5} < 1$, also. So, *now* the quantity in column A is the greater quantity. So, we must mark choice (D). No relationship can be determined. Be careful!

5.8 $\dfrac{1}{1} - \dfrac{x}{y} = \left(\dfrac{1}{1}\right)\left(\dfrac{y}{y}\right) - \dfrac{x}{y} = \dfrac{y}{y} - \dfrac{x}{y} = \dfrac{y - x}{y}$. Choice (C). Again, you could have substituted some numbers. Let $x = 2$, $y = 3$. Then the quantity in column A is $1 - \dfrac{2}{3} = \dfrac{3}{3} - \dfrac{2}{3} = \dfrac{1}{3}$. The quantity in column B is $\dfrac{3 - 2}{3} = \dfrac{1}{3}$. The reason for the statement that $y \neq 0$ is that a fraction cannot have 0 in its denominator.

5.9 Be careful, you "gung-ho" cancelers, otherwise you will probably cross out some x's and y's as well as some 1's, and put down choice (C) as your answer. A *lot* of students do that! You *can* cancel, but only when $xy - 1$ is a factor of the numerator. It is, because $x^2 y^2 - 1 = (xy + 1)(xy - 1)$. See Section 10 if you have forgotten how to simplify quadratic expressions. Therefore, $\dfrac{(xy + 1)\cancel{(xy - 1)}}{\cancel{(xy - 1)}} = xy + 1$, or choice (A). Substitution of some numbers would work well here too. Let $x = 2$, $y = 3$. Then, $\dfrac{2^2 \cdot 3^2 - 1}{(2)(3) - 1} = \dfrac{(4)(9) - 1}{6 - 1} = \dfrac{36 - 1}{5} = \dfrac{35}{5} = 7$. Which answer is 7 when you substitute 2 and 3 for x and y? Choice (A), of course!

5.10 $\left(\dfrac{2}{3}\right)\left(\dfrac{3}{5}\right)\left(\dfrac{x}{1}\right) = 6.$ $\dfrac{2 \cdot 3 \cdot x}{3 \cdot 5 \cdot 1} = 6.$ $\dfrac{2x}{5} = \dfrac{6}{1}$; cross-multiply; $(2x)(1) = (5)(6)$; $2x = 30$, $x = 15$. Therefore, $\dfrac{1}{3}$ of 15 = 5. Choice (B). There is another method that requires no factoring: $\dfrac{2}{3} \cdot \dfrac{3}{5} \cdot x = \dfrac{6x}{15} = \dfrac{6}{1}$. Dividing both sides by 6, $\dfrac{x}{15} = \dfrac{1}{1}$; and multiplying both sides by 15, $x = 15$.

Section 6: Decimals

Addition and Subtraction

To add numbers in decimal form, line up the decimal points and add just as if you were adding whole numbers.

Example: $5.7 + .003 + 45.06 =$

$$\begin{array}{r} 5.7 \\ .003 \\ \underline{45.06} \\ 50.763 \end{array}$$

To subtract two numbers in decimal form, line up the decimal points and subtract just as if you were subtracting whole numbers.

Example: $27.96 - 8.588 =$

$$\begin{array}{r} 27.960 \\ \underline{8.588} \\ 19.372 \end{array}$$

Note: The addition of zeros after the last digit after the decimal point does not change the value of the number: $27.96 = 27.960$. Also, $.3 = .30 = .300$. A whole number is actually a decimal number, but the decimal point is "imaginary": $5 = 5.$, in other words.

Multiplication

To multiply two numbers in decimal form, multiply the numbers just as if they were whole numbers. Then count the number of decimal places (from right to left) in each of the two numbers and find that sum. That number (the sum) is the number of places to count (from right to left again) before placing the decimal point in the product, or the answer.

Example: $(35.87)(5.114) =$

$$\begin{array}{r} 35.87 \quad \text{(2 places)} \\ \underline{5.114} \quad \text{(3 places)} \;+ \\ 14348 \\ 3587 \\ 3\ 587 \\ \underline{179\ 35} \\ 183.43918 \quad \text{(5 places)} \end{array}$$

Note: Sometimes, zeros must be added to account for some places.

$$\begin{array}{r} 5.91 \quad \text{(2 places)} \\ \underline{.011} \quad \text{(3 places)} \;+ \\ 591 \\ \underline{591} \\ .06501 \quad \text{(5 places)} \end{array}$$

To multiply a decimal number by 10, 100, 1,000, and so on, just move the decimal point 1, 2, 3, and so on, places to the *right,* adding zeros as you need to.

Examples: $(3.4)(100) = 340.$ or 340
$(.007)(10) = .07$
$(65)(1000) = (65.)(1000) = 65000.$ or 65000

Perhaps a little justification of the multiplication rules are in order.

$$\frac{3}{10} \times \frac{2}{100} = \frac{3 \times 2}{10 \times 100} = \frac{6}{1000}$$

$$\underset{\text{(1 place)}}{.3} \times \underset{\text{(2 places)}}{.02} = \underset{\text{(3 places)}}{.006}$$

Division

Any division problem can be put into fraction form.

Examples: $56.34 \div 4 = \dfrac{56.34}{4}$

$28.4 \div .04 = \dfrac{28.4}{.04}$

$18 \div 4.5 = \dfrac{18}{4.5}$

$28 \div 16 = \dfrac{28}{16}$

All you have to remember, then, is one rule. Multiply the numerator and the denominator of these fractions by some power of 10 ($10^0 = 1$, $10^1 = 10$, $10^2 = 100$, and so on), which is determined solely by the number of places the decimal point must be moved in the denominator in order to make it a whole number.

Examples (same as above):

$56.34 \div 4 = \dfrac{56.34}{4}$ Since the denominator is already a whole number, just divide

$4\overline{)56.340}$ (the decimal point in the quotient is located directly above the decimal point in the dividend).

14.085

$28.4 \div .04 = \dfrac{28.4}{.04}$ To make the denominator a whole number, it is necessary to multiply it by 100 (move the decimal point 2 places to the right). Therefore, to *not* change the value of the fraction, you must multiply the numerator by the same power of 10, namely 100. That is, you must move the decimal point 2 places to the right in the numerator also.

So, $\dfrac{28.4}{.04} = \left(\dfrac{28.4}{.04}\right)\left(\dfrac{100}{100}\right) = \dfrac{2840}{4} = 4\overline{)2840.}$, or just 710.

$710.$
$\underline{28}$
4
$\underline{4}$
0

$18 \div 4.5 = \dfrac{18}{4.5}$ In this case, you have to multiply both numerator and denominator by 10. (Move the decimal point 1 place to the right.) So, $\dfrac{18}{4.5} = \dfrac{180.}{45.} = 45\overline{)180}$.

4
$\underline{180}$

$$28 \div 16 = \frac{28.}{16.}$$ Since the denominator is a whole number, just divide:

$$
\begin{array}{r}
1.75 \\
16\,)\overline{28.00} \\
\underline{16} \\
12\,0 \\
11\,2 \\
\underline{80} \\
80
\end{array}
$$

Therefore, the one rule takes into account four types of division problems involving decimals:

1. When the dividend (numerator) only is a decimal
2. When the dividend and the divisor (denominator) are both decimals
3. When the divisor only is a decimal
4. When neither dividend nor divisor is a decimal (strictly speaking, we mean a decimal when you *must* have the decimal point)

To Change Any Fraction to a Decimal

Any fraction can be converted into its decimal equivalent by dividing the denominator into the numerator.

Example: $\dfrac{7}{50} = $

$$
\begin{array}{r}
.14 \\
50\,)\overline{7.00} \\
\underline{5\,0} \\
2\,00 \\
\underline{2\,00}
\end{array}
$$

Some decimal equivalents occur so frequently that they should be memorized.

$^{1}/_{8} = .125$ $^{2}/_{3} = .6666666 \ldots$

$^{1}/_{6} = .1666666 \ldots$ $^{2}/_{5} = .4$

$^{1}/_{5} = .2$ $^{3}/_{4} = .75$

$^{1}/_{4} = .25$ $^{4}/_{5} = .8$

$^{1}/_{3} = .3333333 \ldots$ $^{7}/_{8} = .875$

$^{1}/_{2} = .5$

PRACTICE PROBLEMS

See page 204 for instructions on marking your answers.

6.1   If x ranges from .02 to .2, and y ranges from .002 to .02, what is the *maximum* value of the fraction x/y?

    (A) 10   (B) 100   (C) 1   (D) 20   (E) .1

6.2   Of the following, which is the smallest?

    (A) $\dfrac{1}{.5}$ (B) $(.5)^2$ (C) $\dfrac{.5}{5}$ (D) .5   (E) $.5 - .005$

6.3   In a diving competition, Jill received scores of 5.9, 5.8, 6.0, 4.9, and 5.4 for her dives. What was her average score?

    (A) 5.6   (B) 5.5   (C) 5.4   (D) 5.2   (E) 5.95

6.4   If $0.02x - 0.3 = 0.015 + 0.011x$, then $x =$

(A) 2.4   (B) 35   (C) 1.76   (D) 240   (E) 0.035

6.5 $\sqrt{0.0009} =$

(A) 0.03   (B) 0.003   (C) 0.0003   (D) 0.3000   (E) 3.0000

	Column A	Column B	
6.6	$\frac{1}{10}$ of 0.5	$\frac{1}{20}$	A B C D
6.7	$0.2 + 0.8$	$2.1 - 0.1$	A B C D
6.8	$x > y$ $.3x$	$.5y$	A B C D
6.9	$0.9 + 0.09 + 0.0009$	0.999	A B C D
6.10	$1.5x = 3$ $10x$	200	A B C D

ANSWERS AND EXPLANATIONS

6.1 (B)   6.2 (C)   6.3 (A)   6.4 (B)   6.5 (A)
6.6 (C)   6.7 (B)   6.8 (D)   6.9 (B)   6.10 (B)

6.1   To create the largest possible fraction from the values given, you must pick the *largest* value of x for the numerator and the *smallest* value of y for denominator. Using the ranges of values we are given, the largest x is .2, and the smallest y is .002, so the maximum fraction is .2/.002. Multiplying the numerator and denominator by 1,000 gives us 200/2 = 100. Choice (B).

Note: Remember, to create the largest fraction possible, make the denominator as *small* as possible!

6.2 $\frac{1}{.5} = \frac{10}{5} = 2$; $(.5)^2 = (.5)(.5) = .25$; $\frac{.5}{5} = .1$; $.5 = .5$; $.5 - .005 = \begin{array}{r} .500 \\ -\underline{.005} \\ .495 \end{array}$

Thus, comparing 2, .25, .1, .5, and .495, we see the smallest of these decimals is .1. Choice (C).

6.3   To find the average of the five scores, add them up and divide by 5.

$$
\begin{array}{r}
5.9 \\
5.8 \\
6.0 \\
4.9 \\
\underline{5.4} \\
28.0
\end{array}
\qquad
\begin{array}{r}
5.6 \\
5\,\overline{)28.0} \\
\underline{25} \\
30 \\
\underline{30} \\
0
\end{array}
$$

The average is 5.6. Choice (A).

6.4   If you don't like decimals, get rid of them! How? By multiplying both sides of the equation by 1,000. (We use 1,000 because the "worst" decimal is .011. To make that one a whole number we have to move the decimal point 3 places to the right.) So, $.02x - .3 = .015 + .011x$ is equivalent to $20x - 300 = 15 + 11x$; subtracting $11x$ from both sides of the equation, $9x - 300 = 15$. Adding 300 to both sides of the equation, $9x = 315$. Dividing both sides now by 9, we get $x = 35$. Choice (B).

Of course you *could* have done this problem by substituting each of the answers into the original equation. It would have been very messy and time-consuming, though. Another method is to work *with* the decimals for a while: First subtract $.011x$ from both sides to get $.02x - .011x - .3 = .015$. Then add .3 to both sides to get $.02x - .011x = .3 + .015$. So,

$$\begin{array}{rr} & .020x \\ - & .011x \\ \hline & .009x \end{array} \quad \text{and} \quad \begin{array}{rr} + & .300 \\ & .015 \\ \hline = & .315 \end{array}$$

So, $x = \dfrac{.315}{.009} = 9\overline{)315.}^{\,35.}$ It is usually *easier* to multiply both sides of an equation by some power of 10 in order to "clear" *all* of the decimals before you start "manipulating" the equation.

6.5   Which of the answers multiplied by itself will give you .0009?

$$\begin{array}{r} .03 \\ \times\ .03 \\ \hline .0009 \end{array}$$

Choice (A).

6.6   You can do this problem by changing everything to decimals or everything to fractions: $\dfrac{1}{10}$ of $0.5 = \left(\dfrac{1}{10}\right)\left(\dfrac{5}{10}\right) = \dfrac{1 \times 5}{10 \times 10} = \dfrac{5}{100}$; $\dfrac{1}{20} = \left(\dfrac{5}{5}\right)\left(\dfrac{1}{20}\right) = \dfrac{5 \times 1}{5 \times 20} = \dfrac{5}{100}$. So, the quantities are equal. Choice (C). Working with decimals now, $\dfrac{1}{10}$ of $0.5 = .1 \times .5 = .05$; $\dfrac{1}{20} = 20\overline{)1.00}^{\,.05}$. Again, choice (C).

6.7   Do it simply. $.2 + .8 =$
$$\begin{array}{r} .2 \\ +\ .8 \\ \hline 1.0 \end{array} \qquad 2.1 - .1 = \begin{array}{r} 2.1 \\ -\ .1 \\ \hline 2.0 \end{array}$$
So, the quantity in column B is greater. Choice (B).

6.8   Be careful here! Let $x = 10$, $y = 9$. Then $.3(10) = 3$, $.5(9) = 4.5$; $.3x < .5y$.
Let $x = 0$, $y = -10$. Then $.3(0) = 0$, $.5(-10) = -5$; $.3x > .5y$.
It's those pesky negative numbers that seem to cause so much trouble! So, no decision can be reached as to the relationship. Choice (D).

6.9   Simple arithmetic:
$$\begin{array}{l} .9 \\ .09 \\ \underline{.0009} \\ .9909\text{, which is smaller than }.999 \end{array}$$
Choice (B).

6.10   If $1.5x = 3$, then $15x = 30$ and $x = 2$. So, $10x = 20$, which is less than 200. Choice (B).

Section 7: Percentages

$x\%$ is equivalent to $\dfrac{x}{100}$. It is easy to remember this because the % symbol can be thought of as 0/0, 2 zeros and a 1 (yes, a "slanty" 1).

There are three basic types of percent problems, and they cause mass confusion and hysteria because they all "sound" alike.

1. 3% of what number is 9?
2. 9% of 3 is what number?
3. 9 is what % of 36?

Before we "tackle" these problems, it is necessary to know how to change a decimal number into a %, and vice versa.

$$.43 = \frac{43}{100} = 43\%$$

$$.8 = \frac{8}{10} = \frac{80}{100} = 80\%$$

$$2.4 = 2 + .4 = \frac{20}{10} + \frac{4}{10} = \frac{24}{10} = \frac{240}{100} = 240\% \qquad \text{(So, percents } can \text{ be greater than 100!)}$$

To change a decimal number to a %, move the decimal point 2 places to the right and "tack on" the % sign.

More examples:
$$.05 = 5\%$$
$$.545 = 54.5\%$$
$$6 = 600\%$$
$$.001 = .1\%$$

To change a % to a decimal, then, do the reverse! Move the decimal point 2 places to the left and remove the % symbol.

Examples:
$$25\% = 25.0\% = .25$$
$$1\% = 1.\% = .01$$
$$\tfrac{1}{2}\% = .5\% = .005$$
$$125\% = 125.\% = 1.25$$
$$8\tfrac{1}{4}\% = 8.25\% = .0825$$

To change a fraction to a percent, first change it to a decimal, then move the decimal point 2 places to the right and "tack on" the % symbol.

Examples:
$$\tfrac{1}{4} = .25 = 25\%$$

$$\tfrac{7}{8} = .875 = 87.5\%$$

$$\tfrac{1}{3} = \frac{.3333}{100} = 33\tfrac{1}{3}\%$$

$\tfrac{2}{3}$ is then $66\tfrac{2}{3}\%$

Let's go back to our original three problems now. The key to solving these problems is to think of the word *multiply* when you see the word *of,* think of the word *equals* when you see the word *is,* and think of some variable (say, x) when you see the word *what.*

1. 3% of what number is 9?
   Translation: $(.03)(x) = 9$.
   So, $.03x = 9$. Multiply both sides of the equation by 100 to remove the decimal point. $3x = 900$; $x = 300$. So, 3% of 300 is 9.
2. 9% of 3 is what number?
   Translation: $.09 \cdot 3 = x$
   So, $.27 = x$. Therefore, 9% of 3 is .27.
3. 9 is what % of 36?
   Translation: $9 = x\% \times 36$ (remember, "of" with percents means "multiply").
   So, dividing both sides of the equation by 36, we get $^9/_{36} = x\%$; $^1/_4 = x\%$; $.25 = x\%$; $25\% = x\%$; $x = 25$.
   Therefore, 9 is 25% of 36.

PRACTICE PROBLEMS

See page 204 for instructions on marking your answers.

7.1   If 60% of *A* is 20% of *B,* then *B* is what % of *A?*

   (A) 3%   (B) 25%   (C) 30%   (D) 250%   (E) 300%

7.2   If $87\frac{1}{2}\%$ of Jack's weekly salary is $140.00, and if 25% of his weekly salary goes into his savings account, how much money does Jack have left for spending money?

   (A) $40.00   (B) $80.00   (C) $100.00   (D) $120.00   (E) $160.00

7.3   Frank paid $6.40 for a shirt after receiving a discount of 20% off the list price. What was the list price before the sale?

   (A) $6.60   (B) $7.00   (C) $7.40   (D) $8.00   (E) $9.20

7.4   A merchant sells all his articles so that he makes a profit of 15% of his cost. If he sells an article for $287.50, what was the cost to the merchant?

   (A) $200.00   (B) $215.00   (C) $250.00   (D) $272.50   (E) $287.35

7.5   Working on an assembly line, Janet's job is to reject .05% of the parts that come before her. If she rejects 4 parts, how many parts did she examine?

   (A) 8   (B) 80   (C) 800   (D) 8,000   (E) 80,000

7.6   What percent of $^1/_2$ is $^3/_4$?

   (A) 100%   (B) 120%   (C) 125%   (D) 135%   (E) 150%

7.7   If a man's salary is increased from $400.00 to $600.00, what was the percent of increase in his salary?

   (A) 20%   (B) 25%   (C) 30%   (D) 50%   (E) 60%

	Column A		Column B	
7.8	16% of 80		80% of 16	A B C D
7.9	$\frac{1}{4}\%$		.025	A B C D

7.10 What percent of a is b?

(A) $\dfrac{b}{a}$ (B) $\dfrac{a}{b}$ (C) $\dfrac{100b}{a}$ (D) $\dfrac{100a}{b}$ (E) $\dfrac{a}{100b}$

ANSWERS AND EXPLANATIONS

7.1 (E)   7.2 (D)   7.3 (D)   7.4 (C)   7.5 (D)
7.6 (E)   7.7 (D)   7.8 (C)   7.9 (B)   7.10 (C)

7.1 60% of A is 20% of B. Translation: $.60A = .20B$. B is what % of A? Translation: $B = (x\%)(A)$. From the first equation, dividing both sides by .20, we get $\dfrac{.60A}{.20} = B$, or $3A = B$, so $B = (3)(A)$ or $(300\%)(A)$. Choice (E).

7.2 $87\frac{1}{2}\%$ of x is 140. Translation: $(.875)(x) = 140$. Multiply both sides of the equation to get rid of the decimal: $875x = 140,000$. Divide both sides by 875: $875\overline{)140,000}$ with quotient 160. So, Jack's weekly salary is $160.00. Now, 25% of that weekly salary is his savings, so $(.25)(160) = x$; $x = 40$. Therefore, he has left $160 - 40 = 120$. Choice (D).

Note: Sometimes it is much easier to use the fractional equivalents of decimals in problems like these. We shall now do the problem again by this method.

$$87\frac{1}{2}\% \text{ of } x = 140 \qquad \frac{7x}{8} = \frac{140}{1}$$

Cross-multiply, $7x = 1,120$; and divide, $x = 160$. Now, 25% of 160 = savings. $\frac{1}{4}(160) = \text{savings}; 40 = \text{savings}: 160 - 40 = 120$.

7.3 Let $x =$ list price. If Frank received a discount of 20% off the list price, he paid 80% of the list price. That 80% represents $6.40. So, $.80x = 6.40$. Get rid of the decimals: $80x = 640$. Divide: $x = 8$. So, the list price was $8.00, or choice (D). You could have worked backward from the answers fairly simply in this problem. Take 20% off 6.60: $.20(6.60) = 1.32$. $6.60 - 1.32 = 5.28$. So, choice (A) is out, and so on.

7.4 Let the cost of the article be x. His profit is therefore $.15x$. Selling price = cost + profit; therefore, $287.50 = x + .15x. = 1.15x$. Multiply both sides of the equation by 100 (move the decimal points 2 places to the right) to get rid of the decimals: $28,750 = 115x$. Divide both sides of the equation by 115 to get 250, or choice (C). Once again, you could have worked this problem using the answers. Multiply each answer by 1.15 until you reach the required selling price of $287.50.

7.5 Be careful! $.05\% = .0005$, *not* .05. The problem states that Janet rejects .05% of the parts. Therefore, letting $x =$ parts examined: $(.05\%)(x) = 4$; $(.0005)(x) = 4$. $.0005x = 4$; $5x = 40,000$; $x = 8,000$. Choice (D).

7.6   What percent of $^1/_2$ is $^3/_4$?

$$\downarrow \qquad \downarrow \qquad \downarrow \qquad \downarrow$$

$$x \qquad \% \qquad \cdot \ ^1/_2 = \ ^3/_4?$$

$$(x\%)(^1/_2) = \ ^3/_4$$

$$\frac{x\%}{2} = \frac{3}{4}$$

Cross-multiplying, $4x\% = 6$. Dividing by 4, $x\% = \ ^6/_4 = 1.5$. So, $x\% = 150\%$, $x = 150$. Choice (E).

7.7   Percent increase $= \dfrac{\text{amount of increase}}{\text{original amount}}$

Percent increase $= \dfrac{600 - 400}{400} = \dfrac{200}{400} = \dfrac{1}{2} = 50\%$. Choice (D).

7.8 $(.16)(80) = (.80)(16)$ because the digits in the products are exactly the same and the number of decimal places in the products are exactly the same, 2. Choice (C).

7.9 $^1/_4\%$ is equivalent to .25%, which equals .0025. Therefore, the quantity in column B is greater. Choice (B).

7.10   What % of a is b?

$$\downarrow \qquad \downarrow \ \downarrow \qquad \downarrow$$

$$x \qquad \% \ \cdot \ a = b?$$

$$(x\%)(a) = b$$

$$x\% = \frac{b}{a}. \text{ So, it "looks like" choice (A).}$$

However, we must find x, not $x\%$. So,

$$(x\%)(a) = b; \ x\% = \frac{b}{a}$$

$$\frac{x}{100} = \frac{b}{a}$$

$$xa = 100b$$

$$x = \frac{100b}{a}. \text{ Choice (C).}$$

Section 8: Areas, Perimeters, and Volumes

The area of a rectangle is the product of its base and its height.

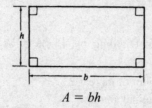

$$A = bh$$

The area of a parallelogram is the product of its base and its height.

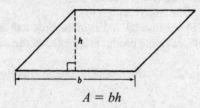

$$A = bh$$

Note: Be careful here! The height *must* be perpendicular to the base. The height of a parallelogram is not one of its sides, unless, of course, that parallelogram happens to be a rectangle.

The area of any triangle is equal to $\frac{1}{2}$ the product of a base and a height (drawn to that base).

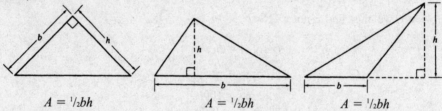

$$A = \frac{1}{2}bh \qquad\qquad A = \frac{1}{2}bh \qquad\qquad A = \frac{1}{2}bh$$

In a right triangle, either leg can be thought of as the base. Then the other leg is the height. Remember, a triangle has 3 bases and 3 heights. Use the most convenient pair.

The area of a square is (side)².

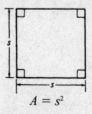

$$A = s^2$$

The area of a square is also equal to $\frac{1}{2}$ (diagonal)².

$$A = \frac{1}{2}d^{\,2}$$

Note: There is a very simple proof for this.

In the square, $d^2 = s^2 + s^2 = 2s^2$. Therefore, $s^2 = \frac{1}{2}d^2$. Because s^2 is the area of the square, $\frac{1}{2}d^2$ is also the area of the square.

The ratio of the area of two similar triangles is equal to the ratio of the squares of corresponding sides, heights, medians, or angle bisectors. Example:

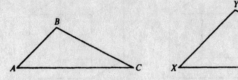

If triangle *ABC* is similar to triangle *XYZ*, then:

$$\frac{AB^2}{XY^2} = \frac{\text{area of triangle } ABC}{\text{area of triangle } XYZ}$$

The area of a circle is equal to the product of π and the (radius)^2.

$$A = \pi r^2$$

(A radius is $\frac{1}{2}$ the length of a diameter.)

The area of a sector of a circle is equal to a fractional part of the area of the whole circle. That fractional part can be determined by taking the ratio:

$$\frac{\text{Central angle}}{360°}$$

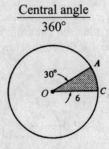

In the preceding diagram, central angle *AOC* of the circle is 30°. Radius *OC* = 6. The area of the entire circle is $\pi 6^2 = \pi 36$ or 36π. Because $\dfrac{30°}{360°} = \dfrac{1}{12}$, the area of the sector is $\dfrac{1}{12}$ the area of the entire circle, or $\dfrac{1}{12} \cdot 36\pi = 3\pi$.

The area of a cube is the sum of the areas of all 6 faces (each of which is a square). Therefore, if the area of one square face is s^2, the surface area of the cube is $6s^2$.

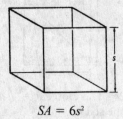

$$SA = 6s^2$$

The volume of a cube is s^3. The volume of any rectangular solid is length $\times$ width $\times$ height. Because each of these dimensions is the same for a cube, the volume is just s^3.

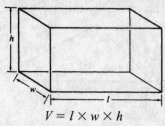 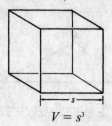

$$V = l \times w \times h \qquad V = s^3$$

The perimeter of a plane geometric figure is simply the "distance around it."

The perimeter of a square, therefore, is $4s$ ($s + s + s + s$).

The perimeter of a triangle is $s_1 + s_2 + s_3$ (the sum of its sides).

The perimeter of a circle is called its circumference. The circumference of a circle is equal to the product of π and the diameter (remember, a diameter is twice a radius, so the formula can be written as $C = \pi 2r$ or $2\pi r$).

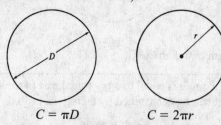

$$C = \pi D \qquad C = 2\pi r$$

To find the arc length of a sector, find the circumference of the circle and multiply it by the fractional part of the circle that the central angle intercepts.

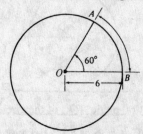

Example: $r = 6$
$\angle AOB = 60°$

$C = 2\pi \cdot 6 = 12\pi$. $\dfrac{60°}{360°} = \dfrac{1}{6}$. Length of arc AB is $\dfrac{1}{6} \, 12\pi = 2\pi$.

The ratio of the areas of two circles is equal to the ratio of the squares of their radii, their diameters, or their circumferences.

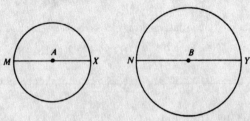

$$\frac{\text{Area of circle } A}{\text{Area of circle } B} = \frac{AX^2}{BY^2} = \frac{MX^2}{NY^2} = \frac{(\text{circumference of circle } A)^2}{(\text{circumference of circle } B)^2}$$

You will find numerical examples in the practice problems that follow.

PRACTICE PROBLEMS

See page 204 for instructions on marking your answers.

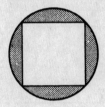

8.1   In the figure above, the perimeter of the square is 40. The area of the shaded region is

(A) $100 - 50\pi$ (B) $100 + 50\pi$ (C) $200 - 50\pi$ (D) $50\pi - 100$
(E) $100\pi - 200$

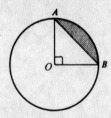

8.2   Find the area of the shaded region if $OB = 6$ in the figure above.

(A) $18 - 9\pi$ (B) $18\pi - 9$ (C) $9\pi - 18$ (D) $9 - 18\pi$ (E) $9\pi + 18$

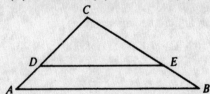

8.3   The area of the triangle CDE above is 12. If $DE \parallel AB$, $DE = 4$, and $AB = 6$, then the area of $ADEB$ is

(A) 10   (B) 12   (C) 15   (D) 18   (E) 27

8.4   What is the area of a circle whose circumference is 4π?

(A) 4π   (B) 8π   (C) 12π   (D) 16π   (E) 24π

8.5   The perimeter of an equilateral triangle is 18. What is the area of this triangle?

(A) 18   (B) 9 √2   (C) 9 √3   (D) 18 √2   (E) 18 √3

8.6   How many tiles 3″ × 3″ are needed to completely cover a floor that is 9′ × 12′?

(A) 12   (B) 108   (C) 144   (D) 1,728   (E) 2,130

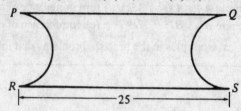

8.7   Each of the semicircles above has diameter 8. *PQ ∥ RS*. The area of the figure is

(A) 200 − 64π   (B) 100 − 16π   (C) 100 − 8π   (D) 200 − 16π
(E) 200 − 8π

	Column A	*Column B*
8.8	Volume of a cube with an edge of 4.	10 times the volume of a cube with an edge of .4. A B C D

Note: Figures are not drawn to scale.

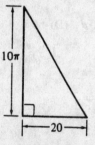   

8.9	Area of the triangle	Area of the circle A B C D

8.10   Cereal boxes that measure 2″ by 8″ by 10″ are to be placed in a large carton, which is 80″ long, 80″ wide, and 40″ high. What is the greatest number of cereal boxes that can fit into the larger carton?

(A) 160   (B) 256   (C) 6,400   (D) 1,600   (E) 40

ANSWERS AND EXPLANATIONS

8.1 (D) 8.2 (C) 8.3 (C) 8.4 (A) 8.5 (C)
8.6 (D) 8.7 (D) 8.8 (A) 8.9 (C) 8.10 (D)

8.1 Practically all of the "shaded region" problems on the SAT are done by subtraction. The clue, in fact, is in the answers. See the minus signs? In this problem, the area of the shaded region is equal to the area of the circle minus the area of the square.

In order to get the area of the square, we need a side (or a diagonal), and in order to get the area of the circle, we need the radius (or the diameter). Because we are told that the perimeter of the square is 40, each side must be 10, since $10 + 10 + 10 + 10 = 40$. So, the area of the square is 100. From this fact alone, and looking at the answers, it is fairly obvious that the answer is (D). However, let's work out the solution. Because the diameter of a circle is also the diagonal of any inscribed square, we can find PQ by using the Pythagorean Theorem. $10^2 + 10^2 = PQ^2$; $100 + 100 = PQ^2$; $200 = PQ^2$; $\sqrt{200} = PQ$; $\sqrt{100 \cdot 2} = PQ$; $10\sqrt{2} = PQ$. (You can reach this point more quickly if you remember that in an isosceles right triangle, the hypotenuse is always

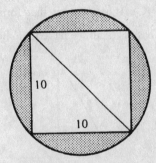

$\sqrt{2} \times$ one of the legs.) Since the diameter is $10\sqrt{2}$, the radius is $5\sqrt{2}$. The area of a circle is πr^2. So, in this case, the area of the circle is $\pi(5\sqrt{2})^2 = \pi(5\sqrt{2})(5\sqrt{2}) = \pi 25\sqrt{4} = \pi \, 25 \cdot 2 = \pi 50$ or 50π. So, the area of the shaded region is $50\pi - 100$, or choice (D).

8.2 The area of this shaded region can also be found by subtraction. Since angle $AOB = 90$, we need to find 90/360, or $\frac{1}{4}$, of the area of the circle. If we subtract the area of triangle AOB from $\frac{1}{4}$ of the area of the circle, we will obtain the shaded area. The radius of the circle is $OB = 6$; therefore the entire circle has an area of $\pi r^2 = \pi(6)^2 = 36\pi$. One-fourth of this area is $\frac{36\pi}{4}$ or 9π. The area of triangle AOB is $\frac{1}{2} B \times H = \frac{1}{2}(6)(6) = 18$. So, the area of the shaded region is $9\pi - 18$. Choice (C).

8.3 Area of $ADEB$ = area of triangle ABC − area of triangle CDE. We are told the area of triangle $CDE = 12$. All we have to do is find the area of triangle ABC. Because $DE \parallel AB$, $\angle A = \angle CDE$ and $\angle B = \angle CED$ (corresponding angles). Therefore, the triangles are similar and their corresponding sides are in proportion. The ratio of the area of two similar triangles is equal to the *squares* of the ratio of corresponding sides, so, $\frac{4^2}{6^2} = \frac{\text{area of triangle } CDE}{\text{area of triangle } ABC}$. $\frac{16}{36} = \frac{12}{x}$; $\frac{4}{9} = \frac{12}{x}$; cross-multiplying, $4x = 108$; $x = 27$. So, the area of $ADEB$ is $27 - 12 = 15$. Choice (C).

8.4 To get the area of a circle we need the radius or the diameter. Since we are told the circumference is 4π, according to the formula $C = \pi d$, the diameter is 4, so the radius is 2. The area of a circle is πr^2, so the area of this circle is $\pi 2^2 = \pi \cdot 4$ or 4π. Choice (A). It's quite *unusual* for the area and the circumference to have the same numerical value. What if the diameter of the circle were any other number but 4? Could the area equal the circumference in any other case?

8.5   Let's draw a diagram:

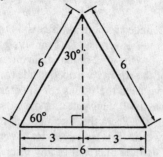

Since the perimeter of this triangle is 18, each of the equal sides is 6. If you remember the formula for the area of an equilateral triangle, $A = \dfrac{s^2}{4} \sqrt{3}$, the area is $\dfrac{6^2}{4} \sqrt{3} = \dfrac{36}{4} \sqrt{3} = 9 \sqrt{3}$. Choice (C). If you forget that formula, use the formula $A = \frac{1}{2}$ (base)(height). Since the base is 6, all we have to do now is find the height. By the Pythagorean Theorem,

$3^2 + h^2 = 6^2$; $9 + h^2 = 36$; $h^2 = \sqrt{27} = \sqrt{9} \sqrt{3} = 3 \sqrt{3}$. So, the area of the triangle is $\frac{1}{2}$ (6)(3 $\sqrt{3}$) = $\frac{1}{2}$(18 $\sqrt{3}$) = 9 $\sqrt{3}$. You could have *avoided* using the Pythagorean Theorem if you remembered the 30°- 60° -90° right triangle relationships:

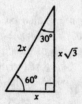

8.6   In a rectangular floor 9′ × 12′ there are 108 square *feet*. Each square foot contains 144 square inches (*not* 12 square inches). So, there are 108 × 144 = 15,552 square inches in the floor. Each 3″× 3″ tile contains 9 square *inches*. So, $\dfrac{15,552}{9} = 1,728$ tiles. Choice (D).

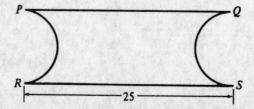

8.7   If you connect P to R and Q to S, you see that PQSR is a rectangle with a length of 25 and a width of 8. The area we want is the area of rectangle PQSR − two semicircles. The area of rectangle *PQSR* is 25 × 8 = 200. This calculation eliminates choices (B) and (C). Two semicircles of diameter 8 are the same as one circle of diameter 8. A circle with a diameter of 8 has a radius of 4 and an area of $\pi(4)^2$ or 16π. So, the area of the figure is $200 - 16\pi$. Choice (D).

8.8 The volume of a cube is given by the formula $V = 5^3$. The volume of the cube described in column A is therefore $4^3 = 4 \times 4 \times 4 = 64$. The volume of the cube described in column B is $(.4)^3 = .4 \times .4 \times .4 = .064$. Ten times this volume is $10(.064) = .64$ Choice (A). The "trap" in this problem is that many students will think the two cubes have the same volume because $10 \times .4 = 4$, but multiplying before using the exponent is working "out of order" and wrong! Exponents must be done *before* multiplication (or division, for that matter) can be done.

8.9 The area of the right triangle is $\frac{1}{2}(10\pi)(20) = \frac{1}{2}(200\pi) = 100\pi$. The area of the circle is $\pi 10^2 = \pi 100 = 100\pi$. So, the quantities in both columns are equal. Choice (C).

8.10 The volume of each cereal box is $2'' \times 8'' \times 10'' = 160$ in^3. The volume of the carton is $40'' \times 80'' \times 80'' = 256,000$. By dividing 256,000 by 160 you find that 1,600 cereal boxes can fit in the large carton. Your calculator will be helpful here because the numbers are big and dividing 256,000 by 160 can be too time-consuming. You could, however, "knock" the numbers down and find the answer quickly without a calculator.

$$\frac{\text{Large carton}}{\text{Cereal box}} = \frac{\overset{20}{\cancel{40}} \times \overset{10}{\cancel{80}} \times \overset{8}{\cancel{80}}}{\underset{1}{\cancel{2}} \times \underset{1}{\cancel{8}} \times \underset{1}{\cancel{10}}} = \frac{20 \times 10 \times 8}{1 \times 1 \times 1} = 1,600$$

Choice (D).

Section 9: Signed Numbers

The absolute value of a number is that number *without* its sign.

Examples: The absolute value of +3 is 3.
The absolute value of −3 is 3.
The absolute value of 0 is 0.

Addition

If the signs of the two numbers are the *same,* add their absolute values and use the same sign in the sum.

Examples: −5 + −7   Add 5 and 7 to get 12. Then use the − sign. So, −5 + −7 = −12.

+5 + +7   Add 5 and 7 to get 12. Then use the + sign. So, +5 + +7 = +12.

Note: In actual use, the + sign before a number is "understood." +5 + +7 is actually written as just 5 + 7.

If the signs are *different, subtract* the absolute values of the numbers and use the sign of the number that had the greater absolute value.

Examples: −5 +   2   "Forgetting" the signs, always subtract the smaller from the greater. 5 − 2 = 3. The absolute value of −5 is 5. The absolute value of 2 is 2. So, "tack on" the − sign in the difference: −5 + 2 = −3.

5 + −8   8 − 5 = 3. The absolute value of −8 is 8. The absolute value of 5 is 5. Use the − sign: 5 + −8 = −3.

5 + −2   5 − 2 = 3. The absolute value of 5 is 5. The absolute value of −2 is 2. Use the + sign (actually, no sign): 5 + −2 = 3.

0 + −3   3 − 0 = 3. The absolute value of −3 is 3. The absolute value of 0 is 0. Use the − sign: 0 + −3 = −3. (Or, simply, "0 + *any* number is that number itself.")

Subtraction

Change the sign of the "second" number and follow the rules for addition.

Examples: −5 − −7   is the same as   −5 + +7 =   2.
−5 − +7   is the same as   −5 + −7 = −12.
+5 − +7   is the same as   5 + −7 = −2.
+5 − −7   is the same as   5 + +7 =   12.

Perhaps a little "gimmick" would come in handy here. Whenever you see two like signs together, circle then and put a + symbol over the circle. Whenever you see two unlike signs together, circle them and put a − symbol above the circle.

Examples: $5 \overset{-}{(+\ -)} 7 = -2$

$5 \overset{-}{(-\ +)} 7 = -2$

$-5 \overset{-}{(+\ -)} 7 = -12$

$5 \overset{+}{(-\ -)} 7 = 12$

$-5 \overset{+}{(-\ -)} 7 = 2$

Multiplication

The product of two numbers with the same sign is positive. The product of two numbers with different signs is negative.

Examples: $(-3)(-5) = 15$
$(-3)(5) \ = -15$

Assuming that you know that $3 + -3 = 0$ (any number plus its additive inverse is zero), $-3 \cdot 0 = 0$ (any number "times" $0 = 0$), the distributive postulate, $a(b + c) = ab + ac$, and the fact that $(-3)(3) = -9$ [because $(-3)(3)$ really means $-3 + -3 + -3 = -9$], then it's really not too hard to present an *intuitive* argument why "two negatives make a positive."

$$a(b + c) = ab + ac$$
$$-3(3\ +\ -3) = -3(3) + (-3)(-3)$$
$$-3(\quad 0\quad) = -3(3) + (-3)(-3)$$
$$0 \quad = -9 + (-3)(-3)$$

but $0 = -9 + 9$; therefore $(-3)(-3)$ *must* be 9.

Division

The quotient of two numbers with the same sign is positive. The quotient of two numbers with different signs is negative.

Examples: $\dfrac{-12}{-6} = 2$

$\dfrac{-12}{6} = -2$

PRACTICE PROBLEMS

See page 204 for instructions on marking your answers.

9.1   If $(-3)^4(-2)^3 = (27)(2)(x)$, then $x =$

(A) -12 (B) -3 (C) 7   (D) 11   (E) 19

9.2 The average of 40, −6, 0, 50, and −10 is

(A) 12.4 (B) 14.8 (C) 22.6 (D) 44.2 (E) 48.4

9.3 Points *P, Q, R,* and *S* are located at −4, −12, 3, and 14 on a number line. $(Q − P) − (R − S) =$

(A) −27 (B) −5 (C) −3 (D) 0 (E) 3

9.4 $(−1)^{51} − (−1)^{50} =$

(A) −2 (B) −1 (C) 0 (D) 2 (E) 101

9.5 The product of −3 and −9 is how much larger than the sum of −3 and −9?

(A) 11 (B) 15 (C) 18 (D) 25 (E) 39

	Column A	Column B	
9.6	$(−2)^7$	$(−2)^6$	A B C D
9.7	$3x − 1$	$3x + 1$	A B C D

$$abc = 0$$
$$a > b$$

	Column A	Column B	
9.8	ac	bc	A B C D

$$x < y$$

9.9	xz	yz	A B C D

$$\frac{x}{y} < 0$$

9.10	xy	$−xy$	A B C D

ANSWERS AND EXPLANATIONS

9.1 (A)   9.2 (B)   9.3 (E)   9.4 (A)   9.5 (E)
9.6 (B)   9.7 (B)   9.8 (D)   9.9 (D)   9.10 (B)

9.1 Do *not* multiply 27 by 2 in this problem. It is unnecessary. $(−3)^4 = 81; (−2)^3 = −8$. Therefore, $(81)(−8) = (27)(2)x$. Divide both sides of the equation by 27 to get $(3)(−8) = 2x$. Divide both sides of the equation by 2 to get $(3)(−4) = x; x = −12$. Choice (A).

9.2 The average of a set of numbers is their sum divided by *n,* where *n* = the number of numbers in the set. The average of 40, −6, 0, 50, and −10 is
$$\frac{(40) + (−6) + (0) + (50) + (−10)}{5} = \frac{74}{5} = 14.8 \text{ Choice (B).}$$

9.3 $(Q - P) - (R - S) = (-12 - -4) - (3 - 14) = (-12 + 4) - (3 - 14) = (-8) - (-11) = -8 + 11 = 3$. Choice (E).

9.4 A negative number raised to an *even power is positive*. A negative number raised to an *odd power is negative*. $(-1)^{51} = -1$. $(-1)^{50} = +1$. Therefore, $-1 - +1 = -1 - 1 = -2$. Choice (A). Remember, 1 raised to any power is still 1.

9.5 The product of -3 and -9 is 27. The sum of -3 and -9 is -12. $27 - -12 = 27 + 12 = 39$. Choice (E).

9.6 There is no need to raise -2 to the sixth and seventh powers to make this comparison. A negative number raised to an *odd* power will always be *negative*. A negative number raised to an *even* power will always be *positive*.

9.7 Any number minus 1 is less than that same number plus 1. Try substituting some numbers. Let $x = -3, 0$, and $+3$. Compare! Choice (B).

9.8 If the product of any amount of numbers is 0, *at least one of them must be 0*. Try some possibilities for *a, b,* and *c*. Remember, though, that *a* is greater than *b*.

a	b	c	ac	bc	abc
3	1	0	0	0	0
-2	-3	0	0	0	0
5	0	-6	-30	0	0

You might as well stop here: *ac could* equal *bc*; *ac could* be less than *bc*. In fact, if $a = 5, b = 0, c = 6$, then $ac = 30, bc = 0$, and *ac* could be greater than *bc*. So, no relationship can be determined. Choice (D).

9.9 Try some numbers (remember, $x < z$).

x	y	z	xz	ya
1	3	+2	2	6
1	3	-2	-2	-6

So, at this point, you can conclude that no relationship can be determined. Remember, $2 < 6$, but $-2 > -6$. Choice (D).

9.10 If $x/y < 0$, *x* and *y* must have different signs. (See the rules for dividing signed numbers, at the beginning of Section 9.) Therefore, the product, *xy,* is negative. Now, $-xy$ is equivalent to $-1(xy)$. Therefore, $-xy$ must be positive. Since a positive number is always greater than a negative number, mark choice (B).

Section 10: Simple Equations

In the booklet *About the SAT,* there is a statement that "the algebra includes linear equations, simple quadratic equations, factoring, and exponents, *but not the quadratic formula.* . . ." That is why we call this section Simple Equations, even though it does include simple quadratic expressions as well as linear equations.

Since there are many *types* of linear equations ("linear" means that no power of the unknown is greater than 1), we feel that the best way to get into solving equations is by presenting some examples.

Examples of Linear Equations

$$\text{If } x + 3 = 5, \text{ then } x = ?$$

Since 3 is "attached" to the unknown, x, by addition, you perform the inverse operation, subtraction, to "get rid" of it. The most important thing to remember in solving equations is that whatever you "do" to one side of an equation, you must do to the other side: $x + 3 = 5; x + 3 - 3 = 5 - 3; x + 0 = 5 - 3; x = 2$.

$$\text{If } 2x - 7 = 5, \text{ then } x = ?$$

Since 7 is "attached" to the term containing the unknown by subtraction, perform the inverse operation, addition, to "get rid" of it: $2x - 7 = 5; 2x - 7 + 7 = 5 + 7; 2x = 12$.

Now, since 2 is "attached" to the unknown by multiplication, perform the inverse operation, division, to "get rid" of it: $2x = 12; \frac{2x}{2} = \frac{12}{2}; x = 6$.

$$\text{If } \frac{3x + 1}{5} = 8 - 2x, \text{ then } x = ?$$

Since 5 is "attached" to the entire left side of the equation by division, we can "get rid" of it by the inverse operation of multiplication. Multiply both sides of the equation by 5:

$$\left(\frac{5}{1}\right)\frac{3x + 1}{5} = 5(8 - 2x) \qquad \frac{5(3x + 1)}{5} = 40 - 10x \qquad 3x + 1 = 40 - 10x$$

Now, you have a choice. First of all, you decide on which side you want the unknown and on which side you want the known (that is, in this case, the numbers). Assume you want the unknown on the left side. So, because there is a $-10x$ on the right side, you must add $10x$ to both sides in order to "get rid" of that $-10x$: $3x + 1 + 10x = 40 - 10x + 10x; 13x + 1 = 40$. Now subtract 1 from both sides to get $13x + 1 - 1 = 40 - 1; 13x = 39$. Divide both sides by 13, and you'll have the answer, 3. You can check your answer by substituting it into the original problem.

If you decide to put the unknown on the right side of the equation, you can subtract $3x$ from both sides first to get $3x + 1 - 3x = 40 - 10x - 3x; 1 = 40 - 13x$. Then subtract 40 from both sides to get $1 - 40 = 40 - 13x - 40; -39 = -13x$. Divide both sides by -13 to get the answer, 3. However, we feel that a little practice will show that fewer mistakes occur when you think a little before you start solving these equations. Try not to get involved with those pesky negative signs. Often, making a foresighted decision about which side you want the unknown on helps avoid that situation.

$$\text{If } \frac{3x + 1}{5} = 8 - 2x, \text{ then } x = ?$$

Yes, this is the same problem. But let's do it a quicker way, although the mathematical principles involved are really the same. Rewrite the problem as $\frac{3x+1}{5} = \frac{8-2x}{1}$. Remember, in the section on fractions, we said that if $\frac{a}{b} = \frac{c}{d}$, then $ad = bc$. So you can cross-multiply here: $(3x+1)(1) = 5(8-2x)$; $3x+1 = 40 - 1x$; and so on. This is probably the best way to start a problem that looks like: $\frac{A}{B} = \frac{C}{D}$.

$$\text{If } \frac{x}{3} + \frac{5x}{6} = 3.5, \text{ then } x = ?$$

You can add the fractions on the left side to get $\frac{2x}{6} + \frac{5x}{6}$ or $\frac{7x}{6}$. Then $\frac{7x}{6} = \frac{3.5}{1}$. Now, cross-multiply to get $7x = 21$; $x = 3$. You could have multiplied each side of the equation by 6 to start with in order to "get rid" of all of the fractions: $\frac{6}{1}\left(\frac{x}{3} + \frac{5x}{6}\right) = \left(\frac{6}{1}\right) 3.5$. This will be equivalent to $\frac{6x}{3} + \frac{30x}{6} = 21$; $2x + 5x = 21$; $7x = 21$; $x = 3$.

Then again, you could have started by "getting rid" of the decimal by multiplying both sides of the equation by 10: $\frac{10x}{3} + \frac{50x}{6} = 35$. Then, you can add the fractions first and then cross-multiply, *or* you can multiply both sides of the equation by 6 in order to "clear" the denominators. There are so many ways of solving a given equation that only by experience will you find the methods that are easiest and quickest for you.

Equations Involving Inequalities

Actually, we should call these *inequations*. For example, "What value(s) for x will satisfy the condition $5x - 3 > 12$?"

$A > B$ means, A is greater than B.

$A < B$ means, A is less than B.

An easy way to remember this is that the arrowhead points to the *smaller* quantity.

If the same number is added or subtracted on both sides of an inequality, the sense (direction) of the inequality remains *unchanged*.

Examples: $-2 > -9$; $-2 + 5 > -9 + 5$, $(3 > -4)$
$-2 < +9$; $-2 - 5 < +9 - 5$, $(-7 < 4)$

If both sides of an inequality are multiplied or divided by the same *positive* number, the sense of the inequality remains unchanged.

Examples: $5 > 2$; $(4)(5) > (4)(2)$, $(20 > 8)$
$12 < 30$; $\frac{12}{6} < \frac{30}{6}$, $(2 < 5)$

However: If both sides of an inequality are multiplied or divided by a negative number, the sense of the inequality is *reversed*.

Examples: $5 > 2$; $(-2)(5) < (-2)(2)$, $(-10 < -4)$

$-8 < +12$; $\dfrac{-8}{-4} > \dfrac{12}{-4}$, $(2 > -3)$

$A \geq B$ means that A is greater than *or* equal to B.

Examples: $6 \geq 4$
$6 \geq 6$

$A \leq B$ means that A is less than *or* equal to B.

Examples: $2 \leq 7$
$2 \leq 2$

$A < x < B$ means that x is less than B but greater than A. In other words, x is between A and B (not including either A or B).

Examples: $-2 < 0 < 5$
$1 < 8 < 12$

$a \not> B$ means that A is *not* greater than B. $5 \not> 7$

Two Equations in Two Unknowns

Sometimes we are given two relationships that exist between two different variables. For example, $3x + 4y = 10$, and $x - 3y = -1$. From the first equation, $3x + 4y = 10$, we can infer that there are an infinite number of solutions, because when $x = 0$, $y = 2.5$; when $x = 2$, $y = 1$; when $x = -2$, $y = 4$; and so on. Likewise, there are an infinite number of solutions for the equation $x - 3y = -1$. However, there is only *one* common solution.

There are two ways to approach a set of equations such as these:

$$3x + 4y = 10$$
$$x - 3y = -1$$

Multiply both sides of the second equation by 3. Let's see what happens:

$$3x + 4y = 10$$
$$3x - 9y = -3$$

Now subtract to "get rid" of one of the variables:

$$\begin{aligned} 3x + 4y &= 10 \\ 3x - 9y &= -3 \\ \hline 13y &= 13 \\ y &= 1 \end{aligned}$$ $(4 - -9 = 13; 10 - -3 = 13)$

Then you can find x by simple substitution in either of the two original equations.

Another method is to solve for one variable in terms of another and then to substitute that variable's equivalent into the other equation.

$$3x + 4y = 10$$
$$x - 3y = -1$$

Solve for x in the *second* equation. (To solve for x or y in the first equation leads to fractions, and you know how we all love fractions! In the second equation, to solve for y, once again you will need to involve fractions.)

So, since $x - 3y = -1$, $x = 3y - 1$. Substitute for x in the "top" equation. Since $3x + 4y = 10$, then $3(3y - 1) + 4y = 10$; $9y - 3 + 4y = 10$; $13y - 3 = 10$; $13y = 13$; $y = 1$. Then find x by substituting 1 for y in either of the two original equations.

Which method to use depends on your experience and practice. Sometimes one method is easier than another depending on the set-up. For example, if you are given

$$3x + 4y = 10$$
$$5x - 7y = \ 3$$

the first method we described would be preferable.

Simplifying Quadratic Expressions

Although you will not be expected to use the quadratic formula, some questions might require factoring quadratic expressions. You have already seen a question of this type in Section 3.7. Remember the following three equations:

1. $a^2 + 2ab + b^2 = (a + b)(a + b)$
2. $a^2 - b^2 = (a - b)(a + b)$
3. $a^2 - 2ab + b^2 = (a - b)(a - b)$

Occasionally you will be faced with a situation where you must simplify an expression such as $x^2 - 5x + 6$ so that you can deal with its factors separately. $x^2 - 5x + 6 = (x - 3)(x - 2)$, as you can discover by a bit of trial and error. Not all quadratic expressions can be factored, of course.

Also remember that

1. $a^2b^2 = (ab)(ab)$
2. $\dfrac{a^2}{b^2} = \left(\dfrac{a}{b}\right)\left(\dfrac{a}{b}\right)$

PRACTICE PROBLEMS

See page 204 for instructions on marking your answers.

10.1 If $5x - 3 > 12$, then

(A) $x^2 < 9$ (B) $x - 4 > 0$ (C) $2x + 1 > 7$ (D) $\dfrac{1}{x} > \dfrac{1}{3}$ (E) $-x > 3$

10.2 If $1 + 0.2x = 1.010$, then $x =$

(A) 0.5 (B) 0.05 (C) 0.005 (D) 0.0005 (E) 0.00005

10.3 If $x + y = A$ and $x - y = B$, then $x =$

(A) A (B) $2A + B$ (C) $2y$ (D) $\dfrac{B - A}{2}$ (E) $\dfrac{A + B}{2}$

10.4 If $ax = dx + g$, then $x =$

(A) $\dfrac{g}{a - d}$ (B) $\dfrac{d + g}{a}$ (C) $\dfrac{g - d}{a}$ (D) $\dfrac{g}{d - a}$ (E) $\dfrac{g + a}{d}$

10.5 If the difference of two numbers is 4 and the difference of their squares is 60, what is the sum of the two numbers?

(A) 64   (B) 56   (C) 15   (D) 44   (E) 76

10.6 If $\dfrac{1}{P} + \dfrac{1}{Q} = \dfrac{1}{R}$, then $P =$

(A) $R + Q$ (B) $\dfrac{RQ}{Q - R}$ (C) $R - Q$ (D) $\dfrac{Q + R}{RQ}$ (E) $Q - R$

10.7 If $\dfrac{a + b + c}{3} = \dfrac{a + b}{3} + 1$, then $c =$

(A) 1   (B) 2   (C) 3   (D) -6 (E) 4

	Column A		Column B	
		$\dfrac{x}{y} = \dfrac{4}{5}$		
10.8	$\dfrac{2x}{y}$		$\dfrac{y}{x}$	A B C D
		$\dfrac{1}{x} < 1$		
10.9	x		1	A B C D
		$2xy = 6xy - 3$		
10.10	$x^2 y^2$		$^5/_8$	A B C D

ANSWERS AND EXPLANATIONS

10.1 (C)   10.2 (B)   10.3 (E)   10.4 (A)   10.5 (C)
10.6 (B)   10.7 (C)   10.8 (A)   10.9 (D)   10.10 (B)

10.1 Add 3 to both sides of the inequality: $5x - 3 + 3 > 12 + 3$; $5x > 15$. Divide both sides by 5: $x > 3$. Now look at all of the answers. (A) $x^2 < 9$. Since we know that $x > 3$, then certainly $x^2 > 9$. So, (A) is out! (B) $x - 4 > 0$ is equivalent to $x > 4$ (adding 4 to both sides). Well, if $x > 3$, then x could be > 4 but *it doesn't have to be!* For example, $3.5 > 3$, then but $3.5 < 4$. $3.677 > 3$, but $3.677 < 4$. There are an infinite number of real numbers that are greater than 3 without being greater than 4! (C) Since $x > 3$, $2x + 1$ represents twice a number greater than 3 that is increased by 1. Twice *any* number greater than 3 gives a result greater than 6. Add 1, and the sum is always greater than 7.

So, our answer is choice (C). However, let's continue. (D) Since $x > 3$, $\dfrac{1}{x}$ is *smaller* than $\dfrac{1}{3}$. For example, $\dfrac{1}{4} < \dfrac{1}{3}$; $\dfrac{1}{3.1} = \dfrac{1}{^{31}/_{10}} = \dfrac{10}{31}$, which is smaller than $\dfrac{1}{3}$, and so on. So, (D) is out! (E) The negative of a number greater than 3 is obviously less than 3: $-5 < 3$, $-10 < 3$. In fact, any negative number is less than 3!

10.2 Subtract 1 from both sides of the equation to get $0.2x = .010$. Multiply by 100 to "get rid" of the decimals: $20x = 1.0$ or just 1. Divide by 20 to get $x = 20 \overline{)1.00}^{\,.05}$. Choice (B). Of course, you could have substituted in all of the answers until one "clicked." But it would be a waste of time in this case. It is easier to do it directly.

10.3
$$x + y = A$$
$$+\ \underline{x - y = B}$$
$$2x\ \ \ \ \ = A + B$$

$$x\ \ \ \ \ = \frac{A + B}{2}\quad \text{Choice (E)}.$$

$x + y = A;\ x - y = B;$
substitute $y = A - x$ into the
second equation to get
$x - (A - x) = B;\ x - A + x = B;$
$2x - A = B;\ 2x = A + B;$
$x = \dfrac{A + B}{2}.$ Choice (E).

If you don't remember either of these two methods, then pick some numbers for x, y, A, and B, such as $x = 1$, $y = 2$. Then, $x + y = 3$. So, $A = 3$. $x - y = 1 - 2 = -1$, so $B = -1$. Now look at all of the answers. (A) A. Well, does $x = A$? Does $1 = 3$? (A) is out! (B) $2A + B$; $2(3) + (-1) = 6 - 1 = 5$. So, $x \neq 2A + B$. (C) $2y$. Does $x = 2y$? Does $1 = 2(2) = 4$? (C) is out! (D) $\dfrac{B - A}{2}$; $\dfrac{-1 - 3}{2} = \dfrac{-4}{2} = -2$. But $x = 1$, not -2. So, (D) is out. (E) must be the answer! But let's check it anyway. $\dfrac{A + B}{2} = \dfrac{3 + (-1)}{2} = \dfrac{3 - 1}{2} = \dfrac{2}{2} = 1$.

10.4 Get every term containing the unknown, x, on one side of the equation. Since $ax = dx + g$, subtract dx from both sides to get $ax - dx = g$. So, if you are going to guess at this point, at *least* guess (A) or (D)! Using the distributive postulate, $ax - dx = (a - d)x$. So, $(a - d)x = g$, and dividing both sides by $(a - d)$ we get $\dfrac{(a - d)x}{(a - d)} = \dfrac{g}{(a - d)}$; $x = \dfrac{g}{a - d}$. Choice (A). Once again, you could substitute numbers for a, d, x, and g in the original "if" statement *and* in all of the answers to see which were equivalent. Be careful! Remember, you should substitute at least two sets of numbers just in case you have some freaky case where you are led astray. For example (and this has nothing to do with the numbers in this problem), suppose you substituted $A = 2$, $B = 1$ into the two expressions $2A - B$ and $3A - 3B$. In the first case you get $2(2) - 1 = 4 - 1 = 3$, and in the second case you get $3(2) - 3(1) = 6 - 3 = 3$. So, if time permits, try at least two sets of numbers and pick them far apart! Otherwise, you could conclude that $2A - B = 3A - 3B$ for all numbers A and B.

10.5 The best way to do this problem is to remember the formula $a^2 - b^2 = (a - b) \times (a + b)$. If the two numbers are a and b, then $a - b$ will be their difference, and $a^2 - b^2$ will be the difference of their squares. It all fits nicely together:

$$a^2 - b^2 = (a - b)(a + b)$$
$$60 = 4(a + b)$$

Therefore, $a + b$, which is the sum we are looking for, is just $^{60}/_4 = 15$. Choice (C).

10.6 So many students get a problem like this one wrong! They start out okay: If $\dfrac{1}{P} + \dfrac{1}{Q} = \dfrac{1}{R}$, then, subtracting $\dfrac{1}{Q}$ from both sides of the equation, they get $\dfrac{1}{P} = \dfrac{1}{R} - \dfrac{1}{Q}$. It is at this point that most of the wrong answers come about. These "wrong" students now invert each term of the equation to get $P = R - Q$.

ERROR. Substitute numbers and you will see that you can't invert fractions any time you want to. For example, $\dfrac{1}{2} + \dfrac{1}{2} = \dfrac{2}{2}$ (or 1, of course). Now invert each fraction to get $\dfrac{2}{1} + \dfrac{2}{1} = \dfrac{2}{2}$. Hmmm! Is it true that $2 + 2 = 1$? You *can* invert fractions when you have a situation such as $\dfrac{A}{B} = \dfrac{C}{D}$, because if $\dfrac{A}{B} = \dfrac{C}{D}$, then

$\frac{B}{A} = \frac{D}{C}$. Example: $\frac{2}{3} = \frac{4}{6}$, $\frac{3}{2} = \frac{6}{4}$. It's that + sign between the fractions that should prevent you from inverting everything in sight. Well, we were down to $\frac{1}{P} = \frac{1}{R} - \frac{1}{Q}$; subtract the fractions on the right side of the equation to get $\frac{1}{P} = \frac{Q - R}{RQ}$. *Now* you have the form $\frac{A}{B} = \frac{C}{D}$, so you *can* invert to get $P = \frac{RQ}{Q - R}$. Choice (B).

Another approach to this problem is to "clear" the fractions by multiplying by PQR. $PQR\left(\frac{1}{P} + \frac{1}{Q}\right) = PQR\left(\frac{1}{R}\right)$. So, $\frac{PQR}{P} + \frac{PQR}{Q} = \frac{PQR}{R}$; $QR + PR = PQ$. Getting all of those terms containing P on one side of the equation: $QR = PQ - PR$. Using the distributive postulate now, $QR = P(Q - R)$. Dividing both sides of the equation by $(Q - R)$ we get, $\frac{QR}{(Q - R)} = \frac{P(Q - R)}{(Q - R)}$. So, $\frac{QR}{Q - R} = P$.

10.7   "Clear" the fractions by multiplying both *sides* of the equation by 3. $3\left(\frac{a + b + c}{3}\right) = 3\left(\frac{a + b}{3} + 1\right)$. This gives you

$$\frac{\cancel{3}(a + b + c)}{\cancel{3}} = \frac{\cancel{3}(a + b)}{\cancel{3}} + 3(1)$$

So, $a + b + c = a + b + 3$. Now, subtract a and then b from both sides to get $c = 3$. Choice (C). It would take a while longer by trial and error to figure out what numbers could fit into the equation.

10.8   Since we are given $\frac{x}{y} = \frac{4}{5}$, then $\frac{2x}{y} = 2\left(\frac{4}{5}\right) = \frac{8}{5}$. Since $\frac{x}{y} = \frac{4}{5}$, then in column B, $\frac{y}{x} = \frac{5}{4}$. $\frac{8}{5} = \frac{32}{20}$; $\frac{5}{4} = \frac{25}{20}$; so, the quantity in column A is greater. Choice (A).

10.9   Since $\frac{1}{x} < 1$, can we conclude that $x > 1$? Substituting some values for x, $\frac{1}{3} < 1$ and $3 > 1$. $\frac{1}{8} < 1$ and $8 > 1$. *But,* what if $x = -2$? $\frac{1}{-2} < 1$ but $-2 \not> 1$. Since we do not know if x is positive or negative, we must mark choice (D). *Try several values of the variable.*

10.10   You could find values of x and y that will "fit" into the equation, but it is just as easy to do this one directly (algebraically). If $2xy = 6xy - 3$, subtracting $2xy$ from both sides, we get $0 = 4xy - 3$. Then, adding 3 to both sides, we get $4xy = 3$. Dividing by 4 we get $xy = \frac{3}{4}$, so that

$$x^2y^2 = (xy)(xy) = \left(\frac{3}{4}\right)\left(\frac{3}{4}\right) = \frac{9}{16}$$

Because $\frac{5}{8} = \frac{10}{16}$, the quantity in column B is greater. Choice (B).

There is a point in this problem at which a lot of students go off course. It is a careless error and we should discuss it. When we are at the point where $4xy = 3$, it is very tempting to say $4x^2y^2 = 9$. *ERROR.* Did you square *both* sides? $3^2 = 9$, but $(4xy)^2 \neq 4x^2y^2$. It is equal to $16x^2y^2$. So, be very careful!

Section 11: Divisibility, Odd and Even Integers

1. Integers are numbers such as -6, -1, 0, 3, and 10.
2. Whole numbers are the nonnegative integers such as 0, 1, 2, and 3, and so on.
3. To say that *X is divisible by Y* means that when you divide X by Y there is *no* remainder.

Examples: 96 is divisible by 8 because $\frac{96}{8} = 12$.
            34 is *not* divisible by 8 because $\frac{34}{8} = 4\frac{1}{4}$.

4. Any number divisible by 2 is called an *even* number: -6, 8, and so on.
5. Any number not even is *odd:* -5, 3, 7, 101, and so on.
6. Any number divisible only by itself and 1 (except 1) is called a *prime* number: 5, 7, 11, and so on.
7. Any number that is not prime is called a *composite* number.

Examples: 2, 3, 29 are prime numbers.
            4, 12, 100 are composite numbers.

8. One number is a multiple of another number if it is divisible by that number.

Examples: 24 is a multiple of 4.
            24 is a multiple of 6.
             6 is a multiple of 2.

9. A factor of a number is any number that will divide into the first number without leaving a remainder.

Examples: 4 is a factor of 24.
            2 is a factor of 6.
            8 is a factor of 8.

Quick Tests for Divisibility

Sometimes, in order to save valuable time on the SAT, it would be helpful to know whether or not one number is divisible by another, without, of course, going through the process of actually dividing and looking for a remainder. For example, is 234,117 divisible by 9? Yes. $234,117 = (26,013)(9)$. Add the digits of 234,117 to get $2 + 3 + 4 + 1 + 1 + 7 = 18$. Since 18 is divisible by 9, 234,117 is divisible by 9. Neat, huh?

A number is divisible by	*If*
2	Its last digit is divisible by 2. (86, 44, 92, 108, 30. Remember, $\frac{0}{2} = 0$.)
3	The sum of its digits is divisible by 3. (27: $2 + 7 = 9$. 9 is divisible by 3, so 27 is divisible by 3. 2,115: $2 + 1 + 1 + 5 = 9$; so, 2,115 is divisible by 3, and so on.
4	The number formed by its last two digits is divisible by 4. (90,724: last two digits form the number 24, which is divisible by 4, so 90,724 is divisible by 4.)

A number is divisible by	If
5	Its last digit is 0 or 5. (25, 605, 900, and so on)
6	It is divisible by 2 and by 3. [324 is divisible by 2 and by 3; so, 324 is divisible by 6. If a number is divisible by *a, b, c, d,* and so on, where these letters represent prime numbers, then the original number is divisible by any product that can be formed by these prime numbers. Example: $210 = (2)(3)(5)(7)$. So, 210 is divisible by 2, 3, 5 and 7. It is also divisible by $(2)(3) = 6$, by $(2)(3)(7) = 42$, and so on.]
7	No quick test
8	The number formed by the last 3 digits is divisible by 8. (237,040: last 3 digits form the number 040, which is divisible by 8; so, 237,040 is divisible by 8.)
9	The sum of its digits is divisible by 9. (See the opening paragraph.)

10. 2 is the *only even* prime number. Any other even number has a factor of 2 and is therefore composite.

11. If k is an integer, $k + 1$, $k + 2$, and so on represent the next consecutive integers.

12. If k is an even integer, the next consecutive even integers are $k + 2$, $k + 4$, and so on.

13. If k is an odd integer, the next consecutive odd integers are (also) $k + 2$, $k + 4$, and so on.

PRACTICE PROBLEMS

See page 204 for instructions on marking your answers.

11.1 If $31 < x < 38$ and $41 < y < 47$ and x and y are prime numbers, then $y - x = $?

(A) 10 (B) 6 (C) 7 (D) 15 (E) cannot be determined

11.2 If the 5-digit number $31,72P$ is divisible by 9, then $P = $

(A) 3 (B) 4 (C) 5 (D) 6 (E) 9

11.3 A boy can divide his baseball cards into equal piles of 3, 4, or 6 cards so that every card is in at least one pile. What is the smallest number of baseball cards he might have?

(A) 68 (B) 72 (C) 18 (D) 12 (E) 24

11.4 Of the following numbers, the one that can be written in the form $3Q$, where Q is an integer, is

(A) 22 (B) 2,222 (C) 22,222 (D) 222,222 (E) 2,222,222

11.5 The average of five consecutive even integers is greater than the least even integer by

(A) 3 (B) 4 (C) 5 (D) 6 (E) cannot be determined from the information given

11.6   If *a, b,* and *c* are three consecutive integers, which of the following is *always* true?

(A) $a + b = c$ (B) $a + b > c$ (C) $a + b = c + 1$ (D) $a + c = 2b$
(E) $2(a + b) > 2c$

11.7   If *N* is a positive integer divisible by 7 without remainder, which of the following must also be divisible by 7 without remainder?

(A) $\dfrac{N}{7}$ (B) $\dfrac{N}{7} + 7$ (C) $3N + 28$ (D) $\dfrac{77}{N}$ (E) $11N + 6$

11.8   If $\dfrac{x^4}{25}$ is not an integer, then *x* could be

(A) 5   (B) 10   (C) 16   (D) 25   (E) $5\sqrt{5}$

	Column A	Column B	
11.9	The average of 7 consecutive odd integers, *a, b, c, d, e, f, g*.	$\dfrac{c + e}{2}$	A B C D

a, b, and *c* are consecutive
odd integers

11.10	*abc*	$a + b + c$	A B C D

ANSWERS AND EXPLANATIONS

11.1 (B)   11.2 (C)   11.3 (D)   11.4 (D)   11.5 (B)
11.6 (D)   11.7 (C)   11.8 (C)   11.9 (C)   11.10 (D)

11.1   The only prime *x* greater than 31 but less than 38 is 37; the only prime *y* greater than 41 but less than 47 is 43. Therefore, $y - x = 43 - 37 = 6$. Choice (B).

11.2   A number is divisible by 9 if the sum of its digits is divisible by 9. $3 + 1 + 7 + 2 + P = 13 + P$. If $P = 5$, then $13 + 5 = 18$, which is divisible by 9. Therefore, 31,725 is divisible by 9. Choice (C).

11.3   Be careful here! What is the *smallest* number divisible by 3, 4, and 6? The answer is 12, choice (D). He can thus make 4 piles of 3 cards each, 3 piles of 4 cards each, or 2 piles of 6 cards each. Many students see that "72" in choice (B); and since 3, 4, and 6 are all factors of 72, they decide on this answer. However, the problem states, "What is the *smallest* number ..." You should really underline important words like these when they come up in a problem.

11.4   Suppose $Q = -2, -1, 0, 3, 7, 9, \ldots$. Then $3Q = -6, -3, 0, 9, 21, 27, \ldots$, which means that $3Q$ is divisible by 3 (because it has 3 as a factor). Which of the answers is divisible by 3? *That* is really the question. A number is divisible by 3 if the sum of its digits is divisible by 3. Try the answers now. (A) 22; $2 + 2 = 4$, 4 is *not* divisible by 3. (B) 2,222: $2 + 2 + 2 + 2 = 8$. No. (C) 22,222; $2 + 2 + 2 + 2 + 2 = 10$. No. (D) 222,222: $2 + 2 + 2 + 2 + 2 + 2 = 12$. Since 12 *is* divisible by 3, then 222,222 is also divisible by 3. Choice (D). Of course, you probably "skipped" right to this answer as you "added up" all those 3s in your mind! Whatever you do, don't try dividing 3 into each of the answers. You'll probably take too much time.

11.5   Consecutive even (or odd) integers can be expressed as $k, k + 2, k + 4, k + 6, k + 8$. For example, if $k = 6$, the five consecutive even integers could be 6, 8, 10, 12, 14. Their average is $\dfrac{6 + 8 + 10 + 12 + 14}{5} = \dfrac{50}{5} = 10$. Suppose $k = -8$. The five consecutive even integers would be $-8, -6, -4, -2$, and 0, and the average would be $\dfrac{-8 + -6 + -4 + -2 + 0}{5} = \dfrac{-20}{5} = -4$. Do you notice anything? Let's take five consecutive even (or odd) integers ($k, k + 2, k + 4, k + 6, k + 8$) and find their average: $\dfrac{k + k + 2 + k + 4 + k + 6 + k + 8}{5} = \dfrac{5k + 20}{5} = \dfrac{5(k + 4)}{5} = k + 4$ (the "middle" integer). So, the average of five consecutive even integers is always 4 greater than the least integer: $k + 4$ is 4 greater than k. Choice (B).

11.6   Let the consecutive integers be $x, x + 1$, and $x + 2$. Then, choice (D), $x + (x + 2) = 2(x + 1)$, is correct because $x + (x + 2) = 2x + 2 = 2(x + 1)$. Of course, you could have substituted numbers. But be careful! $1 + 2 = 3$, choice (A), seems correct. But what about $2 + 3 = 4$? Likewise, in choice (B), $1 + 2$ is *not* greater than 3.

11.7   This is very tricky. If you look at choice (A), it brings about some sort of immediate recognition, doesn't it? But the problem *doesn't* state, "Which of the following shows that N is divisible by 7," it states, "Which of the following *is* divisible by 7?" Is $\dfrac{N}{7}$ divisible by 7? Well, if N is divisible by 7, then N could be $-14, 7, 21$, and so on. Try some of those values to see whether or not $\dfrac{N}{7}$ is divisible by 7. Let $N = 7$. Then $\dfrac{N}{7} = 1$. Is 1 divisible by 7? No. Choice (A) is out! (B) Again, it is easy to let $N = 7$ (in that 7 is certainly divisible by 7). So, is $\dfrac{1}{7} + 7$ divisible by 7? No. On to (C). Letting $N = 7$ again, is $3(7) + 28$ divisible by 7? $21 + 28 = 49$, and because 49 *is* divisible by 7, it *seems* that (C) is the answer. What if you let $N = $ a number other than 7, though? Would $3N + 28$ *still* be divisible by 7? If you had the time to try other Ns, you could make that decision. But because you are rushed for time, your first inclination is probably right. But rather than try other Ns, why not stick to $N = 7$ to see if you can eliminate the other answers. (D) $\dfrac{77}{N}$ is equal to 11 when $N = 7$. Because 11 is *not* divisible by 7, choice (D) is out. (E) $11N + 6 = 83$ when $N = 7$. 83 is *not* divisible by 7, so (E) is out! *So,* choice (C) *was* correct. You probably got nervous because you did not have time to try many sets of values for N, as you were warned to do throughout this book, right? Let's go back though to (C), $3N + 28$. If N is divisible by 7, then $3N$ is divisible by 7, because it contains a factor that is divisible by 7 (N). Because 28 is divisible by 7, the question is, "Is the *sum* of two numbers divisible by 7 if *each number* in the sum is divisible by 7?" The answer to that is yes. The statement is true even if the word *sum* is replaced by *difference* or *product*. It is *not* true if the word is *quotient*. You can see that in choices (A), (B), and (D).

11.8 If $\dfrac{x^4}{25}$ is *not* an integer, then x^4 *can't* be divisible by 25. (A) 5: $5^4 = 5 \times 5 \times 5 \times 5 = 25 \times 25$, which *is* divisible by 25. (B) 10: $10^4 = 10 \times 10 \times 10 \times 10 = 100 \times 100$, which is certainly divisible by 25. (C) 16: $16^4 = 16 \times 16 \times 16 \times 16$. Numbers that are divisible by 25 must have 0 or 5 as their last digit. Examples: 25, 50, 75, 100, 125, 625. $16 \times 16 \times 16 \times 16$ will have a 6 as its last digit when multiplied out. So, $16 \times 16 \times 16 \times 16$ is *not* divisible by 25. Another way of thinking about this is to see if $16 \times 16 \times 16 \times 16$ contains the factors of 25. $\dfrac{16 \times 16 \times 16 \times 16}{5 \times 5} = \dfrac{(2 \times 2 \times 2 \times 2)(2 \times 2 \times 2 \times 2)(2 \times 2 \times 2 \times 2)(2 \times 2 \times 2 \times 2)}{5 \times 5}$. There aren't "two 5s up there." So, $16 \times 16 \times 16 \times 16$ is *not* divisible by 25. What about choice (E), even though we have the answer? Well, $(5\sqrt{5})^4 = (5\sqrt{5})(5\sqrt{5})(5\sqrt{5})(5\sqrt{5}) = (5 \times 5 \times 5 \times 5)(\sqrt{5}\sqrt{5}\sqrt{5}\sqrt{5}) = (25 \times 25)(\sqrt{25}\sqrt{25}) = (25 \times 25 \times 5 \times 5) = 25 \times 25 \times 25$, which is divisible by 25!

11.9 Remember, in problem 11.5 you discovered that the average of an odd number of consecutive even (or odd) integers was indeed the middle integer. So, the average of the seven consecutive odd integers (a, b, c, d, e, f, and g) is d. So, the problem here is really whether or not $\dfrac{c+e}{2}$ is less than, equal to, or greater than d, if in fact that determination can be made. Let's start with 3 odd integers, say, 3, 5, and 7. The average is 5. Now, what is the average of the *two* integers around that average? In other words, what is $\dfrac{3+7}{2}$? How about that? Try five consecutive odd integers, say, 7, 9, 11, 13, and 15. The average of these five integers is $\dfrac{55}{5} = 11$, and the average of 9 and 13 is $\dfrac{9+13}{2} = \dfrac{22}{2} = 11$. Let's take any seven consecutive odd integers, say k, $k+2, k+4, k+6, k+8, k+10$, and $k+12$. The average of these integers is $\dfrac{7k+42}{7} = \dfrac{7(k+6)}{7} = k+6$, the middle term again. The average of the two integers "surrounding" $k+6$ is $\dfrac{(k+4)+(k+8)}{2} = \dfrac{2k+12}{2} = \dfrac{2(k+6)}{2} = k+6$. So, the quantities in column A and column B are equal. Choice (C). This argument works well for consecutive *even* integers, and, in fact, consecutive integers (without being even or odd).

11.10 Substitute some consecutive odd integers: $a = 3, b = 5, c = 7, abc = 105$. $a + b + c = 15$. Again, $a = 1, b = 3, c = 5$. $abc = 15$. $a + b + c = 9$. So, it looks like choice (A). *But* (this time your nervousness paid off) what if some of those odd integers were *negative*? Let $a = -1, b = 1$, and $c = 3$. Then $abc = -3$ and $a + b + c = 3$. Then you would have marked choice (B). Because there is confusion, you *must* mark choice (D); no relationship can be determined. (*Whenever* you're solving a problem by "plugging in," make sure you try negative as well as positive values, unless the conditions of the problem state that all values are positive.)

Section 12: Coordinate Geometry

There are only two formulas you are responsible for:

The *distance* between two points whose coordinates are (x_1,y_1) and (x_2,y_2) is equal to $\sqrt{(x_1 - x_2)^2 + (y_1 - y_2)^2}$. It doesn't matter which of the two points you label (x_1,y_1).

Example: What is the distance between (2,3) and (5,7)?

$$d = \sqrt{(2 - 5)^2 + (3 - 7)^2} = \sqrt{(-3)^2 + (-4)^2} = \sqrt{9 + 16} = \sqrt{25} = 5$$

or

$$d = \sqrt{(5 - 2)^2 + (7 - 3)^2} = \sqrt{(3)^2 + (4)^2} = \sqrt{9 + 16} = \sqrt{25} = 5$$

Remember: $\sqrt{a^2 + b^2} \neq a + b$ for all values of a and b.
Your safest bet is to add the numbers under the square root symbol before you take the square root of the sum. *Do not* take the square roots of the individual summands.

The *midpoint* of the line segment connecting the two points whose coordinates are (x_1,y_1) and (x_2,y_2) has the coordinates $\left(\dfrac{x_1 + x_2}{2}, \dfrac{y_1 + y_2}{2}\right)$.

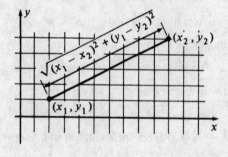 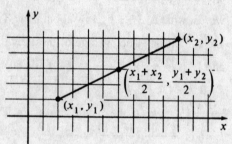

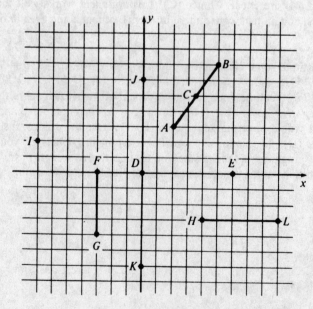

In the diagram opposite, the distance from $A(2,3)$ to $B(5,7)$ is 5. The coordinates of *point C*, the midpoint of *AB*, are $\left(\dfrac{2+5}{2}, \dfrac{3+7}{2}\right) = \left(\dfrac{7}{2}, \dfrac{10}{2}\right) = (3.5,5)$. The *origin* is point $D(0,0)$, where the horizontal x axis and the vertical y axis intersect. Those points located on either of these axes have a 0 for one of their coordinates: $E(6,0)$, $F(-3,0)$, $J(0,6)$, and $K(0,-6)$.

The distance from $H(4,-3)$ to L $(9,-3)$ can be found by the distance formula, $HL = \sqrt{(4-9)^2 + (-3 - -3)^2} = \sqrt{(-5)^2 + (0)^2} = \sqrt{25+0} = \sqrt{25} = 5$. *But, if two points are on the same horizontal line segment, all you have to do is simply "count the boxes." From H to L count 5 boxes. Likewise, the distance from F to G *can* be found by the distance formula, but it would be a waste of time to use it. Again, just count the boxes. $FG = 4$. Just to make sure you know which coordinate comes first and which one comes second, find the coordinates of points H, L, F, G, and I. The answers follow. $H(4,-3)$, $L(9,-3)$, $F(-3,0)$, $G(-3,-4)$, $I(-7,2)$

PRACTICE PROBLEMS

See page 204 for instructions on marking your answers.

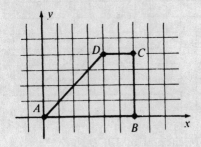

12.1 In the figure above, each box along the x axis represents 2 units and each box along the y axis represents 3 units. Using this scale, what is the area of *ABCD?*

(A) 16   (B) 32   (C) 48   (D) 64   (E) 96

12.2 The distance between point $A(5,0)$ and point B is 8. The coordinates of point B could be any of the following *except*

(A) $(5,8)$ (B) $(-3,0)$ (C) $(13,0)$ (D) $(3,8)$ (E) $(5,-8)$

12.3 Point $M(a,b)$ is the midpoint of the line segment connecting point $A(2a,b)$ and point $B(x,y)$. $x + y =$

(A) a (B) b (C) $a+b$ (D) $a-2b$ (E) $-a$

12.4 If the endpoints of a diameter of a circle are located at (a,b) and $(3a, -b)$, then the area of the circle is

(A) $a^2\pi$ (B) $b^2\pi$ (C) $(a^2+b^2)\pi$ (D) $4a^2\pi$ (E) $2b^2\pi$

12.5 The center of a circle is at point $A(3,2)$. The circle passes through the point $B(5,1)$. What is the area of this circle?

(A) $\sqrt{5}\pi$ (B) 5π (C) 25π (D) 16π (E) 36π

12.6 The points $P(0,0)$, $Q(0,b)$, and $S(a,0)$ are three vertices of rectangle $PQRS$. What must the coordinates of point R be?

(A) (a,b) (B) (b,a) (C) $(b,0)$ (D) $(-a,-b)$ (E) $(-b,-a)$

12.7 Find the area of the triangle PQR whose coordinates are $P(1,3)$, $Q(4,-1)$ and $R(1,-1)$.

(A) 6 (B) 8 (C) 10 (D) 12 (E) 24

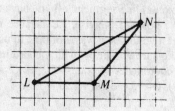

12.8 The area of triangle LMN in the figure above is

(A) 4 (B) 6 (C) 8 (D) 12 (E) 16

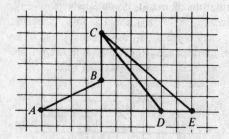

12.9 In the figure above, the area of $ABCD$ is

(A) 12.5 (B) 14 (C) 17.5 (D) 18 (E) none of these

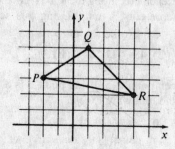

12.10 The area of triangle PQR is

(A) 12.5 (B) 18 (C) 9 (D) 7.5 (E) 11

ANSWERS AND EXPLANATIONS

12.1 (E)   12.2 (D)   12.3 (B)   12.4 (C)   12.5 (B)
12.6 (A)   12.7 (A)   12.8 (C)   12.9 (B)   12.10 (D)

12.1 *If* you remember the formula for the area of a *trapezoid,*

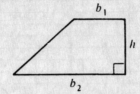

$$A = \tfrac{1}{2}(\text{height})(\text{base}_1 + \text{base}_2)$$

then this problem is fairly easy. Count the boxes from A to B. $AB = 6$. *But* because each box represents 2 units, $AB = 6 \times 2 = 12$. Likewise, $DC = 2 \times 2 = 4$. The height of the trapezoid, $BC = 4 \times 3 = 12$. Therefore, the area of $ABCD$ is equal to $\tfrac{1}{2}(BC) \times (AB + DC) = \tfrac{1}{2}(12)(12 + 4) = 6(16) = 96$. Choice (E).

If you don't remember that formula, *don't worry.* You really don't need fancy formulas for the SAT. Break up the area of $ABCD$ into "convenient figures," that is, figures whose areas are easy to find. In most cases, these "easy" figures are squares, rectangles, and right triangles. See the following figure for one "break-up" of $ABCD$.

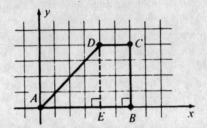

As you can see, $ABCD$ has been broken up into a rectangle, $BCDE$, and a right triangle, AED. $EB = 4$ (remember the *scale*) and $BC = 12$; so, the area of rectangle $BCDE = 12 \times 4 = 48$. The area of right triangle $AED = \tfrac{1}{2}(AE)(ED) = \tfrac{1}{2}(8)(12) = 48$. So, the area of $ABCD = 48 + 48 = 96$. Again, choice (E).

It is not that easy to count the boxes in order to find the area directly, because of that scaling feature of the problem; each box represents more than one unit!

12.2 Every point 8 units from point A lies on a circle whose center is A and whose radius is 8. See the following figure. Since $(5,8)$ is 8 units directly "over" $(5,0)$, choice (A) is 8 units from $(5,0)$. So, (A) is *not* the answer. Since $(-3,0)$ is 8 units to the left of $(5,0)$, choice (B) is *not* the answer. Since $(13,0)$ is 8 units to the right of $(5,0)$, choice (C) is *not* the answer. Since $(5, -8)$ is 8 units directly below $(5,0)$, choice (E) is *not* the answer. So, by elimination, choice (D) is the answer. Of course, you could have used the distance formula here, but that would have taken quite a long time had you tested each of the choices that way. However, let's use the distance formula to prove that $(3,8)$ is *not* 8 units from $(5,0)$: $d = \sqrt{(3 - 5)^2 + (8 - 0)^2} = \sqrt{(-2)^2 + 8^2} = \sqrt{4 + 64} = \sqrt{68} > 8$.

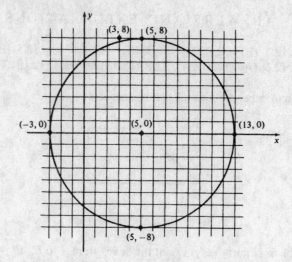

12.3 Use the midpoint formula here. $(a,b) = \left(\dfrac{2a+x}{2}, \dfrac{b+y}{2}\right)$. So, $a = \dfrac{2a+x}{2}$ and $b = \dfrac{b+y}{2}$. Cross-multiplying in each case, we get $2a = 2a + x$; $0 = x$. $2b = b + y$; $b = y$. So, $x + y = 0 + b = b$. Choice (B). You can use the technique of substitution of numbers here, but *unless* you know the midpoint formula, that method *won't help*.

12.4 To find the area of the circle, we need to find the radius. The length of the radius is $\frac{1}{2}$ the length of the diameter. Since (a,b) and $(3a, -b)$ do *not* lie on either a horizontal or vertical line segment, there is no alternative but to use the distance formula here. The length of the diameter is $\sqrt{(a - 3a)^2 + (b - -b)^2} = \sqrt{(-2a)^2 + (2b)^2} = \sqrt{4a^2 + 4b^2} = \sqrt{4(a^2 + b^2)} = \sqrt{4}\sqrt{(a^2 + b^2)} = 2\sqrt{a^2 + b^2}$. So, the length of the radius is $\frac{1}{2}(2)\sqrt{a^2 + b^2}$ or $\sqrt{a^2 + b^2}$. The area of a circle is πr^2. So, in this case, the area of the circle is $\pi \sqrt{(a^2 + b^2)}^2 = \pi(a^2 + b^2)$. Choice (C).

12.5 This problem is easier than 12.4. To get the area of the circle we have to get the length of the radius again. This time, though, the approach is more straightforward. The radius is AB and its length is found by the distance formula: $r = \sqrt{(3 - 5)^2 + (2 - 1)^2} = \sqrt{(-2)^2 + (1)^2} = \sqrt{4 + 1} = \sqrt{5}$. So, the area of the circle is πr^2, which is $\pi \sqrt{5}^2 = \pi \sqrt{5} \sqrt{5} = \pi \sqrt{25} = \pi 5 = 5\pi$. Choice (B). We think you can see why the examiners put choices (A) and (C) in this problem. Don't be careless!

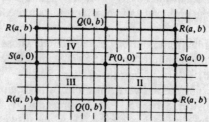

12.6 Given the three points P, Q, and S, you can see that four different rectangles can be formed (labeled I, II, III, and IV in the diagram above). Substituting numbers for a and b will illustrate this fact. Let $a = 6$ and $b = 3$. Then, the coordinates of the rectangle will be $P(0,0)$, $Q(0,3)$, $S(6,0)$, and $R(6,3)$. This is rectangle I. If $a = -6$ and $b = 3$, you get rectangle IV. Point R in this case is located at $(-6,-3)$. If $a = 6$ and $b = -3$, you get rectangle II. But point R is *still* at (a,b), in other words, at $(6,-3)$. We are sure you can see that R is located at (a,b) in rectangle III also. Choice (A).

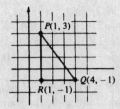

12.7 See the diagram above. Since the figure is a right triangle, its area is $\frac{1}{2}$(leg)(leg) = $\frac{1}{2}(PR)(RQ)$ = $\frac{1}{2}(4)(3)$ = $\frac{1}{2}(12)$ = 6. Choice (A).

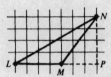

12.8 This is also a fairly easy problem. Since the area of any triangle is $\frac{1}{2}$(base)(height), and because *LM* can be considered a base and *NP* a height, the area of triangle *LMN* is equal to $\frac{1}{2}(LM)(NP)$ = $\frac{1}{2}(4)(4)$ = $\frac{1}{2}(16)$ = 8. Choice (C).

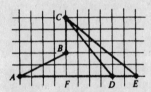

12.9 See the figure above. Perhaps the simplest way of doing this problem is to find the areas of the two right triangles, *ABF* and *DCF*. The area of triangle *ABF* = $\frac{1}{2}(AF)(BF)$ = $\frac{1}{2}(4)(2)$ = $\frac{1}{2}(8)$ = 4. The area of triangle *DCF* = $\frac{1}{2}(DF)(CF)$ = $\frac{1}{2}(4)(5)$ = $\frac{1}{2}(20)$ = 10. Therefore, the area of *ABCD* is 4 + 10 = 14. Choice (B).

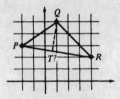

12.10 Unless triangle *PQR* is a right triangle, which would mean we could just take $\frac{1}{2}$(leg)(leg), finding the area of triangle *PQR* presents us with the difficulty of finding its height. (Even if we call *PR* a base, how can we find the precise measurement of height *QT*?) *However,* there is a simple method of finding the area of any "slanted" triangle, that is, a triangle whose base is *not parallel* to either the *x* or the *y* axis.

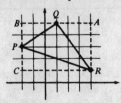

The area of triangle *PQR* is equal to the area of *rectangle RABC* minus the *sum* of the areas of the 3 right triangles, *RAQ, QBP,* and *PCR.* The area of *RABC* = (6)(3) = 18.

The area of triangle
$$RAQ = \tfrac{1}{2}(3)(3) = \tfrac{1}{2}(9) = 4.5$$
$$QBP = \tfrac{1}{2}(3)(2) = \tfrac{1}{2}(6) = 3.0$$
$$PCR = \tfrac{1}{2}(1)(6) = \tfrac{1}{2}(6) = \underline{3.0}$$
$$10.5$$

So the area of triangle $PQR = 18 - 10.5 = 7.5$. Choice (D).

This just *looks* like a lot of work. Since the diagram is drawn for you, it is only necessary to quickly draw the rectangle around the "slanted" triangle and get the areas of the right triangles formed!

SAMPLE TESTS

Mathematical Assessment Test 2

Time—30 Minutes
25 Questions

Notes: 1. The use of a calculator is permitted. All numbers used are real numbers.
2. Figures that accompany problems in this test are intended to provide information useful in solving the problems. They are drawn as accurately as possible, *except* when it is stated in a specific problem that a figure is not drawn to scale. All figures lie in a plane unless otherwise indicated.

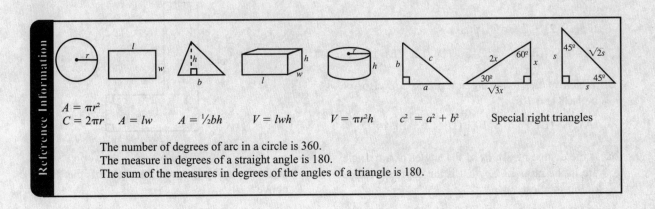

Reference Information

$A = \pi r^2$
$C = 2\pi r$ $\quad A = lw$ $\quad A = \frac{1}{2}bh$ $\quad V = lwh$ $\quad V = \pi r^2 h$ $\quad c^2 = a^2 + b^2$ $\quad$ Special right triangles

The number of degrees of arc in a circle is 360.
The measure in degrees of a straight angle is 180.
The sum of the measures in degrees of the angles of a triangle is 180.

1. Angle *ABC* is bisected by line *DB*. If angle *DBC* = 40°, the measure of angle *ABC* is

   (A) 40   (B) 80   (C) 20   (D) 140   (E) 100

2. When 2 is added to 4 times a number, the result is 18. Which of the following equations represents this statement?

   (A) $2N + 4 = 18$
   (B) $4(N + 2) = 18$
   (C) $2N + 4N = 18$
   (D) $4(4N + 2) = 18$
   (E) $4N + 2 = 18$

3. Marbles are placed into 7 jars, one at a time. The first marble goes into jar 1, the second into jar 2, the third into jar 3, and so on until each jar has one marble. If this pattern is repeated, beginning each time with the first jar, into which jar will the 81st marble be placed?

   (A) Jar 3   (B) Jar 4   (C) Jar 5   (D) Jar 6
   (E) Jar 7

4. If $5(x + 2) - 3x = 20$, then $x =$

   (A) 7.5   (B) 10   (C) 5   (D) 12   (E) 15

5. Which of the following integers is a divisor of both 28 and 70?

   (A) 4   (B) 8   (C) 10   (D) 12   (E) 14

6. If the degree measures of the angles of a triangle are in the ratio 3:4:5, what is the degree measure of the smallest angle?

   (A) 15   (B) 30   (C) 45   (D) 60   (E) 75

7. 10 percent of 90 is equivalent to $^1/_2$ of what number?

   (A) 18   (B) 4.5   (C) 9   (D) 27   (E) 45

8. Of the following fractions, $^2/_3$, $^3/_4$, $^5/_8$, $^{11}/_{12}$, $^{13}/_{24}$, the difference between the largest and the smallest is

   (A) $^7/_{12}$ (B) $^1/_{12}$ (C) $^3/_8$ (D) $^1/_8$ (E) $^5/_6$

9. If the cost of 8 equally priced computer printers is $2,800, what is the total cost of 6 of these printers?

   (A) $1,400   (B) $1,800   (C) $2,000
   (D) $2,100   (E) $2,340

10. The average of 5, 10, 15, 20, and 25 is *not* equal to the average of

    (A) 10 and 20
    (B) 5 and 30
    (C) 5 and 25
    (D) 5, 5, and 35
    (E) 12, 10, and 23

11.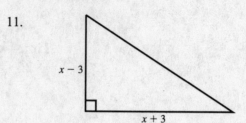

    For which of the following values of *x* does the triangle have an area of 36?

    (A) 9   (B) 8   (C) 6   (D) 4   (E) 3

12.

    What is the perimeter, in feet, of the figure above?

    (A) 44   (B) 47   (C) 50   (D) 88   (E) 91

13. How deep will the sand be in a rectangular sand box with inside dimensions 400 centimeters long, 300 centimeters wide, and 20 centimeters deep if 480,000 cubic centimeters of sand is evenly distributed in it?

    (A) 2 cm   (B) 4 cm   (C) 6 cm
    (D) 8 cm   (E) 20 cm

14. For all integers, let

    $\boxed{X} = X^3$ when X is an even integer
    $\boxed{X} = X^2$ when X is an odd integer
    What is the value of $\boxed{4} - \boxed{3}$?

    (A) 1   (B) 6   (C) 7   (D) 37   (E) 55

15. A certain perfume bottle is completely filled by three perfumes, A, B, and C. If there are equal amounts of A and B, and four times as much C as there is A, what percent of the perfume bottle is filled by C?

    (A) 25% (B) $33\frac{1}{3}$% (C) 40% (D) $66\frac{2}{3}$%
    (E) 80%

16. If a watch is set at 2 P.M. and loses 1.5 minutes every two hours, what will it read when it is actually 2 P.M. the next day?

    (A) 1:30 (B) 1:36 (C) 1:40 (D) 1:42
    (E) 1:51

17. If $Z = \frac{4}{3}x$ and $WZ = \frac{4}{6}x$ for $x \neq 0$, then $W =$

    (A) 2 (B) 4 (C) $\frac{1}{2}$ (D) $\frac{1}{4}$ (E) $\frac{1}{8}$

18. Steve can build a dog house in 1 day. George can build the same type of dog house in 2 days. If they work together, how long will it take them to build 18 dog houses?

    (A) 12 days (B) 10 days (C) 9 days
    (D) 8 days (E) 6 days

19.

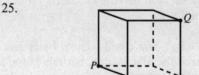

    In the figure above, square *ABCD* has a perimeter of 24. If *E* is the midpoint of *BC,* and *F* is the midpoint of *DC,* what is the area of the shaded region?

    (A) 4.5 (B) 9 (C) 27 (D) 30 (E) 31.5

20. If the radius of a circle is increased by 20%, the area of the circle is increased by

    (A) 20% (B) $33\frac{1}{3}$% (C) 37.5% (D) 44%
    (E) Cannot be determined from the information given

21. If $a = 2b = 5c,$ then the average (arithmetic mean) of *a, b,* and *c* in terms of *a* is

    (A) $17a/30$ (B) $17a/10$ (C) $8a/3$ (D) $8a$
    (E) $17a$

22. A truck can hold 200 cartons of apples or 240 cartons of pears. If the truck is already loaded with 150 cartons of apples, how many cartons of pears can be loaded?

    (A) 40 (B) 60 (C) 70 (D) 80 (E) 90

23. If $D(N)$ is defined to be the sum of the positive integer divisors of *N,* excluding *N,* so that, for example, $D(15) = 1 + 3 + 5 = 9$, then $D(D(6)) =$

    (A) 6 (B) 7 (C) 9 (D) 12 (E) 24

24. A stockbroker keeps 10% of the profit he makes for his client. If the customer received $8,100 from the stockbroker, what was the total profit for the transactions made by the stockbroker?

    (A) 810 (B) 7,290 (C) 10,000 (D) 12,250
    (E) 9,000

25.

    The volume of the cube above is 64. What is the distance from point *P* to point *Q?*

    (A) $4\sqrt{2}$ (B) $4\sqrt{3}$ (C) 12 (D) $3^3\sqrt{12}$
    (E) 16

ANSWERS AND EXPLANATIONS

1. (B)	6. (C)	11. (A)	16. (D)	21. (A)
2. (E)	7. (A)	12. (D)	17. (C)	22. (B)
3. (B)	8. (C)	13. (B)	18. (A)	23. (A)
4. (C)	9. (D)	14. (E)	19. (E)	24. (E)
5. (E)	10. (B)	15. (D)	20. (D)	25. (B)

1. (B) If you sketch the angle *ABC* and draw the bisector *DB*, you can "see" the correct answer.

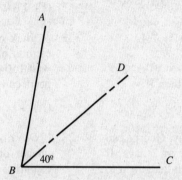

Angle *DBC* is one-half angle *ABC;* therefore, $ABC = 2 \times 40°$ or $80°$.

2. (E) If *N* represents the number, then four times the number is represented as 4*N*. When "2 is added to" the 4*N*, we write $2 + 4N$ or $4N + 2$. The result of this is 18; so, $4N + 2 = 18$.

ERRORS Confusing the placement of the 2 and 4 in the equation, or working out of sequence. The *N* must be multiplied by 4 before the 2 is added. If you work out of sequence, you arrive at choice (B), which states that you add 2 to *N* and multiply that result by 4.

3. (B) You could picture 7 jars and count out one marble for each jar until you reach the 81st marble, but this is too time-consuming! Suppose the problem asked which jar would the 381st marble be deposited into? There is a method. Simply divide 81 by 7 (there are 7 jars) and see that the remainder is 4. This means that the 81st marble goes into the 4th jar (by the way, the 381st marble would go into the 3rd jar ($381/7 = 54$, with a remainder of 3!).

4. (C) Taking $5(x + 2) - 3x = 20$, first multiply the 5 to remove the parentheses. $5x = 10 - 3x = 20$, or $2x + 10 = 20$. Subtract 10 from each side of the equation so that $2x = 10$, or $x = 5$.

ERRORS Incorrectly expanding $5(x + 2)$. Remember, the 5 must multiply *both* the *x* and the 2.

5. (E) Both 28 and 70 are divisible by 7, so both will be divisible by 7×2, or 14. You could quickly divide each of the numbers by each choice using your calculator.

6. (C) $3x + 4x + 5x = 180$; $12x = 180$; $x = 15$. The smallest angle is then 3*x* or $3(15) = 45$.

ERRORS   Forgetting to multiply 15 by 3; getting the largest angle, 75, instead of the smallest.

7. (A)   10% of 90 is 9 (.10 × 90 = 9). 9 is ¹/₂ of the unknown number, or 9 = ¹/₂*N; N* = 18.

8. (C)   ²/₃ = ¹⁶/₂₄; ³/₄ = ¹⁸/₂₄; ⁵/₈ = ¹⁵/₂₄; ¹¹/₁₂ = ²²/₂₄; ¹³/₂₄ = ¹³/₂₄. When fractions have the same denominator, the one with the largest numerator is the largest fraction: the one with the smallest numerator is the smallest fraction. ²²/₂₄ − ¹³/₂₄ = ⁹/₂₄ = ³/₈.

ERRORS   Assuming ²/₃ is the smallest fraction because it has the smallest numerator and denominator in the list; carelessness in changing fractions to their equivalent forms.

9. (D)   Set up a proportion between the number of computer printers and the cost: number/cost: 8/$2,800 = 6/*x*

Cross-multiplying: 8*x* = 6 × 2,800
divide by 8:   8*x*/8 = 6 × 2,800/8
                        x = 3 × 2,800/4 = $2,100

ERROR   Setting up the proportion incorrectly. Make sure that once you decide on the format of the proportion, you stick to it. Here we placed the number of computer printers in the numerator and the cost of these printers in the denominator.

10. (B)   The average of 5, 10, 15, 20, and 25 is 15. If a set of numbers are evenly spaced (each is 5 greater than the next), the average is the middle number. Of course, you could calculate the average by adding the 5 numbers and dividing by 5.   5 + 10 + 15 + 20 + 25 = 75/5 = 15.

The average of 5 and 30 (choice B) is 5 + 30 = 35/2 = 17.5, and this is the only choice that does not have an average of 15.

11. (A)   Substitute each choice into the formula. Area = ¹/₂ base × height. For choice (A), the base will be *x* + 3 or 12 and the height will be *x* − 3 or 6. Area = ¹/₂ *b* × *h* = ¹/₂ (12)(6) = 36.

12. (D)   Since all corners of this figure are 90°, you can find the unknown sides.

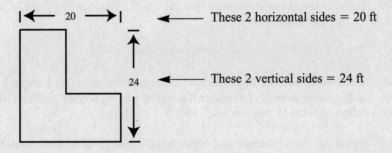

The perimeter is therefore 24 + 24 + 20 + 20 = 88. You may see this more clearly if you mentally "fold out" the inside corner.

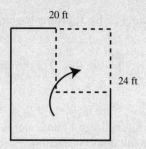

20 ft

24 ft

ERRORS   Forgetting to include two 20-ft lengths and two 24-ft lengths in the total perimeter. If you did this, you would have incorrectly chosen choice (A).

13. (B)   480,000 = length × width × height
480,000 = 400 × 300 × x
480,000 = 120,000x
4 cm = x

ERROR   Using 20 instead of x in the equation. The height of the sandbox is 20, but the sand will rise to a height less than 20.

14. (E)   Follow the definition carefully. $\boxed{4} - \boxed{3} = ?$
Since 4 is an even integer, $\boxed{4} = 4^3 = 4 \times 4 \times 4 = 64$
Since 3 is an odd integer, $\boxed{3} = 3^2 = 3 \times 3 = 9$
$64 - 9 = 55.$

15. (D)   % filled by $C = \dfrac{\text{amount of } C}{\text{total}} = \dfrac{4A}{6A} = \dfrac{2}{3} = 66^2/_3\%$. Total = $A + B + C$.
Since $B = A$, and $C = 4A$, $A + B + C = A + A + 4A = 6A$.

ERRORS   Some students see the word "four" and translate it into 40%; most of the trouble, though, is translating $^2/_3$ into a %. See the Review Guide for a treatment of %.

16. (D)   If a clock loses 1.5 minutes every two hours, how many minutes will it lose in 24 hours? (2 P.M. to 2 P.M. the following day = 24 hours.) Set up a proportion: $\dfrac{1.5}{2} = \dfrac{m}{24}$; cross-multiply, so $1.5 \times 24 = 2 \times m$; $36 = 2m$; $m = 18$ minutes lost. Therefore, at 2 P.M. the following day, the watch will read 18 minutes less than 2 P.M., or 1:42 P.M.

ERROR   Perhaps you thought the time interval was 12 hours rather than 24 hours. You then would have marked choice (E).

17. (C) $Z = {}^4/_3x$ and $WZ = {}^4/_6x$ or $^1/_2$ of $^4/_3x$; therefore, $w = {}^1/_2$.

18. (A)   Since Steve builds 1 dog house in 1 day and George builds 1 every 2 days (that is, $^1/_2$ a dog house each day), together they build 1.5 dog houses each day. It will take 18/1.5 days to build 18 dog houses.   18/1.5 = 12 days.

ERROR   Thinking that if George and Steve work together, they will build 1 dog house each, or two a day.

19. (E)   If the perimeter of the square is 24, the length of one side is 6 ($^{24}/_4 = 6$) and its area is 36 (6 × 6). The small triangle has a height of 3 and a base of 3, and an area of $^1/_2 \times 3 \times 3 = {}^9/_2 = 4.5$. The shaded region has an area of $36 - 4.5 = 31.5$.

20. (D)   "Plug in" again. Let the original radius be 10. Then the new radius will be $10 + .20(10) = 10 + 2 = 12$. So, the area of the old circle is $\pi 10^2 = 100\pi$, and the area of the new circle is $\pi 12^2 = 144\pi$. The % change is figured by taking $\dfrac{\text{change in area}}{\text{original area}} = \dfrac{144\pi - 100\pi}{100\pi} = \dfrac{44\pi}{100\pi} = \dfrac{44}{100} = 44\%$. Try another set of numbers. Let the old radius be 6 and the new one $6 + .20(6) = 6 + 1.2 = 7.2$. Then the old area is 36π, and the new area is 51.84π. The change in the area is $51.84\pi - 36\pi = 15.84\pi$. $\dfrac{15.84\pi}{36\pi} = .44$ or 44%. Obviously the choice of 10 for the radius of the original circle made the solution of this problem much easier.

ERROR   Assuming that if you are not given the radius of the original circle you cannot find out anything about the new circle. Often, with % problems, you don't need any numerical information if the answers are in terms of %.

21. (A)   Putting all variables into terms of a, we get $a = 2b$ or $b = \frac{1}{2}a$ and $a = 5c$ or $c = \frac{1}{5}a$. The average is $(a + \frac{1}{2}a + \frac{1}{5}a)/3$. $(1\frac{7}{10}a)/3 = (\frac{17}{10}a)/3 = 17a/30$

ERRORS   Not applying the average formula correctly. Choice (B) is the total of a, b, and c, but it is not divided by 3. Incorrectly stating the variables in terms of a. For example, because $a = 2b$, $b = \frac{1}{2}a$. b does not equal $2a$.

22. (B)   The ratio of apples to pears is $\dfrac{200}{240}$ or $\dfrac{5}{6}$. So, for every 5 cartons of apples that can be loaded, 6 cartons of pears can take their place. Since there are already 150 cartons of apples on the truck, there is room for 50 more cartons of apples (the truck can hold 200 cartons of apples). Set up a proportion:

$$\frac{\text{Apples that can still be loaded}}{\text{Pears that can be loaded}} = \frac{5}{6} \qquad \frac{50}{p} = \frac{5}{6}$$

Cross-multiply to get $5p = 300$; $p = 60$ or choice (B).

There is a simple way of solving this problem that does not involve ratios. When loaded with 150 cartons of apples, the truck is obviously $\frac{3}{4}$ full $\left(\dfrac{150}{200} = \dfrac{3}{4}\right)$. In the remaining space, $\dfrac{1}{4} \times 240$ cartons of pears will fit; $\dfrac{240}{4} = 60$.

ERRORS   Not understanding proportions; not understanding how to set up the numerators and the denominators; "what goes where?" See the Review Guide for help.

23. (A) $D(D(6))$, according to the definition, is $D(1 + 2 + 3) = D(6) = 1 + 2 + 3 = 6$.

24. (E)   Since the stockbroker takes 10% for himself, the client gets the other 90%. Therefore 90% (profit) = 8,100.

$$\frac{9}{10}p = 8,100$$

$$p = \overset{900}{\cancel{8100}} \times 10/\cancel{9} = 9,000$$
$$ 1$$

25. **(B)**

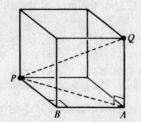

All you need to solve this problem is the Pythagorean Theorem. PQ is the hypotenuse of right triangle PAQ. Since the volume of a cube is (side)³, each side must be $\sqrt[3]{64}$ or 4. So, $AQ = 4$. But in order to use the Pythagorean Theorem you need the length of PA. Aha! PA is the hypotenuse of right triangle PBA, and we know that $BA = 4$ because it's a side of the cube too. In right triangle PBA, then, $PA^2 = PB^2 + BA^2$; $PA^2 = 4^2 + 4^2 = 16 + 16 = 32$. So, $PA = \sqrt{32}$. (Don't simplify the radical. You'll see why later.)

Now that you have the length of PA, use right triangle PAQ. $PQ^2 = PA^2 + QA^2 = (\sqrt{32})^2 + 4^2 = 32 + 16 = 48$. Therefore, $PQ = \sqrt{48} = \sqrt{16 \times 3} = 4\sqrt{3}$, or choice (B). If you got the answer $\sqrt{48}$ but did not see immediately that this is the same as $4\sqrt{3}$, you need to study Section 3 of the *Review Guide* on the arithmetic of square roots.

It is interesting to note here that to find the distance between two points in three-dimensional space, all you need is an extension of the Pythagorean Theorem: $PQ^2 = PB^2 + BA^2 + QA^2$!

ERROR Not being able to visualize a situation in which you can use the Pythagorean Theorem you learned in Geometry and which is reprinted at the beginning of the mathematical section of the SAT.

Mathematical Assessment Test 3

Notes: 1. The use of a calculator is permitted. All numbers used are real numbers.
2. Figures that accompany problems in this test are intended to provide information useful in solving the problems. They are drawn as accurately as possible, *except* when it is stated in a specific problem that a figure is not drawn to scale. All figures lie in a plane unless otherwise indicated.

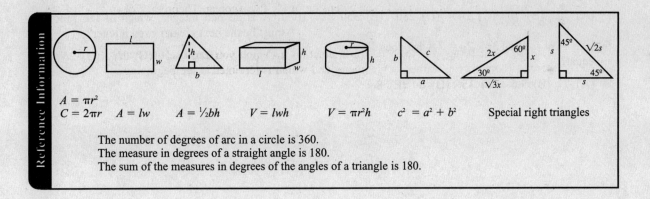

$A = \pi r^2$
$C = 2\pi r$ $A = lw$ $A = \frac{1}{2}bh$ $V = lwh$ $V = \pi r^2 h$ $c^2 = a^2 + b^2$ Special right triangles

The number of degrees of arc in a circle is 360.
The measure in degrees of a straight angle is 180.
The sum of the measures in degrees of the angles of a triangle is 180.

1. An equilateral triangle with a side of 8 has a perimeter twice that of a square. This area of the square is

   (A) 4   (B) 9   (C) 12   (D) 24   (E) 16

2. Two lights, a red one and a green one, blink simultaneously at 1:30 P.M. If the red one blinks every 4 seconds and the green one blinks every 6 seconds, how many *more* times will they blink together in the next two minutes?

   (A) 10   (B) 11   (C) 20   (D) 21   (E) 4

3. If a certain number of shoe boxes are stacked ten boxes to a stack, there are three boxes left over. If they are stacked nine to a stack, one box is left over. How many total boxes are there?

   (A) 13   (B) 10   (C) 63   (D) 72   (E) 73

4. A truck and a car leave from the same location at 9 A.M. The truck travels directly north at 40 miles per hour while the car travels directly east at 30 miles per hour. How far apart are they at 1 P.M.?

   (A) 50   (B) 70   (C) 200   (D) 280   (E) 350

5. If $2x + 3y = 8$ and $3x + 2y = 7$, what does $2x + 2y$ equal?

   (A) 7   (B) 7.5   (C) 15   (D) 6   (E) 8

6. Which of the following numbers will most closely triple its original value if the digits are reversed?

   (A) 92,123   (B) 46,768   (C) 21,446
   (D) 21,475   (E) 31,269

7. The price of a car is increased 10% every 2 years. In 1988, the car cost $16,000. In 1992, a car dealer offered the same car with a $1,500 rebate. How much did the 1992 model cost after this rebate?

   (A) 21,296   (B) 17,700   (C) 17,860
   (D) 14,500   (E) 19,296

8. A gear rotates 90 times every 10 minutes. At the same rate, how many times will it rotate in 4 minutes?

   (A) 9   (B) 12   (C) 24   (D) 30   (E) 36

9. If $3/x = 6$, then $2x - 1 = $?

   (A) 0   (B) 3   (C) 5   (D) 6   (E) 18

10. If N is an odd integer, which of the following must be the next greater even integer?

   (A) $N + 2$ (B) $N + 1$ (C) $2N$ (D) $2N + 1$
   (E) $2N + 2$

ANSWERS AND EXPLANATIONS

1. (B)	6. (C)
2. (A)	7. (C)
3. (E)	8. (E)
4. (C)	9. (A)
5. (D)	10. (B)

1. (B)   First calculate the perimeter of an equilateral triangle with a side equal to 8. $P = 3 \times 8 = 24$. The square will therefore have a perimeter of 12, or one-half the triangle's perimeter. If the square's perimeter is 12, one of its sides is $^{12}/_4 = 3$ and its area will be given by the formula $A = S^2$ or $3^2 = 9$. Choice (B). This is an easy question, but you must know the difference between area and perimeter.

2. (A)   There are actually three patterns in this problem, the red blinks, the green blinks, and the "together" blinks. A chart reveals all three patterns:

Red	4	8	12	16	20	24	28	32	36
Green	6		12		18	24		30	36
Together			↑1			↑2			↑3

The lights blink together every 12 seconds. They will blink 5 times together (after the start of the problem) in each minute. Choice (A).

3. (E)   The number of boxes will give a remainder of 3 when it is divided by 7. Choices (C) and (E) satisfy this condition because $^{63}/_{10} = 6R3$ and $^{73}/_{10} = 7R3$. However when 73 is divided by 9 we get $^{73}/_9 = 8R1$ and when $^{63}/_9$ there is no remainder so our choice is (E).

4. (C)   Since the truck and car move at right angles (directly north and directly east) away from each other, we can use the Pythagorean Theorem to find the distance between them.

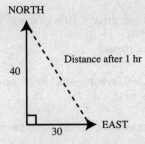

The vehicles travel for 4 hours, so the final diagram will look like this:

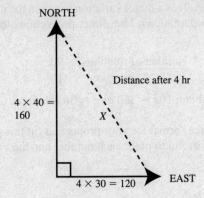

Using the Pythagorean Theorem, we obtain:

$$X^2 = 160^2 + 120^2$$
$$X^2 = 25,600 + 14,400$$
$$X^2 = 40,000$$
$$X = \sqrt{40,000} = 200 \quad \text{Choice (C)}.$$

Although you have your calculator to assist you, it still would be better if you recognized the 3-4-5 triple. Here, the triple is 30-40-50, but choice (A) is not correct because the vehicles travel for 4 hours ($4 \times 50 = 200$)! Be careful.

5. (D) These two equations are called a system of equations. On the SAT, most systems of equations are solved by adding the two equations. If we add these two equations, we obtain:

$$\begin{aligned} 2x + 3y &= 8 \\ + \quad 3x + 2y &= 7 \\ \hline 5x + 5y &= 15 \end{aligned}$$

This is not the answer, but if we divide $5x + 5y = 15$ by 5 we obtain $x + y = 3$. If $x + y = 3$, then $2x + 2y = 6$. Choice (D).

6. (C) In reversing the digits, the last digit will become the first, and so to triple the number, the last digit of the original number should be three times the first digit of the original number. Choices (A), (B), and (D) can be eliminated in this way. Choice (E): 31,269 becomes 96,213, and choice (C): 21,446 becomes 64,412. Choice (C) is closer to three times the original number when the digits are reversed. Choice (C).

7. (C) If the price of the car is increased every 2 years by 10%, the 1990 price = 1988 price + 10% of the 1988 price:
1990 price = 16,000 + .1(16,000)
1990 price = 16,000 + 1,600 = 17,600

The 1992 price will equal the 1990 price + 10% of the 1990 price:
1992 price = 17,600 + .1(17,600)
1992 price = 17,600 + 1,760 = 19,360

If the 1992 price has a $1,500 rebate, the 1992 price is reduced by $1,500. $19,360 - 1,500 = 17,860$. Choice (C).

ERROR Successive 10% increases are *not* the same as one 20% increase. This is not a shortcut!

8. (E) This problem involves a direct variation between the number of rotations and the time needed for these rotations. Use direct proportions to solve direct-variation problems.

$$\frac{\text{Number of rotations}}{\text{Time}} : \frac{90}{10} = \frac{x}{4}$$

Cross-multiplying you obtain $10x = 360$ or $x = 36$ rotations. Choice (E).

Note: Once you "set" the format for your proportion (in this problem we placed rotations "over" time), be careful to place each number and the x in the correct position.

9. (A) By cross-multiplying $3/x = 6$ we obtain $6x = 3$ or $x = 3/6 = 1/2$.

Then $2x - 1 = 2(1/2) - 1 = 0$. Choice (A).

10. (B) If N is odd, $N + 1$ will be the next greater integer and will be even. Choice (B). You can easily solve this problem by choosing an odd integer, say 11. Now substitute $N = 11$ into each choice and see that choice (B) $(N + 1)$ would $= 11 + 1$ or 12, the next greater even integer.

Mathematical Assessment Test 4

Time—30 Minutes
25 Questions

Notes: 1. The use of a calculator is permitted. All numbers used are real numbers.
2. Figures that accompany problems in this test are intended to provide information useful in solving the problems. They are drawn as accurately as possible, *except* when it is stated in a specific problem that a figure is not drawn to scale. All figures lie in a plane unless otherwise indicated.

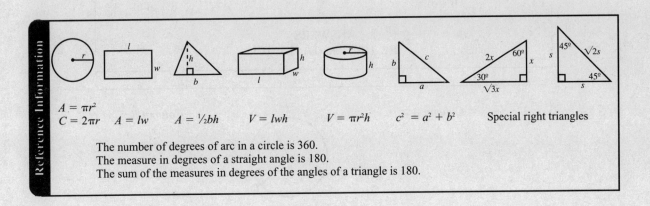

Reference Information

$A = \pi r^2$
$C = 2\pi r$ $A = lw$ $A = \frac{1}{2}bh$ $V = lwh$ $V = \pi r^2 h$ $c^2 = a^2 + b^2$ Special right triangles

The number of degrees of arc in a circle is 360.
The measure in degrees of a straight angle is 180.
The sum of the measures in degrees of the angles of a triangle is 180.

DIRECTIONS FOR QUANTITATIVE COMPARISON QUESTIONS

Questions 1 through 15 each consist of two quantities, one in column A and one in column B. You are to compare the two quantities and on the answer sheet fill in:

A if the quantity in column A is greater
B if the quantity in column B is greater
C if the two quantities are equal
D if the relationship cannot be determined from the information given

Notes: 1. In certain questions, information concerning one or both of the quantities to be compared is centered above the two columns.
2. A symbol that appears in both columns represents the same thing in column A as it does in column B.
3. Letters such as *x, y,* and *n* stand for real numbers.
4. Since there are only four choices, *never mark (E).*

EXAMPLES

Column A	Column B
E1. The average of 3, 5, and 10	9
E2. $x - y$	$y - x$
E3. 6% of 8	8% of 6

ANSWERS
E1. (B), E2. (D), E3. (C)

	Column A		Column B	

Circle with center *O*

1.	*OA*	*OB*	A B C D
2.	number of minutes in 36 hours	number of seconds in 36 minutes	A B C D

$X > 0$

3.	$X + .5$	$2X/4 + 1$	A B C D
4.	The average of 2/5 and 2/7	24/35	A B C D

1 meter = 100 cm

5.	number of cm² in 2 m²	200	A B C D
6.	¹/₄%	.025	A B C D

		$x > 1$	
		$x \neq y$	
7.	y^x	x^x	A B C D
8.	$3\sqrt{16/4}$	$2\sqrt{18/2}$	A B C D

The price of a shirt
is P dollars

9.	The price of the shirt after a 25% discount	$.25P$	A B C D

SQUARE *ABCD:*

10.	The number of square inches in the area of *ABCD*	The number of inches in the perimeter of *ABCD*	A B C D

60 is X% of 30

11.	$3X$	150	A B C D

$0 < a < b < c$

12.	$a + b$	$c - b$	A B C D

13.	x	$y - x$	A B C D

$AB = BC = \sqrt{2}$
O is the center of the circle

14.	$AB + BC$	$AO + OB + OC$	A B C D
15.	Area of circle with radius 7	Area of an equilateral triangle with side 14	A B C D

DIRECTIONS FOR STUDENT-PRODUCED RESPONSE QUESTIONS

Each of the remaining ten questions (16–25) requires you to solve the problem and enter your answer by marking the special grid, as shown in the examples below.

Answer: $\frac{5}{14}$ or 5/14

Answer: 2.5

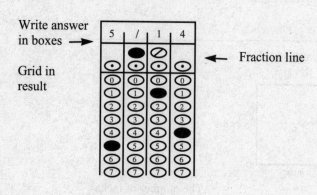

Write answer in boxes →

← Fraction line

Grid in result

Decimal point

Answer: 201

Either position is correct.

• *Decimal Accuracy:* If you obtain a decimal answer, **enter the most accurate value the grid will accommodate.** For example, if you obtain an answer such as 0.666 . . . , you should record the result as .666 or .667. **Less accurate values such as .66 or .67 are not acceptable.**

Acceptable ways to grid $\frac{2}{3}$ = .6666 . . .

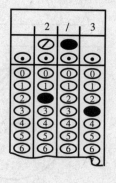
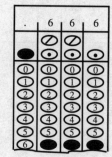
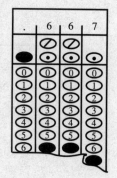

- Mark no more than one oval in any column.
- Because the answer sheet will be machine-scored, **you will receive credit only if the ovals are filled in correctly.**
- Although not required, it is suggested that you write your answer in the boxes at the top of the columns to help you fill in the ovals accurately.
- Some problems may have more than one correct answer. In such cases, grid only one answer.
- No question has a negative answer.
- **Mixed numbers** such as 2½ must be gridded as 2.5 or 5/2.

  (If $\boxed{2\,1\,/\,2}$ is gridded, it will be interpreted as $\dfrac{21}{2}$, not 2½.)

16. If $A + 4 = 14$, then $5A =$

17. Todd bought 14 pens for $6.30. The next day these pens cost $.50 each. How much did Todd save by buying them for $6.30? (Disregard the $ sign when gridding your answer.)

18.

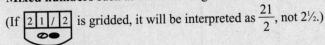

Lines l, m, and n intersect as shown above. What is the value of x?

19. If $4/x = 12/9$, what is the value of x?

20. Seven consecutive integers are listed in increasing order. If the sum of the first three integers is 21, what is the sum of the last two integers?

21. Rainfall of ½ inch is equivalent to 4.25 inches of snowfall. During a storm, 2½ inches of rain fell. If this storm had been a snowstorm, how much snow would have fallen?

22.

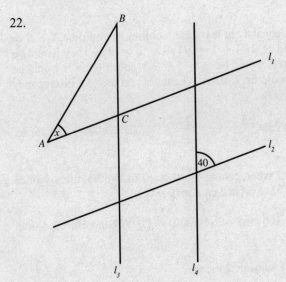

In the figure $l_1 \parallel l_2$ and $l_3 \parallel l_4$, and $AC = CB$. Find x.

23. If 4 DRAX = 5 LINX and 2 LINX = 6 PINX, 24 DRAX will equal how many PINX?

24. The floor plan shown for 3 rooms represents a total space that is 18 m long and 10 m wide. If the living room and dining room are squares, what is the ratio of the area of the kitchen to the area of the living room?

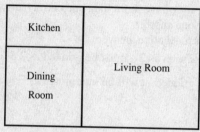

Note: Figure not drawn to scale.

25. A number X is to be multiplied by 3.5, but a mistake is made and X is multiplied by 35 instead. The result obtained is 882 greater than the correct answer. What is the value of X?

ANSWERS AND EXPLANATIONS

1. (C)	6. (B)	11. (A)	16. (50)	21. (21.25)
2. (C)	7. (D)	12. (D)	17. (.70)	22. (20)
3. (D)	8. (C)	13. (D)	18. (25)	23. (90)
4. (B)	9. (A)	14. (B)	19. (3)	24. (4/25)
5. (A)	10. (D)	15. (A)	20. (23)	25. (28)

1. (C) Radii of the same circle are equal. OA and OB are both radii in circle O.

2. (C) Minutes in 36 hours = $36 \times 60 = 2{,}160$.
Seconds in 36 minutes = $36 \times 60 = 2{,}160$.
They are equal.

3. (D) Because $X > 0$, X could equal 1. In that case, column A would be $X + .5$ or $1 + .5 = 1.5$, and column B would be $2x/4 + 1 = 2(1)/4 + 1 = 1\frac{1}{2}$. They would be equal. However, if $X = 2$, column A would be $2 + .5 = 2.5$ and column B would be $2(2)/4 + 1 = 2$, and column A would be greater. Whenever you prove a discrepancy like this, you must choose choice (D).

4. (B) The average of 2/5 and 2/7 is $\dfrac{2/5 + 2/7}{2} = \dfrac{24/35}{2} = 1/2 \times 24/35 = 12/35$; so, column B is larger.

ERROR   Forgetting to divide by 2 when getting the average of two fractions. Notice if you forgot this step, you would have picked choice (C).

5. (A) $2 m^2$ will be $2(100 \text{ cm} \times 100 \text{ cm}) = 2(10{,}000) = 20{,}000$; therefore, column A is larger.

ERROR   Thinking that $2 m^2$ is the same as 2 meters.

6. **(B)** In comparing a percent with a decimal, either convert the % to a decimal or convert the decimal to a %. This will make the comparison easier, provided you convert correctly. Let's look at it both ways. First, $\frac{1}{4}\% = .25\% = .0025$. Column B is larger.

Suppose we did it the other way, converting .025 to a %. Moving the decimal 2 places to the left we obtain $.025 = 2.5\%$. Column B is larger.

7. **(D)** Because $x > 1$ and $x \neq y$, we could have $x = 2$ and $y = 3$. This case would compare 3^2 with 2^3 and column A would be bigger. Suppose we used $x = 2$ and $y = 5$. Then we compare 5^2 with 2^5. $5^2 = 25$ and $2^5 = 2 \times 2 \times 2 \times 2 \times 2 = 32$. Column B is larger in this case and so we must choose choice (D).

8. **(C)** $3\sqrt{16/4} = 3\sqrt{4} = 3 \times 2 = 6$
$2\sqrt{18/2} = 2\sqrt{9} = 2 \times 3 = 6$
They are equal.

9. **(A)** The price of the shirt after a 25% discount is $P - .25P = .75P$. This is a greater amount than $.25P$. You could substitute a value for P and arrive at the same conclusion. Suppose we let $P = \$10$. Then, the discount is $.25 \times 10 = \$2.50$, and the price of the shirt after the discount is $\$10 - \$2.50 = \$7.50$. Column A is $\$7.50$, whereas column B is $\$2.50$.

ERROR Mistaking the price of the shirt after the discount with the actual discount. Read carefully!

10. **(D)** Since *ABCD* is a square, $X = Y$. The area is therefore $X \times X = X^2$ and the perimeter is $4 \times X = 4X$. When $X = 1$, X^2 (the area) is smaller than $4X$ (the perimeter). However, if $X = 5$, then $X^2 = 25$ and $4X = 20$. Therefore, we choose choice (D).

11. **(A)** If 60 is $x\%$ of 30, we can write this as $60 = \left(\dfrac{x}{100}\right)(30) = \dfrac{30x}{100}$. Therefore, $60 = \dfrac{3x}{10}$. Now, cross-multiply to get 3x 5 600; therefore, $3x > 150$, so A > B.

12. **(D)** Let $a = 1, b = 2$, and $c = 3$. Then $a + b = 3$ and $c - b = 1$. So, $A > B$. *But,* if $a = 1, b = 2$, and $c = 10$, then $a + b = 3$ and $c - b = 8$. In this case, $B > A$. So you must mark choice (D).

13. **(D)**

Let $x = 20°$ and $z = 40°$. Then $y = x + z = 60°$. (An exterior angle of a triangle is equal to the sum of the two nonadjacent interior angles.) So, $y - x = 60° - 20° = 40°$. $B > A$. *But,* if you let $x = z = 50°$, then $y = x + z = 100°$ and $y - x = 100° - 50° = 50°$. In this case, $A = B$. Once again, our advice is to substitute several values of the variables, if you have time, before making your conclusion.

14. **(B)**

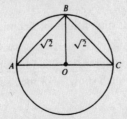

Triangle *ABC* is an isosceles *right* triangle. ($\angle B = \frac{1}{2}(AC) = \frac{1}{2}(180°) = 90°$.) By the Pythagorean Theorem, then, $AC^2 = AB^2 + BC^2 = (\sqrt{2})^2 + (\sqrt{2})^2 = 2 + 2 = 4$. So,

$AC = 2$. Since AC is a diameter, the radii shown, $AO = OB = OC = 1$. Now we are ready to decide which quantity is the greater one. $AB + BC = \sqrt{2} + \sqrt{2} = 2\sqrt{2}$. $AO + OB + OC = 1 + 1 + 1 = 3$. Since $\sqrt{2}$ is approximately 1.4, then $2\sqrt{2}$ is approximately 2.8. Therefore, $B > A$.

15. (A) The area of a circle is πr^2. So, the area of the circle described in column A is $\pi 7^2$ or 49π. The area of an equilateral triangle is $\frac{(\text{side})^2}{4}\sqrt{3}$. So, the area of the equilateral triangle described in column B is $\frac{14^2}{4}\sqrt{3} = \frac{196}{4}\sqrt{3} = 49\sqrt{3}$. Since $\pi > \sqrt{3}$, $49\pi > 49\sqrt{3}$; so, (A) is the correct choice.

16. (50) $A + 4 = 4$; so, $A = 14 - 4 = 10$. Then, $5A$ is $5 + 10 = 50$.

17. (.70) If Todd had paid .50 for each of the 14 pens, he would have spent $14 \times .50 = \$7.00$. Since he only spent \$6.30, he saved $\$7.00 - \$6.30 = .70$ on the purchase.

18. (25)

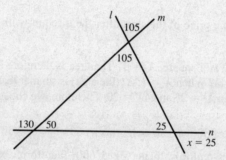

The 105° angle can be "transferred" into the triangle since it is a vertical angle. The supplement of 130° is 50°, and so now we know two angles of the triangle. The third angle is $180 - 105 - 50 = 25°$. Angle x is the vertical angle to the 25° angle and therefore also equals 25°.

19. (3) Cross-multiplying we get $4 \times 9 = 12X$, or $36 = 12X$. $X = 3$.

20. (23) We need to know at what number this list of seven consecutive integers begins. Since the sum of the first three consecutive integers is 21, we can write

$$X + X + 1 + X + 2 = 21$$
$$\text{1st}\quad\text{2nd}\quad\quad\text{3rd}$$

$3X + 3 = 21$, or $3X = 18$. $X = 6$. The seven consecutive integers are 6, 7, 8, 9, 10, 11, and 12. The sum of the last two is $11 + 12 = 23$.

21. (21.25) Placing all of the dimensions in decimal form, we get the following proportion:

$$\frac{.5 \text{ inch rain}}{4.25 \text{ inch snow}} = \frac{2.5 \text{ inch rain}}{X \text{ inch snow}}$$

Cross-multiply and we obtain

$$\frac{.5X}{.5} = \frac{10.625}{.5}$$

$$X = 21.25$$

22. (20)

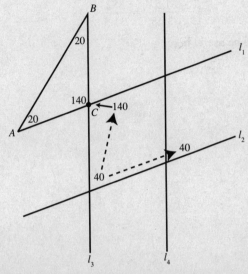

Because $l_3 \parallel l_y$, the 40° angle can be "transferred" as a corresponding angle. Because $l_1 \parallel l_2$, the consecutive interior angles will add up to 180; so, opposite the 40° is 140°. This 140° angle can be transferred by vertical angles into the triangle, leaving 40° to be split between two equal angles ($\triangle$ *ABC* is isosceles) at *A* and *B*. Therefore, *X/A* will equal 40/2 = 20°.

23. (90) This is a compound proportion that can be solved by eliminating one of the variables. Since LINX is in both equations, it can be eliminated as follows:

$$(4 \text{ DRAX} = 5 \text{ LINX}) \times 2 \qquad 8 \text{ DRAX} = 10 \text{ LINX}$$
$$(6 \text{ PINX} = 2 \text{ LINX}) \times 5 \qquad 30 \text{ PINX} = 10 \text{ LINX}$$

So, 8 DRAX is directly equal to 30 PINX. Therefore, 24 DRAX (3 × 8) = 90 PINX (3 × 30).

24. (4/25)

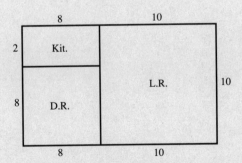

Since the living room and dining room are squares, we can fill in the dimensions as shown. The area of the kitchen is 2 × 8 = 16, and the area of the living room is 10 × 10 = 100. The ratio of kitchen to living room is 16/100 = 4/25.

298 / THE MATHEMATICAL ASSESSMENT TEST

25. (28)   The mistaken product is $35 \times X$, and the correct product is $3 \times 5 \times X$. The difference between the correct answer and the mistake is 882. This can be written as an equation.

$$35X - 3.5X = 882$$
$$31.5X = 882$$
$$\frac{31.5X}{31.5} = \frac{882}{31.5} = 28$$

Your calculator will be useful here.

Mathematical Assessment Test 5

Time—30 Minutes
25 Questions

Notes: 1. The use of a calculator is permitted. All numbers used are real numbers.
2. Figures that accompany problems in this test are intended to provide information useful in solving the problems. They are drawn as accurately as possible, *except* when it is stated in a specific problem that a figure is not drawn to scale. All figures lie in a plane unless otherwise indicated.

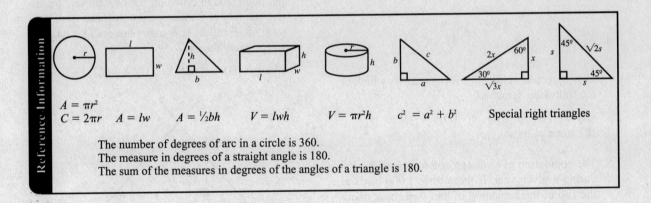

$A = \pi r^2$
$C = 2\pi r$ $A = lw$ $A = \frac{1}{2}bh$ $V = lwh$ $V = \pi r^2 h$ $c^2 = a^2 + b^2$ Special right triangles

The number of degrees of arc in a circle is 360.
The measure in degrees of a straight angle is 180.
The sum of the measures in degrees of the angles of a triangle is 180.

1. How many positive odd integers are greater than 16 but less than 40?

    (A) 12   (B) 13   (C) 14   (D) 23   (E) 24

2. If p people each contribute d dollars to a community fund, what is the total number of dollars contributed by these people?

    (A) p + d   (B) pd   (C) p/d   (D) p − d
    (E) d/p

3.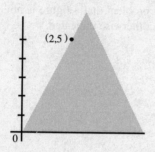

    Which point does *not* lie in the shaded region?

    (A) (1,3)   (B) (2,4)   (C) (3,2)   (D) (5,1)
    (E) (6,1)

4. $\frac{62}{10} \square \frac{27}{5} = 0.8$

    This statement is true if $\square$ is replaced by which of the following symbols?

    (A) +   (B) −   (C) ×   (D) ÷
    (E) none of these

5. The population of birds at a zoo increased by 1% during a given year. If there were 1,000 birds at the zoo in the beginning of that year, how many birds were at the zoo at the end of that year?

    (A) 10   (B) 100   (C) 1,001   (D) 1,010
    (E) 1,100

6. Three lines intersecting at a point form six angles. If the sum of two of these angles is 80°, then the sum of the other four angles is

    (A) 80°   (B) 120°   (C) 160°   (D) 240°
    (E) 280°

7. Two clocks are set to the same time, but one clock loses 1 minute every hour, whereas the other clock gains 2 minutes every 3 hours. After 24 hours, the difference between the times that each clock reads will be how many minutes?

    (A) 24   (B) 40   (C) 48   (D) 60   (E) 72

8. A baseball team wins 5 games for every 3 games it loses. After 48 games have been played, how many more games has the team won than lost?

    (A) 12   (B) 18   (C) 30   (D) 32   (E) 40

9. If the radius of a circle is increased by 10%, its area is increased by

    (A) 10%   (B) 20%   (C) 21%   (D) 32%
    (E) 40 %

10. The average of $4\sqrt{16}$ and $16\sqrt{4}$ is

    (A) $10\sqrt{20}$ (B) $20\sqrt{20}$ (C) 24   (D) 32
    (E) 48

11. If the degree measures of the angles of a quadrilateral are 1x, 2x, 5x and 10x, what is the measure of the largest angle?

    (A) 20°   (B) 60°   (C) 100°   (D) 160°
    (E) 200°

12. Chris walked to the bike store at a rate of 4 miles per hour. She returned on her new bicycle traveling at a rate of 8 miles per hour. If she traveled a total of 16 miles, how many hours did it take her to complete the trip?

    (A) 8   (B) 6   (C) 5   (D) 4   (E) 3

13.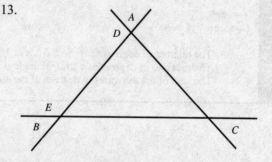

    In the figure above, $\angle C =$

    (A) $B + A$ (B) $180 − (B + A)$
    (C) $180 + (B + A)$ (D) $180 − (D + E)$
    (E) $D + E$

14. Each of the trucks of a delivery company can hold exactly X packages. On a given morning, all of the trucks are loaded so that all of them are filled, except one, and that truck had only 3 packages in it. If a total of 57 packages were loaded on that day, which of the following could be the value of X?

    (A) 5   (B) 7   (C) 8   (D) 9   (E) 12

15. If $\dfrac{4X^2 - 4}{4} = 0$, then X could equal

    (A) 0 (B) 1 (C) -2 (D) 4 (E) -4

16. The posts of a fence are 6 feet apart. The distance from the first post to the last post is 126 feet. How many posts are in the fence?

    (A) 19 (B) 20 (C) 21 (D) 22 (E) 23

17.

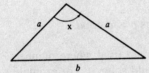

If $90° \le x < 180°$, then in the triangle above, which of the following represents the *smallest* range of values for b?

    (A) $0 < b < a$ (B) $0 < b < 2a$
    (C) $0 < b < a\sqrt{2}$ (D) $a < b < 2a$
    (E) $a\sqrt{2} < b < 2a$

18. If N is decreased by 10%, the result equals 45 increased by 20% of 45. What is the value of N?

    (A) 60 (B) 54 (C) 49.5 (D) 27 (E) 9

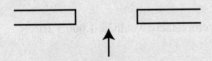

.002 inch gap at 30°F

19. In an electrical device, the gap between two metal prongs is .002 inch when the temperature is 30°F. If each of the metal prongs increases in length at a rate of 1/10,000 inch for each 1°F increase in temperature, at what temperature will the prongs make contact?

    (A) 32°F (B) 40°F (C) 50°F (D) 60°F
    (E) 100°F

20. If $1/X = 3/2$ and $1/N = 4/9$, then $XN - 1/XN = ?$

    (A) 2/3 (B) 5/6 (C) 1 (D) 0 (E) 9/4

21. If a grams of substance 1 is mixed with b grams of substance 2, the percent of substance 1 in the mixture is

    (A) $\dfrac{100a}{b}$ (B) $\dfrac{100b}{a+b}$ (C) $\dfrac{a}{a+b}$
    (D) $\dfrac{100a}{a+b}$ (E) $\dfrac{a+b}{100a}$

22. If $p \# q = 2(p + 2q)$, then if $a \# b = b \# a$, which of the following must be true?

    (A) $a = b$ (B) $a = -b$ (C) $a = b = 0$
    (D) $a = b = 1$ (E) $a = 2b$

23. If $(p + q)(ap - aq) = p^2 - q^2$, then $a =$

    (A) p (B) q (C) 1 (D) 0 (E) -1

24.

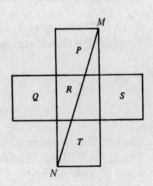

Note: Figure not drawn to scale.

In the figure above, $P, Q, R, S,$ and T are squares.

If the areas of the squares are equal and the perimeter of the figure is 60, then $MN =$

    (A) $5\sqrt{10}$ (B) 17 (C) 20 (D) $10\sqrt{5}$
    (E) $15\sqrt{2}$

25. A cube of volume 1,000 is cut into 125 cubes each of volume 8. The total surface area of the 125 cubes is how much larger than the surface area of the original cube?

    (A) 600 (B) 1,200 (C) 2,400 (D) 2,850
    (E) 3,000

ANSWERS AND EXPLANATIONS

1. (A)	6. (E)	11. (E)	16. (D)	21. (D)
2. (B)	7. (B)	12. (E)	17. (E)	22. (A)
3. (A)	8. (A)	13. (B)	18. (A)	23. (C)
4. (B)	9. (C)	14. (B)	19. (B)	24. (A)
5. (D)	10. (C)	15. (B)	20. (B)	25. (C)

1. (A)   The positive odd integers greater than 16 and less than 40 are those between 17 and 39 inclusive. They are 17, 19, 21, 23, 25, 27, 29, 31, 33, 35, 37, and 39. There are 12 positive odd integers in this range.

2. (B)   If each of p people contributes d dollars, the total is $p \times d$ or pd.

Technique: In these types of problems in which letters are used where numbers should appear, plug in small numbers to see how you would solve it. For example, this problem could read "If *5* people each contribute \$10. ..." Here it is fairly obvious that the total is 5×10, or $p \times d$.

3. (A)   The point (1,3) is slightly above the shaded region. All other points are clearly in the shaded region.

4. (B) $\dfrac{62}{10} = 6^2/_{10} = 6^1/_5;\ \dfrac{27}{5} = 5^2/_5$

$6\,^1/_5 - 5^2/_5 = \dfrac{4}{5} = .8$

The box □ is therefore a −.
Since .8 is 8/10, the □ could not be a +, and since $6^2/_{10} \times 27/5$ would be greater than 1, the □ could not be ×.

5. (D)   Find 1% of 1,000. $.01 \times 1,000 = 10$. Therefore, there would be $1,000 + 10$ birds at the end of the year.

ERROR   Incorrectly changing 1% into its decimal form, .01.

6. (E)   The six angles formed will have a total of 360°. Since two of the angles total 80°, the sum of the other four angles will be $360° - 80° = 280°$.

7. (B)   After 24 hours, clock 1 will be 24×1 min = 24 minutes slow. Since clock 2 runs 2 minutes fast every 3 hours, it will run $2 \times 24/3 = 2 \times 8 = 16$ minutes fast in 24 hours. If one clock is 24 minutes slow and the other is 16 minutes fast, the difference in their times will be $24 + 16 = 40$ minutes.

8. (A)   The ratio of wins to losses is 5:3. Other ratios relate either the wins or the losses to the total games played. The ratio of wins to games played is 5:(5 + 3) or 5:8. Using this information, the following proportion can be set:

$$\frac{\text{Wins}}{\text{Total played}} = \frac{5}{8} = \frac{X}{48}$$

$5 \times 48 = 8X$, or $8X = 240$. $X = 30$.

If the team played 48 games and won 30 games, they therefore lost 18 games. The difference between wins and losses is $30 - 18 = 12$ games.

Technique: The ratio of two quantities, such as wins and losses, can also be related to the total of wins and losses (games played).

9. (C)   Start with a circle with radius $= 1$. Then, its area is $A = \pi r^2 = \pi(1)^2 = \pi$. An increase of 10% in the radius makes the larger radius $= 1 + 10\%(1) = 1 + .1 = 1.1$. The larger area is therefore $A = \pi(1.1)^2 = 1.21\pi$. The area has increased by .21 or 21%.

ERROR   A 10% increase in the radius does not equal a 10% increase in the area because the area formula has r^2 in it.

10. (C) $\dfrac{4\sqrt{16} + 16\sqrt{4}}{2} = \dfrac{4.4 + 16.2}{2} = \dfrac{16 + 32}{2} = \dfrac{48}{2} = 24.$

ERROR   Adding $\sqrt{16} + \sqrt{4}$ and getting $\sqrt{20}$. This addition is not valid because the $\sqrt{}$ must be figured first before the terms can be added. If the square roots were identical, they could be added. For example: $3\sqrt{7} + 2\sqrt{7} = 5\sqrt{7}$.

11. (E)   There are 360° in a quadrilateral; therefore, the following equation can be written: $1x + 2x + 5x + 10x = 360$. $18x = 360$, or $x = 20$. The largest angle is $10x$ or $10(20) = 200$.

12. (E)   Chris traveled 16 miles, but this is the round trip mileage. She traveled 8 miles in each direction. Walking 4 miles/hr, she will cover 8 miles in 2 hours. Biking 8 miles/hr, she will cover the 8 miles, returning in 1 additional hour. Her total time is 2 hours (going) + 1 hour (returning) = 3 hours.

13. (B)

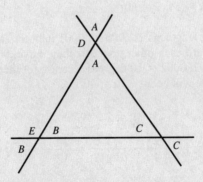

Transfer angles *A*, *B*, and *C* into the triangle (vertical angles of intersecting lines are equal). Since *A*, *B*, and *C* are the three angles of a triangle, $A + B + C = 180$ or $C = 180 - (A + B)$.

14. **(B)** If 3 packages are loaded onto one of the trucks, there are $57 - 3 = 54$ packages to be distributed equally among the other trucks. Since $54/6 = 9$, 9 packages can be loaded on each of the remaining trucks. X could be the total of 6 trucks (each with 9 packages) and 1 truck (with 3 packages). Of the choices given, X could be 7.

15. **(B)** $\frac{4X^2 - 4}{4} = 0$; therefore, the numerator $4X^2 - 4$ must equal 0.
$4X^2 - 4 = 0$ or $4X^2 = 4$, $X^2 = 1$. X could be either $+1$ or -1. Choice (B).

16. **(D)** *Simplify* the problem so that the distance between the first and last posts is 18 feet.

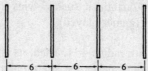

As you can see, dividing 18 by 6 gives you 3, but there are 4 posts. Now coming back to the real problem, if the distance from the first to the last post is 126 feet, there are $^{126}/_6 + 1$ posts, or $21 + 1 = 22$ posts. Be careful in problems such as these.

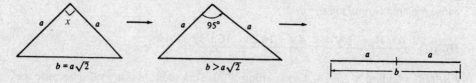

17. **(E)** If $x = 90°$, you have an *isosceles* right triangle. Therefore, $b = a\sqrt{2}$. (Remember, the $45°-45°-90°$ right triangle?) As x increases to $180°$, the triangle progressively "flattens" into a straight line with length of b. When x "hits" $180°$, $b = 2a$. Choices (A), (B), and (C) allow b to be 0. This is impossible. Choice (D) allows b to be equal to a, making the triangle equilateral. Then, *all* angles must be $60°$. But this is not the case, because x is "growing" from $90°$ to $180°$. So, this problem could have been done by the technique of *elimination*.

18. **(A)** $N - 10\% N = 45 + 20\%$ of 45
$$90\% N = 45 + .2(45) = 45 + 9 = 54$$
$$.9N = 54$$
$$N = 54/.9 = 60$$

19. **(B)** Each prong lengthens $1/1,000 = .0001$ inch for each increase of $1°F$. Since the prongs move toward each other, together they move $.0002$ inch for each $1°F$ increase. It will take $.002/.0002 = 10$ degrees increase for the two prongs to touch each other. The temperature will be $30 + 10 = 40°F$.

20. **(B)** $\frac{1}{X} = \frac{3}{2}$; so, $X = \frac{2}{3}$. $\frac{1}{N} = \frac{4}{9}$; so, $N = \frac{9}{4}$.
$$XN - \frac{1}{XN} = \left(\frac{2}{3}\right)\left(\frac{9}{4}\right) - \frac{1}{(^2/_3)(^9/_4)} = \frac{18}{12} - \frac{1}{^{18}/_{12}} = \frac{3}{2} - \frac{1}{^3/_2} =$$
$$\frac{3}{2} - \frac{2}{3}.$$
$$\frac{3}{2} - \frac{2}{3} = \frac{9}{6} - \frac{4}{6} = \frac{5}{6}.$$

21. (D)   Let's assume that there are 10 grams of substance 1 and 30 grams of substance 2. The percent of substance 1 in the *mixture* is $\frac{10}{10+30} = \frac{10}{40} = \frac{1}{4} = .25.$ No matter what numbers you choose, the *fraction* substance 1 is of the entire mixture is $\frac{a}{a+b}$. To change that fraction to a % we must first change it to a decimal and then multiply that decimal by 100 (move the decimal point 2 places to the right). In order to change $\frac{a}{a+b}$ to a %, then, we must multiply it by 100 to get $\frac{100}{1} \times \frac{a}{a+b} = \frac{100a}{a+b}$. So, in the case where $a = 10$ and $b = 30$, $\frac{10}{10+30} = \frac{1}{4}$. Then, $\frac{1}{4} = \left(100 \times \frac{1}{4}\right)$% or 25%.

22. (A)   According to this *invented* operation, #, $a \# b = 2(a + 2b) = 2a + 4b$. $b \# a = 2(b + 2a) = 2b + 4a$. Since $a \# b = b \# a$, $2a + 4b = 2b + 4a$. Subtracting $2b$ from both sides of the equation, $4b = 2b + 2a$. Subtracting $2b$ from both sides of the equation, we get $2b = 2a$. Dividing now by 2, we get $b = a$. Choices (C) and (D) may be true, but not *necessarily* true. Choices (B) and (E) *can* be true if both a and b are 0. But the only conclusion about a and b that *must* be true is that a *must* equal b. So, in a case such as this, you can be led *astray* by the substitution of numbers.

23. (C)   By the distributive postulate, $(ap - aq) = a(p - q)$. So, the problem can be rewritten as $(p + q)(ap - aq) = p^2 - q^2 = (p + q)(a)(p - q)$. Since $(p + q)(p - q) = p^2 - q^2$, $(p + q)(a)(p - q) = a(p^2 - q^2)$. Therefore, a *must* be 1.

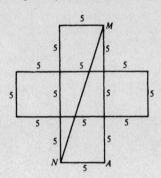

24. (A)   If the perimeter of the figure above is 60, to get from M to M again you must "travel" over 12 equal line segments, each of which must be $^{60}/_{12} = 5$. (The fact that the areas are equal makes those line segments equal.) So, in right triangle *NAM*, $NM^2 = NA^2 + AM^2 = 5^2 + (5 + 5 + 5)^2 = 5^2 + 15^2 = 25 + 225 = 250$. $NM = 250 = \sqrt{25 \times 10} \ \sqrt{25} \ \sqrt{10} = 5\sqrt{10}$.

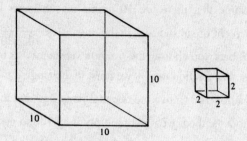

25. (C)   If a cube has a volume of 1,000, each edge must be 10. (Volume = length × width × height. 10 × 10 × 10 = 1,000.) The surface area of a cube is the area of one square "face" × 6 (because there are 6 "faces"). Since the area of one square face is 10 × 10 (length × width = area), the total surface area of the large cube is 100 × 6 = 600. Now, let's look at the small cubes. If the volume of one of the cubes is 8, each edge is 2, 8 = 2 × 2 × 2. The area of one square face is then 2 × 2 = 4. Six such faces gives a total of 24 for the surface area of one cube. Since there are 125 of these small cubes, the total surface area = 125 × 24 = 3,000. So, the total surface area of the 125 cubes is 3,000 − 600 greater than the total surface area of the original big cube.   3,000 − 600 = 2,400.

Mathematical Assessment Test 6

Time—15 Minutes
10 Questions

Notes: 1. The use of a calculator is permitted. All numbers used are real numbers.
2. Figures that accompany problems in this test are intended to provide information useful in solving the problems. They are drawn as accurately as possible, *except* when it is stated in a specific problem that a figure is not drawn to scale. All figures lie in a plane unless otherwise indicated.

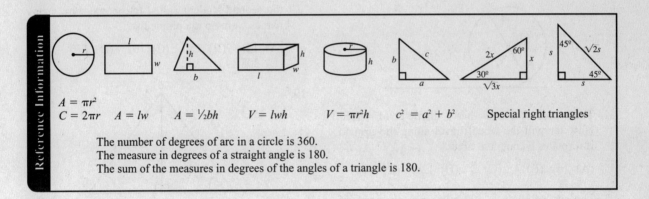

$A = \pi r^2$
$C = 2\pi r$ $A = lw$ $A = \frac{1}{2}bh$ $V = lwh$ $V = \pi r^2 h$ $c^2 = a^2 + b^2$ Special right triangles

The number of degrees of arc in a circle is 360.
The measure in degrees of a straight angle is 180.
The sum of the measures in degrees of the angles of a triangle is 180.

1. The average of 6, 10, 14, and 18 is how much less than the average of 8, 12, 16, and 20?

   (A) 8 (B) 6 (C) 4 (D) 2 (E) 1

2. If 3 inches of a uniform metal rod weighs 8 ounces, how much will 7 inches of the rod weigh?

   (A) 7 oz (B) 18.66 oz (C) 9.66 oz
   (D) 21 oz (E) 24 oz

3.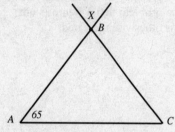

   In triangle ABC, $\overline{AB} = \overline{BC}$. Find X.

   (A) 50 (B) 65 (C) 70 (D) 130 (E) 115

4. The wheel of a truck has a diameter of 4 feet. How far will the wheel travel along the ground if it rotates 6 complete times?

   (A) 16 (B) 4 (C) 2 (D) 12π (E) 24π

5. The city of Boon is 400 miles directly north of the city of Altuna. The city of Clearview is 300 miles directly east of Boon. What is the distance between Altuna and Clearview?

   (A) 700 miles (B) 600 miles (C) 500 miles
   (D) 200 miles (E) 100 miles

6. If X is an odd integer, express the fifth consecutive odd integer greater than X.

   (A) $X + 5$ (B) $X + 6$ (C) $X + 10$
   (D) $X + 11$ (E) $2X + 5$

7. If $X - Y = 3$ and $X^2 - Y^2 = 27$, what is the value of $X + Y$?

   (A) 9 (B) 12 (C) 15 (D) 24 (E) 30

8. Thirty percent of the citizens in a town are registered voters. Of the registered voters, 10% are senior citizens. What percentage of the town's citizens are senior citizens who are registered voters?

   (A) .3% (B) 3% (C) 6% (D) 15%
   (E) 30%

9. Two students were asked to make phone calls notifying others about a school trip. From the phone list they were given, the first student called $^2/_5$ of those listed. The second student called $^7/_{10}$ of those who were not called by the first student. If the second student called 63 people, how many names were on the phone list?

   (A) 126 (B) 150 (C) 162 (D) 170
   (E) 208

10.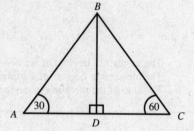

    In triangle ABC, altitude BD is drawn, $\angle A = 30°$ and $\angle C = 60°$. If $\overline{DC} = 2$, what is the length of $\overline{AD}$?

    (A) 1 (B) 2 (C) $2\sqrt{3}$ (D) 6 (E) $6\sqrt{3}$

ANSWERS AND EXPLANATIONS

1. (D)	6. (C)
2. (B)	7. (A)
3. (A)	8. (B)
4. (E)	9. (B)
5. (C)	10. (D)

1. (D)   The average of 6, 10, 14, and 18 is $(6 + 10 + 14 + 18)/4 = 48/4 = 12$.
      The average of 8, 12, 16, and 20 is $(8 + 12 + 16 + 20)/4 = 56/4 = 14$.
Therefore, the average of the first set of numbers is 2 less than the average of the second set of numbers. You might also have noticed that each number of the first set is 2 less than the corresponding number in the second set.

ERROR   Subtracting the sum of the first set from the sum of the second set and dividing this result by 2.

2. (B)   Since the rod is uniform, the length and weight will be directly proportional.

$$\frac{3 \text{ in.}}{8 \text{ oz}} = \frac{7 \text{ in.}}{X \text{ oz}}$$

Cross-multiplying, you get $3X = 7 \times 8 = 56$.
X will equal $56/3 = 18.66$.

3. (A)   Triangle *ABC* is isosceles since $\overline{AB} = \overline{BC}$; therefore, because the base angles of an isosceles triangle are equal, $\angle C = 65°$. There are 180° in a triangle, leaving 50° for angle *B*. Since *X* is the vertical angle at *B, X* will also equal 50°.

4. (E)   The circumference of the wheel is $\pi \times$ diameter $= \pi \times 4 = 4\pi$ feet. The wheel will travel 1 circumference (4π feet) for every complete rotation. Since the wheel rotates 6 times, it travels $6 \times C = 6 \times 4\pi = 24\pi$ feet.

5. (C)   The diagram for this problem looks like this:

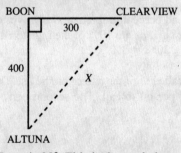

   Note that the angle at Boon is 90°. This is the angle between the cities directly east and directly south of it. Since there is a 90° angle, we can complete a right triangle (by connecting Altuna with Clearview). This distance is the hypothenuse of the right triangle. Using the Pythagorean Theorem,

$$400^2 + 300^2 = X^2$$
$$160,000 + 90,000 = X^2$$
$$250,000 = X^2 \quad \text{or} \quad X = \sqrt{250,000} = 500$$

Technique: You could avoid much computation and spend less time on this problem if you recognize the 3-4-5 triplet. 300-400-*X* is the 3-4-5 triplet with each length being 100 times the value in the triplet. In 300-400-*X,* the *X* will be 5 multiplied by 100.

ERROR Choice (A), 700 miles, is a trap. In the right triangle, you cannot simply add the two sides (300 + 400) to arrive at the value of the hypothenuse.

6. (C) Let X represent the odd integer. Then, $X + 2$ would be the next odd integer. (Remember $X + 1$, the very next number after X, will be even!) The second consecutive odd integer will be $(X + 2) + 2$ or $X + 4$, and so on.

X $\quad$ = original integer
$X + 2$ = 1st consecutive odd integer
$X + 4$ = 2nd consecutive odd integer
$X + 6$ = 3rd consecutive odd integer
$X + 8$ = 4th consecutive odd integer
$X + 10$ = 5th consecutive odd integer

You could do this problem by choosing an odd integer and writing the next five consecutive odds. For example, starting with $X = 5$, we would have 5, 7, 9, 11, 13, and 15.   15 is $X + 10$ or $5 + 10$.

7. (A) There does not seem to be any easy way to solve these equations. We could take $X - Y = 3$ and make it into $X = 3 + Y$, and then substitute that into $X^2 - Y^2 = 27$. This substitution would look like this:

$$X^2 - Y^2 = 27$$
$$(3 + Y)^2 - Y^2 = 27$$

With some work, we would find Y and then eventually find X. However, there is a much more "powerful" technique for solving this problem. $X^2 - Y^2$ is the difference of perfect squares and it factors into $X^2 - Y^2 = (X + Y)(X - Y)$. Since we know $X^2 - Y^2 = 27$ and $X - Y = 3$, we can make the following simple equation:

$$X^2 - Y^2 = (X - Y)(X + Y)$$
$$27 = 3(N)$$
$$9 = N \text{ or } X + Y$$

8. (B) This is a compound percent problem and involves calculating the percent of a percent. Since the senior citizens are 10% of the registered voters (30%), we simply find 10% of 30%. $1/10 \times 30\% = 3\%$.

9. (B) The first student called $^2/_5$ of the names on the list. This left $^3/_5$ $(1 - ^2/_5 = ^3/_5)$ of the people for the second person to call. The second person called $^7/_{10}$ of that $^3/_5$ by calling 63 people.

$^7/_{10} \times ^3/_5 X = 63$ people
$^{21}/_{50} X$ is 63
$X = 63 \times ^{50}/_{21} = 150$

ERROR Forgetting that when one person does $^2/_5$ of the job (like making phone calls), the part remaining is $1 - ^2/_5 = ^3/_5$.

10. (D) This figure consists of three 30-60-90 triangles. They are $\triangle ABD$, $\triangle DBC$, and the entire $\triangle ABC$.

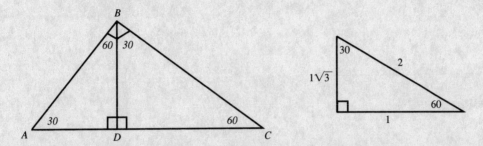

The ratio of the sides in a 30-60-90 triangle is $1 = 1\sqrt{3} = 2$. Since $DC = 2$, BD will equal $2\sqrt{3}$ because it is the side opposite the 60° ($\angle$ C).

Now focus on $\triangle ABD$.

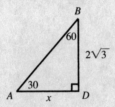

AD, the length we are looking for, will be $\sqrt{3}$ times the side opposite the 30° ($2\sqrt{3}$).
$\sqrt{3} \times 2\sqrt{3} = 2\sqrt{9} = 2 \times 3 = 6$.

Mathematical Assessment Test 7

Time—30 Minutes
25 Questions

Notes: 1. The use of a calculator is permitted. All numbers used are real numbers.
2. Figures that accompany problems in this test are intended to provide information useful in solving the problems. They are drawn as accurately as possible, *except* when it is stated in a specific problem that a figure is not drawn to scale. All figures lie in a plane unless otherwise indicated.

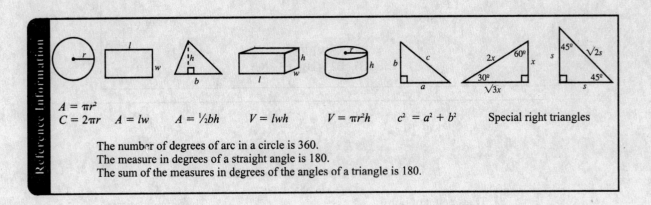

$A = \pi r^2$
$C = 2\pi r$ $A = lw$ $A = \frac{1}{2}bh$ $V = lwh$ $V = \pi r^2 h$ $c^2 = a^2 + b^2$ Special right triangles

The number of degrees of arc in a circle is 360.
The measure in degrees of a straight angle is 180.
The sum of the measures in degrees of the angles of a triangle is 180.

DIRECTIONS FOR QUANTITATIVE COMPARISON QUESTIONS

Questions 1 through 15 each consist of two quantities, one in column A and one in column B. You are to compare the two quantities and on the answer sheet fill in:

A   if the quantity in column A is greater
B   if the quantity in column B is greater
C   if the two quantities are equal
D   if the relationship cannot be determined from the information given

Notes: 1. In certain questions, information concerning one or both of the quantities to be compared is centered above the two columns.
   2. A symbol that appears in both columns represents the same thing in column A as it does in column B.
   3. Letters such as *x, y,* and *n* stand for real numbers.
   4. In that there are only four choices, *never mark (E)*.

EXAMPLES

Column A	*Column B*
E1. The average of 3, 5, and 10	9
E2. $x - y$	$y - x$
E3. 6% of 8	8% of 6

ANSWERS
E1. (B), E2. (D), E3. (C)

Column A	*Column B*

The average yearly
rainfall in Northville
is 68.2 inches.

| 1. | The amount of rain that falls in 1 month in Northville. | The amount of rain that falls in 2 months in Northville. | A B C D |

X is an integer.

| 2. | $X + 3$ | $X - 1$ | A B C D |

$Y - 9 = 10$

| 3. | Y | 1 | A B C D |

$\overline{AB} = \overline{BC}$

| 4. | $\measuredangle C$ | $\measuredangle B$ | A B C D |

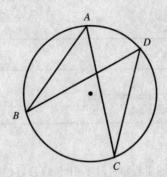

| 5. | ∢ *ABD* | ∢ *ACD* | A B C D |

$$-1 < X < 0$$

| 6. | $5X^4$ | $4X^5$ | A B C D |

| 7. | $\frac{1}{2}\%$ | .05 | A B C D |

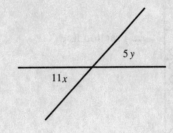

| 8. | *X* | *Y* | A B C D |

$$P * Q = \frac{1}{P} - \frac{1}{Q}$$

| 9. | The value of $P * Q$ when $P = \frac{1}{2}$ and $Q = \frac{1}{3}$ | -1 | A B C D |

50 is *X*% of 25

| 10. | $\frac{1}{10}$ of *X* | 25 | A B C D |

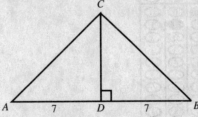

| 11. | Area of △*ACD* | Area of △*CDB* | A B C D |

| 12. | $(p - q)^2$ | $p^2 - q^2$ | A B C D |

For all numbers X,
let $\textcircled{X} = X + 2$

13.	$\textcircled{-X}$		$-\textcircled{X}$	A B C D
14.	8^{16}		4^{32}	A B C D
15.	The perimeter of a rectangle with area 64.		130	A B C D

DIRECTIONS FOR STUDENT-PRODUCED RESPONSE QUESTIONS

Each of the remaining ten questions (16–25) requires you to solve the problem and enter your answer by marking the special grid, as shown in the examples below.

Answer: $\dfrac{5}{14}$ or 5/14

Answer: 2.5

Write answer in boxes →

Grid in result

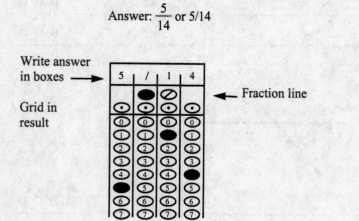

← Fraction line

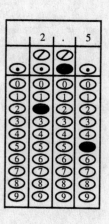

Decimal point

Answer: 201

Either position is correct.

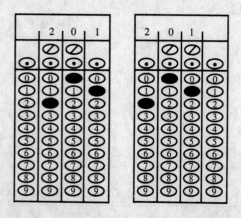

- *Decimal Accuracy:* If you obtain a decimal answer, **enter the most accurate value the grid will accommodate.** For example, if you obtain an answer such as 0.666 . . . , you should record the result as .666 or .667. **Less accurate values such as .66 or .67 are not acceptable.**

Acceptable ways to grid $\dfrac{2}{3}$ = .6666 . . .

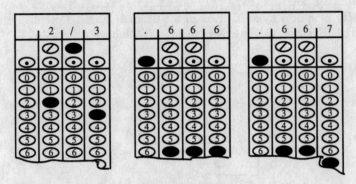

- Mark no more than one oval in any column.
- Because the answer sheet will be machine-scored, **you will receive credit only if the ovals are filled in correctly.**
- Although not required, it is suggested that you write your answer in the boxes at the top of the columns to help you fill in the ovals accurately.
- Some problems may have more than one correct answer. In such cases, grid only one answer.
- No question has a negative answer.
- **Mixed numbers** such as 2½ must be gridded as 2.5 or 5/2.

(If ⬜2⬜1⬜/⬜2⬜ is gridded, it will be interpreted as $\dfrac{21}{2}$, not 2½.)

16. If $R = 2$, $S = 4$, and $T = 1$, then $R^2S/T = $?

17. At a bazaar, twenty-five balloons numbered 1 to 25 in order are attached to a rod. If Bill uses darts to break the first balloon, the last balloon, and the balloons numbered 13 through 16, what fractional part of the remaining balloons are odd-numbered?

18. If $l_1 \parallel l_2$, find the value of $\measuredangle Q$.

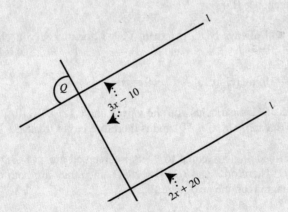

19. Twenty-five percent of 30 percent of 200 is?

20. If the average (arithmetic mean) of 22.5, 14, 3.1, 8.7 and X is 11.7, then $X = $?

21. If $2X + 3Y = 15$ and $3X + 2Y = 10$, then $X + Y = $?

22. If $X + 4$ is 3 more than Y, then $X + 15$ is how much more than $Y + 1$?

23. The floor plan of a room is given in the diagram below. How many tiles, 18 inches by 18 inches, will be needed to cover it completely?

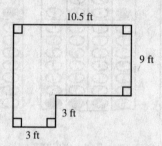

Note: Figure not drawn to scale.

24. If the positive integer X is divided by 4, the remainder is 1; if the positive integer L is divided by 4, the remainder is 3. What is the remainder if XL is divided by 4?

25. A ball bounces up $\frac{1}{2}$ the distance it falls when dropped, and on each bounce thereafter, it bounces $\frac{1}{2}$ the previous height. If it is dropped from a height of 128 feet, how many feet will it have traveled when it hits the ground the fifth time?

ANSWERS AND EXPLANATIONS

1. (D)	6. (A)	11. (C)	16. (16)	21. (5)
2. (A)	7. (B)	12. (D)	17. (9/19)	22. (13)
3. (A)	8. (B)	13. (A)	18. (80)	23. (46)
4. (A)	9. (C)	14. (B)	19. (15)	24. (3)
5. (C)	10. (B)	15. (D)	20. (10.2)	25. (368)

1. (D)   Although we know the average yearly rainfall in Northville, we do not know how it is distributed among the months. We have no means to compare column A and column B, so we choose (D).

2. (A) $X + 3$ will always be larger than $X - 1$ for any X you choose. Even if $X = -7$, then $X + 3 = -7 + 3 = -4$ and $X - 1 = -7 - 1 = -8$. -4 is larger than -8.

3. (A) $Y - 9 = 10$; therefore, $Y = 10 + 9 = 19$.

4. (A)   Since $\triangle ABC$ is isosceles and the vertex angle ($\angle B$) is 40°, both $\angle A$ and $\angle C$ will equal 70° each. $\angle C$ is 70° and is therefore larger than $\angle B$, which is 40°.

5. (C)   An inscribed angle is equal to $\frac{1}{2}$ its intercepted arc. $\angle ABD = \frac{1}{2} AD$ and $\angle ACD = \frac{1}{2} AD$. Therefore, $\angle ABD = \angle ACD$ since they are both equal to $\frac{1}{2}$ the same arc. (See diagram on the next page.)

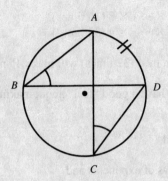

6. (A)   Since $-1 < X < 0$, X is a negative fraction. Pick a typical negative fraction such as $X = -\frac{1}{2}$ and plug in: $5(-\frac{1}{2})^4 = 4(-\frac{1}{2})^5$.

Although you could use your calculator to determine these values, you can immediately conclude that column A is larger because it remains positive, whereas column B will become negative.

$$\left(-\frac{1}{2}\right)^4 = +\frac{1}{16} \quad \left(-\frac{1}{2}\right)^5 = -\frac{1}{32}$$

Note: all negative numbers raised to even powers become positive, whereas all negatives raised to odd powers remain negative.

7. (B)   Converting column B into a %, we obtain $.05 = 5\%$.
5% is larger than $\frac{1}{2}\%$, so we choose column B.

8. (B) $11X = 5Y$ since these values represent a pair of equal vertical angles. Since it takes 11 X's to "balance" only 5 Y's, the X's are smaller than the Y's.

9. (C) $P * Q = 1/P - 1/Q = 1/\frac{1}{2} - 1/\frac{1}{3} = 2 - 3 = -1$

10. (B)   50 is $X\%$ of 25. $50/25 \times 100\% = 200\%$.

$1/10 \times 200 = 20$, which is smaller than column B.

11. (C)   If two triangles have equal bases and the same height (altitude), they have equal area. The base of each triangle is 7. The heights of each $\triangle$ are equal; therefore, their areas are equal.

12. (D)   If $p = q$, then $(p - q)^2 = 0$ and $p^2 - q^2 = p^2 - p^2 = 0$; so, column A = column B. If $p = 2$ and $q = 3$, then $(p - q)^2 = (2 - 3)^2 = (-1)^2 = 1$ and $p^2 - q^2 = 2^2 - 3^2 = 4 - 9 = -5$. In this case, column A > column B. Therefore, we choose (D).

13. (A)   Try substituting several numbers into $\widehat{X} = X + 2$. Be careful.

For $X = 1$ we have
$\widehat{-1} = -1 + 2 = 1$ for column A and $-1 = -\widehat{1}(1 + 2) = -3$ for column B.

Then try $X = -2$:
$\widehat{-2} = -2 + 2 = 0$ for column A and $-\widehat{2} = -(2 + 2) = -4$ for column B.
All substitutions will make column A bigger than column B.

14. (B) $8^{16} = 8 \times 8 \times 8 \times \cdots \times 8$ (16 times)
$4^{32} = 4 \times 4 \times 4 \times \cdots \times 4$ (32 times)

The repeated multiplication by 4 (32 times) will make 4^{32} much bigger than 8^{16}.

Technique: If you do not have a good "feel" about making this comparison, convert each of the bases to 2.

$8^{16} = (2^3)^{16}$ since $8 = 2^3$ and
$4^{32} = (2^2)^{32}$ since $4 = 2^2$.
Now, $(2^3)^{16} = 2^{48}$ by the laws of exponents and
$(2^2)^{32} = 2^{64}$;
$2^{64} > 2^{48}$, column B.

15. (D) There are an infinite number of rectangles with an area of 64. Here are several:

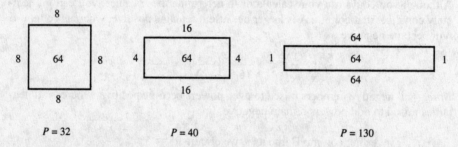

$P = 32$ $P = 40$ $P = 130$

Since some of these rectangles have perimeters less than 130 and at least one rectangle has a perimeter equal to 130, we must choose (D).

16. (16) Substituting $R = 2$, $S = 4$, and $T = 1$ into $R^2 S/T$, we get $(2)^2(4)/1 = 4 \times 4/1 = 16$.

17. (9/19) Bill bursts the first balloon (#1), the last balloon (#25), and #13, 14, 15, and 16. He bursts 6 balloons, so there are $25 - 6 = 19$ remaining balloons. Of these 19, there are 9 odd-numbered balloons (3, 5, 7, 9, 11, 17, 19, 21, and 23). Therefore, the fractional part of the remaining balloons that are odd-numbered is 9/19.

18. (80) Since l_1 is parallel to l_2, $3X - 10 = 2X + 20$, as these are corresponding angles and are therefore equal.

$$3X - 10 = 2X + 20$$
$$3X - 2X = 20 + 10$$
$$1X = 30$$

Angle Q is the vertical angle to $3X - 10$ and is therefore equal to $3X - 10$. Since we know $X = 30$, we can see that $\angle Q = 3X - 10 = 3(30) - 10 = 80$.

19. (15) 25% of 30% of 200 is $1/4 \times 3/10 \times 200/1$.
Canceling we obtain $1/4 \times 3/\overset{}{10} \times \overset{5}{200} = 15$.

20. (10.2) Since there are five numbers (including X) and their average is 11.7, their total will be $5 \times 11.7 = 58.5$. If we add up the four numbers we know, and subtract this sum from 58.5, we will find the value of X.

$$22.5 + 14 + 3.1 + 8.7 = 48.3$$
$$58.5 - 48.3 = 10.2$$
$$X = 10.2$$

21. (5%)   Add the two equations as follows:

$$+ \begin{array}{r} 2X + 3Y = 15 \\ 3X + 2Y = 10 \\ \hline 5X + 5Y = 25 \end{array}$$

If $5X + 5Y = 25$, then by dividing each term by 5 we get

$$\frac{5X}{5} + \frac{5Y}{5} = \frac{25}{5} = 5$$

$$X + Y = 5$$

22. (13)   "$X + 4$ is three more than Y" becomes the equation:

$$X + 4 = Y + 3$$

Since we want to compare $X + 15$ with $Y + 1$, add 11 to each side of this equation.

$$\underset{+ 15}{X + 4 + 11} = Y + 3 + 11 = Y + 14$$

$X + 15 = Y + 14$. The right side of this equation can be rewritten as
$Y + 1 + ⑬$. Therefore, $X + 15 = Y + 1 + ⑬$ or $X + 15$ is 13 more than $Y + 1$.

23. (46)   18-inch tiles are 1.5 ft. (18/12) by 1.5 ft.

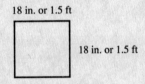

18 in. or 1.5 ft

18 in. or 1.5 ft

The 3-ft $\times$ 3-ft section will take 2 rows of 2 tiles each or $2 \times 2 = 4$ tiles. The rectangular piece 10.5 ft by 9 ft will take 6 rows of 7 tiles each or $6 \times 7 = 42$ tiles. The total number of tiles will be $4 + 42 = 46$ tiles.

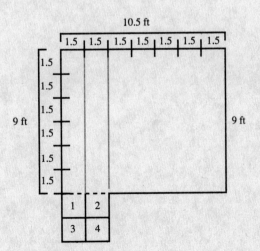

24. (3)   Pick values for X and L that "work." If X is divided by 4, the remainder is 1. X could be 5 because 5/4 = 1R1. L could be 11 because 11/4 = 2R3. XL would be $5 \times 11 = 55$. The remainder when 55 is divided by 4 is 3.   55/4 = 13R3.

25. (368)   You need a diagram to keep track of the bouncing ball!

Start

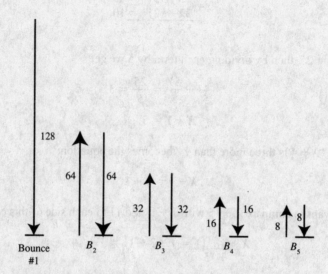

Notice that the diagram accounts for the complete up-and-down motion of the ball. The total distance covered is $128 + 64 + 64 + 32 + 32 + 16 + 16 + 8 + 8 = 368$ ft.

Mathematical Assessment Test 8

Time—30 minutes
25 Questions

Notes: 1. The use of a calculator is permitted. All numbers used are real numbers.
2. Figures that accompany problems in this test are intended to provide information useful in solving the problems. They are drawn as accurately as possible, *except* when it is stated in a specific problem that a figure is not drawn to scale. All figures lie in a plane unless otherwise indicated.

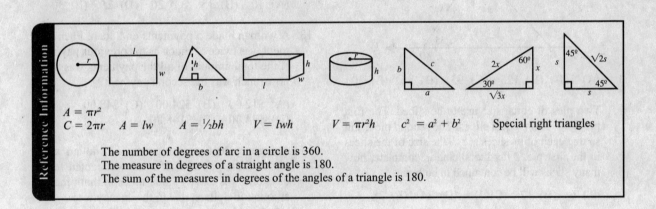

Reference Information

$A = \pi r^2$
$C = 2\pi r$ $\quad A = lw$ $\quad\quad A = \frac{1}{2}bh$ $\quad\quad V = lwh$ $\quad\quad V = \pi r^2 h$ $\quad c^2 = a^2 + b^2$ $\quad$ Special right triangles

The number of degrees of arc in a circle is 360.
The measure in degrees of a straight angle is 180.
The sum of the measures in degrees of the angles of a triangle is 180.

1. If 54 cartons are arranged in 3 equal piles, what is the *least* number of cartons that must be moved to make 6 piles with 9 cartons in each pile?

   (A) 3   (B) 18   (C) 24   (D) 27   (E) 36

2. If $4Q + 3R = 31$ and $2R = 10$, then $Q = ?$

   (A) −2   (B) 2   (C) 4   (D) −4   (E) −16

3. Josh arrived at the library at 3:40 P.M., where he studied for 50 minutes. If he then took 15 minutes to walk home and then watched TV until 7 P.M., how long did he watch TV?

   (A) 2 hr, 5 min   (B) 2 hr, 15 min
   (C) 2 hr, 20 min   (D) 2 hr, 30 min
   (E) 3 hr

4. In the diagram, $l_1 \parallel l_2$, $\angle ABC = 30°$ and $\angle BDC = 55°$. Find the degree measure in X.

   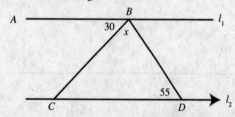

   (A) 150   (B) 125   (C) 95   (D) 85   (E) 30

5. Two pies of equal size are to be sliced. The first pie is cut into 6 equal slices. The second pie is cut so that each of its slices are $1/3$ the size of the slices in the first pie. After the slicing is complete, how many slices will be contained in both pies?

   (A) 6   (B) 12   (C) 18   (D) 24   (E) 28

6. A payroll consists of the salaries of 14 workers and 1 supervisor. Half the workers earn $6.25 per hour, whereas the other half earn $8.00 per hour. The supervisor earns twice the hourly wage of a lower-paid worker. If all 14 workers and the supervisor work 30 hours per week, what will be the total weekly payroll?

   (A) $1,312.50   (B) $1,680   (C) $2,992.50
   (D) $3,367.50   (E) $3,500

7. An apartment building has K floors. Each floor has L apartments and each apartment has R rooms. Express the total number of rooms in the apartment building.

   (A) KLR (B) $K + L + R$
   (C) KL/R (D) RK/L (E) $R(K + L)$

8. Given the number 94,26X, what must X equal for this number to be divisible by 3, 6, and 9?

   (A) 3   (B) 4   (C) 5   (D) 6   (E) 0

9. If X ranges from .0002 to .02 and Y ranges from .002 to .2, what is the *maximum* value of X/Y?

   (A) 2,000   (B) 1,000   (C) 10   (D) 1
   (E) .01

10. $50 is 40 percent of

    (A) $20   (B) $50   (C) $80   (D) $100
    (E) $125

11. How many cubes 7 cm on a side can be cut from a larger cube that measures 28 cm on a side?

    (A) 4   (B) 7   (C) 8   (D) 16   (E) 64

12. Two softballs cost as much as 5 tennis balls. If you have enough money to buy 6 softballs, how many tennis balls could you buy?

    (A) 10   (B) 15   (C) 20   (D) 25   (E) 30

13. A woman made 5 payments on a loan. Each payment was twice as much as the previous payment. If the total amount of all the payments was $372, how much was the second payment?

    (A) $12.00   (B) $24.00   (C) $48.00
    (D) $74.40   (E) $148.80

14. An agency rents cars at a rate of D dollars a day and X cents per mile. If a car was rented for 20 days and was driven 3,000 miles in that time, the amount, in dollars, due to the agency was

    (A) $20D + 3,000X$ (B) $3,000X/20D$
    (C) $20(D + 30 X)$ (D) $10(2D + 3X)$
    (E) $10(2D + 300)$

15. In the figure below, what is the value of X?

    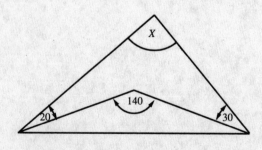

    (A) 40°   (B) 50°   (C) 90°   (D) 100°
    (E) 130°

16. If $A = 2B$, $B = 3C$, and $4C = X$, then what is X in terms of A?

    (A) $A/24$ (B) $2A/3$ (C) $3A/2$ (D) $8A/3$
    (E) $6A$

17. If sugar costs m cents per pound, how many pounds can be bought for $2.00?

    (A) $2m$ (B) $200m$ (C) $2/m$
    (D) $200/m$ (E) $m/200$

18. If p represents the perimeter of an equilateral triangle, and if $\frac{2}{3}p = \frac{8}{15}$, then each side of the triangle is

    (A) $\frac{4}{15}$ (B) $\frac{2}{5}$ (C) $\frac{3}{5}$ (D) $\frac{11}{45}$ (E) $\frac{1}{5}$

19. A class contains twice as many boys as girls. What percent of the class is girls?

    (A) 25%   (B) $33\frac{1}{3}$%   (C) 40%   (D) 50%
    (E) $66\frac{2}{3}$%

20. If $2^{N+1} = 16$, what is the value of 3^N?

    (A) 3   (B) 9   (C) 27   (D) 81   (E) 243

21. A class of 25 students took a test that was scored from 0 to 100. Exactly 15 students received scores greater than 79. If X represents the class average, which of the following is the lowest possible value of X?

    (A) 24   (B) 36   (C) 40   (D) 48   (E) 80

22. How many degrees are there in the angle formed by the hands of a clock at 2:30 P.M.?

    (A) 95   (B) 100   (C) 105   (D) 110
    (E) 120

23.

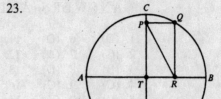

In the circle above, $PQRT$ is a rectangle, and AB and CD are diameters. If $TR = RB = 5$, then $PR =$

    (A) 5   (B) 8   (C) 9   (D) 10
    (E) cannot be determined from the information given

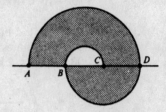

24. In the figure above, if $AB = BC = CD = 4$ and all the arcs are semicircles, find the area of the shaded region.

    (A) 36π (B) 24π (C) 52π (D) 60π
    (E) 72π

25. A 39-foot ladder is placed against a vertical wall of a building so that the ladder is flush with the wall. How far down the wall does the ladder slip after the base of the ladder is 15 feet from the base of the building?

    (A) 3 feet   (B) 4 feet   (C) 4.2 feet
    (D) $4\sqrt{2}$ feet   (E) 5.6 feet

ANSWERS AND EXPLANATIONS

1. (D)	6. (D)	11. (E)	16. (B)	21. (D)
2. (C)	7. (A)	12. (B)	17. (D)	22. (C)
3. (B)	8. (D)	13. (B)	18. (A)	23. (D)
4. (C)	9. (C)	14. (D)	19. (B)	24. (B)
5. (D)	10. (E)	15. (C)	20. (C)	25. (A)

1. (D)   Since there are 3 piles and you wish to make 6 piles, one way to think about this problem is to realize that you must "create" 3 additional piles. Each of these piles will have 9 cartons in it; so $3 \times 9 = 27$. The 54 cartons start out in 3 equal piles; so, each original pile has $54 \div 3 = 18$ cartons in it. If you move 9 cartons from each original pile to create the fourth, fifth and sixth pile, the 54 cartons will be distributed as required.

2. (C)   Starting with the simpler equation, $2R = 10$, we find $R = 5$. Substitute $R = 5$ into $4Q + 3R = 31$; $4Q + 3(5) = 31$.
$4Q = 31 - 15 = 16$. If $4Q = 16$, then $Q = 4$.

3. (B)   Josh was in the library for 50 minutes (3:40 + 50 min = 4:30 P.M.). He walked home in 15 minutes (4:30 P.M. + 15 min = 4:45 P.M.). He watched TV until 7:00 P.M. (7:00 − 4:45 = 2 hr, 15 min).

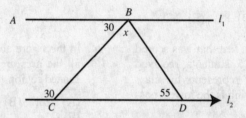

4. (C)   Since $l_1 \parallel l_2$, $\angle BCD = 30°$ because it is the alternate interior angle to $\angle ABC = 30°$. Since there are 180° in a triangle, $X = 180 - (30 + 55)$; $180 - 85 = 95°$.

5. (D)   The first pie will have 6 slices. The second pie will have 3 times as many slices, or 18 slices. Together there will be 24 slices.

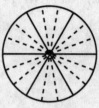

First Pie   +   Second Pie
6   +   18 = 24

6. (D)   There are several calculations you must complete accurately in order to solve this problem, so you might use your calculator here. Since there are 14 workers, 7 will earn $6.25/hr and 7 will earn $8.00/hr. They each work 30 hours, so we have

$$6.25 \times 7 \times 30 = 1,312.50$$
$$8.00 \times 7 \times 30 = 1,680.00$$

By now you probably forgot the supervisor! He makes twice the $6.25 rate per hour, or $12.50 per hour. He works 30 hours, so

$$12.50 \times 30 = 375.00$$

Total 1,312.50, 1,680.00, and 375.00 on your calculator and find the total weekly payroll to be $3,367.50.

7. (A)   If you replace the *K, L,* and *R* with simple numbers, you will see that all you need to do to find the total number of rooms is to multiply, *KLR.* For example, if the apartment building had 10 floors, with 6 apartments on each floor, and each apartment had 4 rooms, the total number of rooms would be $10 \times 6 \times 4$. Since $10 = K$, $6 = L$, and $4 = R$, we have $K \times L \times R$, or *KLR*.

8. (D)   You could substitute each choice into the number and check the divisibility of 3, 6, and 9 using your calculator. However, this will take some time. It's probably faster to remember the "sum-of-the-digits" technique.

• A number divisible by 3 will have digits whose sum is divisible by 3.
• A number divisible by 6 must be even and have digits whose sum is divisible by 3.
• A number divisible by 9 will have digits whose sum is divisible by 9.

$9,426X$ will be divisible by 3, 6, and 9 if $X = 6$.
94,266 is even and has a digit sum of $9 + 4 + 2 + 6 + 6 = 27$, which is divisible by 3 and 9.

9. (C)   To create the largest fraction X/Y, choose the largest X and the smallest Y. This would be $.02/.002 = 20/2 = 10$.

10. (E) $50 = {}^{40}/_{100} X$, or $50 = {}^{4}/_{10} X$. Multiplying both sides by ${}^{10}/_{4}$, you get
$${}^{10}/_{4} \times 50 = {}^{4}/_{10} X \times {}^{10}/_{4}$$
$${}^{500}/_{4} = X = 125$$

You could actually arrive at the correct answer by eliminating the other choices. Since $50 is only 40% of X, neither (A) or (B) make any sense! If $50 were 50% of X, X would equal $100, but 40% is less than 50%, so choices (C) and (D) can't be correct.

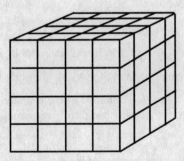

1 layer = 16 cubes

11. (E)   Since the smaller cube is 7 cm on a side, $28/7 = 4$, there will be four cubes in a row of the larger cube. Likewise, there will be $4 \times 4 = 16$ cubes in a "layer" of the larger cube. Since there are "4 layers," each with 16 cubes, the total number of smaller cubes will be 64.

12. **(B)** Form the ratio 2:5 and create a proportion:
softballs/tennis balls:$2/5 = 6/X$
$2X = 30, X = 15$

13. **(B)** Let X represent the first payment. Since each payment was twice as much as the previous payment, the other payments will be $2X$, $4X$, $8X$, and $16X$.
Also, $X + 2X + 4X + 8X + 16X = 372$
$31X = 372$
$X = 372/31 = 12$
   Therefore, the second payment ($2X$) is $2(12) = \$24$.

14. **(D)** The car was rented for 20 days; so, that part of the cost is $20 \times D$, or $20D$. The car was driven 3,000 miles; so, that part of the cost is $3{,}000 \times X/100 = 30X$. (Notice, $X\cent$ converts to $X/100$ dollars).
   The total cost is $20D + 30X$, which factors into $10\,(2D + 3X)$.

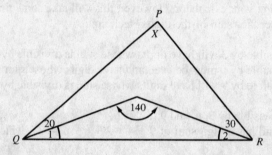

15. **(C)** Since the small triangle has 140° as its vertex, the other two angles ($\angle\,1$ and $\angle 2$) will equal 40°. This means that $\angle\,Q$ and $\angle\,R$ will total $20 + 30 + 40 = 90$. That leaves 90° for X.

16. **(B)** Starting with $X = 4C$, make substitutions for C ($C = B/3$) and B ($B = A/2$).

$$X = 4C = 4\left(\frac{B}{3}\right) = \frac{4(A/2)}{3} = \frac{4A/2}{3} = \frac{2A}{3}$$

17. **(D)** Make a proportion between pounds and cost, but be careful to keep all costs in the same units, either dollars or cents. Here, we converted $\$2.00$ into $200\cent$.
Pounds/cost: $1/m = X/200$
$mX = 200$, or $X = 200/m$

18. **(A)** Each side of an equilateral triangle is $^1/_3$ the perimeter. If $\dfrac{2p}{3} = \dfrac{8}{15}$, then $\dfrac{1p}{3} = \dfrac{4}{15}$. Of course, some of you probably solved for p and then took $^1/_3$ of that answer. If $\dfrac{2p}{3} = \dfrac{8}{15}$; then, cross-multiplying, you get $30p = 24$; dividing both sides of the equation by 30 now, you get $p = {}^{24}/_{30}$ or $^4/_5$. Each side of the triangle is $^1/_3$ of $^4/_5$ or $^1/_3 \times {}^4/_5 = {}^4/_{15}$. Can you see that sometimes a little "insightful" reasoning can save you a lot of time?

19. **(B)** Let $x = $ the number of girls. Then $2x = $ the number of boys.

$$\frac{\text{Girls}}{\text{Total students}} = \frac{x}{x + 2x} = \frac{x}{3x} = \frac{1}{3},$$ which is $33^1/_3\%$.

20. **(C)** $2^4 = 2 \times 2 \times 2 \times 2 = 16$; therefore, if $2^{N+1} = 16$, then $N + 1 = 4$. $N = 3$; $3^N = 3^3 = 3 \times 3 \times 3 = 27$

21. (D)   To arrive at the lowest average, all scores should be as low as possible. Since 15 students received grades greater than 79, assign the lowest possible grade to each of these students. The lowest possible grade for these students is 80. The other 10 students received grades below 79; so, assign them zeros. The average is therefore $(15 \times 80) + (10 \times 0)$ divided by 25 (the total number of students in the class).

$$15 \times 80 = 1,200$$
$$10 \times 0 = \frac{0}{1,200/25} = 48$$

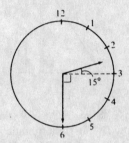

22. (C)   Be careful. The little hand is *on* the 2 only when the big hand is on the 12 (at 2 o'clock). Remember, as the big hand moves *from* 12 around *to* 12 again, the little hand moves (ever so slowly) from 2 to 3. At 2:30 (in this problem) the big hand has gone $\frac{1}{2}$ of the distance around the circle (clock). So, the little hand must have gone $\frac{1}{2}$ the distance between 2 and 3. The angle between any two consecutive hours is 30° $\left(\dfrac{360°}{12} = 30°\right)$. Therefore, the little hand has moved $\frac{1}{2}(30°) = 15°$. So, as you can see in the diagram above, the answer is $90° + 15° = 105°$. Many of you, who forgot that the little hand moves too, probably marked choice (E).

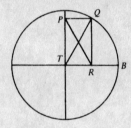

23. (D)   Draw the other diagonal, *TQ*. Since $TB = 5 + 5 = 10$, then $TQ = 10$. *TB* and *TQ* are *radii* of the same circle. Sneaky? Since the diagonals of a rectangle are equal, $PR = TQ = 10$.

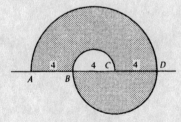

24. (B)   The area of the shaded region is equal to the area of the semicircle whose arc is AD + the area of the semicircle whose arc is BD − the area of the semicircle whose arc is BC. Since $AD = 4 + 4 + 4 = 12$, the radius of the greatest semicircle is 6, so that its area is $\dfrac{\pi 6^2}{2} = \dfrac{36\pi}{2} = 18\pi$. The radius of the semicircle BD is 4, so that

its area is $\dfrac{\pi 4^2}{2} = \dfrac{16\pi}{2} = 8\pi$, and the radius of the smallest semicircle is $\frac{1}{2}(4) = 2$,

so that its area is $\dfrac{\pi 2^2}{2} = \dfrac{4\pi}{2} = 2\pi$. Therefore, the area of the shaded region is $18\pi +$

$8\pi - 2\pi$, or 24π.

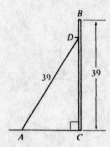

25. (A)   See the diagram above. Since $BC = 39$ (the ladder is "flush" against the wall), we can find BD if we know DC. In right triangle ACD, $AD^2 = AC^2 + DC^2$; $39^2 = 15^2 + DC^2$; $1521 = 225 + DC^2$; $1296 = DC^2$; $DC = 36$. Therefore, $BD = BC - DC = 39 - 36 = 3$. Did you recognize a 5-12-13 right triangle? 15-36-39 is a multiple (3, in fact) of 5-12-13.

Mathematical Assessment Test 9

Time—15 minutes
10 Questions

Notes: 1. The use of a calculator is permitted. All numbers used are real numbers.
2. Figures that accompany problems in this test are intended to provide information useful in solving the problems. They are drawn as accurately as possible, *except* when it is stated in a specific problem that a figure is not drawn to scale. All figures lie in a plane unless otherwise indicated.

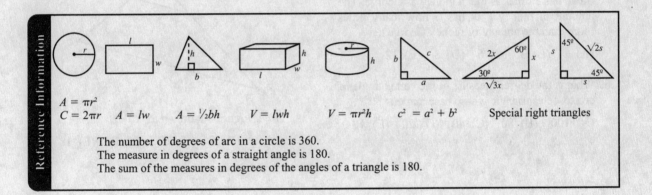

Reference Information

$A = \pi r^2$
$C = 2\pi r$ $A = lw$ $A = \frac{1}{2}bh$ $V = lwh$ $V = \pi r^2 h$ $c^2 = a^2 + b^2$ Special right triangles

The number of degrees of arc in a circle is 360.
The measure in degrees of a straight angle is 180.
The sum of the measures in degrees of the angles of a triangle is 180.

1. If $15X + 3 = 0$, then $X =$

   (A) 3 (B) 5 (C) 0 (D) −5 (E) −¹/₅

2. For two different integers, X and Y, let

   $$X * Y = \frac{2X + Y}{2Y - X}$$

   What is the value of $X * Y$ when $X = -2$ and $Y = 2$?

   (A) ¹/₃ (B) −¹/₃ (C) 0 (D) 1 (E) 2

3. If a student bought 16 pieces of gum for $1.28 and sold all of them for 10¢ each, what was the profit per piece of gum?

   (A) 2¢ (B) 2.5¢ (C) 3¢ (D) 4¢ (E) 5¢

4. 12 is what percent of 50?

   (A) 12% (B) 24% (C) 30% (D) 40
   (E) 50%

5. Paul has 2 times as much money as Steve, and Steve has 3 times as much money as George. The amount of money Paul has is how many times more than the amount of money George has?

   (A) 2 (B) 3 (C) 6 (D) 8 (E) 12

6. What is the degree measure of the vertex angle of an isosceles triangle whose base angle is 80°?

   (A) 100 (B) 80 (C) 40 (D) 20 (E) 10

7. A perfume is made by mixing three fragrances (A, B, and C) in the ratio of 3:1:2, respectively. If there is an unlimited supply of fragrances A and C, but only 1.5 ounces of fragrance B, how many ounces of the perfume can be made?

   (A) 1.5 (B) 4.5 (C) 9 (D) 9.5 (E) 15

8. If .2% of the light bulbs in a shipment are defective, how many defective light bulbs will there be if the shipment contains 20,000 light bulbs?

   (A) 40 (B) 80 (C) 400 (D) 800
   (E) 4,000

9. If $(X + 1/X)^2 = 25$, then $1/X^2 + X^2 = ?$

   (A) 23 (B) 24 (C) 25 (D) 27 (E) 624

10. In triangle *AED*, line *BC* is drawn parallel to side *AD* such that $BE = 2$, $EC = 1$, $CD = 2$, and $BC = 3$. Find the perimeter of trapezoid *ABCD*.

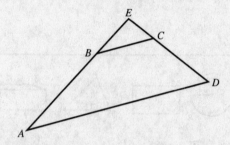

Note: Figure not drawn to scale.

   (A) 6 (B) 8 (C) 10 (D) 12 (E) 18

ANSWERS AND EXPLANATIONS

1. (E)	6. (D)
2. (B)	7. (C)
3. (A)	8. (A)
4. (B)	9. (A)
5. (C)	10. (E)

1. (E) $15X + 3 = 0$; therefore, $15X = -3$ and $15X/15 = -3/15$; $X = -1/5$.

2. (B) "Sub in" $X = -2$ and $Y = 2$ into the "invented" operation:

$$X * Y = \frac{2X + Y}{2Y - X} = \frac{2(-2) + 2}{2(2) - (-2)} = \frac{-4 + 2}{4 + 2} = \frac{-2}{6} = \frac{-1}{3}$$

3. (A) Selling 16 pieces of candy at 10¢ each piece results in $16 \times .10 = \$1.60$. In that the student paid only \$1.28 for the candy, his profit is $1.60 - 1.28 = .32$. The profit on *each* piece is the total profit (\$.32) divided by the total number of pieces (16). $.32/16 = \$.02$ or 2¢ per piece.

4. (B) "12 is what % of 50" can be translated into the following equation:
$12 = X/100 \times 50$.
So, solving we obtain $12 = X/100 \times 50 = X/2$.
$2 \times 12 = X/2 \times 2$, or $X = 24\%$.

Technique: Since percents are based on a denominator of 100, you could have simply doubled 12/50 to obtain 24/100. When you work to make the denominator equal to 100, the resulting numerator *is* the percent. So, 24/100 is 24 %.

5. (C) Thinking algebraically you could write

Paul = 2 Steve, and Steve = 3 George

(1) $P = 2S$ (2) $S = 3G$

Substituting equation (2) into equation (1) you get (1) $P = 2[3G] = 6G$.
This means that Paul has 6 times the money that George has.

6. (D) An isosceles triangle has two equal base angles. The third angle is called the vertex angle. Since there are 180° in a triangle, the vertex angle of this triangle is $(180) - (80 + 80) = 180 - 160 = 20°$.

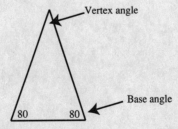

Vertex angle

Base angle

80   80

ERROR Confusing the base angles with the vertex angles in an isosceles triangle. This confusion would lead you to choice (B) by mistake.

7. (C) Start with the fragrance that is in limited supply, which is fragrance B. The original ratio is 3:1:2. Since we use $1\frac{1}{2}$ ounces of B, we have increased the original "recipe" by $1\frac{1}{2}$ times. The original recipe calls for $3 + 1 + 2 = 6$ ounces. So, the final amount of perfume will be $1\frac{1}{2} \times 6$ ounces or $\frac{3}{2} \times \frac{6}{1} = \frac{18}{2} = 9$ ounces.

ERROR Do not *add* $1\frac{1}{2}$ to each fragrance. If you do, you get $4\frac{1}{2} + 1\frac{1}{2} + 3\frac{1}{2} = 9\frac{1}{2}$. This is a *ratio* problem and must be solved by multiplying.

8. (A) We must find .2% of 20,000. .2% is .002 by moving the decimal two places to the left. $.002 \times 20,000 = 40$.

ERROR Thinking that .2% is the same as 2%. Remember .2% is *not* even 1% (.01). It is only a fraction of 1% and must therefore be smaller than 1%.

9. (A) When you face the equation $(X + 1/X)^2 = 25$, there is really only one thing you can do, and that is to expand $(X + 1/X)^2$. It is a binomial expansion of the form $(A + B)^2 = A^2 = 2AB = B^2$. If you do this expansion, some surprising things happen: $(X + 1/X)^2 = (X + 1/X)(X + 1/X) = X^2 + 2(1/X)(X) + (1/X)^2 = 25$. The middle term is $2(1/X)(X)$, which is simply 2! Therefore, $X^2 + 2 + (1/X)^2 = 25$ and $X^2 + (1/X)^2$, which is exactly what we are trying to find, equals $25 - 2 = 23$.

10. (E) When a line segment is drawn parallel to one side of a triangle, it cuts the figure into two similar triangles; $\triangle AED$ is similar to $\triangle BEC$. The corresponding sides of similar triangles are proportional.

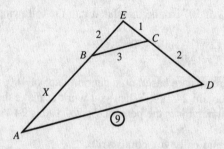

From the dimensions given, we can set a proportion to solve for the other dimensions: $\dfrac{\triangle BEC}{\triangle AED} : \dfrac{1}{3} = \dfrac{3}{AD}$ or $AD = 9$. Using the same proportion, we can find AB. $1/3 = 2/2 + X$ or $2 + X = 6$. $X = 4$. Now we have determined the four sides of the trapezoid $ABCD$. They are 3, 2, 4, and 9. The perimeter is $3 + 2 + 4 + 9 = 18$.

Mathematical Assessment Test 10

Time—30 minutes
25 Questions

Notes: 1. The use of a calculator is permitted. All numbers used are real numbers.
2. Figures that accompany problems in this test are intended to provide information useful in solving the problems. They are drawn as accurately as possible, *except* when it is stated in a specific problem that a figure is not drawn to scale. All figures lie in a plane unless otherwise indicated.

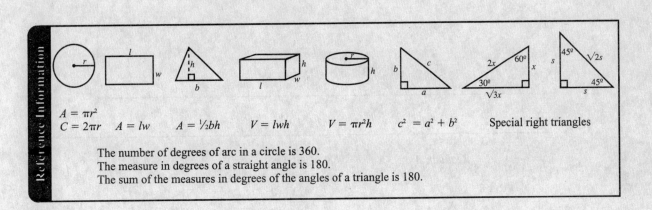

Reference Information

$A = \pi r^2$
$C = 2\pi r$ $A = lw$ $A = \frac{1}{2}bh$ $V = lwh$ $V = \pi r^2 h$ $c^2 = a^2 + b^2$ Special right triangles

The number of degrees of arc in a circle is 360.
The measure in degrees of a straight angle is 180.
The sum of the measures in degrees of the angles of a triangle is 180.

DIRECTIONS FOR QUANTITATIVE COMPARISON QUESTIONS

Questions 1 through 15 each consist of two quantities, one in column A and one in column B. You are to compare the two quantities and on the answer sheet fill in:

- A   if the quantity in column A is greater
- B   if the quantity in column B is greater
- C   if the two quantities are equal
- D   if the relationship cannot be determined from the information given

Notes: 1. In certain questions, information concerning one or both of the quantities to be compared is centered above the two columns.
2. A symbol that appears in both columns represents the same thing in column A as it does in column B.
3. Letters such as *x, y,* and *n* stand for real numbers.
4. Because there are only four choices, *never mark* (*E*).

EXAMPLES

Column A	*Column B*
E1. The average of 3, 5, and 10	9
E2. $x - y$	$y - x$
E3. 6% of 8	8% of 6

ANSWERS
E1. (B), E2. (D), E3. (C)

	Column A	*Column B*	
		$X > 0$	
1.	$X^3 + 1$	$X^3 - 1$	A B C D
2.	.40	4%	A B C D

$$\longleftarrow \!-\!\bullet\!-\!\bullet\!-\!\bullet\!-\!\bullet\!-\!-\!-\!-\!-\! \longrightarrow$$
$$\quad -1 \quad x \quad 0 \qquad 1$$

	Column A	*Column B*	
3.	$4X$	X^4	A B C D
		$1/X > 0$	
4.	X	X^2	A B C D
		$\sqrt{X + 3} = 15$	
5.	X	150	A B C D
6.	$\dfrac{5}{1/5}$	5×5	A B C D

7.	$P < Q < R$	
$P + R$	Q	A B C D

8.	$P/Q = {}^3/_4$	
$\dfrac{4P}{3}$	Q	A B C D

9. | 12 | Area of $\triangle DEF$ | A B C D |
    | :-- | :-- | :-- |

10. | The average of the odd integers from 1 to 100 | The average of the even integers from 1 to 100 | A B C D |
    | :-- | :-- | :-- |

Two marbles are drawn at random from
a bag of 20 colored marbles.

11. | The probability that both marbles drawn are yellow | The probability that both marbles drawn are green | A B C D |
    | :-- | :-- | :-- |

$$0.2X - 1 = 1.1$$

12. | X | 10 | A B C D |
    | :-- | :-- | :-- |

$$x = y = z$$

13. | AB | BC | A B C D |
    | :-- | :-- | :-- |

$$a = 2b$$

14. | b/a | $a/b - 1$ | A B C D |
    | :-- | :-- | :-- |

The sum of 5 consecutive
integers is 0.

15. | The product of the integers | The average of the integers | A B C D |
    | :-- | :-- | :-- |

DIRECTIONS FOR STUDENT-PRODUCED RESPONSE QUESTIONS

Each of the remaining ten questions (16–25) requires you to solve the problem and enter your answer by marking the special grid, as shown in the examples below.

Answer: $\frac{5}{14}$ or 5/14

Answer: 2.5

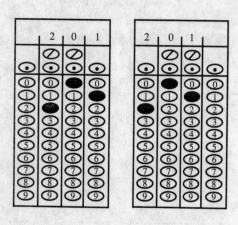

Write answer in boxes →

← Fraction line

Grid in result

Decimal point

Answer: 201

Either position is correct.

- *Decimal Accuracy:* If you obtain a decimal answer, **enter the most accurate value the grid will accommodate.** For example, if you obtain an answer such as 0.666 . . . , you should record the result as .666 or .667. **Less accurate values such as .66 or .67 are not acceptable.**

Acceptable ways to grid $\frac{2}{3}$ = .6666 . . .

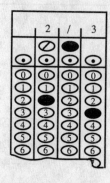
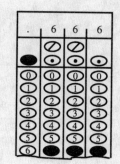
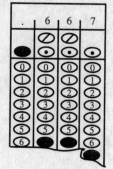

- Mark no more than one oval in any column.
- Because the answer sheet will be machine-scored, **you will receive credit only if the ovals are filled in correctly.**
- Although not required, it is suggested that you write your answer in the boxes at the top of the columns to help you fill in the ovals accurately.
- Some problems may have more than one correct answer. In such cases, grid only one answer.
- No question has a negative answer.
- **Mixed numbers** such as 2½ must be gridded as 2.5 or 5/2.

    (If $\boxed{2\,1\,/\,2}$ is gridded, it will be interpreted as $\dfrac{21}{2}$, not 2½.)

16.

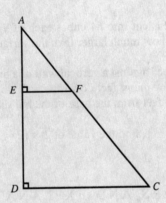

In the figure above, $AE = 3$, $ED = 6$, and $DC = 12$. What is the length of EF?

17. If $3X = 2Y$ and $3Z = 8Y$, then X/Z equals?

18. If $p = q - 4$, then $(p - q)^2 = ?$

19. A businessperson can buy books that have a price range of $3.00 to $6.00 and then mark them with prices between $4.00 and $7.00. What is the maximum profit he would receive if he sold all 100 books he bought? (Do not grid in $).

20. If pipe A can fill a tank in 3 hours, and pipe B can empty it in 4 hours, how many hours will it take for the tank to be one-half full when both pipes are open?

21. In a community of 1,200 residents, 30% are senior citizens. In the last election, 25% of the senior citizens voted. How many senior citizens voted in that election?

22. In the figure that follows, what is the area of triangle ABC?

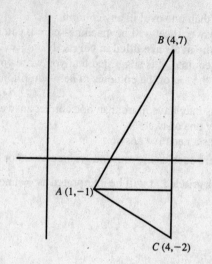

23. A cube of volume 512 is cut into 64 cubes each of volume 8. The total surface area of the 64 cubes is how much larger than the surface of the original cube?

24. A 39-foot ladder is placed against a vertical wall of a building so that the ladder is flush with the wall. How many feet down the wall does the ladder slip after the base of the ladder is 15 feet from the base of the building?

25. If $q \propto t$ is defined as $q^t - 1$, find the value of $2 \propto (2 \propto 3)$.

ANSWERS AND EXPLANATIONS

1. (A)	6. (C)	11. (D)	16. (4)	21. (90)
2. (A)	7. (D)	12. (A)	17. (1/4)	22. (13.5)
3. (B)	8. (C)	13. (D)	18. (16)	23. (1,152)
4. (A)	9. (A)	14. (B)	19. (400)	24. (3)
5. (B)	10. (B)	15. (C)	20. (6)	25. (127)

1. (A)   Any positive number plus 1 will be greater than the same number minus 1. $X > 0$, so $X^3 > 1$ and $X^3 + 1 > X^3 - 1$.

2. (A)   .40 written as a percent is .40 = 40%. 40% is larger than 4%.

ERROR   Incorrectly changing a decimal into a percent. Remember, move the decimal point 2 places to the right.

3. (B) X lies somewhere between 0 and -1. In other words, X is a negative fraction. 4 times X will be a negative fraction, but X^n, or $X \times X \times X \times X =$ will be a *positive* fraction. Let's try this problem by substituting a number between 0 and a negative one, say, $-1/3$.

$$4 \times (-1/3) = -4/3 = -1\,1/3$$
$$(-1/3)^4 = (-1/3)(-1/3)(-1/3)(-1/3) = +1/81$$

4. (A)   If $1/X > 0$, then $X < 1$. For example, $1/(1/2) = 2 > 0$.
Since $X < 1$, then X could be $1/2$. $(1/2)^2 = 1/4$, which is less than $1/4$.

5. **(B)** Solving the equation $\sqrt{X+3} = 15$, we get $\sqrt{X} = 12$. Squaring both sides, we obtain $X = 144$. Remember, the square of a square root "cancels" the root. $(\sqrt{X})^2 = X$.

6. **(C)** $\dfrac{5}{1/5} = 5 \div \dfrac{1}{5} = 5 \times \dfrac{5}{1} = 25$.

7. **(D)** $P < Q < R$. Most students will choose $P = 1$, $Q = 2$, and $R = 3$ to make life easy. In that case, $P + R = 4$, and you would choose (A). However, there are other possibilities. Suppose $P = -3$, $Q = 0$, and $R = 1$. Now $P + R = -3 + 1 = -2$. In this case, you would choose (B). However, because of the uncertainty, you must choose (D). Remember to try negative numbers in problems that involve inequalities.

8. **(C)** By cross-multiplying the given proportion, you get $P/Q = 3/4$. $3Q = 4P$. Divide both sides of this equation by 3 to obtain $Q = 4P/3$; so, these quantities are equal.

9. **(A)** By the Pythagorean Theorem, we find $DF = 3$:

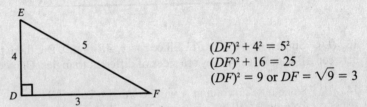

$(DF)^2 + 4^2 = 5^2$
$(DF)^2 + 16 = 25$
$(DF)^2 = 9$ or $DF = \sqrt{9} = 3$

Now, since the area of a triangle is equal to $\frac{1}{2} B \times H$, we find $DEF = \frac{1}{2}(3)(4) = \frac{1}{2}(12) = 6$. 12 is the larger quantity, so we choose column A.

Note: The base of the right triangle could be recognized as the missing piece of the 3-4-5 Pythagorean triple. If you see this, you can solve the problem much faster.

10. **(B)** The odd integers from 1 to 100 are 1, 3, 5, 7, 9, 11, . . . , 99. The even integers from 1 to 100 are 2, 4, 6, 8, 10, 12, ... The longest way to solve this problem is to actually add $1 + 3 + 5 + 7 + \cdots$ and divide it by 50 (in that there are 50 odd integers); then add $2 + 4 + 6 + 8 + \cdots$ and divide that sum by 50 (since there are also 50 even integers). If you do this, you will find $\text{AVE}_{\text{odds}} = 50$ and the $\text{AVE}_{\text{evens}} = 51$. However, this takes too long! There must be a better way. In fact, there are two better ways! First, you could simply add the first odd and the last odd and divide that sum by 2. $1 + 3 + 5 + 7 + \cdots + 97 + 99$; $(1 + 99)/2 = 50$.

Then you could add the first even and the last even and divide that sum by 2. $2 + 4 + 6 + 8 + \cdots + 98 + 100$; $(2 + 100)/2 = 51$.

This averaging technique always works when the numbers to be averaged are *equally spaced;* that is, there is the same "distance" between 5 and 7 as between 11 and 13. The average of equally spaced numbers is one-half the sum of the first number and the last number.

The second method involves solving a "simpler" problem, in this case, the comparison between the average of the odds between 1 and 10 and the average of the evens between 1 and 10.

$$\text{AVE}_{\text{odd}} = \frac{1+3+5+7+9}{5} = \frac{25}{5} = 5$$
$$\text{AVE}_{\text{even}} = \frac{2+4+6+8+10}{5} = \frac{30}{5} = 6$$

This pattern, in which AVE$_{\text{even}}$ > AVE$_{\text{odd}}$, will be true even for numbers from 1 to 100!

11. (D) We have no information about the colors of the marbles, so we can't compare probabilities. Choice (D).

12. (A) A good way to solve an equation with decimals is to "clear" the decimals by multiplying by some factor of 10. In this equation, if all terms are multiplied by 10, we get $2X - 10 = 11$. So, $2X = 11 + 10 = 21$ and $X = 21/2 = 10.5$. Choice (A).

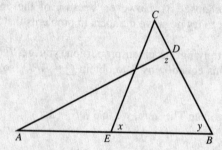

13. (D) Since $x = y$, $CE = BC$. Since $z = y$, $AB = AD$. But there is no relationship between AB and BC since they are sides of different triangles. Choice (D).

14. (B) Since $a = 2b$, column A will be $b/a = b/2b = 1/2$.
Column B will be $a/b - 1 = 2b/b - 1 = 2 - 1 = 1$.
Column B is larger.

15. (C) The five integers whose sum is 0 are $-2, -1, 0, 1$, and 2. The product of these integers is $(-2)(-1)(0)(1)(2) = 0$. The average of these integers is $(-2 + -1 + 0 + 1 + 2)/5 = 0/5 = 0$. Choice (C).

16. (4) Since the angles at E and D are both 90°, $EF \parallel DC$ and $\triangle AEF$ is similar to $\triangle ADC$. Corresponding sides of similar triangles are proportional; so, we can say: $\triangle AEF/\triangle ADC = 3/3 + 6 = EF/12$; $3/9 = EF/12$; $36 = 9EF$; $EF = 36/9 = 4$.

17. (1/4) To find X/Z, make the following substitutions:
Since $3X = 2Y$, then $8Y = 12X$ (multiplying $3X = 2Y$ by 4)
Since $3Z = 8Y$, then $3Z = 12X$

$$\frac{3Z}{Z} = \frac{12X}{Z} \text{ (dividing both sides by } Z)$$

$$\frac{3}{12} = \frac{12X}{12Z} \text{ (dividing both sides by 12)}$$

$$\frac{X}{Z} = \frac{3}{12} = \frac{1}{4}.$$

18. (16) If $p = q - 4$, then $p - q = -4$ and $(p - q)^2 = (-4)^2 = 16$.

19. (400) To get the maximum profit on 100 books, the businessperson must buy the books for the lowest price possible ($3.00) and sell them for the highest price possible ($7.00). The profit on each book is $7 - 3 = 4$. Since he bought 100 books, his total profit would be $4 \times 100 = 400$.

20. (6) Instead of thinking of this problem as having two pipes, think of it as having

one pipe. After 1 hour, this "arrangement" will fill $\frac{1}{3}$ of the tank, but also drain $\frac{1}{4}$ of the tank. We can express this as: After 1 hour = $\frac{1}{3} - \frac{1}{4} = \frac{1}{12}$ full.

Half a tank will require 6 times this amount of time, in that $6 \times \frac{1}{12} = \frac{6}{12} = \frac{1}{2}$ full. So, it will take 6 hours to fill the tank halfway.

21. (90)   First, find the number of senior citizens in the community of 1,200 people. 30% of 1,200 = .3 × 1,200 = 360. Now, 25% of these 360 senior citizens voted in the election. 25% of 360 = .25 × 360 = 90.

22. (13.5)

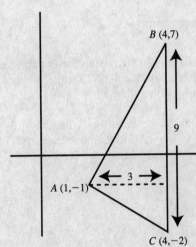

The area of a triangle is $\frac{1}{2} B \times H$.
The base of this triangle is 9 (7 − −2).
The height is 3 (4 − 1).

The area will be $\frac{1}{2}(9)(3) = \frac{27}{2} = 13.5$.

23. (1,152)   The volume of a cube is S^3. Since the large cube has a volume of 512, its side will be 8 (8 × 8 × 8 = 512). The smaller cubes of volume 8 have a side of 2 (2 × 2 × 2 = 8).

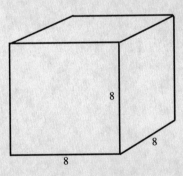

The total surface area of a cube is $6S^2$ (there are 6 faces on every cube). The surface area of the large cube will be $6 \times 8^2 = 6 \times 64 = 384$. The surface area of one of the smaller cubes will be $6 \times 2^2 = 24$. There are 64 small cubes; so, their total surface area is 64 × 24 = 1,536. The difference in the surface areas of the large cube and the 64 smaller cubes is therefore 1,536 − 384 = 1,152.

24. (3)

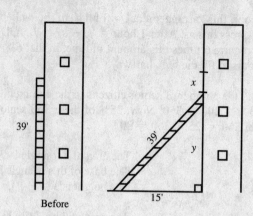

Before

If we find Y, we can answer the question. X will be $39 - Y$. Using the Pythagorean Theorem, we have $39^2 = 15^2 + Y^2$. This triangle employs the 5-12-13 triple, where 15 is 5×3 and 39 is 3×13; so, $Y = 3 \times 12 = 36$. X is therefore $39 - 36 = 3$.

25. (127) Since $q \propto t = q^t - 1$, working inside the parenthesis first, $2 \propto 3 = (2^3 - 1) = (7)$. Now, $2 \propto (7) = 2^7 - 1 = 128 - 1 = 127$. Remember, even with invented operations, the quantity in the parentheses must be calculated first.

Mathematical Assessment Test 11

Time—30 minutes
25 Questions

Notes: 1. The use of a calculator is permitted. All numbers used are real numbers.
2. Figures that accompany problems in this test are intended to provide information useful in solving the problems. They are drawn as accurately as possible, *except* when it is stated in a specific problem that a figure is not drawn to scale. All figures lie in a plane unless otherwise indicated.

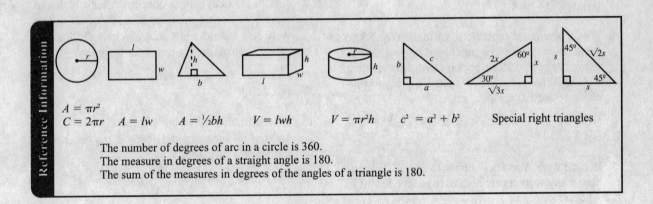

$A = \pi r^2$
$C = 2\pi r$ $A = lw$ $A = \frac{1}{2}bh$ $V = lwh$ $V = \pi r^2 h$ $c^2 = a^2 + b^2$ Special right triangles

The number of degrees of arc in a circle is 360.
The measure in degrees of a straight angle is 180.
The sum of the measures in degrees of the angles of a triangle is 180.

1.

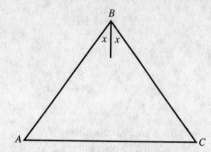

In triangle *ABC*, *AB* = *BC* = *CA*.
What is the value of *x*?

(A) 30   (B) 45   (C) 60   (D) 90   (E) 180

2.

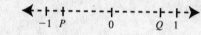

P × *Q* could equal which of the following?

(A) $\frac{3}{4}$ (B) $\frac{1}{2}$ (C) 0   (D) $-\frac{3}{8}$ (E) −1

3. If $4X + 5 = 2Y - 5$, then *Y* = ?

(A) 2*X*   (B) 2*X* + 5   (C) 4*X* + 10
(D) 6*X*   (E) 6*X* + 10

4. When purchased separately, softballs cost $5.50
each. They can also be purchased in packages of
two costing $10.25 or packages of three costing
$14.00. What is the least expensive price to pur-
chase 10 softballs?

(A) $55   (B) $51.25   (C) $50   (D) $48.75
(E) $47.50

5. If it takes 6 workers 4 hours to paint 2 rooms,
how many workers are needed to paint 6 rooms in
4 hours?

(A) 6   (B) 8   (C) 12   (D) 18   (E) 24

6. A car wash charges $5.00 per wash. They also
sell a book of 8 coupons, which can be used for 4
washes. If the coupon book cost $18.00, how
much savings does each coupon represent?

(A) 25¢   (B) 50¢   (C) $1.00   (D) $2.00
(E) $2.25

7. A girl scout collected contributions totaling *D*
dollars from *P* people. What was the average
contribution made by these people?

(A) *DP*   (B) *D* + *P*   (C) *D* − *P*
(D) *D*/*P*   (E) *P*/*D*

8. Two boats leave the same point at the same time.
One travels directly north at 8 miles per hour. The
other boat travels directly east at 6 miles per hour.
How far apart are the two boats after 3 hours?

(A) 10 miles   (B) 14 miles   (C) 30 miles
(D) 42 miles   (E) 44 miles

9. If $p \times r \times m > 0$, then *r* could not equal

(A) 2   (B) $\frac{1}{2}$ (C) −1   (D) 0   (E) 4

10. Which of the following numbers is divisible by 2,
5, and 9?

(A) 37,255   (B) 95,472   (C) 265,490
(D) 451,180   (E) 531,360

11. In a certain office, $\frac{3}{4}$ of the workers are married
and $\frac{3}{4}$ of these workers have children. What fraction of the workers in the office are married without children?

(A) $\frac{1}{16}$ (B) $\frac{3}{16}$ (C) $\frac{1}{4}$ (D) $\frac{1}{2}$ (E) $\frac{9}{16}$

12. During the first hour of business, the box office
sold $\frac{1}{2}$ the tickets for a concert. After 400 tickets
were sold during the next hour, $\frac{1}{3}$ of all tickets
were left unsold. How many tickets did the box
office have before it opened for business?

(A) 800   (B) 1,000   (C) 1,200   (D) 1,600
(E) 2,400

13. Which of the following numbers would be decreased by approximately 50% if the order of its
digits were reversed?

(A) 7,002   (B) 4,802   (C) 6,423   (D) 9,195
(E) 3,321

14. After losing a library book, a student was charged
$31.50 to replace the book and $3.50 late fee.
What percent of the total charge was the replacement cost of the book?

(A) 90%   (B) 70%   (C) 50%   (D) 15%
(E) 10%

15. If 5 pounds of flour costs *D* dollars, what is the
cost of $1\frac{1}{2}$ pounds, in cents?

(A) .3*D*   (B) 30*D*   (C) 150*D*   (D) *D*/30
(E) *D*/150

16. If 40% of *X* + *Y* is 80 and *X* = 240, what is the
value of *Y*?

(A) −40   (B) 0   (C) 120   (D) 160
(E) 208

17. If $1,100 is divided among Al, Bill, and Chuck in the ratio 9:8:5, respectively, what amount will Bill receive?

    (A) 50 (B) 150 (C) 200 (D) 400
    (E) 450

18. If the radius of a circle is 8, and is increased by 20%, the area of that circle is increased by

    (A) 1.6π (B) 16π (C) 28.16π (D) 32π
    (E) 91.16π

19. A company pays its salespeople a commission of 6% on all sales up to and including $500, and then 10% on all sales above $500. If one of the salespeople made $130 in commissions, what were her total sales?

    (A) $800 (B) $1,000 (C) $1,300
    (D) $1,500 (E) $2,400

20.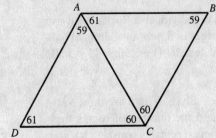

    Note: Figure not drawn to scale.

    If the angles of *ABCD* have the measures indicated, which is the longest line segment?

    (A) *BC* (B) *AB* (C) *AC* (D) *AD*
    (E) Cannot be determined from the information given

21. If one bell rings every 12 minutes, and another bell rings every 10 minutes, the first time both bells ring at the same time is after how many minutes?

    (A) 140 (B) 120 (C) 80 (D) 60 (E) 48

22. If *N* is a positive integer, which of the following is always odd?

    (A) $19N+6$ (B) $18N+4$ (C) $19N+5$
    (D) $18N+5$ (E) $19N^2+5$

23. If *X* students attain an average of *p*, and *Y* students attain an average of *q*, the average of $X+Y$ students is

    (A) $X+\dfrac{Y}{2}$ (B) $p+q$ (C) $p+\dfrac{q}{2}$
    (D) $pX+\dfrac{qY}{X}+Y$ (E) $p+\dfrac{q}{X}+Y$

24. A cubic foot of water is poured into a rectangular box whose base is 12 inches by 18 inches. How high up will the water rise?

    (A) 4 inches (B) 6.5 inches (C) 8 inches
    (D) 12.5 inches (E) 18 inches

25. If the volume of a cube is 8, the sum of the lengths of its edges is

    (A) 8 (B) 24 (C) 16 (D) 32 (E) 64

ANSWERS AND EXPLANATIONS

1. (A)	6. (A)	11. (B)	16. (A)	21. (D)
2. (D)	7. (D)	12. (E)	17. (D)	22. (D)
3. (B)	8. (C)	13. (C)	18. (C)	23. (D)
4. (E)	9. (D)	14. (A)	19. (D)	24. (C)
5. (D)	10. (E)	15. (B)	20. (A)	25. (B)

1. (A) $AB = BC = CA$; therefore, $\triangle ABC$ is equilateral. Each angle of an equilateral triangle equals 60°. Angle $B = 60° = 2x$, $x = 30$.

2. (D) Since P is a negative number and Q is a positive number, $P \times Q$ must be negative ($- \times + = -$). This eliminates choices (A) and (B) because they are positive. For the answer to be 0 (choice C) either P or Q must be zero. So, choice (C) is out. Since $P > -1$ and $Q < 1$, then $P \times Q$ could not equal -1 exactly. Choice (E) is wrong. We are left with choice (D).

3. (B) $4X + 5 = 2Y - 5$. Adding 5 to both sides of this equation, we get $4X + 10 = 2Y$. Dividing both sides by 2, we see $Y = 2X + 5$.

4. (E) Since the packages of softballs are cheaper than individual softballs, we must use as many packages of three as possible. Three packages of 3 plus an additional ball will be the cheapest way to purchase 10 balls. This will cost $3(14) + 5.50 = 42 + 5.50$. The 10 balls can be purchased for $47.50, choice (E).

5. (D) This problem seems more difficult than it actually is. There are three variables: the number of workers, the time they work, and the number of rooms they paint. However, for the question they ask, the time (4 hours) remains constant; so, you can eliminate it from your thinking. The other two variables, the number of workers and the number of rooms painted, vary directly and can be placed into a direct proportion.

No. of workers / No. of rooms painted ($6/2 = X/6$)
Cross-multiplying, $36 = 2X$ or $X = 18$. Choice (D).

6. (A) Since 8 coupons can purchase 4 car washes, each wash costs 2 coupons. Two coupons cost $2 \times \$18/8 = 2 \times \$2.25 = 4.50$. Since the regular price of a car wash is $5.00, you save 50¢ by using 2 coupons ($5.00 - 4.50$). Each coupon is therefore worth 50¢/2 = 25¢. Choice (A).

7. (D) Divide the total amount contributed by the total number of people who contributed, D/P. Choice (D).

Technique: In literal problems such as this, try substituting your own numbers to see if you can get a better idea of how to proceed. For example, if the girl scout collected $100 ($D$) from 20 people ($P$), we can see that the average contribution would be 100/20 (D/P). Choices (A), (B), and (C) would be easily eliminated if you used this technique.

8. (C) Since one boat goes directly north and the other goes directly east, their paths make a right triangle. (See diagram on the next page.)

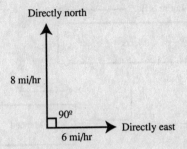

The distance between them will be the hypotenuse of the right triangle. Be careful and remember that the boats travel for 3 hours; so, the hypotenuse we need is the one in the following triangle.

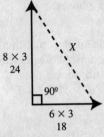

Using the Pythagorean Theorem will be "messy," but it states $(24)^2 + (18)^2 = X^2$.

$$576 + 324 = X^2$$
$$900 = X^2$$
$$30 = \sqrt{900} = X$$

You could arrive at the correct answer more quickly if you recognize that 6-8-10 is a Pythagorean triple. Since boats travel for 3 hours, the final answer will be $3 \times 10 = 30$. Choice (C).

9. (D)   Since the product of $P \times R \times M$ is greater than O, R could not be O. If $R = 0$, then $P \times R \times M = 0$. Choice (D).

10. (E)   Numbers divisible by 2 must be even; so, eliminate choice (A). Numbers divisible by 5 end in zero or 5; so, eliminate choice (B). It is relatively easy to use the "sum of the digits" technique on the other choices. Remember, for a number to be divisible by 9, the sum of its digits must be divisible by 9.

265,490: $2 + 6 + 5 + 4 + 9 + 0 = 26$. Choice (C) is out.
451,180: $4 + 5 + 1 + 1 + 8 + 0 = 19$. Choice (D) is out.

   Choice (E) is the correct answer by process of elimination, but let's check.

531,360: $5 + 3 + 1 + 3 + 6 + 0 = 18$. 18 is divisible by 9.

11. (B) $^3/_4$ of all workers are married. Of the married workers, $^3/_4$ have children. This means that $^1/_4$ of the married workers do not have children. $^1/_4 \times ^3/_4 = ^3/_{16}$, married without children. Choice (B). Be careful not to confuse fractions that relate to the entire office and fractions that relate to just the married workers. (Diagram is overleaf.)

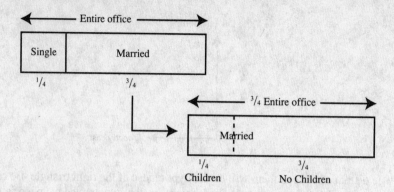

12. (E) Set up the following equation:
1st hour + 2nd hour = sold after 2 hours
$\frac{1}{2}T + 400 = \frac{2}{3}T$

Be careful with the right side of this equation! The problem stated that after 2 hours, $\frac{1}{3}$ of the tickets (T) were unsold. This means that $T - \frac{1}{3}T = \frac{2}{3}T$ were sold. Our equation relates what was sold; so, we use $\frac{2}{3}T$ on the right side.
$\frac{1}{2}T + 400 = \frac{2}{3}T$, $400 = \frac{2}{3}T - \frac{1}{2}T = \frac{4}{6}T - \frac{3}{6}T = \frac{1}{6}T$, $6 \times 400 = 2400 = T$
Choice (E).

13. (C) Decreasing a number by 50% means cutting it in half.

Original	Reversed
7,002	2,007
4,802	2,084
6,423	3,246	← This reversal approximately reduces the original
9,195	5,919	number by 50%.
3,321	1,233

14. (A) Answer the question asked. What % of the *total charge* was the *replacement cost?*

$$\frac{\text{Replacement cost}}{\text{Total charge}} \times 100\% = \frac{31.50}{35.00} \times \frac{100}{1} = \frac{630}{7} = 90\%$$

If you chose 10% [choice (E)], you did not read the question carefully.

15. (B) Set up a direct proportion and be careful to express all costs as cents.

$$\frac{\text{Pounds}}{\text{Cents}} = \frac{5}{D \times 100} = \frac{1.5}{X}$$

Cross-multiplying, $5X = 150D$

$$X = \frac{150D}{5} = 30D$$
Choice (B).

16. (A) First, find the value of $X + Y$. Since 40% of $X + Y$ is 80, we have

$.40 (X + Y) = 80$

$$\frac{.40}{.40} (X + Y) = \frac{80}{.40} = 200, \text{ dividing by } .40$$
$$X + Y = 200$$

Since $X = 240$, we have $240 + Y = 200$, or $Y = 200 - 240 = -40$.

17. (D)   Al + Bill + Chuck = 1,100

$$9X + 8X + 5X = 1,100$$
$$22X = 1,100$$
$$X = \frac{1,100}{22} = 50$$

Bill receives $8X$ or $8(50) = \$400$. Choice (D).

18. (C)   If the radius is 8, the original circle has an area of πr^2 or $\pi(8)^2 = 64\pi$. Increasing the radius by 20%, we get a new radius equal to $8 + .20(8) = 8 + 1.6 = 9.6$. The area of a circle with a radius 9.6 is $\pi(9.6)^2 = 92.16\pi$. The increase in area will be $92.16\pi - 64\pi = 28.16\pi$.

19. (D)   Let x represent the total sales. Then, $.06(500) + .10(x - 500) = 130$. Multiply by 100 (move the decimal points 2 places to the right) in order to "get rid" of the decimal points to get $6(500) + 10(x - 500) = 13,000$. Now, $3,000 + 10x - 5,000 = 13,000$; $10x - 2,000 = 13,000$; adding 2,000 to both sides of the equation, $10x = 15,000$; dividing by 10 now, $x = 1,500$. *Or,* work your way backward from the answers. First, subtract 500 from the total sales represented by each of the answers. For example, (C) $1,300 - 500 = 800$. The salesperson gets 10% of this or $80. She also gets 6% of 500 or $30: $80 + 30 = 110$. *No good.* We need 130. Obviously, then, the total sales have to be greater than $1,300. This eliminates (A), (B), and (C).

20. (A)   The longest side of a triangle is opposite the greatest angle. In triangle *ADC*, then, *AC* is the longest side. In triangle *ABC*, *BC* is the longest side; so, it is longer than *AC*. It certainly doesn't look that way from the diagram—but remember that the figure isn't drawn to scale.

21. (D)   Find the least number that is divisible by 12 and 10.

$12 \times 5 = 60 = 10 \times 6$. The bells will ring at the same time after 60 minutes (also after 120 minutes, and so on). The important word in this problem is *first.*

22. (D)   18 times a positive integer will always be positive. Then, a positive integer plus 5 will always be odd.

23. (D)   If $\dfrac{10}{x}$ students had an average of $\dfrac{70}{p}$ and $\dfrac{20}{y}$ students had an average of $\dfrac{40}{q}$, the $\dfrac{30}{x+y}$ students will have a combined average of $\dfrac{10(70) + 20(40)}{10 + 20} = \dfrac{700 + 800}{30} = \dfrac{1500}{30} = 50$. Algebraically, then, the answer is $\dfrac{x(p) + y(q)}{x + y}$.

24. (C)

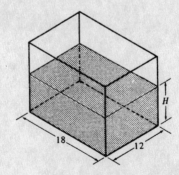

One cubic foot measures $12'' \times 12'' \times 12''$. If this cubic foot of water is poured into a box (shown above) whose base measures $12'' \times 18''$, the water will reach a height, H. Since it is assumed that no water is lost in the transfer, $12 \times 12 \times 12 = 12 \times 18 \times H$. Divide both sides of the equation by 12×18 to "isolate" H:

$$\frac{\cancel{12} \times \cancel{18} \times H}{\cancel{12} \times \cancel{18}} = \frac{\cancel{12} \times \overset{2}{\cancel{12}} \times \overset{4}{\cancel{12}}}{\underset{3}{\cancel{12} \times \cancel{18}}} \qquad \text{so, } H = 8''$$

25. (B)

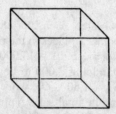

The volume of a cube is (edge)³. In this problem, then, (edge)³ = 8; so, edge = 2. Since there are 12 edges in a cube (4 for the top, 4 for the bottom, and 4 for the sides), the sum of the edges is $12 \times 2 = 24$.

Mathematical Assessment Test 12

Time—15 minutes
10 Questions

Notes: 1. The use of a calculator is permitted. All numbers used are real numbers.
2. Figures that accompany problems in this test are intended to provide information useful in solving the problems. They are drawn as accurately as possible, *except* when it is stated in a specific problem that a figure is not drawn to scale. All figures lie in a plane unless otherwise indicated.

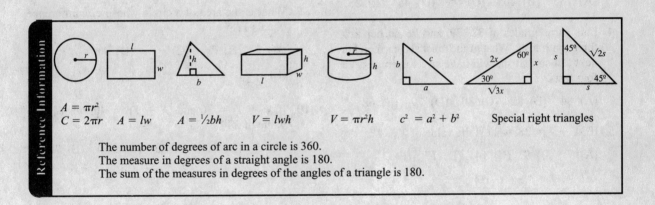

$A = \pi r^2$
$C = 2\pi r$ $A = lw$ $A = \frac{1}{2}bh$ $V = lwh$ $V = \pi r^2 h$ $c^2 = a^2 + b^2$ Special right triangles

The number of degrees of arc in a circle is 360.
The measure in degrees of a straight angle is 180.
The sum of the measures in degrees of the angles of a triangle is 180.

1. What is the value of $(X + Y)^2$ when $X = -3$ and $Y = 3$?

   (A) 9 (B) 6 (C) 3 (D) 0 (E) -3

2. What is the greatest common factor of 27 and 54?

   (A) 18 (B) 9 (C) 6 (D) 3 (E) 2

3. If $l_1 \parallel l_2$ and l_3 is not parallel to l_4, find the value of X.

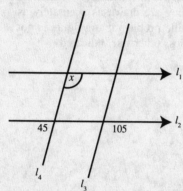

   (A) 135 (B) 105 (C) 95 (D) 45 (E) 25

4. Lois earns grades of 82, 79, and 96 on her first three math tests. What grade must she earn on her next test so that she will have an 84 average after four tests?

   (A) 84 (B) 82 (C) 80 (D) 79 (E) 68

5. If $3X + 7 = 28$, what is the value of $X + 7$?

   (A) 7 (B) 9 (C) 14 (D) 17 (E) 21

6. Two cities are 105 miles apart. If John takes 8 hours to make a round-trip between the cities and takes 4½ hours to go one way, what is his rate, in miles per hour, for his return trip?

   (A) 3.5 (B) 30 (C) 35 (D) 50 (E) 60

7. The weekday rate for a telephone call is 40¢ for the first 2 minutes and 12¢ for each additional minute. The weekend rate is 50% less for the first 2 minutes and 33⅓% less for each additional minute. How much do you save if you make a 5-minute phone call on Sunday rather than Monday?

   (A) 76¢ (B) 60¢ (C) 48¢ (D) 32¢
   (E) 20¢

8. The men's department of a department store employs 40 people. If the store employs 60 people in the men's department during the holiday season, what is the percent increase in the staff?

   (A) 33⅓% (B) 50% (C) 66⅔% (D) 133⅓%
   (E) 150%

9. What is the area of a circle whose circumference equals 1?

   (A) 2 (B) 2π (C) $\dfrac{1}{2\pi}$ (D) 4π
   (E) $\dfrac{1}{4\pi}$

10. If $X^2 + Y^2 = 30$ and $(X + Y)^2 = 40$, what is the value of XY?

   (A) 5 (B) 10 (C) 70 (D) 350 (E) 700

ANSWERS AND EXPLANATIONS

1. (D)	6. (B)
2. (B)	7. (D)
3. (A)	8. (B)
4. (D)	9. (E)
5. (C)	10. (A)

1. (D) When $X = -3$ and $Y = 3$, $(X + Y)^2$ will be $(-3 + 3)^2 = 0^2 = 0$.

2. (B) The greatest common factor of 27 and 54 is the largest number that divides evenly into both numbers. 18 will divide evenly into 54, but it does not divide evenly into 27; so, it cannot be the greatest common factor. However, 9 (choice B) divides evenly into both 27 and 54 and is the largest common factor.

3. (A) The 45° angle can be "moved" inside the parallel lines. Two consecutive angles inside parallel lines add up to 180°.

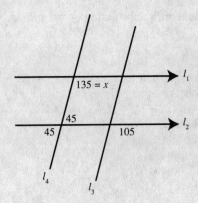

$45 + X = 180$
$X = 135°$. Choice (A).

4. (D) Lois' final average will be $\dfrac{82 + 79 + 96 + X}{4} = 84$.

$X + 257 = 84.4 = 336$
$X = 336 - 257 = 79$.

5. (C) $3X + 7 = 28; 3X = 28 - 7 = 21$, and $X = 7$.
Therefore, $X + 7 = 7 + 7 = 14$. Choice (C).
Be careful to provide the answer to $X + 7$ and not simply X.

6. (B) Since the trip in one direction took $4^1/_2$ hours, the return trip takes $8 - 4^1/_2$ or $3^1/_2$ hours. The two cities are 105 miles apart; so, John's rate, in miles per hour, for the return trip is

$\dfrac{105 \text{ miles}}{3.5 \text{ hrs}} = 30 \text{ mi/hr}$ Choice (B).

7. (D) A 5-minute call on Monday costs $40¢ + 3(12¢) = 76¢$.
                     1st two   additional
                     minutes   minutes

The same 5-minute call on Sunday will cost less. It is 50% less for the first two minutes; so, instead of 40¢ for 2 minutes it will cost 50% of 40 or 20¢. The additional 3 minutes will cost 66 ⅔% of 36¢ or 24¢. So, the Sunday call costs 44¢. The savings are 76 − 44 = 32¢. Choice (D).

8. (B) The increase for the holiday season is 20 people (60 − 40 = 20). The % increase is 20/40 × 100% = 50%.

ERROR Finding the % of 20/60 × 100% = 33⅓%. The percent increase answers the question, "increased from what?" The denominator must be the number of people employed *before* the holidays. So, the correct % is

$$\frac{20 \text{ people increase}}{40 \text{ staff before holidays}} \times \frac{100}{1}\% = 50\%$$

9. (E) Starting with the circumference formula $C = 2\pi R$, we have $1 = 2\pi R$. Solving for R, we get $\dfrac{1}{2\pi} = R$.
The area of the circle is πR^2. Substituting $A = \pi R^2 = \pi\left(\dfrac{1}{2\pi}\right)^2$, $A = \dfrac{\pi}{4\pi^2} = \dfrac{1}{4\pi}$. Choice (E).

10. (A) Using the expansion formula $(X + Y)^2 = X^2 + 2XY + Y^2$, we can make the following substitutions:

$$(X + Y)^2 = X^2 + 2XY + Y^2$$
$$40 = 30 + 2XY$$
$$10 = 2XY$$
$${}^{10}/_2 = XY = 5. \text{ Choice (A)}.$$